VISUAL ARTS IN POLAND

VISUAL ARTS IN POLAND

*An Annotated Bibliography of Selected
Holdings in the Library of Congress*

JANINA W. HOSKINS

LIBRARY OF CONGRESS ○ WASHINGTON
1993

Library of Congress Cataloging-in-Publication Data

Library of Congress.
    Visual arts in Poland : an annotated bibliography of selected holdings
in the Library of Congress / Janina W. Hoskins.
        p.   cm.
    Includes index.
    ISBN 0-8444-0741-0
    ——— ———— Copy 3 Z663.77   .V58   1992
        1. Art, Polish—Bibliography—Catalogs.   2. Library of Congress—
    Catalogs.   I. Hoskins, Janina W.   II. Title.
    Z5961.P57L5   1992
    [N7255.P6]
    016.7'09438—dc20   92-27991
                                                                             CIP

The paper used in this publication meets the minimum requirements of American National
Standard for Information Sciences—Permanence of Paper for Printed Library Materials,
ANSI Z39.48-1984.

For sale by the U.S. Government Printing Office
Superintendent of Documents, Mail Stop: SSOP, Washington, DC 20402-9328
ISBN 0-16-041650-7

Contents

✻

Foreword

❊

Janina W. Hoskins has served the Library of Congress as its Polish —and often more broadly as its East European—area specialist since 1952. During those nearly four decades, she has played a major and sustained role, through her know-how and finesse in acquisition matters, in shaping the Library's Polish collection, which ranks as one of the largest and most diverse outside of Poland. She helped Librarian of Congress L. Quincy Mumford and the director of the Library's Overseas Office negotiate the Public Law 480 program with the Polish government, and later had the satisfaction of actually selecting titles for eighteen American university libraries from among the books given by Poland under that program as "in-kind" donations in repayment of post-World War II U.S. aid.

She has traveled officially to Poland for the Library and the State Department on several occasions, both for acquisitions and to lecture on the Library's Slavic collections and the history of Slavic studies in the United States, and has often appeared on Voice of America broadcasts to Poland. As an area specialist in the Library's European Division, Dr. Hoskins has provided specialized reference service to Congress (where, incidentally, she was a staffer for two years before coming to the Library), and to academics, other libraries, the diplomatic community, and the general public. The Library of Congress has formally recognized her superior performance with a Meritorious Service Award.

Among her initiatives to promote broader awareness of the Library's rich Polish and East European holdings, Dr. Hoskins has prepared numerous exhibits and displays on historical themes (such as "The Millenium of the Baptism of Poland in 966") or major figures (Nicolaus Copernicus, Tadeusz Kościuszko, Kazimierz Pułaski). She has written articles ("Thomas Jefferson Views Poland;" "Printing in Poland's Golden Age") and books, some to accompany her exhibits, others of a historical or bibliographic nature (*Early and Rare Polonica of the 15th–17th Centuries in American Libraries*, published by G.K. Hall; *Polish Books in English 1945–1971*) or focusing on a research area (*Polish Genealogy and Heraldry: An Introduction to Research*). Still lending her skills on occasion to the Library after retiring in 1989, Dr. Hoskins was recently invited to write a number of informative pieces for the Library of Congress *Information Bulletin* to mark the bicentenary of the Polish Constitution of 3 May 1791.

In her professional activities—she is a member of the American Historical Association, the American Association for the Advancement of Slavic Studies, and the Polish Institute of Arts and Sciences in New York—Dr. Hoskins has often lectured at scholarly

❀

organizations and colleges, and has been active in both national and
international conventions of historians and Slavic specialists. She has
contributed to books and professional journals, and has written book
reviews for *The American Historical Review, The Mississippi Valley
Historical Review, Jahrbücher für Geschichte Osteuropas,* and other
scholarly journals.

Visual Arts in Poland affords Dr. Hoskins an opportunity to
weave together a number of strands: her unmatched familiarity with
the Library's Polish collection, her thorough knowledge of Polish
history and culture, and an early and continuing interest in the arts
that dates back to her student days in Kraków (she holds masters and
doctoral degrees from the Jagiellonian University, where she taught
and majored in history, and minored in art).

David H. Kraus
Assistant Chief
European Division, Library of Congress

Karl Friedrich Schinkel's design for the centrally planned hunting lodge of Prince Antoni Radziwiłł in Antonin includes this great hall, intended as a place of entertainment and rest after the hunt. This remarkable lodge built of timber in 1827 reflects Schinkel's attempt to adapt the principles of Durand's treatise to wooden structures. It is one of the great tourist attractions today. Interior from K.F. Schinkel, *Sammlung architektonischer Entwürfe* (Berlin, 1866). For 1988 English-language edition of this classic work—which has the complete German text, as well— see bibliographic entry 237.

Introduction

❀

As events of major historical significance have unfolded over the past several years in the countries of Eastern Europe—events which, in fact, began in Poland—public and press attention have focused on the drama of political and economic struggle and change. But the breakup of the Soviet Union has allowed for a resurgence of local, regional, and national identities, and increasingly, scholars will be interested in studying the cultural and intellectual history of the region.

Visual Arts in Poland offers the researcher a useful tool for understanding one aspect of that history. The Library of Congress holds in its collections excellent resources on the visual arts in Poland: the history, the achievements, and the interactions of its people and residents with the arts and artists of other lands and cultures. The purpose of the book is to introduce the researcher to these materials and to provide guidance in their use.

To understand the art and cultural life of Poland, a brief bit of history is useful. Poland and the Grand Duchy of Lithuania were united in 1385, with the Grand Duke of Lithuania becoming the king of Poland. In 1569, a constitutional union of the countries was enacted, with one parliament, one jointly elected king, and one currency, but with separate armies, administrations, and laws. The united countries became the Polish-Lithuanian commonwealth ("Respublica") and by that union, Poland became a multicultural state.

Then, in three turbulent stages within the relatively brief period from 1772 to 1795, Poland was divided among Russia, Prussia, and Austria, until it finally ceased to exist as a separate country. The small Grand Duchy of Warsaw, created in 1807 by Napoleon—with Frederick-August, the king of Saxony, as Grand Duke—was dissolved after Napoleon's downfall. The 1815 Congress of Vienna created the "Congress Kingdom of Poland," with the Russian tsar as king. This "kingdom" was abolished after an unsuccessful uprising in Poland in 1830–31. Its lands became part of the Russian Empire. After the 1830–31 uprising and a second uprising in 1861–63, many artists, intellectuals, writers, and politically active people left their country and emigrated, mostly to Western Europe.

In 1918 Poland once more emerged as an independent state, lasting through the interwar years, but in September 1939 the country was occupied, first by Germany and later by the Soviet Union. At the Teheran, Yalta, and Potsdam conferences in 1943 and 1945, the boundaries of contemporary Poland were determined. Territories that Poland had held after World War I—Western Belorussia, part of

Lithuania, and the Western Ukraine—were incorporated into the Soviet Union. In 1945 Poland became the Polish Peoples Republic (Polska Rzeczpospolita Ludowa), dominated by the Polish Workers [Communist] Party. The Communist Party endured until 1989, when the political victory of Solidarity at the polls restored the multiparty system and the name Republic of Poland [Rzeczpospolita Polska].

This bibliographic survey of materials in the collections of the Library of Congress encompasses selected publications that deal with the visual arts in Poland, published either in Poland or in the West. It includes books and periodicals—and occasionally individual articles—published since the nineteenth century. A few ancillary reference works were added in Chapter XI to provide the researcher with information about sources on the area's geography, history, and literature. The majority of the works listed were acquired by the Library of Congress after World War II. Most of them are in Polish, but works in English, French, German, and Italian are also included. Book titles in Polish are followed by English translations. Excluded from this work are microfilms, microfiche, manuscripts, and calendars.

The survey lists 868 selected entries organized by subject into eleven chapters, five of which are subdivided into topical sections. To allow for browsing by subject or art category, a few entries are repeated in later chapters or sections, as appropriate. In each of their later occurrences, these entries retain the unique item number assigned to them in their first occurrence. For example, *Katalog zabytków sztuki w Polsce* [Catalog of art monuments in Poland], an indispensable source published since 1953 (a second series since 1977), cuts across several of the categories of materials that are treated in this survey, including descriptions and photographs of buildings of architectural significance, paintings, sculptures, prints, and decorative art objects. Each volume covers one province and consists of numerous sections for counties and towns (see entry 32).

A few books that became available after the initial survey was completed in 1989 have been added to related existing entries, without being separately numbered. The citations of books in this work include Library of Congress call numbers. The bulk of the entries will be found in the chapters on architecture, painting, prints, and in the initial chapter, "Historical, multimedia, and thematic surveys."

The rendering of Polish place names can present problems— most often as a consequence of changing political borders. In this survey, the names of Polish cities and towns are spelled in Polish, except for the nation's capital, which appears in the familiar English version, Warsaw. The city of Vilnius is spelled in the Polish form, Wilno.

I am thankful for the help and courtesies that I received from many staff members of the Library of Congress during the preparation of this publication.

✻

Special thanks are due Mr. David H. Kraus, Acting Chief of the European Division (of which I was a member until my retirement in 1989) for his editorial advice in the early stages of this work and for his continuing interest.

I wish to acknowledge, as well, the editorial assistance of Mrs. Roberta Goldblatt, former editor of the *American Bibliography of Slavic and East European Studies*, who also input some of the entries into the computer.

Mr. Grant Harris, senior reference librarian in the European Division's Reading Room, could always be counted on to help, especially in my struggles with the computer while searching for obscure or old publications.

The staff of the Prints and Photographs Division of the Library was unfailingly courteous and helpful in aiding my research.

Dr. Agnieszka Morawińska, Curator of the Gallery of Polish Art at the National Museum in Warsaw, kindly shared with me, during a visit to Washington, her knowledge of the arts and art publications in Poland.

Janina W. Hoskins

I. Historical, Multi-Media, and Thematic Surveys

**Queen Bona Sforza (1494–1557),
the wife of King Sigismund I
(The Elder). Woodcut after
Maciej Miechowitta,** *Chronica
Polonorum.* **Kraków, 1521. From
Feliks Kopera,** *Malarstwo w
Polsce od XVI do XVIII wieku.*
vol. 2, 1966

I. Historical, Multi-Media, and Thematic Surveys

❋

1. ANDERS, Henryk.
Rytm; w poszukiwaniu stylu narodowego. [Rhythm; in search of a national style] Warszawa, Arkady, 1972. 245p. illus. (part color). N7255.P6A52
   Bibliography: p. 238–41.
   Bibliographic references.

"Rytm," a visual arts movement of the years 1922–32, cultivated an art deco style that widely exemplified Polish pictorial and sculptural expression. Adaptation of Polish subject matter. Deals with the artists and their works in paintings and sculpture, architectural friezes, and posters, as well as tapestries and scenic decoration.

2. Ars auro prior: studia Ioanni Białostocki sexagenario dicata. Warszawa, Państwowe Wydawnictwo Naukowe, 1981. 767 p. illus. N7442.B5 1981
   Editorial Committee: Juliusz A. Chrościcki, et al.
   English, French, German, Italian, Polish, Russian, and Spanish.
   Bibliography of Jan Białostocki's works: p. 757–68.
   Bibliographic references.

Collected essays. The title, from Ovid, affirms the superiority of skilled workmanship over precious metals. The essays address the honoree's polymathic range: from conceptual problems of creativity (William S. Heckscher) to the iconography of antiquity, the Byzantine, Early Christian, and High Renaissance eras

(Ernst H. Gombrich); and from Renaissance art theory (James S. Ackerman) to connoisseurship (Pierre Rosenberg). The emphasis is on Northern and Western European schools of art. With over one hundred essays, this is an impressive publication.

3. ASKANAS, Kazimierz.
Sztuka Płocka. [The art of Płock] Płock Towarzystwo Naukowe Płockie, 1974. 553 p. illus. N7255.P62P462
   Summary in English, French, German, and Russian.
   Bibliography: p. 247–66.

Text divided into customary historical periods. The town is best known for its rich metalwork of Romanesque and Gothic periods, from which numerous manuscript illuminations also emerged. Considerable and interesting architecture and works of art from Baroque through 1900.

4. BANACH, Andrzej.
Les "Enfers" Domaine Polonais. Paris, Jean-Jacques Pauvert, 1966. 245 p. illus. (Bibliothèque Internationale d'Erotologie, no. 17. J.M. Lo Duca, ed.) N6991.B3

Eroticism, fifteenth to twentieth century, illustrated in all art media, including photography. Arranged thematically (attire) and symbolically (siren), rather than historically.

5. BANACH, Jerzy.
Ikonografia Wawelu. [Icono-

graphy of the Wawel] Kraków, 1977. 2 v. illus. (Źródła do dziejów Wawelu, vol. 9, parts 1 and 2) DK4735.W3Z76 v. 9
   Summary in French in v. 2.
   Bibliographic references.

In vol. 1, panoramas and long views of the buildings from various vantage points. In vol. 2, the buildings and interiors in detail. A work of great interest that assembles and describes the subject matter of prints, drawings, watercolors, and photographs, from the sixteenth to the nineteenth century. Full scholarly apparatus. A delightful compendium.

6. BANACH, Jerzy.
Tematy muzyczne w plastyce polskiej. [Musical themes in Polish visual arts] Kraków Polskie Wydawnictwo Muzyczne, 1956–60. 2 v. illus. (part color). N8226.B3
   Vol. 1: Painting, Sculpture;
   Vol. 2: Prints, Drawings.
   Also available in German.

A valuable reference offering delightful genre subjects, allegories, costumes of all periods, from the twelfth century to the present. The reader is introduced to an enormous variety of works, most of which are little known, by both Polish and foreign artists. Many enlarged details.

7. BARANOWICZ, Zofia.
Polska awangarda artystyczna, 1918–1939. [Polish artistic avant garde, 1918–1939] Warszawa, Wydawnictwa Artystyczne i

Filmowe, 1975. 262 p. illus. (part color). N7255.P6B37

Bibliography: p. 252–55.

8. BIAŁOSTOCKI, Jan.

The art of the Renaissance in Eastern Europe: Hungary, Bohemia, Poland. Oxford [Eng.], Phaidon, 1976. xxiv, 312 p. illus. (part color). (The Wrightsman lectures, delivered under the auspices of the New York University Institute of Fine Arts, vol. 8) N6817.B52 1976b

Bibliography: p. 281–306.

Synthesizes East European architectural, ornamental, and sculptural achievements from the fifteenth to the seventeenth century. Unique in scope and authority, the study traces the conversion of sober, intellectual Florentine forms to exuberant, optical Mannerism.

9. BIAŁOSTOCKI, Jan.

Mannerism and "Vernacular" in Polish art. *In Georg Kauffmann, ed. Walter Friedlaender zum 90. Geburtstag Berlin, Walter de Gruyter, 1965. p. 47–57. N7443.K34

Bibliographic references.

Characterizes as vernacular, Polish mannerist structures that lack the typical Italian qualities of tension, conflict, refinement, and sophistication. Polish examples are marked by spontaneity, naïveté, and profusion of forms. The chief example cited is Krzyżtopór Castle in Ujazd, Kielce province. Its architect, Lorenzo Muretto de Sent, interpreted Vignola and achieved scenographically a "powerful play of monumental masses." Originally published in the author's Pięć wieków myśli o sztuce (Warsaw, 1959).

10. CHRZANOWSKI, Tadeusz, *and* Marian Kornecki.

Sztuka Śląska Opolskiego od średniowiecza do końca w XIX. [The art of Opole Silesia from the Middle Ages to the end of the nineteenth century] Kraków, Wydawnictwo Literackie, 1974. 506 p. illus. N7255.P62D662

Bibliography: p. 475–77.
Bibliographic references.

In the territory of Opole Silesia—as elsewhere in Poland—architecture is the most distinguished art by an overwhelming margin; outstanding Gothic, Renaissance, Baroque, and Neoclassical buildings, mostly sacred, some secular. Extravagant sculpture even by Baroque standards in Baborów, Kluczbork, and Głogówek. Nysa and Brzeg are two cities with consistently the most important art and architecture. The book is divided by periods, then subdivided by architecture and other fields of art. A chapter is devoted to notable wooden architecture dating from the early 1060s.

Can be supplemented by: Katalog zabytków sztuki w Polsce [Catalog of art monuments in Poland] Vol. IV, parts 1–14: Województwo Opolskie. [Opole Province] Warszawa, Polska Akademia Nauk, Instytut Sztuki, 1960–67. illus. (N6991.K36)

11. CHRZANOWSKI, Tadeusz, *and* Marian Kornecki.

Sztuka Ziemi Krakowskiej [Art of Kraków Province] Kraków Wydawnictwo Literackie, 1982. 743 p. illus. N7255.P62K73 1982

Bibliography: p. 683–99.

Divided into periods, from pre-Romanesque to twentieth century.

Covers architecture, including a chapter on wooden buildings, painting, sculpture, and decorative arts. A fabulous compendium of the highest scholarly interest; material unique to this important book. Most revealing may be the examples of architecture —Baroque, neoclassical, neo-Gothic to Secession—because they are least well known abroad. Buildings are remarkable for their number and architectural interest.

Additional illustrative material can be found in Katalog zabytków sztuki w Polsce. Vol. 1, parts 1–2: Województwo Krakowskie [Catalog of art monuments in Poland. Vol. 1, Kraków Province] Warszawa, Państwowy Instytut Sztuki, 1953. 574 p. 835 illus. (N6991.K36 v. 1) A collective work edited by Jerzy Szablowski. Description and illustrations of monuments in fifteen counties in Kraków province.

12. CONSTRUCTIVISM in

Poland 1923–1936: BLOK, Praesens, a.r. Museum Folkwang Essen 12.5–24.6.1973. Rijksmuseum Kröller-Müller Otterlo, 14.7–2.9.1973. [Stuttgart, Dr. Gantz'sche Druckerei, 1973.] 208 p. illus., ports. N7255.P6C66

Catalog of the exhibition by Ryszard Stanisławski, et al.

Foreword and introduction in Dutch, English, and German; text in English.

Bibliography: p 148–54.

The earliest self-assertions of constructivists were preceded by activities of those artists identified as "formists." A survey of the activities of Polish avant-garde artists between the two world wars—the first Western European exhibition of their

❀

work. The output of Mieczysław Szczuka, Katarzyna Kobro, Władysław Strzemiński, and Henryk Stażewski. The leading artists' paintings, sculpture, architectural compositions, and graphics could not be fully represented since most of the works were lost during the war. The artists' activities and publications in the BLOK group (1924–26), the Praesens group (1926–39), and the "a.r." group (the revolutionary artists, 1929–36), including the first constructivist exhibition (Wilno 1923), and the first Praesens group exhibition (1926). The first permanent collection of international modern art was established in 1931 in the Museum of Art in Łódź.

13. Contemporary art from Poland. Walter Phillips Gallery July 5–28, 1985. Banff, The Walter Phillips Gallery, 1986. 60 p. illus. N7255.P6C67 1986
Exhibition catalog featuring the works of four invited performing artists who took part in the exhibition. Catalog of the work of other artists in the show: artists' books, posters, and prints. Essay by Bożenna Stokłosa on contemporary Polish art, including a section on art in the period of Solidarity: martial law and present trends, 1980–86.

14. Cracow, city of museums; the most beautiful works of art from seven museums. Warsaw, Arkady, 1976. 54 p. 183 plates (part color). AM70.P63K7413
A collective work edited by Jerzy Banach.
Translation by Neil Jones and C.S. Acheson-Waligórska of *Kraków, miasto muzeów.*
Incorporates the collections of the

Wawel (Royal Halls and Chambers, Cathedral Treasury, Oriental art, Armory), the National Museum (including the Czartoryski collection), the Jagiellonian University Museum and Library, the Museum of Archeology and Ethnography, and the Historical Museum of the City. Museums were concentrated in Kraków, the center of arts and sciences in Poland, in the last decades of the nineteenth century. Highly literate text, and large-scale, generally good reproductions.

15. DOBROWOLSKI, Tadeusz. Sztuka Krakowa. [The art of Kraków] 5th rev. ed. Kraków, Wydawnictwo Literackie, 1978. 622 p. illus. (part color), plates. N7255.P62K74 1978
Summary in French and Russian.
Bibliography: p. 533–74.
A carefully detailed account of architecture, sculpture, painting, and a few examples of decorative arts dating from the pre-Romanesque period to the present. Many rare works are reproduced in more than 375 excellent photographs. Architectural representations of all periods, including the nineteenth century, are especially notable.

Additional illustrative material can be found in Katalog zabytków sztuki w Polsce. [Catalog of art monuments in Poland] Vol. IV, parts 1–4. Miasto Kraków. Warszawa, Polska Akademia Nauk, Instytut Sztuki, 1965–87. (N6991.K36)

16. DOBROWOLSKI, Tadeusz. Sztuka Młodej Polski. [The art of Młoda Polska] Warszawa, Państwowe Wydawnictwo

Naukowe, 1963. 453 p. 295 illus., 1 color plate. N7255.P6D63
Bibliography: p. 428–36.
Traces the early twentieth-century movement of renewal called Młoda Polska, which had ideals in common with Art Nouveau and the Arts and Crafts Movement. A large number of rare and fascinating works of architecture, painting, sculpture, prints, and decorative arts from about 1890 to 1914, primarily in Kraków, are illustrated, regrettably in poor reproductions.

A work dealing with the same period—but a decidedly different art form—is Józef Kozłowski's Proletariacka Młoda Polska. Sztuki plastyczne i ich twórcy w życiu proletariatu polskiego 1878–1914 [The Proletarian Young Poland. Visual arts and their creators in the life of the Polish proletariat 1878–1914]. Warszawa, Arkady, 1986. 229 p. illus. part color (N8243.S65K6 1986). Summary in English, German and Russian. Bibliography: p. 204–220. Published in the series Sztuka jako świadectwo czasu [art as a witness of the times]. Has many illustrations of paintings, drawings, prints, books, and also periodical illustrations.

17. DOBROWOLSKI, Tadeusz. Sztuka polska od czasów najdawniejszych do ostatnich. [Polish art from the earliest period to the present] Kraków, Wydawnictwo Literackie, 1974. 769 p. 581 illus. N7255.P6D615
Bibliography compiled by Józef Lepiarczyk: p. 693–721.

Architecture, sculpture, painting, and he decorative arts, from Romanesque to the mid twentieth century. Illustrations chosen with an invariably keen

*eye for stunning but lesser-known
examples, touching on Romanesque
sculpture in Trzebnica, great Gothic
church interiors in Strzegom,
Gniezno, and Nysa, and exuberant
eighteenth-century sculpture in
Stanisławów.*

18. Dzieje sztuki polskiej.

[History of Polish art] 2d ed.
Warszawa, Wydawnictwa
Szkolne i Pedagogiczne, 1987.
367 p. 133 illus. (part color).
N7255.P6D914 1987

Collective work edited by
Bożena Kowalska.

Bibliographic references.

*A collection of twenty studies on
Polish visual arts. The emphasis is on
the history of the modern period,
especially after World War II. The
last study deals with industrial art
designs. The book originated from
lectures given in Warsaw at the Art
Studium for teachers, and approved
by the Ministry of Education.*

19. Expressiv: mitteleuropäische

Kunst seit 1960. Central European Art since 1960. Museum
moderner Kunst/Museum des 20.
Jahrhunderts, Wien/Vienna
30.11.1987–26.01.1988. Hirshorn
Museum and Sculpture Garden,
Washington, D.C. 18.02.1988–
17.04.1988. Wien, Museum
moderner Kunst, 1987. 279 p.
illus. N6758.E98 1987

Organization, coordination,
and Catalog by Katharina
Theodorakis-Pratscher.
Collaborators: Gabriele Hobart
and Maria Stipsicz.

Text in German and English.
Bibliographic references.

*Based on the thesis that Central
European art of the post-World War
II era has common forms of*

*expression, and on the creative
strength of that expression. Six
Polish artists, each of whom has a
distinct artistic character: Magdalena
Abakanowicz, Jerzy Bereś, Edward
Dwurnik, Izabella Gustowska,
Władysław Hasior, and Józef
Łukomski. Short statements by or
about the artists with respect to their
works, and an essay by Mariusz
Hermansdorfer (Wrocław) on
Poland's artistic traditions. A well-
chosen, important exhibition and
catalog.*

20. Galerie Asbaek.

Modern Polish art.
Copenhagen, Galerie Asbaek,
1979. 48 p. illus. (part color),
N7255.P6G34 1979

An exhibition catalog.
"Galerie Asbaek, Copenhagen,
January 9–27, 1979."

Edited by Teresa Rostkowska.
English and Danish.

Includes biographies and
works of Magdalena
Abakanowicz, Marek Chlanda,
Jan Dobkowski, Stefan
Gierowski, Marzenna
Kawalerowicz, Zbigniew
Makowski, Andrzej Sapija, and
Ryszard Winiarski.

*Features eight individual artists.
Some, like Magdalena Abakanowicz,
are of international reputation and
began their careers in the 1960s, while
others are recent art school graduates.
Capsules on the aesthetic character of
their art. Excellent reproductions.*

21. GIEYSZTOR, Aleksander,

**Michał, Walicki, *and* Jan
Zachwatowicz.**

Sztuka polska przedromańska i
romańska do schyłku XIII
wieku. [Polish pre-Romanesque
and Romanesque art before the

end of the thirteenth century]
Warszawa, Państwowe
Wydawnictwo Naukowe, 1971.
914 p. illus. (part color), leaves of
plates. (Dzieje Sztuki Polskiej,
vol. 1, part 1–2) N7255.P6G53
v. 1

Sponsored by the Art Institute
of the Polish Academy of
Sciences.

Bibliography (p. 796–839) and
catalog by Maria Pietrusińska.

List of illustrations in English
and Russian.

*A sumptuous scholarly publication
that begins with artifacts of the early
Middle Ages, town planning, and
architectural sculpture. There is an
extensive section on manuscript illumination, book bindings, and ecclesiastical and courtly objects of art. Excellent reproductions. English translation of the table of contents and a
twenty-one-page list of illustrations on
over twelve hundred black and white
plates, plus eight in color. Of the
significant works of art that have
survived from the period before the
end of the thirteenth century, virtually
every one has been included here.*

22. GRYGLEWICZ, Tomasz.

Groteska w sztuce polskiej
XX wieku. [The grotesque in
Polish twentieth-century art]
Kraków, Wydawnictwo
Literackie, 1984. 190 p. 56 p. of
plates, illus. N7255.P6G83 1984

Bibliographic references.

*The grotesque is traced from the
Domus Aurea to Polish art of the
1970s. Different facets of the subject
are examined, from lyrical and
expressionistic grotesquerie to the
avant-garde. Among the many artists
included are two who were active
around 1900, Leon Chwistek and
Witold Wojtkiewicz, and two*

moderns, Stefan Żechowski and
Bronisław Linke.

23. HARASIMOWICZ, Jan.

Treści i funkcje ideowe sztuki
śląskiej Reformacji (1920–1650).
[Content and ideological function
of art in the Silesian Reformation
(1520–1650)] Wrocław,
Wydawnictwo Uniwersytetu
Wrocławskiego, 1986. 233 p. 159
illus. (Acta Universitatis
Vratislaviensis, no. 819. Historia
Sztuki, II) N7971.P6H37 1986

Summary in German: "Ideen-
programme und ideologische
Funktionen der Kunst der
schlesischen Reformation (1520–
1650)," p. 194–205.

Bibliography: p. 175–86.
Bibliographic references.
Place index (Polish and
German).

*Systematized and characterized
contents and decorations of Protestant
churches from the period of the
Reformation in Silesia, including
altars, choir stalls, ceiling and wall
paintings, epitaphs, and stalls.*

24. Historia kultury materialnej
Polski w zarysie. [An outline of
the history of Polish material
culture] Wrocław, Zakład
Narodowy im. Ossolińskich,
1978–79. 6 v. DK4110.H56

Sponsored by the Institute of
Material Culture of the Polish
Academy of Sciences.

Collective work edited by
Witold Hensel and Jan Pazdur.
Bibliographies.

*A precise, detailed examination of
material culture divided into categories
such as habitations and gardens, agri-
culture, transportation, crafts and
itinerant trades, schools and hospitals,
and attire. In sections arranged chron-*

ologically from the seventeenth century
*to 1918. The text is illustrated by
contemporary representations of the
subject or object, or by the work
objects themselves, utilitarian and
ornamental objects, whether on a
small scale or monumental, in metal,
wood, stone, ceramic, or other
material.*

25. Historia Pomorza.

[A history of Pomerania]
Poznań, Wydawnictwo
Poznańskie, 1969–84. 2 vols. in 4
parts. illus., maps. DD491.P75H5

Collective work edited by
Gerard Labuda.

Covers the period from prehistoric times to 1815. Projected in
4 vols.

Table of contents in English
and Russian.

Bibliographic references.
——— 2d. rev. ed. Poznań,
Wydawnictwo Poznańskie, 1972.
vol. 1, part 1–2. DD491.P75H52

*Contains information on
architecture, sculpture, painting.*

26. Historia Śląska.

[A history of Silesia] Wrocław,
Zakład Narodowy im.
Ossolińskich, 1960–85. 3 vols. in
7 parts. illus. maps.
DK4600.S425H58 1960

Sponsored by the Polish
Academy of Sciences, Institute of
History.

Collective work edited by
Karol Maleczyński.

Bibliographies.
Contents: vol. I: To the year
1763; v. II: 1763–1850; v. III:
1850–1918.

*Each volume contains information
about architecture, sculpture, paintings, and decorative arts.*

May be supplemented by Historia

Śląska od najdawniejszych
czasów do roku 1400. *[A history
of Silesia from the earliest times to
the year 1400]* Kraków, Polska
Akademia Umiejętności, vol. 3,
1936. 886 p. illus.
(DD491.S46H5) *Collective work
edited by Władysław Semkowicz.
Summaries of individual chapters in
French. Bibliographic references.*

27. Historia sztuki polskiej w
zarysie. [An outline of the
history of Polish art] Kraków,
Wydawnictwo Literackie, 1962.
3 v. illus., color plates, plans.
N7255.P6H5

A collective work by Helena
Blumówna, et al, edited by
Tadeusz Dobrowolski and
Władysław Tatarkiewicz.

Vol. 1. Sztuka średniowieczna.
[Medieval art]; v. 2. Sztuka
nowożytna. [Modern art]; v. 3.
Sztuka nowoczesna. [Contempo-
rary art]

Bibliographies in each
volume. Bibliography for all 3
vols.: v. 3, p. 431–50.

*In this collaborative, wide-ranging
work dealing with architecture, urbanism, sculpture, painting, printmaking, and the decorative arts from the
medieval period to the mid-twentieth
century, chapters are devoted to
uncommon subjects such as Russo-
Byzantine art (1040–1500) and
popular art. Illustrations throughout
are of poor quality.*

28. KARPOWICZ, Mariusz.

Barok w Polsce. [The Baroque
in Poland] Warszawa, Arkady,
1988. 338 p. 262 illus., 30
drawings, 24 color plates. DLC

Comments to illustrations:
p. 277–316.

Bibliography: p. 325.

The author traces the beginning of the Baroque in Poland to the architectural style of the Jesuits Church in Nieśwież, on which construction started in 1582. Discusses other churches in the Baroque style. Of the secular architecture, the royal palace in Warsaw (1599–1619) is seen as the most interesting. Two chapels, those of the Boim Family in Lwów, and St. Kazimir in Wilno Cathedral, are picked as the most beautiful examples of the Baroque in Poland. Good reproductions of paintings and sculptures of the period.

29. KARPOWICZ, Mariusz.
Sztuka Oświeconego Sarmatyznu. Antykizacja i klasycyzacja w środowisku warszawskim czasów Jana III. [The art of Enlightened Sarmatism. Antiquation and classicization in the milieu of Warsaw in the time of John III] 2d rev. ed. Warszawa, Państwowe Wydawnictwo Naukowe, 1986. 191 p. 104 p. of plates, illus. N7255.P62W336 1986

Summary in English.
Bibliographic references.

Neo-classicism was introduced into the court, among the rich and powerful connected with it, and among Warsaw's élite of the period 1672–1711. Investigation of the architectural and decorative programs of three palaces, that includes visual prototypes and literary sources (Livy, Virgil, Horace). Discusses the prevailing culture that affected this movement.

30. KARPOWICZ, Mariusz.
Sztuka polska XVII wieku. [Polish art of the seventeenth century] Warszawa,
Wydawnictwo Artystyczne i Filmowe, 1975. 220 p. illus. (part color). N7255.P6K37

Bibliography: p. 213–14.

31. KARPOWICZ, Mariusz.
Sztuka Warszawy czasów Jana III. [Art in Warsaw in the period of Jan III] Warszawa, Państwowe Wydawnictwo Naukowe, 1987. 299 p. illus. N7255.P62W3349 1987

Bibliographic references.

Deals with the patronage of King Jan III Sobieski, 1674–96, and the art that followed his reign to 1710. Primary attention is to architecture and sculpture, but paintings and prints are also surveyed. Architects include Tylman of Gameren (born in Utrecht) and J. Piola (born in Como). Painters such as Claude Callot, younger brother of Jacques Callot, are represented, as well as Polish-born artists such as Jerzy Eleuter Szymonowicz-Siemiginowski. A scholarly, well-illustrated work.

32. Katalog zabytków sztuki w Polsce. [Catalog of art monuments in Poland] Vols. I–IX, 1953–1982; Seria nowa. [New Series] vol. 1 + Warszawa, Polska Akademia Nauk, Instytut Sztuki, 1977 + illus. maps. N6991.K36

This topographical catalog records buildings of architectural significance, exterior and interior furnishings and decorations, paintings, sculpture, sacral goldsmithery, and vestments.

Each volume of the original series of the Katalog zabytków sztuki w Polsce covers one province (województwo) and consists of numerous sections (zeszyty) published on various dates. In 1977, a new series of
this catalog was instituted, based on the reorganized administrative divisions of the country. Originally, there were seventeen provinces, now there are forty-nine. The new series does not duplicate the original, but covers territories not previously included in the original series.*

Each section includes an index of names and an up-to-date list of volumes and sections published, as well as places covered. Some sections contain hundreds of good, small photographs.

33. KĘBŁOWSKI, Janusz.
Dzieje sztuki polskiej; panorama zjawisk od zarania do współczesności. [A history of Polish art; a panorama of representative examples from the earliest period to the present] Warszawa, Arkady, 1987. 285 p. illus. (part color). N7255.P6K39 1987

Bibliography: p. 218–30.
Index of places and monuments.

A remarkable and stimulating work. The author has assembled architecture, sculpture, and painting (from wall-size to miniature) to represent all principal historical phases of art, and sociological/political viewpoints. Most importantly, the author's aesthetic judgments are unassailable except perhaps with respect to contemporary works. He has sought out for discussion—in 651 plates—works seldom reproduced elsewhere. Worthy of mention here are a Crucifixion, Szamotuły, c. 1380–1390; sculptural detail, façade of City Hall, Wrocław, c.1585; Bishop's Palace, Poddębice, 1610–1617; and an aerial view of Krzyżtopór Castle, Ujazd, 1627–1644. Unfortunately, the production quality of the book itself is entirely unworthy of its important contents.

34. KĘPIŃSKA, Alicja.

Nowa sztuka, sztuka polska w latach 1945–1978. [The new art. Polish art in the years 1945–1978] Warszawa, Auriga, 1981. 279 p. illus. (part color). N7255.P6K46

Bibliographic references.

Devoted to the avant-garde movement of 1945–1978, and to analyses of Polish art during that period. Intellectual and aesthetic context, as demonstrated by chapters on the polyphonic model of art in the 1960s and "Space and Light: parameters of the new sensibility." Very well-chosen, interesting illustrations: 183 in black and white, fifteen in color.

35. KOSTROWICKI, Jerzy.

Poland; nature, settlement, architecture. Warsaw, Arkady, 1973. 545 p. illus. (part color), maps. DK408.K615513

Translation by Doreen Heaton Potworowska of *Polska. Przyroda—Osadnictwo—Architektura.*

This attractive album explores the architecture and landscape of Poland in the context of its natural environment, cultural development, and socio-economic transformation. A comprehensive historical introduction, followed by six chapters that deal with the major geographical regions of Poland: the Carpathian Mountains and sub-Carpathian upland; the central plains; the Sudeten Mountains and Silesia; the Greater Poland plateau; the Mazovian lowlands; and the seaboard and lakelands. Includes 452 illustrations.

36. KOZAKIEWICZ, Stefan, *and* Stanisław Lorentz.

Poland. *In* Encyclopedia of world art. Vol. 11. New York, McGraw-Hill, 1966. p. 376–414. N31.E4833

Bibliography.

A rather authoritative, comprehensive, detailed, clear, and engaging presentation of Polish art and architecture in English. Arranged in two main sections: "Cultural and Artistic Periods" and "Monumental Centers." The first section provides an exposition of architecture and building, painting, and sculpture, each to the degree appropriate for the period. The second section is arranged by provinces (województwo), then by cities within each province. It gives the urban history, and lists important buildings and their architects, and the buildings' contents and surrounding areas, for each historically and artistically significant city. There is a bibliography on each of the cities.

37. KOZAKIEWICZ, Stefan.

Polish art. *In* New Catholic Encyclopedia. Vol. 11. New York, McGraw Hill, 1967, p. 490–96. illus. BX841.N44 1967

Bibliographic references.

38. KOZAKIEWICZOWA, Helena, *and* Stefan Kozakiewicz.

The Renaissance in Poland. Warsaw, Arkady, 1976. 329 p. illus. (part color), map. N7255.P6K6613

Translation by Doreen Heaton Potworowska of *Renesans w Polsce.*

Bibliography: p. 323–25.

An outstanding album for the English-language reader. In an excellent English translation, 252 fine black and white photographs and eight

plates in color are magisterially discussed. The authors call attention to works of art rarely illustrated and details generally overlooked. Lengthy essays trace developments from 1500 to 1640. Contains numerous drawings of plans and a map of all sites mentioned. Reproductions show the most beautiful Renaissance buildings, such as the Town Hall in Poznań (converted from the Gothic style, 1550–1560) by the architect Giovanni Battista Quadro from Lugano. Another Town Hall, built during the years 1570 to 1572 and well preserved, is in Brzeg (Silesia), by the architect Giacomo Pario from Como; also, the Cloth Hall (Sukiennice) in Kraków with its attica. The magnificent Sigismund Chapel in the Wawel Cathedral by the architect Bartolomeo Berrecci, and the Wawel Royal Castle with courtyard galleries, are reproduced in great detail. An abundance of illustrations of paintings, tapestries, tombs, and sculptures, among them—the tomb of Bishop A. Zebrzydowski at Wawel by Jan Michałowicz.

39. KOZAKIEWICZOWA, Helena.

Renesans i manieryzm w Polsce. [The Renaissance and Mannerism in Poland] Warszawa, Auriga, 1978. 173 p. illus. (part color). N7255.P6K65

A brief history of what was principally architectural and sculptural expression, illustrated by fine photographs of infrequently reproduced monuments such as the tomb of the Mazovian knights, 1526–1528 (figs. 13–14), the Castle gateway at Brzeg, 1551–1553 (fig. 74), and the tomb of the Firlej family, c. 1600, in Bejsce (figs. 96–97).

40. Kraków. Muzeum Narodowe. L'art à Cracovie entre 1350 et 1550; exposition organisée à l'occasion du sixième centenaire de la fondation de l'Université Jagiellone. Cracovie, 1964. 386 p. 105 plates. N6997.K7K714

Catalog by Maria Kopffowa, et al.

Bibliography: p. 251–72.

Catalog from the exhibition of medieval and Renaissance Polish art, on the 600th anniversary of the founding of the Jagiellonian University, Kraków. A total of 313 entries; covers decorative art from the fifteenth and sixteenth century, ranging from goldsmithery and metalwork to textiles. The lengthy introduction (57 p.) by Maria Kopffowa discusses the history as well as the intellectual and cultural life of Kraków.

41. Krakowscy malarze, rzeźbiarze i graficy w 40 lecie Polski Ludowej, lipiec-sierpień 1985. [Cracovian painters, sculptors and printmakers on the fortieth anniversary of Peoples' Poland [exhibition catalog] July–August 1985] Kraków, Urząd miasta Krakowa, Biuro Wystaw Artystycznych, 1985. 1 vol. illus. N7255.P62K777 1985

Edited by Joanna Radzikowska.

Photographs by Krzysztof Rzepecki.

Includes paintings, sculptures, and prints by Polish artists. Addresses of the artists are given as well as a list of the most important events in the visual arts in Kraków from 1945 to 1985, arranged chronologically.

42. Kultura ocalona. Katalog wystawy poświęconej kulturze Żydów polskich. [A culture rescued. Catalog of an exhibition on the cultural heritage of Polish Jewry] Warszawa, Muzeum Narodowe w Warszawie, 1983. 58 p. 77 plates, illus (part color). N7255.P6K85 1983

Introduction in Polish and English.

Catalog by Barbara Askanas, et al.

Illustrates the splendor of the Jewish tradition and its artists within the Polish milieu. The first part illuminates Jewish culture as produced by Jewish artists; the second part enriches the knowledge of Polish culture through Jewish subjects originating with Polish artists. Covers manuscripts, gold and other metalwork, weaving, numismatics, paintings, and drawings. Good reproductions.

43. Kunstdenkmäler in Polen; ein Bildhandbuch. Herausgegeben von Reinhardt Hootz. Krakau und Südostpolen. Berlin, Deutscher Kunstverlag, 1984. 501 p. illus. (part color), map. N7255.P6K87 1984 v. 1

Introduction, text, and photograph selection by Jerzy Z. Łoziński.

Translation from the Polish by Renate Böning.

Bibliography: p. 498–500.

Outstanding photographs, 349 in black and white, 16 in color, of many architectural, sculptural, and painted monuments.

Pictures and explanatory text arranged alphabetically by city. Many floor plans and two maps.

For the Polish language edition, see entry 129.

44. Kunst in Polen von der Gotik bis heute. [Ausstellung] Kunsthaus Zürich. 26 Juni bis 8. September 1974. Zürich, Kunsthaus Zürich, 1974. 317 p. chiefly illus. (part color). N7255.P6K86

Catalog of exhibition by Tadeusz Dobrzeniecki, et al.

Bibliography: p. 11–13.

Nearly three hundred objects chosen with highly discriminating taste and knowledge, resulting in choice rarities such as The Building of a Temple *(1602), by the Gdańsk painter, Anton Moeller, and seventeenth- and eighteenth-century Polish portraits. Catalog, but only eighty-six works reproduced.*

45. LORENTZ, Stanisław, *and* Andrzej Rottermund. Klasycyzm w Polsce. [Classicism in Poland] Warszawa, Arkady, 1984. 304 p. illus. (part color). N7255.P6L67 1984

Also available in English, see next entry

46. LORENTZ, Stanisław, *and* Andrzej Rottermund. Neoclassicism in Poland. Warsaw, Arkady, 1986. 309 p. illus. (part color). N7255.P6L6713 1986

Translation by Jerzy Bałdyga of *Klasycyzm w Polsce.*

Bibliography: p. 237–38.

In Poland, the neoclassical style had its greatest reverberation in architecture. The authors provide a complex and fascinating exposition: through French contacts, the style was initiated about 1760 and nourished in Rome by Polish architects (F. Smuglewicz engraved the decorations of the Golden House of Nero, 1776) and by the archaeologist, S.K. Potocki. Palladio's villas were an important influence, and S.M.

Maggiore provided the model for the façade of the Church of St. Anne, Warsaw, 1786–1788. Further, C.N. Ledoux's buildings were sources for E. Szreger and S.B. Zug. The discussion begins with an introductory essay; the catalog is based on more than 250 plates. Sculpture, painting, and the decorative arts are included.

47. ŁUKASZEWICZ, Piotr, and Jerzy Malinowski.

Ekspresjonizm w sztuce polskiej. [Expressionism in Polish art] Wrocław, Muzeum Narodowe we Wrocławiu, 1980. 100 p. 100 black and white illus., and 6 color plates. N7255.P6L814

Exhibition catalog.
Summary in English.
Bibliography: p. 52–54.

The exhibition included paintings executed between 1912 and 1937. The catalog lists over 600 works, of which 206 are reproduced. Traces the history of the movement and foreign artists' influences, and provides a chronology of the activities of the Polish Expressionists.

48. MAŃKOWSKI, Tadeusz.

Dawny Lwów; jego sztuka i kultura artystyczna. [The old city of Lwów, its art and artistic culture] Londyn, Nakładem Fundacji Lanckorońskich i Polskiej Fundacji Kulturalnej, 1974. 422 p. illus. N7255.P62L885

Introduction by Karolina Lanckorońska.
Bibliographic references.

The manuscript was written about 1938 and eventually condensed for this 1974 publication on the city of Lwów. A scholarly, well-produced, well-illustrated history of the city's architecture, both ecclesiastical and

secular (including elevations and plans, altars and tombs), its paintings, sculpture, and decorative arts from the fourteenth century through the Renaissance, Baroque, and Classical. A major work of reference for the city.

49. MAŃKOWSKI, Tadeusz.

Influence of Islamic art in Poland. *In* Ars Islamica, vol. 2, pt. 1, 1935, p. 93–117. illus. N6260.A13 v. 2

Bibliographic references.

Islamic influences entered through Armenians who settled in Lwów. Early manifestations were in architecture (fourteenth century), but primary objects were rugs and sashes, both first imported from Persia and Turkey, then made in Poland by Armenians working in Persian and Turkish styles. Commerce and manufacture were on a vast scale. Jewelry and arms were imported in lesser numbers.

50. MAŃKOWSKI, Tadeusz.

Mecenat artystyczny Stanisława Augusta. [The artistic patronage of (King) Stanislaus Augustus] Warszawa, Państwowe Wydawnictwo Naukowe, 1976. 384 p. illus. N5280.P72S865

Edited by Zuzanna Prószyńska.
Introduction by Władysław Tatarkiewicz.
Summary in English.
Bibliographic references.

The present critical edition of a work written in the 1926–1938 era. Updates the status of research and makes the literature current. The text examines one of the most important of all royal patrons in Polish history and considers six

aspects of his influence: (1) the spirit of the Enlightenment, where patronage functioned to improve the general welfare, while the King's refined personal taste promoted the creation of architectural masterpieces; (2) the King's agent, August Moszyński, who purchased prints, drawings, medals, and antiquities on an enormous scale; (3) the King's classicizing and Western taste as opposed to traditional Sarmatism, with the expansion of Greco-Roman taste being taken into account; (4) the production of porcelain in the Belvedere; (5) the program for the Knight's Hall to commemorate important events and persons in Polish history (inter alia with bronze busts, many of which are extant); (6) and—in the King's mercantile interest—the production of waist sashes.

51. MAŃKOWSKI, Tadeusz.

Orient w polskiej kulturze artystycznej. [The Orient in Polish artistic culture] Wrocław, Zakład Narodowy im. Ossolińskich, 1959. 255 p. plates, illus. (part color). N7255.P6M36 1959

Summary and table of contents in French.
Bibliographic references.

The influence may be divided between the Byzantine ascendance, from the Middle Ages to the fall of Constantinople in 1453, and the Islamic dominance, from that date to the nineteenth century. During the first period, painting in particular, in various media, was charged with Near Eastern styles through Armenian influence. During the second period, rugs especially, but also fabrics, arms, and armor, were imported from Persia by way of Turkey. Polish artists and architects were also active in Turkey and Transylvania.

52. MAŃKOWSKI, Tadeusz.

Sztuka Islamu w Polsce w XVII i XVIII wieku. [Islamic art in Poland in the seventeenth and eighteenth centuries] Kraków, Gebethner and Wolff, 1935. 126 p. illus. 40 plates. (Polska Akademia Umiejętności. Wydział Filologiczny. Rozprawy, vol. 64, no. 3) AS142.K85

Bibliographic references.

A study in seven chapters covering topics such as the infiltration of Eastern art, especially Islamic, into Poland from the Middle Ages to the Baroque, through trade, war, or other mechanisms; Persian carpets collected by Polish kings from Sigismund Augustus to Augustus III; Eastern and Western influences on Polish seventeenth-century weaving; Eastern and Polish sashes; production in Lwów of arms, embroidery, and clothing, with their particular styles and ornamentation.

53. MAŃKOWSKI, Tadeusz.

Sztuka Ormian lwowskich. [Art of the Armenians of Lwów] Polska Akademia Umiejętności. Prace Komisji Historji Sztuki, vol. 6, no. 1, 1934, p. 61–163. illus. N6991.P633 v. 6 folio

Summary in French.
Bibliographic references.

Armenians, settled in southeastern Poland since at least the beginning of the thirteenth century, have gradually assimilated with the Polish population, while still retaining elements of their national culture. Lwów has been their intellectual center. The author analyzes the influence of Armenian artistic monuments on the art of the region. Architectural ornament has

Islamic characteristics. Manuscript illumination flourished.

54. Mille ans d'art en Pologne,

Petit Palais, Paris, avril–juillet 1969. Paris, Petit Palais, 1969. 1 v. (unpaged) illus., color plates. N6991.M5

Bibliographic references.
Exhibition catalog.

Within the wide chronological span, the widest diversity in materials and quality. Great objects of Gothic sculpture, goldsmithery, ecclesiastical vestments, and Renaissance tapestries. Also portraits and other paintings— Gothic to the present—and decorative arts. A summary catalog.

Reviews in the French press by André Chastel, Le Monde *(May 3, 1969), Pierre du Colombier,* L'Amateur de l'Art *(April 24, 1969), Pierre Schneider,* L'Express *(May 26–June 1, 1969), and others.*

55. Obóz koncentracyjny Oświęcim w twórczości artystycznej. [The Oswięcim concentration camp in art] 2d ed. Oświęcim, Wydawnictwo Państwowego Muzeum, 1961–62. 4 v. in 1. illus. (part fold.). N7255.P6026 1961

Text by Kazimierz Smoleń.
Text in Polish, English, French, German, and Russian.
Contents: Vol. 1–3. Malarstwo [Painting]—v. 4 Rzeźba. [Sculpture].

The first volume (xviii, 79 p.) reproduces drawings in coal by Jerzy Adam Brandhuber; the second (xxii, 40 p.), drawings and a woodcut by Mieczysław Kościelniak; and the third (iii, 61 p.), drawings by Maria Hiszpańska-Neumann, Janina Tollik, Franciszek Jaźwiecki, Tadeusz Myszkowski, Jerzy

Potrzebowski, and Władysław Siwek. The fourth volume (74 p.) presents photographs of sculptures by Mieczysław Stobierski, Hanna Raynoch, Tadeusz Myszkowski, Vida Jocić, Hubert van Lith, and G.W. Mizandari. All the artists were professionals, and all were prisoners at Oświęcim. Their works reveal the daily experiences of hunger, exhaustion, torture, and death. Eleven penetrating portraits by Franciszek Jaźwiecki were drawn from life at the camp.

56. Ogólnopolska wystawa

Młodej Plastyki pod hasłem "Przeciw wojnie—przeciw faszyzmowi," zorganizowana z okazji V Światowego Festiwalu Młodzieży i Studentów. Malarstwo—rzeźba—grafika. Lipiec—wrzesień 1955 Warszawa, "Arsenał." Exposition de la jeune peinture, sculpture et gravure. Contre la guerre —contre le fascisme, organisée a l'occasion du V Festivale Mondial de la Jeunesse et des Etudiants. Peinture—sculpture— gravure. Juillet–Septembre 1955 Varsovie, "Arsenal." Warszawa, Centralne Biuro Wystaw Artystycznych, [1955]. 47 p. [47] plates. N6991.A47

Catalog of the exhibition in Polish and French.
Introduction by Andrzej Jakimowicz.

Lists 499 exhibited items; only 47 reproduced. Arranged with the State Museum Majdanek. Over 80 young artists express themselves against war in general and against human destruction by the Nazis. Some images are conventionally abstract or symbolic, while others are of individual artistry.

57. OLSZEWSKI, Andrzej K.
Dzieje sztuki polskiej 1890–
1980 w zarysie. [An outline
history of Polish art 1890–1980]
Warszawa, Wydawnictwo Interpress, 1988. 186 p. 282 illus. (part
color) N7255.P6044 1988
Bibliography: p. 166–72.

*This study is divided into five periods
— 1980–1925, 1925–1933, 1933–
1949, 1949–1955, and 1955–1980.
Beginning with the influence of impressionism, the author continues
through the avant-garde, follows with
the wartime art of the concentration
camps and prisons and postwar
socialist realism, and concludes with
contemporary abstract art.*

*An English translation of this
work was published in 1989 in
Warsaw, under the title:* An Outline history of Polish twentieth-
century art and architecture.

58. O polskiej sztuce religijnej;
praca zbiorowa. [Polish religious
art; a collective work] Katowice,
Nakładem Związku Artystów
Śląskich, 1932. 383 p. illus.
N7971.P602
A collective work by Helena
Abancourt de Franqueville, et al.
Edited by Jerzy Langman.
Bibliography: p. 191.

*Works of the nineteenth and twentieth
century: paintings, sculpture, mosaics,
stained glass, weaving, book binding.
Important for lesser-known works of
major painters (Józef Mehoffer, Jan
Matejko) and outstanding works by
lesser-known artists (Karol Hukan,
altar of the Queen of Angels, Jesuit
Church, Kraków). Illustrates the
widespread and fine production of
stained glass, as by S. Wyspiański,
J. Mehoffer, Karol Maszkowski, and
J. Piasecki. Eight original woodcuts*

*by Zdzisław Gedliczka, Stanisław
Jakubowski, Wanda Korzeniowska,
and Paweł Steller.*

59. Pamiątki Zamku
Królewskiego w Warszawie.
[Historical relics of the Royal
Castle in Warsaw] 3d rev. ed.
Warszawa, Krajowa Agencja
Wydawnicza, 1976. 88 p. illus.
(part color). DK4645.R6P35
Edited by Stanisław Lorentz,
Andrzej Rottermund, and Jan
Sarnecki.
Summaries and list of illustra-
tions in French and English
inserted.

*Although unattractively produced,
this book illustrates highly interesting
works: paintings, sculpture, and the
decorative arts. Jean Baptiste Oudry's
portrait of Stanisław Leszczyński
(1730) is reproduced (p. 39).*

60. PASIERB, Janusz S.
Ochrona zabytków sztuki
kościelnej. [Preservation of eccle-
siastical art monuments] Poznań,
Pallotinum, 1971. 239 p. illus.
N9041.P6P37 1971
Table of contents also in
French and German.
Bibliography: p. 151–53.

*Provides citations to, and excerpts
from, the articles of ecclesiastical and
civil laws governing the preservation of
churches and the works of art within,
as well as the theoretical and juridical
foundations of the laws. Chapters are
devoted to the pathology of physical
materials, the installation of modern
equipment, and traditional subjects or
methods of preserving church fabric
and accessories.*

61. PIWOCKI, Ksawery.
Historia Akademii Sztuk
Pięknych w Warszawie, 1940–

1964. [History of the Academy of
Arts in Warsaw, 1904–1964]
Wrocław, Zakład Narodowy im.
Ossolińskich, 1965. 238 p. illus.
ports. N332.W3P5
Sponsored by the Art Institute
of the Polish Academy of
Sciences.

*Includes a list of students for the years
1904–1963/64.*

**62. Poland, Komisariat
Generalny.**
Nowojorska Wystawa
Światowa, 1939–1940. Offical
catalogue of the Polish Pavilion
at the World's Fair in New York
1939. Warsaw, Drukarnia Polska,
1939. 503 p. illus. (part color),
plates, ports., maps, plans, diagrs.
T785.G1P7 1939
[Polish Pavilion] p. 97–242,
290–92, 449–76.

*Interesting for the 1939 viewpoint
with respect to contemporary styles
and values in art. Reproductions,
some in color, of historical and
diagrammatic works of art in the
Hall of Honor, such as the* Victory
at Vienna *and—by Arthur
Szyk—the* Poles in America.
*Masterful essay by Michał Walicki
on the art of Poland before the
partitions. Lists of exhibited paintings, prints, decorative arts, and folk
art. The catalog itself is a fine
example of book design.*

63. POLLAKÓWNA, Joanna.
Formiści. [The Formists]
Wrocław, Zakład Narodowy im.
Ossolińskich, 1972. 199 p. illus.
(Studia z Historii Sztuki, vol. 14)
N7255.P6P64
Sponsored by the Polska
Akademia Nauk, Instytut Sztuki.
Summary in French.
Bibliographic references.

Panorama of the city of Kraków in the early seventeenth century, from Pierre d'Avity's *Neuwe Archontologia Cosmica* (Frankfurt, 1649). The medallions adorning it, from left to right, show St. Florian, whose protection was sought against fire; the coats of arms of the city, the Duchy of Milan, the Kingdom of Poland, and the Grand Duchy of Lithuania; and the crowned "K" for Kazimierz or Casimir the Great. Library of Congress, Geography and Map Division

Pollakówna's work is one of the first on Formiści (the Formists) to provide a broad picture of that short-lived movement. The first use of the name Formists to denote the group was at the second exhibition of Polish Expressionists, in August 1918. The following year an exhibition of Formist art was held in Warsaw. Especially notable among the Formists were Stanisław Ignacy Witkiewicz, Leon Chwistek, Tytus Czyżewski, Zbigniew Pronaszko, and Andrzej Pronaszko.

64. Polska, jej dzieje i kultura od czasów najdawniejszych do chwili obecnej. [Poland, her history and culture from the earliest times to the present] Warszawa, Trzaska, Evert i Michalski, 1927–32. 3 vols. illus., ports., maps. DK414.P84 ERR

Edited by Stanisław Lam. Bibliographies.

A valuable survey covering the entire span of Polish history and culture to 1930. The arrangement is chronological: vol. 1, to 1572; v. 2, to 1795; and v. 3, from 1796 to 1930. Comprises articles by leading scholars as such as Aleksander Brückner, historian of Polish culture, and art historians Feliks Kopera and Mieczysław Treter. Includes much information about Polish architecture, painting, sculpture, decorative arts, and arms and armor.

65. Polska w krajobrazie i zabytkach. [Poland in landscapes and historical monuments] Warszawa, T. Złotnicki, 1930. 2 v. illus. DK407.P6

Text by Aleksander Janowski et al.

Photographs by Jan Bułhak and others.

Immensely useful for placing the architectural and sculptural monuments in their geographical locale, the subjects are arranged by pre-World War II regional divisions (województwa). Volume I covers Warsaw, Łódź, Gdańsk, and their regions and those of Kielce, Lublin, Białystok, Pomorze, Poznań, and Silesia. Volume II covers Kraków and is particularly valuable for its coverage of the cities of Lwów and Wilno. Rzeszów, Jarosław, and Przemyśl are included in the Lwów region. Other regions now within the U.S.S.R.: Stanisławów, Tarnopol, Wołyń, Polesie, among others, are included. Splendid choice of subjects, on all levels of culture and artistry, and all periods from the late medieval. Castles, churches, synagogues, and country houses are individually discussed in some detail. Nearly 1,500 photographs, including natural landscapes.

66. Polskie życie artystyczne w latach 1890–1914. [Polish artistic life in the years 1890–1914] Wrocław, Zakład Narodowy im. Ossolińskich, 1967. 270 p. illus. N7255.P6P676

Sponsored by the Historical Institute of the Polish Academy of Sciences.

Collective work edited by Aleksander Wojciechowski.

Prodigious documentation—including photographs—on art education, institutions devoted to promoting the arts, as well as exhibitions, organizations of artists, commercial aspects, and art periodicals.

67. Polskie życie artystyczne w latach 1915–1939. [Polish artistic

life in the years 1915–1939] Wrocław, Zakład Narodowy im. Ossolińskich, 1974. 738 p. illus. N7255.P6P677

Sponsored by the Art Institute of the Polish Academy of Sciences.

Collective work edited by Aleksander Wojciechowski.

Bibliographies.

More than half the volume is devoted to a chronology of the major artistic events throughout the country and Polish art events abroad (United States, United Kingdom, France, Germany, Latin America). Covers competitions, with names of submitting artists, exhibitions and their participants, dedications of monuments, publications of illustrated books, and theatrical productions of artistic significance. Special chapters on architecture, art education, and artists' organizations. The editors are sensitive to the participation of women in the arts. Numerous photographs.

68. PORĘBSKI, Mieczysław.
Interregnum; studia z historii sztuki polskiej XIX i XX w. [Interregnum; studies in the history of Polish art of the nineteenth and twentieth centuries] Warszawa, Państwowe Wydawnictwo Naukowe, 1975. 309 p. illus. N7255.P6P68

Bibliographic references.

The first half deals with problems in nineteenth-century historicism, the iconography of Hope from Ripa to Wojniakowski, and battle subjects and heroes (Don Quixote by H. Daumier and P. Michałowski). The second half treats contemporary subjects, such as the surrealist painter S.I. Witkiewicz.

69. PORĘBSKI, Mieczysław.
Pożegnanie z krytyką. [Farewell to criticism] Kraków, Wydawnictwo Literackie, 1966. 259 p. illus. N6991.P647

Bibliographic references.

Collected essays, originally published during the years 1956 to 1965, mainly in Polish periodicals, by a leading critic of contemporary art. The first half contains twenty-four profiles of Polish artists, including Maria Jarema (d. 1958), Andrzej Wróblewski (d. 1957), Janina Kraupe, and Stanisław Wojtowicz. The second half comprises reflections evoked by international exhibitions (Venice, Moscow, Sao Paulo), a theoretical essay entitled "Art and Information," and an "Introduction to Metacriticism."

70. Presences polonaises.
Witkiewicz, Constructivisme, les contemporains: L'art vivant autour du Musée de Łódź. Centre Georges Pompidou, 23 juin—26 septembre, 1983. [Exhibition catalog] Paris, Le Centre, 1983. 335 p. illus. (part color). NX571.P6P74 1983

Exhibition catalog.

A French tribute to the Museum of Art, Łódź, which was inaugurated in 1931 and is among the first museums of modern art in Europe, and to the multidisciplinary exponents of modern art movements: Stanislaw Ignacy Witkiewicz, visual artist, dramatist, writer, originator of "Czysta Forma" (Pure Form), and his contemporary Bruno Schulz; the many practitioners of Constructivism, also in architecture, and of Futurism. Modern conceptual visual artists, writers, dramatists, composers. Biographies, oeuvres catalogs, collection of the Łódź Museum. An important investigation and analysis of modern art in Poland.

71. PTAŚNIK, Jan.
Cracovia artificum, 1300–1550. Kraków, Polska Akademia Umiejętności, 1917–1936. 2 v. (Źródła do historyi sztuki i cywilizacyi w Polsce, tom 4, 5 zesz. 1) NK1036.P6K7
    Vol. 2 edited by Marian Friedberg.
————— ————— Supplementa. [1] + Wrocław, Zakład Narodowy im. Ossolińskich, 1985 + DK4721.C73
The first volume (151 p.), edited by Bolesław Przybyszewski, includes texts of sources for the years 1410–12 and 1421–24, which were not listed in the earlier edition by Ptaśnik. The next volumes will include sources for the years 1433–50.

72. PTAŚNIK, Jan.
Kultura włoska wieków średnich w Polsce. [Italian culture of the Middle Ages in Poland] 2d ed. Warszawa, Państwowe Wydawnictwo Naukowe, 1959. 332 p. illus. DK411.P78 1959
    Bibliography: p. 313–25.
One chapter is devoted to artists and artisans—wall painters, manuscript illuminators, sculptors, goldsmiths—active mainly in Kraków. Other chapters treat bankers, physicians, engineers, merchants, scholars, military men, and others. "Poles in Italy" forms a separate chapter.

73. RHODES, Anthony.
Poland. p. 130–171 *in* Art treasures of Eastern Europe. New York, G.P. Putnam's Sons, 1972. 278 p. illus. (part color),
maps. N6750.R47
    Bibliography: p. 273.
    Biographical notes on artists: p. 266–271.
Excellent photographs.

74. Rokoko. Studia nad sztuką 1. połowy XVIII w. [Rococo. Studies in the art of the first half of the eighteenth century] Warszawa, Państwowe Wydawnictwo Naukowe, 1970. 325 p. illus. N7255.P6R6
    Materiały Sesji Stowarzyszenia Historyków Sztuki zorganizowanej wspólnie z Muzeum Śląskim we Wrocławiu. Wrocław, październik 1968. [Papers delivered at the meeting organized by the Association of Art Historians and the Silesian Museum, Wrocław, October 1968]
    Introduction by Jan Białostocki.
    Summary and table of contents in English.
    Bibliographic references.
Important studies which include articles on the formation and genealogy of European Rococo with examples from Poland (Lwów, Dominican Church, architect Jan Witt; Berezwecz, Orthodox Church, architect Jan K. Glaubitz). Four articles are devoted to developments in Silesia: churches, and the ducal hall in the cloister of Lubiąż (Leubus). One article discusses churches where pillars are the principal expressive form ("Kościoły ściennofilarowe"); another discusses catafalques, projected and executed.

75. ROZANOW, Zofia, *and* Ewa Smulikowska.
Skarby kultury na Jasnej Górze. [Cultural treasures at Jasna Góra] 2d rev. ed. Warszawa, Interpress,
1979. 211 p. color illus. N7255.P62C937 1979
    Introduction by Władysław Tomkiewicz.
    Bibliography: p. 209–10.
    Photographs by Jan Michlewski and Janusz Rosikoń.
Also available in English translation (see next entry).

76. ROZANOW, Zofia, *and* Ewa Smulikowska.
The cultural heritage of Jasna Góra. 2d rev. ed. Warsaw, Interpress, 1979. 211 p. color illus. N7255.P62C936 1979
    Introduction by Władysław Tomkiewicz.
    Translation by Stanisław Tarnowski.
    Bibliography: p. 209–11.
    Photographs by Jan Michlewski and Janusz Rosikoń.
Art treasures at the Pauline Monastery in Częstochowa. Lavish gifts were bestowed on Jasna Góra by the kings of Poland: croziers and chalices, a reliquary crucifix of 1510, the scepter of the Jagiellonians of 1500, a silver repoussé antependium of the early eighteenth century, and many more. Seventeenth-century paintings of the history of the monastery, including the Hussite attack in 1430, when the picture of the Madonna was slashed.

77. Rubens, Niderlandy i Polska.
[Rubens, The Netherlands, and Poland] Łódź, Muzeum Sztuki, 1978. 177 p. 32 leaves of plates, illus. N6973.R9S47 1977
    Edited by Jacek Antoni Ojrzyński.
    Summaries and table of contents in English.
    Bibliographic references.
    Materiały Sesji Naukowej,

Łódź 25–26 lutego 1977. [Papers from the Scholarly Sessions Held at Łódź on February 25–26, 1977]

Eighteen essays on the 400th anniversary of Rubens's birth. Papers on works by Rubens and his atelier in Polish collections (Poznań, Warsaw, Kraków); on Polish travelers in the Low Countries; on the influence of Netherlandish ornament through prints (H. Wierix), through objects (tapestries, goldsmithery); and by immigrant artists (Hans Vredeman de Vries).

78. Sarmatia artistica.

Księga pamiątkowa ku czci Profesora Władysława Tomkiewicza. [Sarmatia artistica. Essays in honor of Professor Władysław Tomkiewicz] Warszawa, Państwowe Wydawnictwo Naukowe, 1968. 291 p. illus. N7443.S29

Bibliographic references.
Bibliography of W. Tomkiewicz's works: p. 7–15.
Table of contents in English.

Covering the sixteenth to nineteenth century, includes a study by S. Sawicka on a drawing by Antoine Caron (Fogg) of festivities in France for Polish envoys, 1573; one by N. Miks, who investigates G.B. Gisleni, a seventeenth-century Polish architect (drawings in the Soane Museum); and one by A. Dobrzycka on Thorvaldsen and his Polish patron.

79. Secesja. Wystawa ze zbiorów Muzeum Mazowieckiego w Płocku.

Katalog wystawy. [Secession: An exhibition from the collections of the Masovia Museum in Płock. Catalog] Płock, Muzeum

Mazowieckie w Płocku, 1979. 24 p. illus., ports. N6465.A7M88 1979

Introduction by Tadeusz Zaremba.

Paintings, prints, drawings, sculpture, medals, ceramics, glass, metalwork, furniture, and costume. Orientation of Polish style to that of Austria and Germany evident from preponderantly Austro German origins of objects represented. Other works shown are by Czechoslovak, Russian, French, and Belgian artists. Famous names include E. Gallé and M. Thonet. Lesser-known Polish artists include the painters K. Krzyżanowski, K. Stabrowski, and W. Wojtkiewicz; the sculptor W. Szymanowski; and the ceramicist J. Szczepkowski.

80. STARZYŃSKI, Juliusz.

Polska droga do samodzielności w sztuce. [The Polish road to originality in art] Warszawa, Państwowe Wydawnictwo Naukowe, 1973. 183 p. 189 illus. N7255.P6S75

Summary in English and Russian.
Bibliography: p. 141–58 by Maria Liczbińska.

81. Stowarzyszenie Historyków Sztuki. Sztuka XIX wieku w Polsce. Naród—Miasto. [The art of the nineteenth century in Poland. The nation—the city] Warszawa, Państwowe Wydawnictwo Naukowe, 1979 272 p. illus. N7255.P6S8 1979

Materiały Sesji Stowarzyszenia Historyków Sztuki, Poznań, grudzień 1977.
Bibliographic references.

Fourteen essays selected from the many papers delivered at a session of

the Association of Art Historians held in Poznań in December 1977. The theme of the session was the history of art during the period of the partitions. An essay by Maria Janion discusses "The Romantic artist and the national 'sacrum.'" History painting is represented by an essay on Jan Matejko's three canvases collectively entitled "The Allegory of Poland" that discusses "Father Skarga's Sermon," "Rejtan at the Warsaw Sejm in 1773," and "Poland shackled." "Residential architecture of the Warsaw grande bourgeoisie," "capitalist architecture in Łódź," and "The 'National Historism' of the years 1919–1929 as an expression of romantic throught" are some of the other essay titles.

82. Stowarzyszenie Historyków Sztuki. Sztuka około 1900. [Art circa 1900]. Warszawa, Państwowe Wydawnictwo Naukowe, 1969, 276 p. illus. N7255.P6S8 1969

Table of contents in English.
Bibliographic references.
Materiały Sesji Stowarzyszenia Historyków Sztuki, Kraków, grudzień 1967. [Papers delivered at the meeting of the Association of Art Historians held in Kraków, December 1967]

The book consists of sixteen essays, ranging from Andrzej Jakimowicz on Jacek Malczewski's self-portraits and Janina Wiercińska on book design and ornament in the 1980s, to Karol Estreicher on Zakopane as an art center during the years 1900 to 1914 and the popularity and application of the Zakopane style in sculpture, architecture, painting, furniture, rugs, and other art forms. Among the artists influenced by the Zakopane style were Władysław Skoczylas,

Zofia Stryjeńska, Pafał Malczewski, and Zbigniew Pronaszko.

83. Stowarzyszenie Historyków Sztuki. Sztuka około roku 1600. [Art circa 1600] Warszawa, Państwowe Wydawnictwo Naukowe, 1974. 353 p. illus. N7255.P6S8 1974

Bibliographic references.

Materiały Sesji Stowarzyszenia Historyków Sztuki zorganizowanej przy współpracy Wydziału Kultury Prezydium Wojewódzkiej Rady Narodowej w Lublinie. Lublin, listopad 1972.

Seventeen essays including, for example, those of Jerzy Kowalczyk on Polish contacts with Venetian artists; Józef T. Frazik on artists and craftsmen in the Przemyśl and Sanok regions around 1600; Karol Majewski on architects from Lublin active from 1571 to 1625; and Ewa Różycka-Rozpędowska on Late Renaissance manor houses in Silesia. Other essays include studies on architecture of the sixteenth and seventeenth century; Jan Skuratowicz on the beginning of the Netherlandish trend in sculpture in the second half of the sixteenth century in Silesia; and Maria Glińska on Netherlandish stonecutters active in West Pomerania at the turn of the sixteenth century.

84. Stowarzyszenie Historyków Sztuki. Sztuka Pobrzeża Bałtyku. [The art of the Baltic Coast] Materiały Sesji Stowarzyszenia Historyków Sztuki, Gdańsk, listopad 1976. [Papers from the Sessions of the Association of Art Historians, Gdańsk, November 1976] Warszawa, Państwowe Wydawnictwo Naukowe, 1978. 437 p. illus. N7255.P62B346

Edited by Hanna Fruba.
Table of contents also in English.
Bibliographic references.

Twenty essays on the art and architecture of an historically important and culturally fruitful region. Included are studies on the castles of the Teutonic Knights; an entry into Gdańsk (1646) as an example of interaction between that city and Antwerp; Netherlandish elements in art in Gdańsk (about 1600); a predella of Philip Bischof and problems in the late medieval iconography of death, with a regional artistic overview by J. Białostocki.

85. Studia Renesansowe. [Renaissance Studies] Wrocław, Zakład Narodowy im. Ossolińskich, 1956–64. 4 v. illus.

Sponsored by the Art Institute of the Polish Academy of Sciences.
Edited by Michał Walicki.
Summaries in French and Russian.
Vols. 2–4 (1957–64) include extensive bibliographies on the Renaissance in Poland.

Major articles by authoritative scholars. Poland's fine architecture, sculpture, and decorative arts of the period. Also articles on contemporary painting and manuscript illumination.

86. STYCZYŃSKI, Jan. The artist and his work. Warsaw, Interpress, 1977. 148 p. chiefly illus. (part color). NX571.P6S8513

Edited by Grażyna Hartwig.
Translation by Krystyna Kęplicz.

Twenty-nine artists, internationally known: painters, fiber artists, graphic artists, sculptors, architects, com-posers, theater and film directors. Insightful photographs of the artists at work and of their works, in mutually enhancing juxtapositions. Included are M. Abakanowicz, J. Młodożeniec, W. Sadley, H. Stażewski, J. Szajna, T. Kusielewicz, W. Świerzy.

87. SUCHODOLSKA, Maria, and Bogdan Suchodolski. Polska, naród a sztuka. Dzieje polskiej świadomości narodowej i jej wyraz w sztuce. [Poland, the nation and its art. A history of Polish national consciousness and its expression in art] Warszawa, Arkady, 1988. 470 p. illus. (part color). N7255.P6S86 1988

An album that illustrates historical subjects and universal allegories applied to Poland, and taken from literature on seven themes (such as Kingdom and Republic, Fatherland, Military Service, and Daily Life). Texts introducing the chapters are integrated thematically with the illustrations, but lack specific plate numbers. Among the wide array of pictures of art and architecture are many beautiful and little-known works, e.g., triptych Pławna, no. 121; tympanum, Strzegom, no. 335; relief sculpture, tomb of Piotr Tomicki, no. 362.

Also available in English (see next entry).

88. SUCHODOLSKA, Maria, and Bogdan Suchodolski. Poland: nation and art; a history of the nation's awareness and its expression in art. Warsaw, Arkady, 1989. 477 p. illus. (part color), facsims., ports. DLC

Translation of *Polska, naród a sztuka* by Magdalena Iwińska and Piotr Paszkiewicz

89. SUCHODOLSKI, Bogdan.
Dzieje kultury polskiej. [History of Polish culture] Warszawa, Interpress, 1980. 637 p. illus. (part color) DK4100.S918

Also available in English (see next entry).

90. SUCHODOLSKI, Bogdan.
A History of Polish culture. Warsaw, Interpress, 1986. 256 p. illus. (part color). DK4110.S919 1986

Translated by E. J. Czerwiński.

Consists principally of 411 excellent reproductions of works of art: architecture, sculpture, painting, manuscript illumination, prints, a few objects of decorative art. Chosen with artistic discrimination, the selection is balanced in all periods from medieval to modern. The text is geared not to artistic styles but to social, economic, and political factors instrumental in shaping Polish culture.

91. ŚWIECHOWSKI, Zygmunt.
Sztuka romańska w Polsce. [Romanesque art in Poland] Warszawa, Arkady, 1982, 279 p. illus., maps, plans. (Dzieje sztuki w Polsce) N7255.P6S93 1982
Bibliography: p. 275.

Also available in English (see next entry).

92. ŚWIECHOWSKI, Zygmunt.
Romanesque art in Poland. Warsaw, Arkady, 1983. 279 p. illus. N7255.P6S9313 1983
Translation by Alina Kozińska-Bałdyga and Jerzy Bałdyga of *Sztuka romańska w Polsce.*
Bibliography: p. 275.

A bountifully literate, readable, and scholarly text accompanied by over two hundred black-and-white and eight color photographs and plans. Only a few great monuments of outstanding quality survive. At the close of the Romanesque period, Legnica was the ruler's impressive residence in Eastern Europe along with Prague and Estergom. The author deals with influences from the Rhine, Meuse, Saxony, Thuringia, and Lorraine, as well as monuments that are "integral parts of a specifically Polish historical process." Covers architecture, sculpture in stone and wood, metal art, and wall painting.

93. Symbolae historiae artium;
studia z historii sztuki Lechowi Kalinowskiemu dedykowane. [Symbolae historiae artium; studies in art history dedicated to Lech Kalinowski] Warszawa, Państwowe Wydawnictwo Naukowe, 1986. 506 p. illus. N7442.K35 1986
Edited by Jerzy Gadomski, et al.
In Polish, English, French, and German.
Bibliographic references.

To commemorate the eightieth birthday of Lech Kalinowski, thirty-three essays on Romanesque, Gothic, and early Renaissance architecture, manuscript illumination, and wall painting, in Poland or by Polish artists. Also, an article by A. Gieysztor on Polish masters at the University of Paris in the fifteenth century, and articles on theory and iconography.

94. Sztuka dworu Wazów w Polsce. Wystawa w Zamku Królewskim na Wawelu, maj-czerwiec 1976. Katalog. Art of the court of the Vasa dynasty in Poland. Exhibition in the Wawel Castle in Cracow, May– June 1976. Catalogue. Kraków, Państwowe Zbiory Sztuki na Wawelu, 1976. 209 p. 55 leaves of plates, illus. (part color), ports. N7255.P6S97
Edited by Andrzej Fischinger.
Text in Polish and English.
Bibliography: p. 133–38.

An important exhibition of collections formed over some eighty years during the reigns of three Polish monarchs, descendant in the male line from the Swedish Vasa dynasty and in the female line from the Polish-Lithuanian Jagiełło family: Sigismund III (1587–1632), Władysław IV (1632–1648), and Jan Kazimierz (1648–1668). Loans from thirteen European and American collections, together with holdings of paintings, medals, jewelry, arms and armor from thirty-one Polish collections.

95. Sztuka i historia; księga pamiątkowa ku czci Michała Walickiego. [Art and history; A festschrift in honor of Michał Walicki] Warszawa, Wydawnictwa Artystyczne i Filmowe, 1966. 232 p. illus. N7443.S95
Editorial Committee: Jan Białostocki, Andrzej Ryszkiewicz, Juliusz Starzyński, Jerzy Toeplitz, and Władysław Tomkiewicz.
Bibliography of M. Walicki's works by Anna Wiercińska.

Essays by twenty-three authors, on subjects ranging from Romanesque sculpture, Gothic architecture and reliquaries, and a drawing by Esaias van de Velde, to iconography of Vertumnus and Pomona, and from the eighteenth-century architect Efraim Szreger to the pre-World War II architect Oskar Sosnowski;

all works of art of Polish execution or in Polish collections.

96. Sztuka sakralna w Polsce
na Ziemiach Zachodnich i Północnych. [Sacred art in Poland in the western and northern territories] Warszawa, Ars Christiana, 1976. 53 p. illus., maps. N7971.P6S9

By Jerzy Dobrzeniecki.
Maps by Lidia Müllerowa.
Bibliographic references.

Many well-known churches and monuments are treated (Gniezno, the Basilica of the Primate; Szczecin; Wrocław), along with a number of others of perhaps equal distinction but less publicized. Periods covered are from the Romanesque (such as the Gothic parish church at Pyrzyce, near Szczecin) to the Baroque (Church of St. Joseph at Krzeszów). A scholarly, descriptive paragraph is given for each of the 250 churches, with mention of altarpieces, icons, paintings, free-standing sculpture, funerary monuments, and reliquaries. The main substance of the book lies in the 250 fine photographs. The maps are not cross-referenced in the text.

97. Sztuka Warszawy. [The art of Warsaw] Warszawa, Państwowe Wydawnictwo Naukowe, 1986. 479 p. illus. [208] p. of plates. N7255.P62W37 1986

Collective work by Juliusz A. Chrościcki, Mariusz Karpowicz, Maria I. Kwiatkowska, Marek Kwiatkowski, Adam Miłobędzki, Teresa Mroczko, and Andrzej Olszewski.

Edited by Mariusz Karpowicz.
Bibliographic references.

A carefully assembled and finely produced volume of authoritative essays on painting, sculpture, and architecture. In addition to chapters on the medieval period, the Renaissance, and Baroque, two chapters are devoted to art and architecture under the Saxon monarchy. This is followed by essays on the nineteenth century in two chronological phases. A chapter on the period 1890 to 1939 closes the work. Features uncommon illustrations such as those of buildings taken from incidental portrait backgrounds, and of seldom-reproduced drawings and manuscripts. Buildings and interiors in contemporary photographs offer opportunities to study such outstanding sculptors as Jan Jerzy Plersch (1704–1774), among a wealth of others.

98. Sztuka Wrocławia. [The art of Wrocław] Wrocław, Zakład Narodowy im. Ossolińskich, 1967. 508 p. illus. map. N6886.B75S9

Collective work edited by Tadeusz Broniewski and Mieczysław Złat.

Foreword in English, p. 16–23.

Bibliography: p. 468–72.

The survey is divided into the following periods: Romanesque (1000–1250), Gothic (1250–1500), Renaissance and Mannerism (1500–1650), Baroque (1650–1750), Classicism (1750–1850), art during 1850–1945, and art from 1945 to 1965. Included are architecture, sculpture, painting, and decorative arts. An index of artists and Wrocław monuments; 420 inadequate illustrations.

99. I Tesori dell'antica Polonia;
dai Veneti ai re di Cracovia. Skarby Polski starodawnej; od Wenetów po czasy królów dynastji Piastowskiej. Padova, Palazzo della Ragione 13 aprile–31 luglio 1985. Modena, Panini, 1985. 187 p. 197 illus. (part color). DK4090.T47 1985

Bibliographies.
Exhibition catalog.

One of the most extensive and scholarly exhibitions ever assembled on Polish art from prehistoric times to the medieval period. It comprised 2,500 objects from forty-seven institutional collections in Poland: codices, sculpture, textiles, arms, coins, and jewelry. Ten essays investigate the linguistic and cultural ties between the Wends and the Veneti, between Poland and northern Italy.

100. TUROWSKI, Andrzej.
Konstruktywizm polski. Próba rekonstrukcji nurtu (1921–1934). [Polish Constructivism. An attempt at reconstruction of the trend 1921–1934] Wrocław, Zakład Narodowy im. Ossolińskich, 1981. 360 p. 373 illus. N7255.P6T87 1981

Bibliography: p. 243–64.
Bibliographic references.

Sponsored by the Polish Academy of Sciences, Art Institute. List of exhibitions of Polish Constructivists, 1919–39. Summary and list of illustrations in English.

101. Varsavia; immagine e storia di una capitale. Catalogo della mostra. Ferrara, Chiesa di San Romano, Palazzina di Marfisa d'Este 27 giugno–6 settembre 1987. Ferrara, 1987. 372 p. illus. (part color). DK4611.V37 1987

Exhibition catalog edited by Gabriele Corbo.

An outstanding exhibition that traces the history of the city, from the medieval period to the present, through paintings, prints, sculpture, drawings, medals, objects of decorative arts, and photographs. Highly informative on architecture of the nineteenth and twentieth century. Includes photographs of pre-World War I Warsaw showing buildings altered or demolished before 1939. Rich in portraits. Prints especially well chosen, showing them as a potent vehicle for historical information. Catalog of nearly five hundred objects, plus essays on subjects covered in the exhibition such as the Vistula in the history of the city and the Jews in Warsaw during the Nazi occupation.

102. WALLIS, Mieczysław.
Secesja. [Secession] Warszawa, Arkady, 1967. 343 p. illus. N6496.N6W4
Summary in English.
Bibliography: p. 322–25.
Bibliographic references.

A well-illustrated history of the Secession movement, which may be most valuable for its information on Polish artists. Besides the well-known figures (Wyspiański, Mehoffer), this history includes the painters W. Wojtkiewicz, E. Okuń, and F. Ruszczyc; the sculptor K. Laszczka; the ceramicist J. Szczepkowski; and the architects W. Sadłowski (Lwów) and G. Landau Gutenteger (Łódź). Drawings for unrealized architectural projects in Warsaw by D. Lande. Also valuable is a list of European Secession periodicals, reproductions of initial letters, and a list of artists, their metier, and dates.

————.
Secesja [Secession] 2d ed. Warszawa, Arkady, 1974. 250 p. illus. N6465.A7W34 1974

Summary in English.
Bibliography: p. 238–39.
Bibliographic references.
Also available in German.

103. Warsaw. Muzeum Narodowe w Warszawie. Sztuka warszawska od średniowiecza do połowy XX wieku. Katalog wystawy jubileuszowej zorganizowanej w stulecie powstania Muzeum 1862–1962. Warszawa, Maj–Wrzesień 1962. [Warsaw's art from the Middle Ages to the mid-twentieth century; Catalog of the jubilee exhibition organized on the hundredth anniversary of the establishment of the Museum 1862–1962] Warsaw, May–September 1962. Warszawa, Muzeum Narodowe, 1962. 2 parts in 1 vol. N6991.W26
Introduction by Stanisław Lorentz.
Contents: Part 1. Od Średniowiecza do Baroku. [From the Middle Ages to the Baroque] by Tadeusz Dobrzeniecki, Janina Ruszczycówna, et al. LI, 122 p. 49 illus.
Part 2. Od Oświecenia do połowy XX wieku. [From the Enlightenment to the middle of the twentieth century] A collective work edited by Stefan Kozakiewicz. LXX, 593 p. 183 illus.
Bibliographies.

Catalogue raisonné of the exhibition of paintings, sculpture, and decorative arts.

104. Warszawa, jej dzieje i kultura.
[Warsaw, its history and culture] Warszawa, Arkady, 1980. 667 p., illus. (part col.), plans. DK4630.W36
A collective work edited by Aleksander Gieysztor and Janusz Durko.

An informative handbook on Warsaw, organized chronologically, from the Middle Ages to 1945. Includes architecture, painting, sculpture, and decorative arts. Thirty two color and 668 black and white illustrations.

105. Warszawa w wieku Oświecenia. [Warsaw in the period of the Enlightenment] Wrocław, Zakład Narodowy im. Ossolińskich, 1986. 323 p. illus. (part color), facsims., ports. DK4631.W385 1986 folio
Collective work edited by Andrzej Zahorski.
Bibliography: p. 298–303.

The period of the Enlightenment coincides with the reign of King Stanisław Poniatowski from 1764 to 1795. The great cultural fecundity of this period in Poland was due in large measure to this monarch. A brilliant elucidation in fourteen chapters, covering political, social, economic, and cultural conditions. Profusely illustrated with typical Bellotto views and other city scapes, portraits, genre subjects (Cries of Debucourt after Norblin), and book illustration. The chapters on the visual arts and architecture reproduce many drawings of royal projects (e.g., the castle of Ujazdów by E. Schreger and Bellotto), and buildings for magnate patrons as well as for the public. In addition to the famous works, the chapter on paintings includes decorative painting by J.B. Plersch, numerous fine portraits, and a wide variety of works by J.P. Norblin.

106. WŁODARCZYK, Wojciech.
Socrealizm. Sztuka polska w
latach 1950–1954. [Socialist realism. Polish art during the years
1950–1954] Paris, Libella, 1986.
135 p. 12 illus. (Historia i
teraźniejszość, 11) N7255.P6W57
1986
*Looks at socialist realism as a
worldwide phenomenon. Examines its
theory and sources under headings such
as "Tradition" and "Mysticism of
Architecture." Then looks at applications (as in the Academy of Fine
Arts, Warsaw). The third section is
titled "Irreconcilable Strategies." A
scholarly work that draws together
politics, visual arts, architecture, and
literature.*

**107. Współczesna sztuka
polska.** [Contemporary Polish
art] Warszawa, Arkady, 1981. 413
p. illus. (part color), ports.
N7255.P6W7
Collective work edited by
Andrzej Ryszkiewicz.
Biographical sketches of artists
by Helena Szustakowska.
*Twenty-three artists—painters,
sculptors, poster artists, theatrical
designers—whose styles range from
expressive realism to abstraction. For
the most part, the artists are
well-known from exhibitions and
publications. The material is presented in essays, short biographical
sketches, and good illustrations.*

108. Wystawy jubileuszowe
150-lecia Akademii Sztuk
Pięknych w Krakowie 1818–
1968. Katalog. Part I: 1818–1918.
Part II: 1919–1939. [Jubilee exhibition of one-hundred-fifty years
of the Academy of Fine Arts
in Kraków, 1818–1968. Catalog.

Part I: 1818–1918. Part II: 1919–
1939] Kraków, Muzeum
Narodowe w Krakowie, 1969.
141 p. 61 plates. N7255.P6W97
"History of the Fine Arts
Academy" by Helena Blum.
Exhibition catalog by Zofia
Kucielska, Bożena Szajna-
Sierosławska, Zofia Tobiaszowa,
and Sławomir Wojak.
*Within the major chronological spans
of Part I (first hundred years) and
Part II (next fifty years), the catalog
is arranged according to a finer
chronology. Part I includes a gallery
on Matejko and his epoch (thirty-two
painters, five sculptors) including, for
example, T. Ajdukiewicz and S.
Bieszczad; a gallery of Moderns such
as Mojżesz (Moïse) Kisling, Julian
Fałat, Władysław Lam, and T.
Niesiołowski; and a section on the
prints of fifty-one artists, including
Ludwik Markus (Marcoussis). Part
II is grouped according to art
movements or styles; e.g., the
"Sztuka" Group and the Colorists,
Modern Classicism, and Romantic
Tradition; a section on prints includes
Z. Karolak and A.S. Majcher; and,
finally, a group of six architects and
theatrical designers. Reproductions
are poor.*

109. Wzory sztuki
średniowiecznej i z epoki
Odrodzenia po koniec wieku
XVII w dawnej Polsce. Monuments du Moyen-Age et de la
Renaissance dans l'ancienne Pologne depuis les temps les plus
reculés jusqu'à la fin du XVII
siècle. Warszawa, Paris, Zakład
Chromolitograficzny M. Fajansa;
Drukarnia J. Ungra, 1853–1858.
2 vols. illus. (part color).
N7255.P6W98 1986

Edited by Alexander
Przezdziecki and Edward
Rastawiecki.
Text in French and Polish.
Reprinted in 1986 by
Wydawnictwa Artystyczne i
Filmowe.
Originally published in
sections for subscribers.
*The first work that extensively
discusses the decorative arts of ancient
Poland from medieval and Renais-
sance times through the Seventeenth
Century.*

110. ŻARNECKI, George.
Polish art. [Birkenhead, Eng.]
Polish Publications Committee
(Great Britain), 1945. 48 p. illus.
N6991.Z3
Introduction by Tancred
Borenius.
*A short introduction to Polish art
from the Romanesque to about 1930,
by the distinguished medievalist at the
Courtauld Institute, London.*

**111. Źródła do Dziejów Sztuki
Polskiej.** [Sources for the history
of Polish, arts] Vol. 1 +
Wrocław, Zakład Narodowy im.
Ossolińskich, 1951 + illus., ports.
N6991.Z7
Sponsored by the Art Institute
of the Polish Academy of
Sciences.
*A monographic series that is an
indispensable reference. Tabulations
such as art exhibitions and their
contents held in Warsaw (1819–45),
with reviews and a bibliography;
inventories of works of art and
furnishings in castles; archival documents of various kinds; a glossary of
obsolete terms; and documents on
individual artists and groups, including correspondence and notebooks.*

II. Architecture

St. John Cathedral in Warsaw.
Built in the fourteenth century,
originally as a parochial church, it
was rebuilt in 1839–42 according
to the plans of Adam Idźkowski.
It was severely damaged during
World War II and rebuilt after the
war. A number of important
events took place in the church,
including the coronations of
kings Stanisław Leszczyński and
Stanisław August Poniatowski.
The oaths on the May 3, 1791
Constitution were taken here.
Photo by K. Jaworski from *Sztuka
polska* by Tadeusz Dobrowolski.
Kraków, Wydawnictwo
Literackie, 1974

II. Architecture

✺

112. BUJAK, Adam.
Nekropolie królów i książat polskich. [The Necropolises of Polish kings and princes] Warszawa, Wydawnictwo Sport i Turystyka, 1988. 35, 14 p. 258 photographs (color). DK4131.B85 1988

Text by Michał Rożek.

Summary and description of illustrations in English, German, and Russian.

Bibliography.

An album of artistic photography covering royal burial places that range from the Poznań and Płock Cathedrals, and Kraków Cathedral at Wawel, to the Cistercian Abbey at Lubiąż.

113. BUXTON, David.
The wooden churches of Eastern Europe. An introductory survey. Cambridge, Cambridge University Press, 1981. 405 p. illus., maps. NA5450.B89 1981

Bibliography: p. 395–97.

Sets the subject in the perspective of historical and political changes and shifting frontiers. In Chapter 6, "Catholic Churches in Poland and Czechoslovakia," the author examines the stylistic features of each church. Structures from the sixteenth century remain, although, in most cases, rebuilding took place every century. Chapter 7, "Protestant Churches of the Margins. Poland and Slovakia," deals with widely scattered Lutheran churches, unified only by design. Appendix II, "The Vanished

Synagogues," describes some of the 120 synagogues destroyed by the Nazis.

114. CHROŚCICKI, Juliusz A., and Andrzej Rottermund.
L'Architecture de Varsovie. Atlas. Varsovie, Arkady, 1977. 245 p. illus. (part color), plans. NA1455.P62W762714

The format is like that of the guides published by the American Institute of Architects. The Atlas is arranged alphabetically by street name with all notable monuments being listed thereunder, except for outstanding suburban sites or palaces (Muranów, Natolin, Wilanów, for example) which are inserted in the alphabetical register. A short historical survey with over 350 photographs.

[10]. CHRZANOWSKI, Tadeusz, and Marian Kornecki.
Sztuka Śląska Opolskiego od średniowiecza do końca w. XIX. [The art of Opole Silesia from the Middle Ages to the end of the nineteenth century] Kraków, Wydawnictwo Literackie, 1974. 506 p. illus. N7255.P62D662

Bibliography: p. 475–77.

Bibliographic references.

In the territory of Opole Silesia—as elsewhere in Poland—architecture is the most distinguished art by an overwhelming margin; outstanding Gothic, Renaissance, Baroque, and Neo-classical buildings, mostly sacred, some secular. Extravagant sculpture,

even by Baroque standards, in Baborów, Kluczbork, and Głogówek. Nysa and Brzeg are two cities with consistently the most important art and architecture. The book is divided by periods, then subdivided by architecture and other fields of art. A chapter is devoted to notable wooden architecture dating from the early 1060s.

Can be supplemented by: Katalog zabytków sztuki w Polsce [Catalog of art monuments in Poland]. Vol. IV, parts 1–14: Województwo Opolskie. [Opole Province] Warszawa, Polska Akademia Nauk, Instytut Sztuki, 1960–67. illus. (N6991.K36)

115. CIOŁEK, Gerard.
Ogrody polskie. [Polish gardens] 2d revised ed. Warszawa, Arkady, 1978. 296 p. illus. SB466.P6C5 1978

Edited by Janusz Bogdanowski.

Bibliography: p. 266–72.

A history of gardens in Poland, divided into eight chronological categories. Under "Medieval" are subtitles such as "the myth of paradise" and "the cult of the tree". "Renaissance" comprises Italian-style gardens and their elements—walls, labyrinths, parterres, and fountains. The English garden is discussed under "Revolutionary changes of style;" the book ends with modern parks. Over 550 very good illustrations: photographs, plans, drawings, prints—not always fully identified.

116. DEGEN, Kurt.
Die Bau- und Kunstdenkmäler des Landkreises Breslau. Frankfurt am Main, W. Weidlich, 1965. 548 p. illus., maps, plan, plates. (Bau- und Kunstdenkmäler des deutschen Ostens. Reihe C. Schlesien. Vol. 1)
NA1086.B85D4
Bibliographies.

Every town in the nearly nine-hundred-square kilometer Breslau/Wrocław region is listed alphabetically; buildings and monuments—from the Romanesque to the nineteenth century—are described in exhaustive detail. Included are important objects of sculpture and painting in churches like that in Zobten am Merge/Sobótka. Choice architectural monuments, such as the castle at Romberg/Samotwór by Karl Gotthard Langhans (after 1776) and the castle at Rosenthal/Mirosławice by W. Bode, A. Raschke, and G. Winkler (c. 1800). German place names are retained in the text, the manuscript having been completed before World War II. Addenda give Polish equivalents, current bibliography, and names of artists, artisans, and architects.

117. DMOCHOWSKI, Zbigniew.
The architecture of Poland. An historical survey. London, Polish Research Centre, 1956. xxvi, 429 p. illus. NA1191.D6
Bibliography: p. 411–16.
Recommended for its clarity in presenting major monuments and sites (Lwów, Wilno), although recent research has made many particulars obsolete. Emphasis on the period before World War II.

[15.] DOBROWOLSKI, Tadeusz.

Sztuka Krakowa. [The art of Kraków] 5th rev. ed. Kraków, Wydawnictwo Literackie, 1978. 622 p. illus. (part color), plates. N7255.P62K74 1978
Summary in French and Russian.
Bibliography: p. 553–74.
A carefully detailed account of architecture, sculpture, painting, and a few examples of decorative arts dating from the pre-Romanesque period to the present. Many rare works are reproduced in more than 375 excellent photographs. Architectural representations of all periods, including the nineteenth century, are especially notable.
Additional illustrative material can be found in Katalog zabytków sztuki w Polsce. [Catalog of art monuments in Poland] Vol. IV, parts 1–4. Miasto Kraków. Warszawa, Polska Akademia Nauk, Instytut Sztuki, 1965–87. (N6991.K36)

118. GUERQUIN, Bohdan.
Zamki Śląskie. [Silesian castles] Warszawa, Budownictwo i Architektura, 1957. 87 p. 354 illus. NA7740.G8
Sponsored by the Institute of History of Polish Architecture, of the Wrocław Polytechnic.
Following an introduction the sites are listed alphabetically, each with a description of the building and related literature. This section is interspersed with architectural plans and cross sections, and reproductions of early prints, drawings, and watercolors, and is followed by more than 230 excellent photographs. The map is not adequate.

119. GUERQUIN, Bohdan.
Zamki w Polsce. [Castles in

Poland] 2d ed., revised. Warszawa, Arkady, 1984, 346 p. illus. (part color). DK4043.G84 1984
Edited by Stefan Muszyński.
Bibliography: p. 77–80.

Research dating from the late eighteenth century into the castles of Poland. Some castles are retained as ruins to enhance the panorama. The purpose and location of castles determined their design, whether fortifications or habitations, independently situated or connected with a town. Instituted first by knights, royalty, and religious orders, they were later built by the rich and powerful. The earliest stone-built castles date from 1230. Arranged alphabetically by place, with brief scholarly notes added. Emphasis on lesser-known castles. Monuments in formerly Polish territory now in the U.S.S.R. are omitted. Over 450 excellent photographs, plans, and graphic representations dating back to the fifteenth century.

120. JAROSZEWSKI, Tadeusz.
The book of Warsaw palaces. Warsaw, Interpress, 1985. 168 p. illus. DK4734.J37 1985
Photographs by Edmund Kupiecki.
Translated by Stanisław Tarnowski.
Bibliography: p. 174.
Has over one hundred crisp, well-reproduced, recent photographs of fifty palaces, with a synoptic history and data on the building style for each. Highly recommended.

121. KALINOWSKI, Konstanty.
Conservation and protection of historical treasures in People's Poland. Polish Western Affairs,

❁

vol. 15, no. 1, 1974, p. 46–62.
DK443.P618 v. 15
Bibliographic references.

Sets out the principles according to which protection and conservation are extended to all cultural property within certain categories, whether historical, scientific, or artistic. Lists the hierarchy of values and the administrators. Reviews the spectacular achievements in the area of postwar buildings and urban reconstruction and restoration.

[32]. **Katalog zabytków sztuki w Polsce.** [Catalog of art monuments in Poland] Vols. I–IX, 1953–1982; Seria nowa. [New Series] vol. 1+ Warszawa, Polska Akademia Nauk, Instytut Sztuki. 1977+ illus. maps. N6991.K36

This topographical catalog records buildings of architectural significance, exterior and interior furnishings and decorations, paintings, sculpture, sacral goldsmithery, and vestments.

Each volume of the original series of the Katalog zabytków sztuki w Polsce *covers one province (województwo) and consists of numerous sections (zeszyty) published on various dates. In 1977, a new series of this catalog was instituted, based on the reorganized administrative divisions of the country. Originally, there were seventeen provinces, now there are forty-nine. The new series does not duplicate the original, but covers territories not previously included in the original series.*

Each section includes an index of names and an up-to-date list of volumes and sections published as well as places covered. Some sections contain hundreds of good, small photographs.

122. KEYSER, Erich.
Die Baugeschichte der Stadt Danzig. Köln. Wien, Bohlau, 1972. 552 p. illus. maps (in pocket) (Ostmitteleuropa in Vergangenheit und Gegenwart, no. 14) NA1455.P62D365
Edited by Ernst Bahr.
Bibliographic references.

A comprehensive history of the architecture of Gdańsk from the earliest times to the beginning of the twentieth century. Included are churches, public secular buildings, as well as fortification architecture. Crisp, clear, small illustrations.

123. KNOX, Brian.
The architecture of Poland. London, Barrie & Jenkins, 1971. 161 p. 214 illus., map, plans. NA1455.P6K55 1971b
Bibliography: p. 152–55.

An introduction to the subject useful for the English-language reader because of its informal and genial style of writing. A personal view of the "Polishness" of Polish art is presented. Monuments of architecture, which may appear in better photographs in other publications, are here accompanied by helpful maps of the country dating from the tenth to the twentieth century and by many ground plans. Lacks scholarly apparatus.

[36]. **KOZAKIEWICZ, Stefan, *and* Stanisław Lorentz.**
Poland. *In* Encyclopedia of world art. Vol. 11. New York, McGraw-Hill, 1966. p. 376–414.
Bibliography.

A rather authoritative, comprehensive, detailed, clear, and engaging presentation of Polish art and architecture in English. Arranged in two main sections: "Cultural and

Artistic Periods" and "Monumental Centers." The first section provides an exposition of architecture and building, painting, and sculpture, each to the degree appropriate for the period. The second section is arranged by provinces (województwo), then by cities within each province. It gives the urban history, and lists important buildings and their architects, and the buildings' contents and surrounding areas, for each historically and artistically significant city. There is a bibliography on each of the cities.

124. KRASSOWSKI, Witold.
Architektura drewniana w Polsce. [Wooden architecture in Poland] Warszawa, Arkady, 1961. 170 p. (chiefly illus.) (Biblioteka Zakładu Architektury Polskiej Politechniki Warszawskiej, vol. 11) NA4110.K7
Summary and list of illustrations in English and Russian.

Represented are cottages, manor houses, houses of worship, gates, farm buildings, granaries, and windmills. Originally, wooden and masonry buildings shared the same forms. From about 1650 to the eighteenth century, wooden buildings were endowed with features that could only be attained with timber construction.

125. KRAUZE, Andrzej, *ed.*
Sztuka sakralna w Polsce; architektura. [The sacral art in Poland; Architecture] Warszawa, Ars Christiana, 1956. 366 p. illus. (part color). NA5691.K7 folio
Editorial Committee: Teodor Bursze, Jan Dąbrowski, Stanisław Szymański.

Also available in English (see next entry).

126. KRAUZE, Andrzej, *ed*.
The sacral art in Poland; Architecture. Warsaw, Ars Christiana, 1956. 366p. illus. (part color). NA5691.K713 folio
   Editorial Committee: Teodor Bursze, Jan Dąbrowski, Stanisław Szymański.
   Translated by Krystyna Dąbrowska.
Churches, architectural sculpture, window frames, tombs, doors, of all periods: Romanesque, Gothic, Renaissance, Baroque, Classical, nineteenth-century, and modern, in splendid photographs. Brief scholarly introduction and catalog of 308 illustrations.

127. KUPIECKI, Edmund, *and* Jerzy Dobrzycki.
Cracow; landscape and architecture. Warsaw, Arkady, 1967. 55 p. illus. (part color), 184 plates. N6836.K8K813
   Text by Jerzy Dobrzycki.
   Translation by Marek Łatyński.
   Photography by Edmund Kupiecki.
Book of photographs, loosely arranged; Includes some buildings and details seldom reproduced, such as two Art Nouveau monuments, the Helena Modrzejewska Old Theater and the Palace of Art.

128. ŁOZIŃSKI, Jerzy Z., *and* Adam Miłobędzki.
Guide to architecture in Poland. Warsaw, Polonia, 1967. 286 p. illus., maps. N6991.L713
In format, resembles the guidebooks of the American Institute of Architects. Arranged alphabetically by city, under which 3,500 monuments are listed and succinctly described. Nearly

four hundred excellent photographs. Sixteen large, legible maps. An admirable publication.

129. ŁOZIŃSKI, Jerzy Z.
Pomniki sztuki w Polsce. Tom 1. Małopolska [Art monuments in Poland. Vol. 1. Małopolska] Warszawa, Arkady, 1985. XIX, 489 p. illus., maps. NA1455.P6L69 1985 vol. 1
Emphasizes architecture but also includes paintings, sculpture, and decorative arts. Covers the period from the eleventh through the nineteenth century. Provides lists of artists, artisans, and photographers. Reproduced are 349 objects of art.
   Includes a brief history of art for each period: Romanesque and Gothic, Renaissance and Mannerism, Baroque and Rococo, Classicism and styles of the nineteenth century.
   It is the first of three planned volumes that will cover the entire territory of Poland.
   For a German-language edition, see entry 43.

130. MALECZYŃSKI, Karol, Marian Morelowski, *and* Anna Ptaszycka.
Wrocław; rozwój urbanistyczny. [Wrocław; urban development] Warszawa, Budownictwo i Architektura, 1956. 333 p. illus. plans, maps. DD901.B87M28
   Bibliographic references.
Half of the book is devoted to the period up to the end of World War II, when Polish administration was resumed. The Middle Ages was a time of expansive building (the Cathedral, the Churches of the Magdalen and of the Holy Cross, the Hospital of St. Anne). The years 1526 to 1807 are treated collectively.

Particularly remarkable is the eighteenth-century university. The second half of the book deals with the reconstruction of the devastated city; the City Hall, Cathedral, Market Square, and elsewhere.

131. MIŁOBĘDZKI, Adam.
Zarys dziejów architektury w Polsce. [An outline of the history of architecture in Poland] 3d ed. Warszawa, Wiedza Powszechna, 1978. 366 p. illus., 171 plates, plans. NA1455.P6M54 1978
   Bibliography: p. 320–22.
   Index of places and monuments.
Authored by a prominent architectural historian, the work is divided into seven chapters, beginning with the eighth century. Chapter 4 deals with the architecture of the Counter Reformation (c. 1570–1650); chapter 5 is on the architecture of the Baroque (c. 1650–1795). The volume ends with the year 1914. General bibliography. Useful index by place name that gives the principal phases or building features, and includes specific bibliographic references. Also, an index of persons. There is no index by building type, hence no way to locate, for example, a discussion of Baroque synagogues (p. 217–20) other than through place names.

132. MIŁOBĘDZKI, Adam.
Zarys dziejów architektury w Polsce. [An outline of the history of architecture in Poland] 4th rev. ed. Warszawa, Wiedza Powszechna, 1988. 364 p. illus. 171 plates, plans. NA1455.P6 1988
   Bibliography: p. 318–20.
   Index of places and monuments.

*Revisions in this 4th edition include
Chapter 4, "Architecture of the
Counter Reformation Period" which
now encompasses the years c. 1570 to
1670; Chapter 5, "Baroque" covers
the period c. 1670 to 1795. The final
chapter closes with four pages on the
history of post-World War II to
1950. Some revisions on Jesuit
architecture and the architect Maciej
Trappola appear in Chapter 4, but
the main revisions occur in Chapter 5.
Titles have been added in the General
Bibliography, and some deleted. Infe-
rior to the 3d (1978) edition in
the quality of printed text and
illustrations.*

133. The Old Town and the
Royal Castle in Warsaw. Warsaw,
Arkady, 1988. 63 p. of text, 24
illus., 159 color plates, plans.
DK4637.S7S7313 1988
Edited by Bożena Wierzbicka.
Translated by Jerzy A.
Bałdyga.
*Four essays on the history and
reconstruction of Warsaw's Old Town
and the Royal Castle by Jan
Zachwatowicz, Piotr Biegański,
Stanisław Lorentz, and Aleksander
Gieysztor. Good illustrations of the
interior of the castle—its furnishings,
sculptures, paintings, clocks, candela-
bra, etc. Also available in Polish,
Stare Miasto i Zamek Królewski
w Warszawie (1988).*

**134. PIECHOTKA, Maria, and
Kazimierz Piechotka.**
Bożnice drewniane. [Wooden
synagogues] Warszawa,
Budownictwo i Architektura,
1957. 219 p. illus. NA4690.P5
*Also available in English (see next
entry).*

**135. PIECHOTKA, Maria, and
Kazimierz Piechotka.**
Wooden synagogues. Warsaw,
Arkady, 1959. 219 p. illus., map.
NA5691.P513
Translation by Rulka Langer
of *Bożnice drewniane.* (1957)
*A history of Jewish settlements,
beginning in the eighth century, on
territory that was to become the
Polish state; an immigration that
culminated in about 1600 when half
of all European Jews lived in Poland.
Their influence on urban development
and architecture. An account of the
evolution of the synagogue in Poland,
with emphasis on wooden buildings,
photographs of which are arranged
alphabetically by locality. A map
pinpoints locations.*

136. PILCH, Józef.
Zabytki architektury Dolnego
Śląska. [Architectural monu-
ments of Lower Silesia]
Wrocław, Zakład Narodowy im.
Ossolińskich, 1978. 375 p. of
text, 158 illus. NA1455.P62S567
Bibliography: p. 351–53.
*Treats an area that includes
Wrocław, Wałbrzych, and Legnica.
Lists the sites in alphabetical order,
giving each a short paragraph on its
outstanding buildings, their dates, and
notable features. No summary.
Ninety-nine drawings of plans and
159 photographs.*

**137. Podług nieba i zwyczaju
polskiego.** Studia z historii
architektury, sztuki i kultury
ofiarowane Adamowi
Miłobędzkiemu. [According to
heaven and Polish customs.
Studies in the history of architecture, art, and culture presented to
Adam Miłobędzki] Warszawa,
Państwowe Wydawnictwo

Naukowe, 1988. 685 p. illus.
N7255.P6P57 1988
Edited by Zbigniew Bania,
Andrzej Baranowski, Maria
Brykowska, Juliusz A.
Chróścicki, Andrzej Grzybowski,
and Adam Małkiewicz.
Bibliographies.
Table of contents in German
and Russian.
*Eighty studies, primarily by Polish
scholars, written in honor of Adam
Miłobędzki, a distinguished scholar of
the history of Polish architecture, and
prepared by his friends and students
in honor of his sixtieth birthday. The
first part of the title refers to a
seventeenth-century Polish textbook on
architecture by Łukasz Opaliński,
edited by Miłobędzki, and published
in 1957.*

138. SEWERYN, Tadeusz.
Kapliczki i krzyże przydrożne
w Polsce. [Roadside chapels and
crosses in Poland] Warszawa,
Instytut wydawniczy PAX, 1958.
illus. NA4875.S4
Bibliographic references.
*Presents the history and tradition of
placing shrines and crosses along
roadsides. Nearly four hundred illustrations of work done entirely by local
villagers. Discusses the rich variety of
wooden shrines—and occasional stone
shrines—with the figures of Christ
and saints also sculptured in wood.
These were placed usually inside the
shrines but, at times, above crosses.
Some shrines were linked to legends,
others were created as an act of
thanksgiving, or as a prayer for help
or forgiveness, while still others were
erected to honor the dead, including
those killed in battle.*

139. STĘPIŃSKA, Krystyna.
Pałace i zamki w Polsce,

dawniej i dziś. [Palaces and castles in Poland in the past and today] Warszawa, Krajowa Agencja Wydawnicza, 1977. 2 vols. illus. DK4044.S73

Summary of introduction, table of contents, and descriptions of illustrations in English and Russian.

Bibliography: vol. 2, p. 151–57.

Excellent handbook. Buildings are arranged alphabetically by name, and a history and description of each accompanies well-chosen photographs. Synopsis of the catalog into in English.

140. THULLIE, Czesław.
Zabytki architektoniczne województw katowickiego i opolskiego. Przewodnik. [Architectural monuments of the Katowice and Opole provinces. A guide] Katowice, Wydawnictwo "Śląsk," 1969. 270 p. illus. map. NA1455.P62K37

Bibliography: p. 227–28.

An introduction covers such subjects as fortifications, palaces and country houses, city and town markets, seats of government, and sacral architecture. Fifty routes are offered through the two provinces. Listed for each site, are important monuments, their plan and style, and date of building and architect. Over one hundred small, but clear photographs.

141. Vilniaus àrchitektùrà.
[Architecture of Wilno] Vilnius, "Mokslas," 1985. 384 p. illus. NA1197.V52V543 1985

Edited by Klemęnsas Cerbulenas, J. Glemzfia, and A. Jankevicfiiene.

In Lithuanian.

Summary in Russian, German, and English.

Bibliography: p. 367–73.

Discusses the urban and architectural development of Wilno. Lists 195 buildings and groups of buildings of historical and architectural significance. The order is alphabetical according to location. Excellent photographs and plans give access to outstanding architectural monuments from the Romanesque to the nineteenth century.

142. Warsaw. Politechnika.
Zakład Architektury Polskiej. Polish architecture up to the mid-19th century. Warsaw. Budownictwo i Architektura, 1956. 30 p. of text. 499 illus., map. NA1191.W313 1956 folio

By Jan Zachwatowicz.

A brief, highly informative introduction, in a fine translation, provides an overview of the evolution of the country's architecture. Followed by 499 excellent photographs of superb buildings extant throughout the country. A map identifies the sites. An outstanding book.

143. Zabytki urbanistyki i
architektury w Polsce; odbudowa i konserwacja. [Urban and architectural monuments in Poland; restoration and conservation] Vol. 1+ 1986+ Edited by Wiktor Zin. NA109.P7Z33 1986 v. 1

Vol. 1: Miasta historyczne. [Historical cities] Warszawa, Arkady, 1986. 645 p. illus.

Collective work by Piotr Biegański and others.

Edited by Wojciech Kalinowski.

A superior study of the issue involved in restoration—for example, his-toricism versus functionalism, documentation, and evaluation of cultural worth—as applied to twenty-three Polish cities. Includes the less often publicized cities of Grudziądz, Lanckorona, and Tarnów. Illustrated with nearly one thousand diagrams, drawings, and prints from all periods, old and modern.

144. ZACHWATOWICZ, Jan.
Polish architecture. Warsaw, Arkady, 1967. 526 p. map, plans, 346 plates. NA1191.Z313

Translation by Marek Łatyński of *Architektura polska*.

Valuable for outstanding photographs of buildings of all periods. Baroque, classical, romantic, Eclectic, and Art Nouveau are allotted equal space as with earlier, better-known monuments. Brief introductory texts.

145. ZACHWATOWICZ, Jan.
Protection of historical monuments in Poland. Warszawa, Polonia, 1965. 147 p. illus. N6991.Z28 1965

Translation by Christina Cenkalska.

Sets forth the principles and methods for the protection of monuments. Recounts the procedures used in the reconstruction of Warsaw, Gdańsk, Szczecin, and other cities demolished in World War II. Relates the means used to conserve movable works of art.

146. ZUBRZYCKI-SAS, Jan K.
Skarb architektury w Polsce. [A treasury of architecture in Poland] Kraków, A. Koziański, 1907–1916. 4 v. illus., plans. NA1191.Z8 folio

Table of contents for each chapter in Polish and French.

Issued in parts for subscribers.

Photographs and drawings of exteriors and interiors of buildings, and sometimes of their ruins. Architectural and ornamental details. Valuable for the many photographs of structures before their destruction in two World Wars.

147. BIAŁOSKÓRSKA, Krystyna.

Polish Cistercians [sic] architecture and its contacts with Italy. Gesta, vol. 4, 1965, p. 14–22. 20 figs. N6280.G4 v. 4

Under the auspices of the Bishop of Kraków, Iwo Odrowąż, Italian art became increasingly influential during the first half of the thirteenth century. Master Simon, who was among the first to arrive, is thought to be the architect of the abbeys of Wąchock, Koprzywnica, Sulejów, and Jędrzejów. The author brings research on Wąchock up to date and expands the number of churches credited to Cistercian influence.

148. BOROWIEJSKA-BIRKENMAJEROWA, Maria.

Barbakan Krakowski.
[Kraków barbican] Kraków, Wydawnictwo Literackie, 1979. 207 p. illus. (Cracoviana. Seria I: Zabytki) DK4735.B37B67
Summary in English.
Bibliography: p. 196–202.

A three-year investigation (1969–1971) of the fortifications of Kraków, the medieval and Renaissance capital of Poland. A Summary of the archaeological, architectonic, and urban evidence as well as a list of the cartographic and manuscript sources. The author, who participated in the studies, proposes Wit Stwosz as a major architect of the Barbican.

149. BUJAK, Adam.

Kościół Mariacki w Krakowie. [St. Mary's Church in Kraków] Warszawa, Sport i Turystyka, 1987. 52 p. 226 color illus. NA5955.P62K7263 1987
Summary and list of illustrations in English, French, German, and Russian.
Photographs by Adam Bujak, text by Michał Rożek.

The church, which embodies Kraków's history, has a Gothic exterior with Renaissance and Baroque interior additions. During the years 1889 and 1891, the interior was restored to its mainly Gothic character by Tadeusz Stryjeński. Over two hundred excellent color photogrphs of interior furnishings, many in rare detail: bronze Gothic baptismal font; town councillors' stalls (1516–1521); Renaissance ciborium, presbytery stalls (1635–1637); Jan Matejko's polychrome decorations.

The church also houses the famous altar by Wit Stwosz.

150. CHODYŃSKI, Antoni Romuald.

Zamek Malborski w obrazach i kartografii. [Malbork Castle in pictures and on maps] Warszawa, Państwowe Wydawnictwo Naukowe, 1988. 176 p. 67 illus. (part color). N8217.C26C46 1988
Bibliography: p. 141–46.

A collection of the views of Malbork Castle, including a history of its construction and various remodelings, as well as the contemporary renovation. Summary in English.

151. CROSSLEY, Paul.
Gothic architecture in the reign of Casimir the Great. Church architecture in Lesser Poland 1320–1380. Kraków, Ministerstwo Kultury i Sztuki. Zarząd Muzeów i Ochrony Zabytków, 1985. 492 p. 240 illus. maps. (Biblioteka Wawelska, 7) NA5955.P62M345 1985
Bibliography: p. 459–65.
Abbreviated version in Polish: p. 369–458.

Written by a British architectural historian, this is the first analytical survey of fourteenth-century Polish Gothic architecture. Concentrates on the Kraków Cathedral of Sts. Wacław and Stanisław on the Wawel and the parish church of St. Mary, Kraków. Rebuilding of the Romanesque cathedral, site of the coronations and burials of Władysław Łokietek and Casimir the Great, began in the 1320s. Acknowledges the patronage of three Polish bishops on the work of reconstruction in the Wawel, and that of the merchants of Kraków on St. Mary's church. The author gives a history of the iconography and influences of the buildings; defines the architecture under King Casimir—its purposes, styles, and influences; and places the royal churches in the style of Central European Late Gothic (Sondergotic). He also examines eighteen additional churches, all in Małopolska, built for King Casimir the Great, who was greatly interested in secular and military architecture. This work is a revised version of the author's doctoral dissertation written at Cambridge University, England. Includes all the scholarly apparatus.

Reviewed by Amanda Simpson in Burlington Magazine, vol. 129 no. 1013, (Aug. 1987), p. 539, and by Paul W. Knoll in The Polish Review, v. 33, no. 4, 1988, p. 469–71.

152. DROST, Willi.
Kunstdenkmäler der Stadt Danzig. Unter Mitarbeit von Gregor Brutzer, Irmagard Koska und Hans Bernhard Meyer. [Stuttgart] W. Kohlhammer [1957–72] 5 v. illus. (part color), facsims., plans, ports. (Bau- und Kunstdenkmäler des deutschen Ostens. Reihe A)
N7255.P62D363

Vol. 5 edited by Franz Swoboda.

Bibliographic references.

Contents: 1. Sankt Johann.—2. Sankt Katharinen.—3. Sankt Nikolai. St. Joseph. Königl. Kapelle. Hl. Leichnam. St. Salvator.—4. Die Marienkirche in Danzig und ihre Kunstschätze.—5 St. Trinitatis. St. Peter und Paul. St. Bartholomai. St. Barbara. St. Elisabeth. Hl. Geist. Engl. Kapelle. St. Brigitten.

Romanesque, Gothic, and Baroque churches and chapels in Gdańsk. Important interior furnishings: choir stalls, tombs, epitaphs, carved and painted altarpieces, lanterns, and treasures. Exhaustive scholarly account of all exterior and interior features, lavishly illlustrated.

153. GUERQUIN, Bodan.
Zamek w Malborku. [The castle of Malbork] Warszawa, Arkady, 1960. 107 p. illus. plans.
NA7741.M3G8

Summary and list of illustrations in English, German, and Russian.

Bibliography: p. 107.

Monastery fortress built by the Teutonic Knights beginning around the end of the thirteenth century. In 1309, became the capital of the Order, and eventually comprised three fortified castles. Between 1457 and 1772, was

in the Polish kingdom. Devastated under the Prussians. Serious reconstruction started after 1850 the architect Konrad Steinbrecht. Good photographs, despite octavo format.

154. Katedra Gnieźnieńska.
[Gniezno Cathedral] Poznań, Księgarnia św. Wojciecha, 1968– 70. 2 v. illus. (part color), plates.
NA5955.P62G555

Collective work by Jan Zachwatowicz, et al.

Edited by Aleksandra Świechowska.

Summary in English.

Bibliographic references.

An important scholarly work on the history of the building and its contents. The capital of Poland when the country adopted Christianity in 966, Gniezno remains the titular see of the Polish Primate. Three successive structures were built on the site, beginning in the tenth century, and there was an important rebuilding, after the fire of 1760, by the architect Ephraim Schreger. This was the site of the cult of St. Adalbert, and the famous Romanesque doors of the Cathedral represent scenes from his life. The volumes also treat the sculpture and treasures. Numerous plans, cross-sections, diagrams and photographs.

155. KORNECKI, Marian.
Gotyckie kościoły drewniane na Podhalu. [Gothic wooden churches in Podhale] Kraków, Wydawnictwo Literackie, 1987. 148 p. illus. NA5955.P62P645 1987

Summary in English and German.

Bibliography: p. 130–32.

The five oldest timber churches of the Podhale region in the foothills of the

Tatra Mountains retain, to varying degrees, their original fifeteenth-century construction. The towers, however, are mainly seventeenth-century. The churches in Dębno, Łopuszna, Harklowa, Grywałt, and Nowy Targ, still hold notable Gothic panel paintings, carvings, and fragments of patterned wall painting. The church at Dębno has the most extensive patterned interior decoration.

156. MROCZKO, Teresa.
Architektura gotycka na Ziemi Chełmińskiej. [Gothic architecture in the Chełmno region] Warszawa, Państwowe Wydawnictwa Naukowe, 1980. 360 p. 40 leaves of plates, illus. NA5955.P62C475

Bibliography: p. 323–33.

Scholarly publication with all apparatus. Covers the period from the first half of the thirteenth century. A map indicates the forty or more buildings discussed. Numerous drawings of elevations and plans. The photographic illustrations are adequate.

157. Poland. Zarząd Muzeów i Ochrony Zabytków. Stare Miasto w Poznaniu. [The Old Town of Poznań], Poznań, Wydawnictwo Poznańskie, 1971. 222 p. illus. (part color). (*Its Teka Konserwatorska, no. 6*)
NA1191.A25 no. 6

By Henryk Kondziela.

Summary in English: p. 213– 21.

Bibliography: p. 109–10.

One of the finest concentrations of medieval buildings in all of Poland is in the Old Town of Poznań. The town was prosperous until the beginning of the seventeenth century, but fell to Swedish invaders in 1655. Extensively destroyed in 1945, the

Collegium Novum of the
Jagiellonian University in
Kraków, built in 1883–87 in the
neogothic style by architect Feliks
Księżarski (1820–1884), who also
designed the Credit Bank in
Lwów and the sarcophagus of
King Michał Wiśniowiecki in the
Cathedral at Wawel, Kraków. From
*Cracow, the Royal Capital of
Ancient Poland, its History and
Antiquities* by Leonard Lepszy.
London, T.F. Unwin, 1912

*Old Town has been restored to its
pre-nineteenth century appearance.
The book chronicles the rebuilding and
recounts the principles of preservation.*

158. ŚWIECHOWSKI, Zygmunt, and Jan Zachwatowicz.

L'Architecture cistercienne en
Pologne et ses liens avec la
France. Biuletyn Historii Sztuki,
vol. 20, no. 2, 1958, p. 139–73.
illus. N6.B5 v. 20

　　Bibliographic references.

*The earliest Cistercian foundations
date from the twelfth century, and as
many as thirty existed in the
thirteenth century. This was due in
part, to the devotion of the Piast
lords, but also to the Order, which
had an eye to eastward expansion.
The building models were French,
since most monastic establishments
were of French origin. A helpful map
traces the routes. Analyses of some of
the buildings, a certain number of
which were architecturally inspired,
while others were fortified; sixty
photographs, plans, and diagrams.*

159. ŚWIECHOWSKI, Zygmunt.

Budownictwo romańskie w
Polsce; Katalog zabytków.

[Romanesque architecture in Poland; a catalog of relics] Wrocław, Zakład Narodowy im. Ossolińskich, 1963. 438 p. 919 illus., map. (Źródła do historii kultury materialnej) NA5691.S89
    Summary in French.
    Bibliographies.
Buildings are listed alphabetically by location. Significant dates, architectural characteristics, and descriptions of materials, building history, and bibliography are provided for each. Many site and building plans. Captions and a one-paragraph summary of each monument (in French).

160. WIDAWSKI, Jarosław.

Warszawski dom mieszkalny w średniowieczu. [Warsaw residences in the Middle Ages] Warszawa, Politechnika Warszawska, 1985. 177 p. illus., plans. (Prace naukowe Politechniki Warszawskiej, Budownictwo, no. 90: Architektura) TH4.W3715 no. 90
Consists of two parts: the private residence in Central Europe in the Middle Ages, and urban construction in Warsaw in the Middle Ages. Plans, drawings of reconstructions, and a list of 150 brick buildings located in Warsaw before about 1600.

[8]. BIAŁOSTOCKI, Jan.

The art of the Renaissance in Eastern Europe: Hungary, Bohemia, Poland. Oxford [Eng.], Phaidon, 1976. xxiv, 312 p. illus. (part color). (The Wrightsman lectures, delivered under the auspices of the New York University Institute of Fine Arts, vol. 8) N6817.B52 1976b
    Bibliography: p. 281–306.
Synthesizes East European architectural, ornamental, and sculptural achievements from the fifteenth to the seventeenth century. Unique in scope and authority, the study traces the conversion of sober, intellectual Florentine forms to exuberant, optical Mannerism.

161. BIEGAŃSKI, Piotr.

Frombork città di Copernico. Architettura e tradizione. Wrocław, Zakład Narodowy im. Ossolińskich, 1973. 17 p. illus. (Accademia Polacca delle Scienze. Biblioteca e Centro di Studi a Roma. Conferenze, fasc. 60) NA1455.P62F72
Copernicus lived and worked in Frombork from 1512 to 1516 and again from 1521 to 1543. A report on the history of the archeological excavations and the reconstruction of the bishop's fortified palaces, especially the restoration of the defensive tower to its appearance in the years when Copernicus resided there.

162. BOCHNAK, Adam.

Kaplica Zygmuntowska. [The chapel of King Sigismund] Warszawa, Auriga, 1960. 34 p. 63 illus. NA5697.K67B6 1960
    Bibliography: p. 32.
Useful for the illustrations: the altar wall, the wall of the throne, and the details of the marble relief sculptures in the tympani, the three-dimensional sculptures in the niches, the half-figures in relief in the rondels, and the funerary sculptures.

163. DOBROWOLSKI, Tadeusz.

Zamek na Wawelu. Dzieło architektury polskiej. [The castle of Wawel. A masterpiece of Polish architecture] *In* Studia Renesansowe, vol. 1, 1956, p. 140–85. 27 figs. N6991.S87 v. 1
    Summary in French and Russian.
    Bibliographic references.
Argues that, despite its Italian origins, the castle incorporates more features of local tradition—a plan used in Poland in the fifteenth century, arcades higher than in Italian construction, and so forth—thus constituting more of a Polish than Italian masterpiece.

164. ESTREICHER, Karol.

Polish Renaissance architecture. Burlington magazine, vol. 86, no. 502, January 1945, p. 4–9. illus. N1.B95 v. 86
The author traces the Florentine origins of Polish Renaissance architecture (the cortile surrounded by an arcade in the Royal Castle, Wawel, 1506–1516) and recounts the continuance of the Florentine style until 1595, when it was superseded by the Baroque. Renaissance architecture came to Poland from Hungary, then spread to East Prussia, the Baltic states, and Sweden. The author enlarges upon the decorative motif of the parapet, the earliest being that of the Kraków Cloth Hall (Sukiennice), 1556.

165. FIOCCO, Giuseppe.

Il Mosca a Padova. *In* Venezia e la Polonia nei secoli dal XVII al XIX. Edited by Luigi Cini. Venezia, Istituto per la collaborazione culturale, 1965, p. 43–52. 2 illus. NX371.P6V4
Establishes the identity of the architect-sculptor active in Poland, Giovanni Maria Padovano, called Il Mosca.

166. FISCHINGER, Andrzej.

Santi Gucci; Architekt i rzeźbiarz królewski XVI wieku.

[Santi Gucci; royal architect and sculptor of the XVI century] Kraków, Ministerstwo Kultury i Sztuki, Zarząd Muzeów i Ochrony Zabytków, 1969. 193 p. 112 p. of plates. (Biblioteka Wawelska, 3) N6923.G825F57 1969

Summary in French.
Bibliographic references.

The first full-scale study since 1933 of Santi Gucci, the prolific architect and sculptor, born in Florence c. 1530, and active in Poland from around 1550. Worked in Kraków for royal patrons and others (tombs of Sigismund Augustus and his sister Anna, Sigismund Chapel, Wawel), Grodno (now in the U.S.S.R.), Baranów, and elsewhere. His castles, churches, and tombs are shown in photographs, plans, elevations, and drawings of the seventeenth, eighteenth, and nineteenth centuries. Analogous contemporary Italian material: B. Bandinelli, B. Ammanati, B. Buontalenti, Michelangelo, and others.

167. FRAZIK, Józef Tomasz.
Zamek w Krasiczynie. [The castle of Krasiczyn] Kraków, Politechnika Krakowska, 1968. 252 p. illus., plans. (Zeszyty Naukowe Politechniki Krakowskiej. Architektura, no. 22) NA17.K7

Summary also in English and Russian.

Bibliography: p. 234–43.
Bibliographic references.

A historical and scientific analysis of the methodology of construction from the sixteenth century to the present. Codifies a new method of analysis of materials, techniques, and stratification of walls and plaster. Reconstructs the

building in each of its phases from its overall composition and the function of its parts to the details of decoration (sgraffito and painted). Places the fortified castle in the historical development of such bastioned structures. Eight good analytical elevation drawings. Otherwise, poorly reproduced plates in this important study.

The castle of Krasiczyn, located in the province of Rzeszów, holds an important position among the monuments of Polish architecture of the Renaissance-Mannerism style.

168. GRUNDMANN, Günther.
Burger, Schlösser und Gutshäuser in Schlesien. Frankfurt am Main, Wolfgang Weidlich, 1982–87. 2 v. illus. (part color), plans. (Bau- und Kunstdenkmäler im Östlichen Mitteleuropa, vol. 1, 3) NA7763.G78 1982

Vol. 1. Die mittelalterlichen Burgruinen, Burgen und Wohntürme, bearbeitet von Dieter Grossmann unter Mitarbeit von Hanna Nogossek; v. 2. Schlösser und Feste Häuser der Renaissance, bearbeitet und erweitert von Dieter Grossmann.

Bibliography: v. 1, p. 173–77; v. 2, p. 138–40.

Volume 1 covers nearly 500 medieval castles, ruins of castles, and towers for habitation. Categories include Piast residences, castles surrounded by water, and others. Most of them are described in detail, reviewing the evidence of excavations, additions to the building since its origin, and the literature. Illustrations include floorplans, elevations, reconstructions, manuscript illumination of the fourteenth and fifteenth centuries, prints and drawings of the seventeenth through the ninteenth century and

photographs. Volume 2 covers Renaissance castles and banquet halls categorized by town castles (sixteen, of which the most important are Brzeg (Brieg) and Oleśnica (Oels)); hill castles, including Gorzanów (Graferort); and valley castles, the most numerous category. Findings from excavations, descriptions of structure, and earlier scholarly findings are provided for each. A chapter is devoted to the ornamental decorations, sculpted and sgraffito. Over 250 photographs of sites are supplemented by nineteenth-century illustrations, floor plans, elevations, and reconstructions.

169. Kazimierz; praca zbiorowa. [Kazimierz; a collective work] Warszawa, Państwowe Wydawnictwo Naukowe, 1987. 225 p. illus. (Kraków. Wędrówki w przeszłość. Cracow. A journey to the past.)

Edited by Sławomir Wojak.
In Polish and English.
Bibliography: p. 34–36.

A study of Kazimierz, the town lying on the shore of the Vistula opposite Kraków, as seen through extensive pictorial records in the Kraków Historical Museum and the Public Archives of the Kraków Voivodship. The earliest surviving view is in the Nuremberg Chronicle (1493). Nineteenth-century photographs constitute the primary documentation. Nearly three hundred illustrations, grouped in seven categories, including the Market Place, Paulites' Monastery and Church on the Rock, Synagogues, and Cemeteries.

170. KORNECKI, Marian.
Zamki i dwory obronne Ziemi Krakowskiej [Castles and fortifi-

cations in the Province of Kraków] Kraków, Wydział Kultury Prezydium WRN w Krakowie, Wojewódzki Konserwator Zabytków, 1966. 90 p. illus. DK511.K58K6

The modest format belies the high interest of the subject matter. Thirty-five sites in ninety evocative photographs, prints, and drawings.

171. KOWALCZYK, Jerzy.

Zamość, città ideale in Polonia. Il fondatore Jan Zamoyski e l'architetto Bernardo Morando. Wrocław, Zakład Narodowy im. Ossolińskich, 1986. 56 p. illus. (Polska Akademia Nauk. Stacja Naukowa w Rzymie. Conferenze, fasc. 92) NA1455.P62Z365 1986

Bibliography: p. 51–53.

Jan Zamoyski (d. 1605), educated in Padua ("Patavium virum me fecit"), and Grand Chancellor to the crown, by 1580 had in his possession the design by Morando of Zamość, the ideal city, fortified and in hexagonal form. History of its construction near Lublin with referents for the design to Francesco di Giorgio, Bramante (Vigevano), and Serlio.

[38]. KOZAKIEWICZOWA, Helena, *and* Stefan Kozakiewicz.

The Renaissance in Poland. Warsaw, Arkady, 1976. 329 p. illus. (part color), map. N7255.P6K6613

Translation by Doreen Heaton Potworowska of *Renesans w Polsce.*

Bibliography: p. 323–25.

An outstanding album for the English-language reader. In an excellent English translation, 252 fine black and white photographs and eight plates in color are magisterially discussed. The authors call attention to works of art rarely illustrated and details generally overlooked. Lengthy essays trace developments from 1500 to 1640. Contains numerous drawings of plans and a map of all sites mentioned. Reproductions show the most beautiful Renaissance buildings, such as the Town Hall in Poznań (converted from the Gothic style, 1500–1560) by the architect Giovanni Battista Quadro from Lugano. Another Town Hall, built during the years 1570 to 1572 and well preserved, is in Brzeg (Silesia), by the architect Giacomo Pario from Como; also, the Cloth Hall (Sukiennice) in Kraków with its attica. The magnificent Sigismund Chapel in the Wawel Cathedral by the architect Bartolomeo Berrecci, and the Wawel Royal Castle with court-yard galleries, are reproduced in great detail. An abundance of illustrations of paintings, tapestries, tombs, and sculptures, among them—the tomb of Bishop A. Zebrzydowski at Wawel by Jan Michałowicz.

[39]. KOZAKIEWICZOWA, Helena.

Renesans i manieryzm w Polsce. [The Renaissance and Mannerism in Poland] Warszawa, Auriga, 1978. 173 p. illus. (part color). N7255.P6K65

A brief history of what was principally architectural and sculptural expression, illustrated by fine photographs of infrequently reproduced monuments such as the tomb of the Mazovian knights, 1526–1528 (figs. 13–14), the Castle gateway at Brzeg, 1551–1553 (fig. 74), and the tomb of the Firlej family, c. 1600, in Bejsce (figs. 96–97).

172. KUPIECKI, Edmund.

Gdańsk. Landscape and architecture of the town complex. Warsaw, Arkady, 1972. 24 p. of text, 180 illustrations. DD901.D24K793 1972

By Jerzy Stankiewicz and Bohdan Szermer.

Photographs by Edmund Kupiecki.

A history of the city, especially its modern political vicissitudes, and its construction from about the year 1000. The Netherlandish character of its buildings date from the second half of the sixteenth and the seventeenth century, when Dutch and Flemish architects and artists were imported. The most interesting example of the Gdańsk Mannerist trend in building and decorations is the Arsenal (1602–1605) by the architect van Opbergen. An abundance of well-photographed examples.

173. LEWICKA, Maria.

Bernardo Morando. *In* Saggi e memorie di storia dell'arte. Vol. 2. Venezia, 1959. p. 141–55. illus. N4.S2 v. 2

Bibliographic references.

The architect Bernardo Morando was born in Padua and worked in Poland for his patron, Jan Zamoyski, from 1578 until his death in about 1600. His design of the fortified city of Zamość is one of the best Renaissance urban concepts in Europe. Similar projects had previously been carried out in Poland on a small scale. The author discusses the palace, the Church of the Annunciation and St. Thomas, the city gates of Lwów and Lublin, and other design features.

174. LEWICKA, Maria.

Mecenat artystyczny Jana Zamoyskiego. [The artistic pat-

ronage of Jan Zamoyski] *In*
Studia Renesansowe, vol. 2,
1957, p. 303–39. illus.
N6991.S87 v. 2
Summary in French.
Zamoyski (1542–1605) was a
statesman and Great Chancellor of
the Crown from 1578, and Com-
mander in Chief of the Polish Army
for 1581. His organizational abilities
are demonstrated in the construction
of the fortified city, Zamość.
Archival evidence demonstrates his
attention to the smallest details of the
building. He ordered paintings from
the Tintoretto workshop, specifying
themes, compositions, and colors.

175. ŁOZIŃSKI, Jerzy Z.
Grobowe kaplice kopułowe w
Polsce 1520–1620. [Funerary
chapels with cupolas in Poland
1520–1620] Warszawa,
Państwowe Wydawnictwo
Naukowe, 1973. 308 p. 284 illus.,
map. NA5955.P6L67
Discusses burial traditions in Poland.
Includes eastern territories now ceded
to the USSR. Map with all sites
marked. Index by place. Many
drawings of plans and cross-sections.
Over three hundred fascinating photo-
graphs, not all well-produced.

176. ŁOZIŃSKI, Władysław.
Sztuka lwowska w XVI i
XVII wieku. Architektura i
rzeźba. (The art of Lwów in the
sixteenth and seventeenth centuries. Architecture and sculp-
ture] Lwów, H. Altenberg, 1901.
228 p. illus. NA3571.P62L84
Buildings characterized by marked
plastic qualities, built by architects
native to Lwów as well as Italians
and Germans. Many arresting exam-
ples, such as the gateway to the

Arsenal (fig. 34), and Boim's
Chapel, exterior and dome (figs.
76–77). Four chapters each on
architecture and sculpture. An old-
fashioned book recommended for its
subject matter; the text has 103
illustrations.

177. MAJEWSKI, Alfred.
Zamek w Baranowie. [The
castle in Baranów] Warszawa,
Arkady, 1969. 104 p. illus., plans.
NA7764.B3M3
Photography by Emil
Rachwał.
Summary in English, French,
German, and Russian.
Bibliography: p. 81–82.
A brief account, with sixty high-
quality photographs, of an important
Polish Renaissance secular building.
The architect of this magnificent
castle, built for the Leszczyński
family, was probably Santi Gucci.
The castle, with its four-wing type
rectangular plan, has ionic columns on
both levels and a galleried courtyard.
The west wing was enlarged by
Tylman of Gameren during the years
1695 to 1700 after the castle was
purchased by the Lubomirski family.
Fine seventeenth-century stucco
decorations.

178. MAMUSZKA, Franciszek.
Droga Królewska w Gdańsku.
[The Royal Road in Gdańsk]
Wrocław, Zakład Narodowy im.
Ossolińskich, 1972. 186 p. illus.
map. DK4683.D75M35
Bibliography: p. 120–22.
A 63-page supplement is included,
which contains summaries in English,
Russian, French, and German, to-
gether with lists of illustrations in
those languages.
Polish kings made their entry into

the city of Gdańsk through the
Renaissance High Gate, the principal
entrance into the city, and proceeded
by way of Long Road into the Long
Market. The author traces the history
of this thoroughfare, which extended
inland to the productive heart of the
country, and connected it with the
Baltic port. The principal focus is on
the architecture of famous buildings,
such as the Artus' Court, the main
Town Hall, and the residences of
patricians, that lined the Royal
Road.

179. POKORA, Jakub.
Sztuka w służbie Reformacji:
Śląskie ambony, 1550–1650. [Art
in the service of the Reformation:
Silesian pulpits, 1550–1650]
Warszawa, Państwowe
Wydawnictwo Naukowe, 1982.
334 p. 170 illus. map.
NA5955.P62S58 1982
Summary in German: "Die
Kunst im Dienste der Reforma-
tion: die schlesischen Kanzeln,
1550–1650," p. 323–34.
Bibliography: p. 130–36.
Bibliographic references.
A study of church 114 pulpits,
mainly protestant, listed alphabeti-
cally by geographic location of the
churches. Provides a history of each
pulpit, its style and condition, and
names of the artists, when available;
also the iconographic themes of pulpit
decorations.
A revised doctoral dissertation
(Wrocław University, 1978), this is
a pioneering work on this subject in
Polish arts literature.

180. ROŻEK, Michał.
Mecenat artystyczny
mieszczaństwa krakowskiego w
XVII wieku. [The artistic patronage of Kraków burghers in the

seventeenth century] Kraków, Wydawnictwo Literackie, 1977. 420 p. illus. tables. (Biblioteka Krakowska, no. 118) DK4700.B52

Bibliography: p. 370–86. Bibliographic references.

A study based on municipal records, which provide information on the activities of the patrons. Artistic patronage extended to the building of chapels, altars, parish churches, as well as vestments, chalices, candlesticks, carpets, crosses, and chasubles.

181. ROŻEK, Michał.

The Royal Cathedral at Wawel. Warsaw, Interpress, 1981. 177 p. illus. (part color). NA5955.P62W384 1981

Translation by Bogna Piotrowska of *Królewska Katedra na Wawelu.*

Photographs by Stanisław Markowski.

Bibliography: p. 177–78.

Also available in French, German, and Polish.

A scholarly and spirited introduction to an edifice imbued with national history. Earliest construction dates back to 1020s. Excellent illustrations focusing on interiors with Gothic, Renaissance, and Baroque tombs, screens, altarpieces, choir stalls, and treasures. Interior and exterior architectural ornament and sculpture. A deceptively modest format for a substantial text.

182. SIKORSKI, Jerzy, *and* Tadeusz Piaskowski.

Frombork. Olsztyn, Pojezierze, 1972. 182 p. illus. NA1455.P62F77

Summary and list of illustrations in English and German.

Bibliography: p. 155–56.

A popular picture book featuring ninety-nine fine photographs of Frombork, the natal city of Copernicus (d. 1543), where he authored his "De revolutionibus orbium coelestium" and in whose cathedral he is buried. A history of the city, and of the cathedral-fortress (fortified against the Teutonic knights), its furnishings (altars, sculpture, paintings, tombs), and the canonries or residences.

183. SINKO, Krystyna.

Santi Gucci Fiorentino i jego szkoła. [Santi Gucci Fiorentino and his school] Kraków, Gebethner i Wolff, 1933. 82 p. illus. (Biblioteka Historji Sztuki, no. 3) N6923.G825S5 1933

Summary in Italian.

Concerns the architect and sculptor who died before February 1600, and for whom G. Milanesi discovered evidence in Florentine archives. The author also adds information from Polish archival records for the years 1558, 1568, 1575, and 1577. Examines the constructions of Łobzów, Castle 1585–86, and the Myszkowski family castle, among other projects. Defines Santi Gucci's style and contrasts it with that of his collaborators and pupils.

[85]. Studia Renesansowe.

[Renaissance Studies] Wrocław, Zakład Narodowy im. Ossolińskich, 1956–64. 4 v. illus. N6991.S87

Sponsored by the Art Institute of the Polish Academy of Sciences.

Edited by Michał Walicki.

Summaries in French and Russian.

Vols. 2–4 (1957–64) include

extensive bibliographies on the Renaissance in Poland.

Major articles by authoritative scholars. Poland's fine architecture, sculpture, and decorative arts of the period. Also articles on contemporary painting and manuscript illumination.

184. VECCHI, Mariapia.

Polonia 2° millennio. Milano, Silvana editoriale d'arte, 1970, 221 p. illus. (part color) DK4043.F36

Photographs made with a fresh eye: about one hundred pages devoted to architectural subjects, including interior medieval and Renaissance halls of Jagiellonian University (p. 142–143), and old houses at Bydgoszcz (p. 157).

185. Wawel. Katedra i Zamek Królewski. [Wawel. The Cathedral and Royal Castle] Kraków, S.A. Krzyżanowski, 1939. 24 p. 70 illus. (part color). NA5691.W3

Introduction by St. Świerz-Zaleski.

Notable are the pre-World War II photographs of interiors, such as the presbytery of the cathedral, and chambers with Renaissance and Baroque furnishings. Remarkable reliquaries, chasuble, tapestries. No description of illustrations.

186. Zamość, miasto idealne:

400 lat Zamościa. Studia z dziejów rozwoju przestrzennego i architektury. [Zamość, an ideal city: four hundred years of Zamość. Studies in its spatial and architectural development] Lublin, Wydawnictwo Lubelskie, 1980. 289 p. illus., maps, plans. NA9241.P62Z359

Edited by Jerzy Kowalczyk.

Bibliographic references.

Catalog of plans and maps of Zamość: p. 258–78.

Nine essays on seventeenth century and Rococo building activities, on Armenian building, and on construction during the period of the Congress Kingdom. Also, plans and maps of the city of Zamość from the seventeenth to the twentieth century.

187. ZŁAT, Mieczysław.

Attyka renesansowa na Śląsku. [The Renaissance parapet in Silesia] Biuletyn Historii Sztuki, vol. 17, 1955, p. 48–79. N6.B5

The attica, a decorative parapet wall covering the roof, was found in classical, Gothic, and Italian Renaissance architecture. A distinctive feature of the Polish Renaissance as well, it first appeared in the architecture of Kraków, notably in the City Cloth Hall (1556–1557). It was eventually used throughout Poland (in town houses, burghers' mansions, the castles of magnates), and also in Silesia, Moravia, and Slovakia.

188. ZŁAT, Mieczysław.

Zamek w Krasiczynie. Źródła i stan badań. [The castle in Krasiczyn. Sources and the state of research] Studia Renesansowe, vol. 3, 1963, p. 5–149. illus. N6991.S87

Summary in French and Russian.

Bibliographic references.

The quadrilateral castle near Przemyśl, with four cylindrical corner bastions and an interior court, was begun about 1592 by an unknown architect, and completed in 1614 by Galeazzo Appiani for the Krasicki family. Later neglected, it was restored by the Sapieha family, and again after World War I. Analysis of the unified expression that resulted

from a latent medieval building design and Renaissance forms. Opulent Renaissance interior carvings in doorways and window frames. Inventories reprinted from 1637, 1687, 1787, 1792, and 1811.

189. Barocco fra Italia e Polonia. Warszawa, Państwowe Wydawnictwo Naukowe, 1977. 428 p. illus. NX571.P6B37

Atti del IV Convegno di Studi promosso ed organizzato dal Comitato degli studi sull'arte dell'Accademia polacca delle scienze e dalla Fondazione Giorgio Cini di Venezia (Varsavia, 14–18 ottobre 1974)

Edited by Jan Ślaski.

A collection of highly original studies such as "Il filone Italiano dell'arte polacca del seicento ed i suoi rappresentanti maggiori," by Mariusz Karpowicz, in which he charts the course of the triumph of Baroque art and architecture in Poland; he attributes that triumph to the activities of the Jesuits, the preferences of the king and court, the widespread knowledge of Italy among the elite, and the traditional influx of Italian artists into Poland. Other studies are "Ultimo periodo dell'architettura tardobarocca in Polonia e gli architetti italiani" by Tadeusz S. Jaroszewski, and "Architettura e decorazione dei funerali polacchi in Italia dal cinquecento al settecento," by Juliusz A. Chrościcki. Elena Bassi, in "Contributi della cultura veneta all'arte polacca," reviews sixteenth through eighteenth century architects and artists who were born Venetian or Venetic and died Polish, such as Giambattista da Venezia, architect of the Warsaw Barbican, and Bernardo Morando. The name of the

Warsaw quarter of Muranów is derived from Morando's name.

190. CYDZIK, Jacek, *and* Wojciech Fijałkowski.

Wilanów. Warszawa, Arkady, 1975. 304 p. illus. (part color), plans. NA7764.W5C93

Sponsored by the Ministerstwo Kultury i Sztuki. Ośrodek Dokumentacji Zabytków.

Summary and list of illustrations in English, French, and Russian.

Bibliography: p. 120–21.

Photographs by Edmund Kupiecki.

An account of the reconstruction and restoration of the palace, as well as a history of the early construction. Reproduces many early plans, drawings, and photographs of work in progress. Has over 130 excellent photographs of the reconstructed palace, with many details, as well as the gardens and park.

191. DALBOR, Witold.

Pompeo Ferrari 1660–1736. Działalność architektoniczna w Polsce. [Pompeo Ferrari 1660–1736; his activity in Poland as an architect] Warszawa, Wydawnictwo Kasy im. Mianowskiego, 1938. 210 p. illus. NA1123.F43D35 1938

Summary in Italian.

Bibliographic footnotes.

Born in Rome, Ferrari arrived in Poland in 1696 to work for Stanisław Leszczyński at Rydzyna, where forty years later he died. His children were citizens of Poznań. As a recognized architect he built in Gniezno, Poznań, and Leszno. His best known work is the chapel of the Gniezno Cathedral named for Primate Potocki.

**192. FIJAŁKOWSKI,
Wojciech.**
Wnętrza pałacu w Wilanowie.
[Interiors of the Palace at
Wilanów] Warszawa, Państwowe
Wydawnictwo Naukowe, 1986.
207 p. illus (part color).
NA7764.W5F44 1986
 Summary in English, French
and Russian.
 Bibliographic references.
*Art and ideology of the present
structure, built from 1677 to 1696
for King Jan III Sobieski. Plans,
decorations, and interiors developed
under later royal patrons. Contributions of foreign artists. Excellent
illustrations accompany this scholarly
study.*

193. HEMPEL, Eberhard.
Baroque art and architecture in
Central Europe: Germany, Austria, Switzerland, Hungary,
Czechoslovakia, Poland. Baltimore, Penguin Books, 1965.
xxiii, 370 p. illus., maps, plans.
200 plates. N6756.H413
*An account of Renaissance architec-
ture in Poland that is defective with
respect to monuments, development,
causes, and chronology. The author's
assessment of the great Baroque
buildings, sculpture, and painting of
Poland is inadequate.*

194. HENTSCHEL, Walter.
Die sächsische Baukunst des
18. Jahrhunderts in Polen. Berlin,
Henschelverlag Kunst und
Gesellschaft, 1967. 2 v.
NA1191.H4
 Vol. 1: Text. 552 p.; v. 2: 581
illustrations.
 Extensive bibliographic refer-
ences in v. 1.
*Twelve architects who came from
Saxony to Poland are discussed*

*individually. Among the most active
were Johann Christoph Naumann,
Joachim Daniel Jauch, Carl
Friedrich Pöppelmann, Johann
Friedrich Knobel, Ephraim Schreger
(b. Toruń), and Simon Gottlieb Zug.
This is followed by three chapters on
new and reconstructed palaces, gardens, churches, and other buildings in
Warsaw, Grodno, Białystok, and
elsewhere for King Augustus the
Strong, Augustus III, Count Brühl,
and Polish patrons, and on Polish
inspiration and Saxon achievement.
Extensive documentation—
principally from Dresden and
Staatsarchiv. An outstanding work of
scholarship.*
 *Reviews by Stanisław Lorentz and
others in* Biuletyn Historii Sztuki,
vol. 32, no. 3–4, 1970, p. 349–89.

195. KALINOWSKI, Konstanty.
Architektura Barokowa na
Śląsku w drugiej połowie XVII
wieku. [Baroque architecture in
Silesia in the second half of the
seventeenth century] Wrocław,
Zakład Narodowy im.
Ossolińskich, 1974. 245 p. 172
plates, illus., map. (Studia z
historii sztuki, 21).
NA1455.P62S564
 Summary, table of contents,
and list of illustrations in German.
 Bibliographic references.
*A presentation of architects and
builders and their production of
residential buildings (especially castles), sacral buildings from
monasteries to parish churches, and
civic buildings. The chief figures
include Giovanni Seregni, Carlo
Rossi, Marcin Urban, Mateusz
Kirchberger, and Giacomo Scianzi.
The presentation is in three sections,
by period (1640–1670, 1670–1680,*

*1680–1700). A chronological table
lists 340 buildings, 187 of which are
new constructions. The state of
research is assessed. Plans and cross-
sections; a good map.*

196. KALINOWSKI, Konstanty.
Architektura doby Baroku
na Śląsku. [Architecture of the
Baroque period in Silesia]
Warszawa, Państwowe
Wydawnictwo Naukowe, 1977.
382 p. illus. NA1455.P62S565
 Summary in German.
 Bibliographic references.
*Renews consideration of the 1640–
1680 decades (section one), and the
1680–1710 decades (section two);
concentrates on the years 1710–1760
(section three). In section two, the
discussion is divided according to
cloisters, Roman Catholic churches,
Protestant churches, residences, and
the architects who span the century.
Section three is similarly arranged,
with the addition of important
buildings outside the categories: one
each by J.B. and J.E. Fischer von
Erlach, one each by K. and K.I.
Dientzenhofer. Work by the eight
leading architects of the 1700–1760
period is summarized.*

197. KALINOWSKI, Konstanty.
Lubiąż. Wrocław, Zakład
Narodowy im. Ossolińskich,
1970. 205 p. illus. (Śląsk w
zabytkach sztuki). N7255.P62L85
 Bibliography: p. 195–97.
*The volume is chiefly devoted to the
spectacular Baroque-style Cistercian
complex of cloisters, cloister church,
and palace, the latter built between
1681 and 1739. Sculptural decorations by Franz Joseph Mangoldt. In
the twelfth century, the Cistercians
were brought by Prince Bolesław to
Lubiąż, a village now in Wrocław*

province. In 1945, Lubiąż was returned to Poland.

[28]. KARPOWICZ, Mariusz.
Barok w Polsce. [The Baroque in Poland] Warszawa, Arkady, 1988. 338 p. 262 illus., 30 drawings, 24 color plates. DLC
  Comments to illustrations: p. 277–316.
  Bibliography: p. 325.
The author traces the beginning of the Baroque in Poland to the architectural style of the Jesuits Church in Nieśwież on which construction started in 1582. Discusses other churches in the Baroque style. Of the secular architecture, the royal palace in Warsaw (1599–1619), is seen as the most interesting. Two chapels, those of the Boim Family in Lwów, and St. Kazimir in Wilno Cathedral, and picked as the most beautiful examples of the Baroque in Poland. Good reproductions of paintings and sculptures of the period.

[31]. KARPOWICZ, Mariusz.
Sztuka Warszawy czasów Jana III. [Art in Warsaw in the period of Jan III] Warszawa, Państwowe Wydawnictwo Naukowe, 1987. 299 p. illus. N7255.P62W3349 1987
  Bibliographic references.
Deals with the patronage of King Jan III Sobieski, 1674–96, and the art that followed his reign to 1710. Primary attention is to architecture and sculpture, but paintings and prints are also surveyed. Architects include Tylman of Gameren (born in Utrecht) and J. Piola (born in Como). Painters such as Claude Callot, younger brother of Jacques Callot, are represented, as well as Polish-born artists such as Jerzy

Eleuter Szymonowicz-Siemiginowski. A scholarly, well-illustrated work.

198. KOWALCZYK, Jerzy.
Sebastiano Serlio a sztuka polska. O roli włoskich traktatów architektonicznych w dobie nowożytnej. [Sebastinao Serlio and Polish art. On the role of Italian architectural treatises in the modern period] Wrocław, Zakład Narodowy im. Ossolińskich, 1973. 358 p. illus. (Studia z Historii Sztuki, no. 16) NA1455.P6K68
  Summary in Italian.
  Bibliographic references.
A very important study focused on Serlio, whose six books on architecture were, for Polish practice, the most influential of all treatises. In 216 plates, the author compares illustrations from Serlio with buildings and details as executed in Poland. Traces evidence of influence of treatises by Vitruvius, Alberti, Vignola, Palladio, and Scamozzi on architectural and artistic cultural development in Gdańsk, Toruń, Poznań, Lwów, and elsewhere, and accounts for influx of ideas from Holland and of nordic classicism. Gives provenances of Italian architectural treatises in Polish libraries.
  Review by Konstanty Kalinowski published in Artium Questiones, *vol. 2, 1983, p. 179–82.*

199. KRĘGLEWSKA-FOKSOWICZ, Ewa.
Barokowe rezydencje w Wielkopolsce. [Baroque residences in Wielkopolska] Poznań, Wydawnictwo Poznańskie, 1982. 130 p. illus. NA7763.K73 1982
A brief introduction to fifteen Baroque palaces built between 1640

and 1780. Photographs of exteriors and interiors; reproductions of original plans and elevations.

200. KRÓL, Aleksander.
Zamek Królewski w Warszawie od końca XIII wieku do roku 1944. [The royal castle in Warsaw from the thirteenth century to 1944] Warszawa, Państwowy Instytut Wydawniczy, 1969. 249 p. illus., plans. NA7764.W3K7
  Bibliographic references.
The study begins with the proposed reconstruction of the earliest building on the site (the city having been settled early in the twelfth century); continues with construction under the various kings (Sigismund Augustus 1548–1572; the Vasa dynasty 1587–1668; the Saxon dynasty kings 1697–1763; and the Stanisław August Poniatowski, who abdicated in 1795). It continues through the nineteenth century, and closes with the post-1944 rebuilding. The author provides much information about the architects and artists who contributed to the splendor of the castle, and enumerates castle treasures rescued from the destruction of the war.

201. LILEYKO, Jerzy.
Zamek warszawski: rezydencja królewska i siedziba władz Rzeczypospolitej 1569–1763. [The Castle of Warsaw: Residence of the king and seat of government of the Republic 1569–1763] Wrocław, Zakład Narodowy im. Ossolińskich, 1984. 304 p. 110 p. of plates, illus. (Studia z historii sztuki, vol. 35) DK4645.Z35L55 1984
  Summary and table of contents also in French.
  Bibliography: p. 301–10.

Ideological, architectural, and decorative program of the castle. Its architectural forms reflect juridical and constitutional principles as well as the parliamentary system. Comparable to the Palazzo Ducale in Venice, for being simultaneously the residence of the doge and seat of the republic's authority. Scholarly, copious study of the architecture. Vincenzo Scamozzi, in Poland from 1592 to 1598, may have been among its many architects.

202. LORENTZ, Stanisław.
Il Castello reale di Varsavia. L'opera e il contributo di artisti e architetti italiani nella sua storia. Wrocław, Zakład Narodowy im. Ossolińskich, 1972. 47 p. illus. (Polska Akademia Nauk. Stacja Naukowa w Rzymie. Conferenze, fasc. 52) NA7764.W3L67

The small format notwithstanding, a succinct and detailed account of the building of the palace since the Renaissance. Emphasis placed on Italian architects who built, designed, advised, or just passed through, such as Vincenzo Scamozzi in 1598. Several grand projects of the 1700s reproduced. Interesting asides, such as the presentation of Shakespeare in the theater during Shakespeare's lifetime. An excellent reference.

203. LORENTZ, Stanisław.
Efraim Szreger, architekt polski XVIII wieku. [Efraim Szreger, Polish architect of the eighteenth century] Warszawa, Państwowe Wydawnictwo Naukowe. 1986. 354 p. illus. NA1455.P63S974 1986

Summary, list of illustrations, and table of contents in English and German.

Bibliographic references.

Large-scale monographic study on Szreger, the Baroque and rococo architect (1727–1784) who had an enormous and diverse practice for ambitious patrons, from whom he gained major commissions. He built for the king (Royal Castle, in Warsaw, and Castle Ujazdów), and for two successive primates of Poland (reconstructing Gniezno Cathedral), as well as for the Czartoryski family.

204. LORENTZ, Stanisław.
Jan Krzysztof Glaubitz, architekt wileński XVIII w. Materiały do biografii i twórczości. [Jan Krzysztof Glaubitz, architect of Wilno in the eighteenth century; materials on his biography and art] Warszawa, 1937. 44 p. illus., plans. (Towarzystwo Naukowe Warszawskie, Prace z historii sztuki, 3) NA1199.G5L6

Summary in German.

An architect (d. 1767) who built extensively in Wilno and its vincinity, Glaubitz was chief architect and designer of the stucco interiors of the Evangelical-Augsburg Church, 1738–1743. Playing a similar role at the Church of St. Catherine, during the years 1741 to 1746, he turned to restoration for the Jesuit church of St. John. Ouside Wilno he built the Church of the Knights of Malta and the Dominican Church and Cloister. The Baroque style governed his work during the period 1738 to 1750, and the Rococo thereafter.

205. MIŁOBĘDZKI, Adam.
Architektura polska XVII wieku. [Polish architecture of the seventeenth century] Warszawa, Państwowe Wydawnictwo Naukowe, 1980. 2 vols. illus.

(part color), maps, plans. (Dzieje sztuki polskiej, v. 3, 4) NA1455.P6M536

Volume 1: text; v. 2: illustrations.

Bibliography: v. 1, p. 437–73, compiled by Adam Małkiewicz. Summary and lists of illustrations in English and Russian.

A period in Poland of extraordinary fecundity in building and architectural ornament; over 1,300 photographs of utmost fidelity and legibility. The churches and monasteries, castles, and palaces, are shown in elevation, with their fa.ades, towers, gateways, pediments, ballustrades, naves, domes, ceilings, windows, walls, doorways, altars, tombs, iron grills, fireplaces, stucco decorations: a wealth of details on the architecture and ornamental sculpture. Contemporary prints and drawings supplement the photographs. Included are Wilno and Lwów. Three indices to the text volume: by person, date, and rank or profession; by place or monument; and by iconography.

206. MOSSAKOWSKI, Stanisław.
Tylman z Gameren; architekt polskiego Baroku. [Tylman van Gameren; architect of the Polish Baroque] Wrocław, Zakład Narodowy im. Ossolińskich, 1973. 350 p. illus. (Polska Akademia Nauk. Instytut Sztuki. Studia z Historii Sztuki, vol. 17) NA1455.P63T675

Summary in English.

List of illustrations in English. Bibliographic references.

One of the most eminent Baroque architects practicing in Poland, Tylman was born in Utrecht around 1630 and died in Warsaw in 1706. This is a peerless study of his secular and sacral architecture and interior decoration. His humanistic, mainly

Venetian, education shaped monumental buildings. He consistently found logical, rational, symmetrical solutions. Yet he designed interiors in the high Baroque style. His work was molded by the specific economic and social style of Poland as well as by Polish architectural tradition. Over four hundred drawings and photographs of buildings are reproduced. The extended English summary is first-rate.

207. Nieborów, Arkadia.
Warszawa, Wydawnictwo Sport i Turystyka, 1988. 212 p. 27 black and white and 166 color illus.

Text by Włodzimierz Piwkowski; photographs by Krzysztof Jabłoński.

Summary and list of illustrations in English, French, German, and Russian.

Bibliography.

Currently a national museum, Nieborów—located eighty kilometers southwest of Warsaw—has undergone numerous reconstructions since its beginnings, in the sixteenth century, as a simple two-story brick manor house. By the end of the seventeenth century, it had become transformed into a palace designed by Tylman van Gameren. After more reconstruction, first in the Rococo style, and then in the Neo-classical style (by Szymon Bogumił Zug), architect Leandro Marconi in 1886 altered some of the decorations, making them neo-Rococo. Under Janusz Radziwiłł, the last owner of Nieborów and the park Arkadia, the palace was once more rebuilt, this time according to the design of the architects Romuald Gutt and Kazimierz Skórewicz. Nieborów escaped the destruction of World War II, and after the war became

a national art museum. Arkadia, founded by Helena Radziwiłł in 1778, had a lake and was decorated with garden pavilions, such as the Temple of Diana and the Gothic House with Sybil's grotto. The park was eventually redesigned, changing it from a neo-classical into a Romantic garden.

208. PASIERB, Janusz S., *and* Jan Samek.
The shrine of the Black Madonna at Częstochowa. 2d enlarged ed. Warsaw, Interpress, 1985. 224 p. facsims., illus. (mostly color). N7971.P62C976 1985

Bibliography: p. 223–24.

Photographs by Janusz Rosikoń, Chris Niedenthal, and Józef Jurkowski.

Translation by Bogna Piotrowska.

The first edition was published in 1980.

The introduction sketches the history of the icon and of the church building. The icon is of Byzantine origin, a replica of a lost original (another copy being in S.M. Maggiore, Rome). It arrived two years after the founding of the monastery in 1382, and was repainted in 1434. The present church dates from after 1690, only the Denhoff family chapel (built by F. Zaor and J. Napora between 1644 and 1676) having survived the pre-1690 fire. The architectural plan of the monastery is said to be a perfect specimen of Baroque residential architecture. Fortifications that withstood Swedish invaders in 1655 were pulled down by order of Tsar Aleksander I. The spire of 1690 was rebuilt in 1900. Summary discussion of interiors of the church (stucco vault of 1962–1695) and high altar (1725–1728), by the Wrocław workshop of

J.A. Karinger on the design of J.A. Buzzini. A volume of popular taste, illustrating the treasures in enlarged details.

209. Poland.
Zarząd Muzeów i Ochrony Zabytków. Puławy; praca zbiorowa. [Puławy (palace); collective work] Warszawa, Arkady, 1962. 117 p. illus. (*Its Teka konserwatorska, no. 5*) NA1191. A25 no. 5

Collective work edited by Stanisław Lorentz.

Summaries in French and Russian.

Bibliographic references.

A detailed and coherent account of the palace at Puławy (region of Lublin) as architectural monument. Built in the Baroque style by Tylman van Gameren around 1675 and torched by the Swedes in 1706, it was reconstructed in the Rococo style by Jan Zygmunt Deybel. Having among the oldest Rococo interiors in Poland, its Salle d'Or was designed by J.A. Meissonier. The garden pavilions were constructed between circa 1750 and 1810; Chinese pavilion, Doric orangerie, small Maryńska palace, Gothic house, Temple of the Sibyl, and others. Under the formidable Izabella Czartoryska, and the architect C.P. Aigner, it was reconstructed once more beginning in 1796. In the nineteenth century, another structural transformation was carried out by J. Górecki and J. Ankiewicz. A wealth of illustrations and scholarly notes.

210. ROŻEK, Michał.
Katedra Wawelska w XVII wieku. [Wawel Cathedral in the seventeenth century] Kraków, Wydawnictwo Literackie,

1980. 335 p. illus. (Biblioteka krakowska, no. 121) DK4700.B52 no. 121

Bibliography: p. 296–314.
Bibliographic references.

Archives and unpublished manuscripts were the author's primary sources, with sixteenth- and seventeenth-century printed books as his secondary references for this distinguished work of scholarship. Illustrations are taken from the manuscripts (e.g., the funerary catafalque of Władysław IV, d. 1648, designed by Giovanni Battista Gisleni) and from contemporary prints (the coronation of Augustus II in 1967). Chapters are devoted to the arrangement of the nave and ambulatory, the royal chapel of the Vasa, and the chapels of the cathedral.

211. SPELSKIS, Antanas.

Po baroko skliantais. [Under the Baroque ceiling] Vilnius, Vaga, 1967. 183 p. illus. (part color). NA5697.V48S58

In Lithuanian.

Summary and list of illustrations in English, French, German, and Russian.

Bibliography: p. 173.

The book is composed of 155 photographs of the Church of St. Peter and St. Paul in Wilno, which was begun soon after 1668 with the arrival of the Italian architect Jan (Giovanni) Zaor (Zaur) from Kraków. The opulent stucco interiors were executed in 1683 by Pietro Beretti and Giovanni Galli. The patron was the Grand Hetman of Lithuania and Governor of Wilno, Michał Kazimierz Pac (d. 1682). Early in the nineteenth century, there was another redecoration. Eight plans and elevations.

212. SZABLOWSKI, Jerzy.

Architektura Kalwarji Zebrzydowskiej (1600–1702). [Architecture of the Kalwarja Zebrzydowska (1600–1702)] *In* Rocznik Krakowski, vol. 25, 1933, p. 1–118. illus. DB879. K8R58 v. 25

Summary in German.
Bibliographic references.

In the Province of Kraków is a calvary, begun in the period of the Counter-Reformation, which consists of the Franciscan Cloister and small churches and chapels devoted to the Passion of Christ (His tomb recalling that in Jerusalem) and of His Mother (Her house in the shape of a heart). Styles initially Lombard Renaissance (Giovanni Maria Bernardoni), then Flemish (Paul Baudarth). Models of Vredeman de Vries are visible.

213. TATARKIEWICZ, Władysław.

Dwa Baroki, Krakowski i Wileński., [Two Baroques, Kraków and Wilno] Polska Akademia Umiejętności, Prace Komisji Historii Sztuki, vol. 8, no. 2, Kraków, 1946, p. 183–224. illus. N6991.P633 folio

Summary in French.
Bibliographic references.

The author contrasts the Baroque architectural style as practiced in seventeenth-century Kraków with that of Wilno, where it appeared some time later. The style in Kraków originated in Rome, whereas in Wilno the style came from the Piedmont. In Kraków, architects and decorators were primarily Italians: Giovanni Trevano, Francesco Solari, Giovanni Battista Falconi, Baltazar Fontana. Building and decorating in Wilno was carried out principally by Poles, some of whom were members of monastic orders: Aleksander Osikiewicz, Tomasz Żebrowski, Ludwik Hryncewicz, and K. Kamieński. The author claims that the architecture of Wilno is of superior originality and artistic value.

214. WRABEC, Jan.

Barokowe kościoły na Śląsku w XVIII wieku. Systematyka typologiczna. [Baroque churches in Silesia in the eighteenth century. Typological systematics] Wrocław, Zakład Narodowy im. Ossolińskich, 1986. 210 p. illus., plans, map. (Studia z historii sztuki, vol. 37) NA5955.P62S587 1986

Summary, list of illustrations, and table of contents in German.

Bibliography: p. 159–67.

This study of Catholic churches and chapels covers the territory of Silesia, except Czech Silesia. The author selects for analysis sixty well-preserved objects from these churches. Criteria for selecting the objects included artistic value and representation of style. Austria, Bohemia, and Moravia were stronger influences on church architecture than Italy. Czech influences were especially strong in Upper Silesia in the second half of the eighteenth century.

215. ZACHWATOWICZ, Jan, *and* Piotr Biegański.

The Old Town of Warsaw. Warszawa, Budownictwo i Architektura, 1956. 16 p. of text. 124 illus. (part color). DK651. W2Z3

Translated by Cecylia Wojewoda.

History of the rebuilding, partly in text, but mainly in photographs.

The Cathedral in Wilno, rebuilt according to designs by the architect **Wawrzyniec Gucewicz (1753–1798)** who, while studying in Paris, was greatly influenced by the work of C.N. Ledoux (1736–1806), a great architect of romantic classical design. From *Sztuka polska* by Tadeusz Dobrowolski. Kraków, Wydawnictwo Literackie, 1974

Fold-out street and building plans, and twenty-one street elevations. Photographs of destroyed buildings and their reconstruction, including splendid doorways, courtyards, staircases, halls, stucco façade ornaments, wrought iron balconies, and shop signs.

216. Zamek Królewski w Warszawie. Architektura, ludzie, historia. [The Royal Castle in Warsaw; Architecture, people, history] Warszawa, Państwowe Wydawnictwo Naukowe, 1973. 323 p. illus. NA7764.W3Z35 1973

Collective work by Stanisław Herbst, Stanisław Lorentz, Władysław Tomkiewicz, and Jan Zachwatowicz.

Edited by Aleksander Gieysztor.

Summary in English and French, p. 253–85.

Bibliography: p. 237–43.

Five essays on the evolution of the building, from the thirteenth and fourteenth centuries—the Piast and Jagiellonian dynasties—to the reconstruction of the castle after World War II. A concise book written by authorities in the field.

217. BARTCZAKOWA, Aldona.

Franciszek Maria Lanci, 1799–1875.

Warszawa, Budownictwo i Architektura, 1954. 114 p. illus. NA1199.L3B3

A prolific architect, born at Fano (Marches), died in Warsaw. An eclectic, he built in the neogothic style (e.g., the Golden Chapel of the Cathedral of Poznań), in the Egyptian revival style, and in Italian villa and Classicial revival styles (carriage house, Wilanów). Maps with sites of executed work in Poland, including Warsaw.

218. BARTCZAKOWA, Aldona.

Jakub Fontana, architekt warszawski XVIII wieku. [Jakub Fontana, Warsaw architect of the eighteenth century] Warszawa, Państwowe Wydawnictwo Naukowe, 1970. 350 p. illus., facsims., ports. NA1455.P63F64

Summary in French and Russian.

Bibliographic references.

Scholarly monograph on Jakub Fontana (1710–1773), who was the architect of sumptuous baroque buildings, influenced by Italian and Saxon styles, and built under noble, royal, and clerical patronage.

219. BATOWSKA, Natalia, Zygmunt Batowski *and* Marek Kwiatkowski.

Jan Chrystian Kamsetzer architekt Stanisława Augusta. [Jan Christian Kamsetzer Architect of Stanisław August] Warszawa, Państwowe Wydawnictwo Naukowe, 1978. 306 p. illus. port. NA1455.P63K3532

Some articles in French and German.

Summary and table of contents in English and Russian.

Bibliographic references.

A scholarly work on the Dresden-born architect (1753–1795) who arrived in Warsaw in 1773. Appointed architect to King Stanisław August Poniatowski, he worked on royal projects—the palace, Łazienki, and Ujazdów—for the rest of his life. His neo-classical style is punctuated with Turkish and Chinese follies. Illustrations consist mainly of projects as drawn.

220. CHRZANOWSKI, Tadeusz.

Karczmy i zajazdy polskie. [Polish taverns and hostels] Warszawa, Arkady, 1958. 82 p. illus. NA7850.P6C4

Bibliography: p. 81–82.

Traces the history and architecture of the institutions. Illustrated with prints, drawings, and photographs. Alphabetical list of fifty-eight selected taverns and hostels from the eighteenth century.

221. CZERNER, Olgierd.

Rynek Wrocławski. [The Market Square of Wrocław] Wrocław, Zakład Narodowy im.

Ossolińskich, 1976. 233 p. illus. (Teka Konserwatorska, 8) NA1191.A25

Summary in English.

Bibliography: p. 145–46.

Bibliographic references.

The Market Square and adjacent areas: the history and function of every secular building is discussed individually. A wealth of illustrations of interiors and exteriors, eighteenth to twentieth centuries. There is an account of the destruction during World War II, and of subsequent reconstruction in the postwar period.

222. JAROSZEWSKI, Tadeusz S.

Architektura doby Oświecenia w Polsce. Nurty i odmiany. [The architecture of the Enlightenment in Poland. Currents and variants] Wrocław, Zakład Narodowy im. Ossolińskich, 1971. 253 p. 175 illus. (Studia z Historii Sztuki, vol. 13) NA1455.P6J36

Summary in French.

Bibliographic references.

Neoclassicism appeared in Poland in the 1760s. Traces the importance and influence of French seventeenth-century architecture, of Palladio, the Pantheon, by direct contact with France and England, and by indirect contact through publications.

223. JAROSZEWSKI, Tadeusz S.

Chrystian Piotr Aigner. Architekt Warszawskiego Klasycyzmu. [Christian Piotr Aigner. Architect of Warsaw Classicism] Warszawa, Państwowe Wydawnictwo Naukowe, 1970. 334 p. illus. NA1455.P63A56 1970

Summary in Russian and English.

Bibliographic references.

Christian Piotr Aigner (1756–1841) was an enormously prolific architect. Unfortunately, the reconstruction of his oeuvre has been hampered by the loss, during World War II, of his principal collection of drawings. He worked for the magnates: the Potockis at Puławy, an important intellectual center, and for the Czartoryskis and Lubomirskis at Łańcut. He functioned as a military architect and as Master General of Construction in the Kingdom of Poland. He was the author of historical and theoretical treatises, and is entitled to be seen as the creator (with Antonio Corazzi) of the classical face of Warsaw.

224. JAROSZEWSKI, Tadeusz S., *and* Andrzej Rottermund.

Jakub Hempel, Fryderyk Albert Lessel, Henryk Ittar, Wilhelm Henryk Minter, architekci polskiego Klasycyzmu. [Jakub Hempel, Fryderyk Albert Lessel, Henryk Ittar, Wilhelm Henryk Minter, the architects of Polish Classicism] Warszawa, Państwowe Wydawnictwo Naukowe, 1974. 256 p. illus. NA1455.P6J37

Four architects, born between 1762 and 1777. Minter received his education in Prussia. In Warsaw in about 1800—as an officer in the Corps of Engineers—he built his outstanding and influential grain storehouse in a functional form, rejecting historical styles. The three other architects were trained in Rome, and worked in neo-classical and historical styles for magnates and the gentry in Poland. Ittar's circus at the Radziwiłł Arkadia was inspired by Piranesi. Separate sections are devoted to each of the four architects, and each section is summarized in English.

225. JAROSZEWSKI, Tadeusz S.
O siedzibach neogotyckich w
Polsce. [Neogothic residences in
Poland] Warszawa, Państwowe
Wydawnictwo Naukowe, 1981.
369 p. illus. NA7412.P6J37 1981
　Summary in Russian and
English.

　Bibliographic references.
　Catalog of 100 selected
neogothic residences, p. 171–327.
*Neogothic was the most popular
historical style in nineteenth-century
Poland, flourishing especially from the
1840s to the 1860s and again around
1900. The text is divided according to
three building types. The first type is
palaces, to which an irregular plan
gave greatest opportunities for the
picturesque. Henryk Marconi was one
of the most productive architects
(Dowspuda palace near Suwałki,
1820–23, owned by General Ludwik
Pac [1780–1835]). Others were
F.M. Lanci and F. Jaszczołd. The
author presents research on this
little-known group in the northeast
and southeast of Poland. The second
type is castles, many of them restored
medieval manors. Outstanding examples are Łańcut, with its façade by
K.F. Schinkel, and other plans by
A. Raczyński. After it was rebuilt
by Aigner, Łańcut was one of the
most spectacular examples of the
neogothic style. The third type is the
villa. The author argues that,
although English designs were followed
(A.W. Pugin, J. Nash), German
and Austrian models were especially
influential (K.F. Schinkel, F.A.
Stuler). A scholarly, well-illustrated
book.*

**226. KOSSAKOWSKA-
SZANAJCA, Zofia, *and*
Bożena Majewska-
Maszkowska.**

Zamek w Łańcucie. [The castle
of Łańcut] Warszawa, Arkady,
1964. 469 p. illus. NA7764.L3K6
　Summary in French, English,
and Russian.

　Bibliographic references.
*The castle of Łańcut, near Rzeszów
in southeastern Poland, was transformed in the 1770s and 1780s into a
splendid residence. The work was done
principally by the architects Christian
Piotr Aigner and Vincenzo Brenna.
The scholarly text is in keeping with
the importance of the castle and its
art collections, but the illustrations
are wholly inadequate. The collection
includes antiquities as well as modern
sculpture (Canova, Thorvaldsen),
paintings by Garafalo Sofonisba,
Anguissiola, Watteau, Boucher,
Fragonard, and F. Winterhalter, and
tapestries, furniture, and other decorative arts.*

227. KWIATKOWSKI, Marek.
Łazienki and Belweder.
Warsaw, Arkady, 1986. 37 p. 77
plates (part color), illus.
DK4641.L39K95
　Color photographs by
Krzysztof Jabłoński.
　Also available in Polish.

*The book, in English, is essentially a
tourists' souvenir. The text lacks a
clear exposition of the history of
construction on the site. Belvedere was
built as a residence before 1663 and
Łazienki was one of its pavilions.
The present buildings date from the
eighteenth century. Reproductions of
paintings, drawings, and plans show
the now demolished Ujazdów Castle
and other no-longer-extant structures,
such as the Chinese gate. Schematic
map of buildings and monuments.*

**[45]. LORENTZ, Stanisław,
and Andrzej Rottermund.**

Klasycyzm w Polsce. [Classi-
cism in Poland] Warszawa,
Arkady, 1984. 304 p. illus. (part
color). N7255.P6L67 1984
*Also available in English, see next
entry.*

**[46]. LORENTZ, Stanisław,
and Andrzej Rottermund.**
Neoclassicism in Poland.
Warsaw, Arkady, 1986.
309 p. illus. (part color).
N7255.P6L6713 1986
　Translation by Jerzy Bałdyga
of *Klasycyzm w Polsce.*
　Bibliography: p. 237–38.

*In Poland, the neoclassical style had
its greatest reverberation in architecture. The authors provide a complex
and fascinating exposition: through
French contacts, the style was initiated about 1760 and nourished in
Rome by Polish architects (F.
Smuglewicz engraved the decorations
of the Golden House of Nero.
1776) and by the archaeologist,
S.K. Potocki. Palladio's villas were
an important influence, and S.M.
Maggiore provided the model for
the façade of the church of St.
Anne, Warsaw, 1786–1788. Further, C.N. Ledoux's buildings were
sources for E. Szreger and S.B. Zug.
The discussion begins with an introductory essay; the catalog is based on
more than 250 plates. Sculpture,
painting, and the decorative arts are
included.*

228. LORENTZ, Stanisław.
Natolin. Warszawa, Nakładem
Towarzystwa Naukowego
Warszawskiego, 1948. 340 p.
illus., ports. NA7764.N3L6
　Summary in French.

*Originally a pheasantry in the park
of Wilanów, the small palace was
rebuilt at the beginning of the*

nineteenth century, principally by the architect C.P. Aigner. The patrons were Alexander and Anna Potocki. All the rooms are described, as are the structures in the park and later monuments. Natolin was destroyed by the Nazis and reconstructed after 1945. Over 230 illustrations.

229. MALINOWSKA-KWIATKOWSKA, Irena.

Stanisław Zawadzki 1743–1806. Warszawa, Państwowe Wydawnictwo Techniczne, 1953. 122 p. illus. (Mistrzowie Architektury polskiej) NA1455.P63Z355

Bibliography: p. 42.

The Polish counterpart of Robert Adam. Brief introduction, chronological table of works, and two schematic maps of places where the architect worked. The book is composed chiefly of photographs of extant buildings, including interiors, plans, elevations, and old views.

230. MASZKOWSKA, Bożena.

Mecenat artystyczny Izabelli z Czartoryskich Lubomirskiej (1736–1816). [Artistic patronage of Izabella Lubomirska, née Czartoryska (1736–1816)] Wrocław, Zakład Narodowy im. Ossolińskich, 1976. 635 p. illus., plans. (Studia z Historii Sztuki, vol. 22) N5280.P72L825

Bibliography: p. 401–27.
Summary in English.

Immensely wealthy, intellectually well endowed, and widely traveled, the "Princesse Marechale" sustained Poland's cultural standing in Europe. Architecture was the principal object of her patronage, Łańcut and Wilanów were among here residences. Robert Adam designed a villa for her

(drawings in the Soane Museum). She collected paintings and books. This exhaustive scholarly work with 252 illustrations has an excellent English-language summary.

231. OSTROWSKA-KĘBŁOWSKA, Zofia.

Architektura pałacowa drugiej połowy XVIII wieku w Wielkopolsce. [The architecture of palaces in the second half of the eighteenth century in Wielkopolska] Poznań, Państwowe Wydawnictwo Naukowe, 1969. 319 p. illus. (Poznańskie Towarzystwo Przyjaciół Nauk. Prace Komisji Historii Sztuki, vol. 8, no. 2) NA7763.O78 v. 8

Summary in French.

A superior work of scholarship which draws the closest parallels between architectural production in Wielkopolska and initially that of France but principally of England. In this westernmost part of Poland, after 1750, the French style was imitated by admirers of the exiled King Leszczyński. Sometimes it was modified by trends emanating from the Habsburg lands, as at Ciążeń: J.F. Blondel cum François Cuvilles. The most potent influences were classicist, Palladian, and English. Pawłowice is the first example of Classicism in Wielkopolska. Designed by Karl Gotthard Langhans between 1779 and 1783, its great hall is framed by corinthian columns as in Robert Adam's Syon and Kedleston. During the years 1780 to 1785 the English park was introduced, supplanting the French garden. Houses were built on a smaller scale, as by the architect Stanisław Zawadzki: Śmiełów, Dobrzyca (whose English park with pantheon, pavilions, and

Gothic ruin is still extant), and Lubostroń.

232. OSTROWSKA-KĘBŁOWSKA, Zofia.

Budownictwo i architektura. (Building and architecture) *In* Dzieje Wielkopolski. [History of Wielkopolski] Poznań, Wydawnictwo Poznańskie, 1973. Vol. 2, p. 275–96. illus. DK511.W55D94

Vol. 2 edited by Witold Jakóbczyk.

Describes trends in architectural styles in Wielkopolska from 1815 to 1870. Among notable buildings erected during that period were a church in Rogalin, designed after the style of the temple in Nîmes, the Raczyński family library in Poznań (currently serving as the municipal library) designed by Karl Schinkel; the Gold Chapel (Złota Kaplica) in the cathedral in Poznań (built in the byzantine style); and the palace of Tytus Działyński in Kórnik (which houses a museum and library) in a neogothic style. At the same time, the Prussian government erected in Poznań a fortress-prison and barracks, using the French architectural style from J.N.L. Durand's treatise. (The fortress no longer exists.)

233. OSTROWSKA-KĘBŁOWSKA, Zofia.

Pałace Wielkopolskie z okresu klasycyzmu. [Palaces of Wielkopolska from the period of Classicism] Poznań, Wydawnictwo Poznańskie, 1970. 141 p. illus. NA7763.O8

Wielkopolska in the eighteenth century was the westernmost province of Poland. It comprised the voivodeships of Poznań, Kalisz, and Gniezno. In a brief and highly informative text, seventeen great palaces are described, for which the designs of Robert Adam, Lord Burlington, and Colin Campbell are evoked. The palace at Pawłowice was built between 1779 and 1783 by the Silesian architect Karol Gotthard Langhans, and decorated by the Warsaw architect Jan Christian Kamsetzer between 1789 and 1793. The arthitect Stanisław Zawadzki built both the palace at Śmiełów (1776–1782) and the one in Lubostroń (1795–1800), the former having a Pompeian room with a painting by Franciszek Smuglewicz, the latter based on Palladio's Villa Rotonda via Chiswick and Mereworth Castle. Good, if small, photographs of exteriors and interiors.

234. OSTROWSKA-KĘBŁOWSKA, Zofia.
Siedziby Wielkopolskie doby Romantyzmu. [Residences of Wielkopolska during the period of Romanticism] Poznań, Wydawnictwo Poznańskie, 1975. 129 p. illus. NA7763.O83
Bibliography: p. 126.

Each of four chapters is devoted to a palace in the baronial or castellated Gothic revival style, the fifth chapter to classical villas. Between 1821 and 1838, Karl Friedrich Schinkel (1781–1841) built for Antoni Radziwiłł a hunting lodge and mausoleum. Schinkel projected a castle in Kórnik after 1830. Other projects there are reminiscent of Strawberry Hill by Antonio Corazzi and Enrico Marconi. An island castle for Klaudyna Potocka was designed by her brother, the architect Tytus Działyński. Such Polish and other European nineteenth-century castellated buildings are discussed. The

revival styles are briefly, but contextually treated. Well illustrated.

235. OSTROWSKI, Wacław.
Działalność urbanistyczna Stanisława Leszczyńskiego w Nancy i jej pozycja w dziejach budowy miast. [The town planning activity of Stanisław Leszczyński and its position in the history of urbanism] Kwartalnik Architektury i Urbanistyki; teoria i historia. Vol. 2, no. 3/4, 1957, p. 179–98. illus. NA6.K9
Summary in English and German.
Bibliographic references.

The construction in Nantes by the abdicated Polish King Stanisław Leszczyński, beginning in 1752, is extraordinary for the number of public buildings he built. His ideas were linked to his literary utopian program. The formal plan may have analogies to earlier examples in Poland.

236. SCHINKEL, Karl Friedrich.
Collection of architectural designs: including designs which have been executed and objects whose execution was intended. New complete edition. New York, Princeton Architectural Press, 1989. 54, 11 p., 174 p. of plates: ill.; 23 × 29 cm. NA1088.S3 1989

Translation of: Sammlung architektonischer Entwürfe [Berlin, 1866] An introductory analysis and descriptions of each design, written by the architect and translated into English by Karin Cramer, accompany the plates; original German text and prefatory essays also included.

237. SCHINKEL, K.F.
Sammlung architektonisher Entwürfe. Rev. Ed., Berlin, Verlag von Ernst & Korn, 1866. 11 p. of text, 174 plates. NA2630.S3 1866 folio

238. STOWARZYSZENIE Historyków Sztuki.
Klasycyzm. Studia nad sztuką polską XVIII i XIX wieku. [Classicism. Studies in Polish art of the eighteenth and nineteenth centuries] Wrocław, Zakład Narodowy im. Ossolińskich, 1968. 272 p. illus. (Studia z Historii Sztuki, vol. 11) N7255.P6S8
Materiały Sesji Stowarzyszenia Historyków Sztuki. Poznań, październik 1965.

Seven essays including, for example, the reception of the Palladian style in Poland in the second half of the eighteenth century (T. Jaroszewski), the patronage of Izabella Lubomirska in architecture (Majewska-Maszkowska), the beginning of the Enlightenment style in Poland (S. Lorentz), and Antiquity in the works of Tylman of Gameren (S. Mossakowski). Some articles have French summaries.

239. Stowarzyszenie Historyków Sztuki.
Sztuka l. połowy XVIII wieku.
[The art of the first half of the eighteenth century] Warszawa, Państwowe Wydawnictwo Naukowe, 1981. 371 p. illus., plans, ports. N7255.P6S968
Table of contents in English.
Bibliographic references.
Materiały Sesji Stowarzyszenia Historyków Sztuki. Rzeszów, listopad 1978.

❁

Eight out of twenty-two papers delivered at the meeting of Polish art historians, held in November 1978 in Rzeszów, are devoted to Polish architecture. Adam Miłobędzki discusses the architectural designs of Pompeo Ferrari, Poppelman, Kasper Bażanka, and Jan Spazzio. Others deal with residences in Wielkopolska in the first half of the eighteenth century, Baroque churches in Wielkopolska, and neo-Baroque architecture in Poland.

240. SZYDŁOWSKI, Tadeusz, *and* Tadeusz Stryjeński.

O pałacach i dworach z epoki po Stanisławie Auguście i budowniczym królewskim Jakóbie Kubickim. [On country palaces and residences from the post-Stanisław August period, and on the royal architect Jakób Kubicki] Kraków, Gebethner i Wolff, 1925. 49 p. illus. NA7763.S98 1925

Four country palaces by the outstanding neo-classical architect Jakób Kubicki (1758–1833): in Igołomia, Pławowice, Białaczew, and Bejsce, and two residences. Twenty-three good photographs of exteriors and interiors; plans and elevations. Kubicki, a pupil of Merlini, also studied in France and Italy. He had a strong influence on the Polish neo-classical architecture of small palaces, and his style was often imitated.

241. TATARKIEWICZ, Władysław.

Dominik Merlini. Warszawa, Budownictwo i Architektura, 1955. 192 p. (chiefly illus.) NA1199.M4T3

Merlini, a preeminent eighteenth-century architect in Poland, was born in 1730 near Lugano. By 1750 he was active in Poland, and from 1761 architect to the crown. A well-defined presentation of the royal palace, Warsaw, Łazienki, and other palaces in Warsaw and its territory; drawings of elevations and plans; photographs. Other commissions and projects. A visual glossary of Merlini's forms and motifs in forty-six figures: façades, interior elevations, windows, capitals, etc.

242. TATARKIEWICZ, Władysław.

Łazienki Warszawskie. [The Warsaw Łazienki (palace)] Warszawa, Arkady, 1972. 286 p. illus. (part color), plans. NA7764.W2T3 1972

Summary and list of illustrations in English, French, and Russian.

Bibliographic references.

Photographs by Edmund Kupiecki.

The first half of the book covers the history of the former palace of Ujazdów, which was rejected by King Stanisław August Poniatowski as a residence in favor of one of the pavilions. Łazienki was the name of a bathing pavilion that had been built by Tylman van Gameren in the 1680s. The King renovated and reconstructed the palace between 1775 and 1776. Merlini was the architect. The second half of the book consists of 260 splendid photographs.

243. TŁOCZEK, Ignacy F.

Polskie budownictwo drewniane. [Polish wooden buildings] Wrocław, Zakład Narodowy im. Ossolińskich, 1980. 200 p. 132 p. of plates. illus. (part color). NA1455.P6T57

Bibliography: p. 193–94.

The buildings exhibit extraordinary, rich, geometrical structures, the shingle style in Baroque expositions, or modernism avant-la lettre. Constructions date mostly from the fifteenth to eighteenth centuries. Copious illustrations: over sixty drawings; 138 photographs, of which eight are in color. Glossary of terms used in wood construction.

244. TRZEBIŃSKI, Wojciech.

Działalność urbanistyczna magnatów i szlachty w Polsce XVIII wieku. [The urban activity of magnates and nobles in Poland in the eighteenth century] Warszawa, Państwowe Wydawnictwo Naukowe, 1962. 177 p. illus., 6 fold-out plans. NA9212.P6T7

Sponsored by Zakład Historii Architektury i Urbanistyki of the Polish Academy of Sciences.

Bibliography: p. 161–67.

Bibliographic references.

Some eighty new settlements were established in Poland between 1710 and 1795 and about thirty-five more were projected. The book is divided into new and rebuilt towns, and gives a critical overview based on archives (to which extensive references are given), demographics, and other data. Chronological table of names of settlements, dates and owners. The study includes Warsaw and Białystok.

245. Varsavia 1764–1830: de Bellottto a Chopin. Venezia, Arsenale, 1985. 171 p. illus. (part color). N7255.P6V37 1985

Bibliography: p. 169–71.

Exhibition catalog prepared by Wojciech Fijałkowski, Marek Kwiatkowski, Alberto Rizzi.

Highly important and innovative exhibition held at Ca' Rezzonico.

❋

Essays on the history of Warsaw and its art patronage, on the architectural-urbanistic evolution (1764–1830), and on Venetians and Venetophiles in Warsaw— eighteenth and nineteenth centuries. A fully illustrated, scholarly catalog. Especially noteworthy are the numerous reproductions of architectural projects by Domenico Merlini, Vincenzo Brenna, Giacomo Quarenghi, and others.

246. WEGNER, Jan.

Arkadia. Warszawa, Muzeum Narodowe w Warszawie, 1948. 74 p. of text, 38 illus., map, port. DK651.N33W4

Bibliography: p. 67–71.

A classical and romantic pastoral park recreated near Warsaw by Helena Radziwiłł between 1778 and 1821. An early design was by the royal architect Szymon Bogumił Zug; later contributors were Henryk Ittar, the decorative sculptor Giochino Staggi, and the painter Jan Piotr Norblin. Structures, some extant, were a temple of Diana, an amphitheater, an aqueduct, and a Swiss cottage.

247. AFTANAZY, Roman.

Materiały do dziejów rezydencji. [Materials on the history of residences.] Warszawa, Polska Akademia Nauk, Instytut Sztuki, 1986 + NA7412.P6.A38 1986

Edited by Andrzej J. Baranowski.

Part I: Wielkie Księstwo Litewskie, Inflanty, Kurlandia. [The Grand Duchy of Lithuania, Livonia, Courland]

Vols. 1–2 (1986) cover former provinces of Połock, Vitebsk,

Mscisław, Minsk, Brest-Litovsk, and Nowogródek.

Vols. 3–4 (1987) include former provinces of Troki, the Duchy of Samogitia, Polish Livonia, the Duchy of Courland, and Wilno.

Each volume consists of 2 sections: (A) text, and (B) illustrations.

Publication in progress.

The first two of nine projected volumes on the castles, palaces, great country houses, and lesser manors in the territory of the ancient Kingdom of Poland and Grand Duchy of Lithuania. For each property the author has researched the history of the locality, of ownership, architecture, and construction, and has described the exterior and interior— including furnishings—and the gardens and parks. Former owners are the source for most of the information. Their photographs have been supplemented by the author's. Other photographs come from the National Museum of Art in Warsaw and Kraków, and the Art Institute of the Polish Academy of Sciences.

248. Arka Pana. [Roman

Catholic Church in Nowa Huta] Paris, Editions du Dialogue, 1988. 103 p. illus. NA5955.P62N694 1988

Text by Józef Gorzelany.
Photographs by Adam Bujak.
Book design by Witold Urbanowicz Sac.

Text in Polish, French, and German.

A book celebrating the Church at Nowa Huta, which was constructed between 1967 and 1977 after a hard-won struggle to secure permission from the government to build. It was consecrated in 1977 by Cardinal

Karol Wojtyła (now Pope John Paul II). The architect was Wojciech Pietrzyk (his inspiration was Le Corbusier's church at Ronchamp). Sculptures include six variations on the Pietà by Antoni Rząsa (1929– 1980) and a Crucifixion by B. Chromy.

249. BRYKOWSKI, Ryszard.

Łemkowska drewniana architektura cerkiewna w Polsce, na Słowacji i Rusi Zakarpackiej. [Wooden Orthodox church architecture of the Lemko people in Poland, Slovakia and Carpathian Rus] Wrocław, Zakład Narodowy im. Ossolińskich, 1986. 195 p. 156 illus. map. NA5955.P62L493 1986

Summary in English.
Bibliography: p. 176–78.

Not until 1924 was the name of the Lemko ethnographic group linked with the architectural style of the churches. The origins of the group, and of the styles, have yet to be determined. A catalog of more than one hundred churches, dating from the late seventeenth century, arranged by place.

250. BRYKOWSKI, Ryszard, *and* Marian Kornecki.

Drewniane kościoły w Małopolsce Południowej. [Wooden churches of southern Małopolska] Wrocław, Zakład Narodowy im. Ossolińskich, 1984. 176 p. 140 illus., map. NA5955.P62M344 1984

Summary in English and German.

Bibliography: p. 63–64.

Alphabetical list of places where wooden churches stand, and a brief description of them. Many photo-

❁

*graphs of interiors and details, such as
doors and windows.*

251. Building and architecture

in Poland 1945–1966. Warsaw,
Interpress, 1968. 116 p. illus.
NA1191.B813
  Edited by Przemysław
Trzeciak.

*Architectural construction and town
planning, as implemented according to
a collective industrial and social
program. Articles on buildings for
education, sport, transportation, and
health care, among others, with some
technical data.*

252. CEMPLA, Józef.

Wawel. Katedra Królewska.
[Wawel. The Royal Cathedral]
Kraków, "Starodruk," 1957. 6 p.
16 plates of drawings.
NA5691.C4 folio

*Sixteen drawings by Józef Cempla,
fifteen of which are in pencil, one in
charcoal. Most are on paper that is
tinted yellow, with white highlights
reserved.*

253. GARLIŃSKI, Bohdan.

Architektura polska 1950–
1951. [Polish architecture 1950–
1951] Warszawa, Państwowe
Wydawnictwa Techniczne, 1953.
209 p. illus., plans. NA1191.G35
folio
  Sponsored by the Instytut
Urbanistyki i Architektury.

*Official buildings, such as those in
Warsaw, of the Polish Communist
Party: the Finance Ministry, the
Mausoleum of the Red Army,
housing in the area of
Marszałkowska Street, the buildings
in Nowa Huta, and elsewhere in the
country. Illustrated in plans,
elevations, models, and photographs on
576 plates.*

254. HEYMAN, Łukasz.

Nowy Żoliborz 1918–1939;
Architektura—urbanistyka.
[Nowy Żoliborz 1918–1939;
Architectural forms—town plan-
ning] Wrocław, Zakład
Narodowy im. Ossolinskich,
1976. 258 p. 36 leaves of plates,
illus. (Studia z historii sztuki,
vol. 25) NA1455.P62Z644
  Sponsored by the Art Institute
of the Polish Academy of
Sciences.
  Summary and list of illustra-
tions in English.
  Bibliographic references.

*Deals with the residential quarter of
Warsaw; a review and assessment of
policies and ideologies. There were
severe housing problems immediately
after World War I. Large-scale
plans were governed chiefly by social
objectives—historicism (recreating
the "Joli bord" from which the Polish
name is derived). Influences upon the
planners and planning bodies. Inadequate map.*

255. Karl Friedrich Schinkel i Polacy.

[Karl Friedrich Schinkel
and the Poles] [Exhibition cata-
log] Warszawa, Muzeum
Narodowe w Warszawie, 1987.
196 p. 54 plates. NA1088.S3K365
1987
  Collective work by Waldemar
Baraniewski, Tadeusz S.
Jaroszewski, Anna Kozak, and
Zofia Ostrowska-Kębłowska.
  Bibliography: p. 192–96.
  Bibliographic references.

*Nine essays on Karl Friedrich
Schinkel (1781–1841), the Berlin
architect, plus two appendices and a
catalog of fifty-six plans, elevations,
and other drawings, some by the
architect himself, along with objects
associated with Schinkel's work in
Poland, such as portraits of his
patrons. Among the subjects of the
essays are the Golden Chapel in the
Cathedral of Poznań; Antonin, the
hunting lodge built for Antoni
Radziwiłł; the Krzeszowice and
Kwilcz palaces; the Zawada and
Kórnik castles; and scenography for
the opera "Faust" (with music by
Antoni Radziwiłł). The exhibition, held at the National Museum
(Warsaw), included original drawings from the following repositories:
the National Museums of Kraków,
Wrocław, Poznań; the Museums of
Kórnik and Łańcut; and the National Archives in Kraków.*

256. KONDEK, Wacław.

Łódzkie pałace. Album. [An
album on the palaces of Łódź]
Łódź, Wydawnictwo Łódzkie,
1973. 172 p. illus. NC312.P63K66
folio

*Presents 171 drawings by the author,
documenting thirty-eight palaces and
villas (exteriors, interiors, and details); a brief text touches on the
preponderantly nineteenth-century history of the buildings. While the
sketches are intended to convey impressions rather than information,
they do bring out material not
otherwise available.*

257. Kościoły Warszawy w odbudowie.

[The rebuilt
churches of Warsaw] Warszawa,
Rada Archidiecezjalna
Odbudowy Kościołów
Warszawy, 1956. 40 p. of text, 51
leaves of illus. (part color).
NA5691.K6
  Text by Władysław Jan
Grabski.
  Description of illustrations by
Antoni S. Tomaszewski.
  Bibliographies.

❁

*Brief historical accounts of the
construction of fifty-five churches.
Photographs of the churches before
World War II, in their destroyed and
rebuilt states.*

258. Kościoły w Polsce
odbudowane i wybudowane,
1945–1965. [Rebuilt and newly
built churches in Poland, 1945–
1965] Warszawa, Ars Christiana,
1966. 255 p. illus. (part color).
NA5691.K59

Collective work by Marcin
Bukowski and others.

*Two hundred forty-five photographs,
of which two thirds are before-and-
after shots of buildings once destroyed
and then rebuilt; the remaining third
is of new buildings. Brief descriptive
catalog. Alphabetical listing of
churches.*

**259. KRÓL-KACZOROWSKA,
Barbara.**
Teatry Warszawy: Budynki i
sale w latach 1748–1975.
[Theaters of Warsaw: Buildings
and auditoria in the years 1748–
1975] Warszawa, Państwowy
Instytut Wydawniczy, 1986. 279
p. 130 illus. NA6840.P6W237
1986

Bibliography: p. 254–57.
List of theaters: p. 258–62.

*A cultural rather than architectural
history of nearly two hundred professional theaters constructed over a
period of two-hundred years. Good
illustrations of exteriors, interiors,
and plans.*

260. MAŁACHOWICZ, Edmund.
Stare miasto we Wrocławiu.
Zniszczenie, odbudowa,
program. [The Old City of
Wrocław. Its destruction, re-
building, program] Warszawa,

Państwowe Wydawnictwo
Naukowe, 1976. 262 p. illus.
NA1455.P62W765

Summary in English and
German.

Bibliography: p. 233–35.

*The author sketches the history of the
Wrocław area, where settlements date
from 2500 B.C. Ever-important
strategically, hence fortifications. Emphasis is placed on the reconstruction
of the city after World War II. The
buildings and streets are illustrated in
two hundred photographs and drawings from the nineteenth century to the
present.*

261. OLSZEWSKI, Andrzej K.
Nowa forma w architekturze
polskiej 1900–1925. Teoria i
praktyka. [New form in Polish
architecture 1900–1925. Theory
and practice] Wrocław, Zakład
Narodowy im. Ossolińskich,
1967. 221 p. 122 illus.
NA1191.O35

Summary in English.

*Presents the first synthesis of the
architecture of the period. Characterizes the Kraków Art Nouveau as
akin to the English Arts and Crafts
Movement, and that of Warsaw as
rationalistic in construction. Rare
photographs of Art Nouveau in
Łódź, Lwów, and Poznań. Covers
historiography and theoretical writings
by architects. For example, the
1920s were marked by decorative
modernism, as in the Polish pavilion
(Paris) by Józef Czajkowski and the
Church of St. Roch (Białystok) by
Oskar Sosnowski, with the views of
Le Corbusier gradually taking over
through the Blok group (Mieczysław
Szczuka, Teresa Żarnower) and the
Praesens group (Barbara Brukalska
and Stanisław Brukalski, Helena
Syrkus and Szymon Syrkus).*

262. Poland. Archiwum Główne.
Katalog rysunków
architektonicznych Henryka i
Leandra Marconich w Archiwum
Głównym Akt Dawnych w
Warszawie. [A catalog of archi-
tectural drawings of Henryk and
Leandro Marconi in the Main
Archive of Old Acts in Warsaw]
Warszawa, Państwowe
Wydawnictwo Naukowe, 1977.
307 p. illus. (Biblioteka
muzealnictwa i ochrony
zabytków. Series A, vol. 11)
AM70.P6B5

By Tadeusz S. Jaroszewski and
Andrzej Rottermund.

*The drawings of Henryk Marconi
(1792–1863), who came to Poland
in 1822, and his son Leandro
(1834–1919), who was born in
Warsaw. They were prolific architects
with official commissions (court
houses, jails) and private commissions
(churches, palaces) working in neogothic, neoclassical, and Renaissance
styles; 164 plates.*

**263. POPŁAWSKA, Irena, and
Stefan Muthesius.**
Poland's Manchester: 19th-
century industrial and domestic
architecture in Łódź. Journal of
the Society of Architectural
Historians, vol. 45, no. 2, June
1986, p. 148–60. illus. NA1.A327
v. 45

Bibliographic notes.

*Łódź, the foremost monument of
nineteenth-century industry, was the
preeminent Polish city for industrial
growth. Factories for textile manufacture, workers' houses, and owners'
mansions remain largely intact. The
textile factory buildings of Israel
Kalmanowicz Poznański
(1833–1900) serve as an example.
His large spinning mill was con-*

structed in 1859 and, after the fire of 1890, was reconstructed—along with some additional buildings—according to designs by Hilary Majewski (1837–1897), the Łódź municipal architect from 1872 to 1892. Majewski also designed the residence for the owner of the I.K. Poznański textile factory.

264. PURCHLA, Jacek.
Jan Zawiejski, architekt przełomu XIX i XX wieku. [Jan Zawiejski, Fin-de-siècle architect] Warszawa, Państwowe Wydawnictwo Naukowe, 1986. 404 p. illus. NA1455.P63Z3737 1986

Summary in English and German.

Bibliographic references.

A splendid study on Jan Zawiejski (1854–1922), the important architect—trained in Vienna under H. von Ferstel—who shaped the face of Kraków in his day. Documents his work and addresses subjects such as European vs. Polish architectural tradition c. 1900, as well as socio-economic influences on fin-de-siècle architecture. Fluent and detailed English summary; 301 illustrations.

265. Stowarzyszenie Historyków Sztuki. Sesja (30th: 1980: Warsaw, Poland) Sztuka dwudziestolecia międzywojennego. [Art in the interwar period.] Warszawa, Państwowe Wydawnictwo Naukowe, 1982. 345 p. illus. N7255.P6S8 1980

Edited by Anna Marczak.
Bibliographic references.
Table of contents in English.
Materiały Sesji. Warszawa, październik 1980. [Papers delivered at the meeting held in Warsaw, October 1980]

Among the subjects covered by the Session were the architecture of mountain resorts and residences in Wielkopolska [Great Poland] in the 1919–1939 period; the production of glass at the "Niemen" foundry (on the river Niemen in Lida county), the art of the national parks; and theories of art.

266. Stowarzyszenie Historyków Sztuki. Sztuka XX wieku. [Art of the twentieth century] Warszawa, Państwowe Wydawnictwo Naukowe, 1971. 254 p. illus. N6485.S75

Collection of studies.
Bibliographic references.
Materiały Sesji Stowarzyszenia Historyków Sztuki. Słupsk, październik 1969.

Of particular interest are the articles on architecture, such as Piotr Krakowski on the reception of the Bauhaus in Poland between the wars, Krzysztof K. Pawłowski on town planning in that same period, and the evolution of residential design.

267. SYRKUS, Helena.
Ku idei osiedla społecznego 1925–1975. [Toward the idea of community housing development 1925–1975] Warszawa, Państwowe Wydawnictwo Naukowe, 1976. 455 p. illus., plans, ports. NA1455.P6S87

Bibliographic references.

An account of the author's and her husband's (Szymon Syrkus, 1893–1964) work as architects in Warsaw. Both concentrated on urban community housing at times when there was a shortage of housing, first after World War I and again after World War II. Describes the international congresses of modern architecture in

which they participated, the activity of CIAM (Congrès Internationaux d'Architecture Moderne, 1928–1956, an international organization of avant-garde architects and urbanists), and the active part some Polish architects played in that organization. Discusses many prominent modern architects and urbanists with whom they had contact (e.g., Le Corbusier, Pierre Jennert, P. Behrens). Numerous plans and illustrations reproduced from private collections.

268. SZAFER, T. Przemysław.
Nowa architektura polska. Diariusz lat 1971–1975. [Contemporary Polish architecture. Diary for the years 1971–1975] Warszawa, Arkady, 1979. 372 p. illus. NA1455.P6S93

Bibliographies.

Divided into seven sections, including residential architecture, buildings for education, culture, communications, sports, and health care. Covers both rural and urban structures, and the restoration of historic structures. A brief text introduces each section. The heart of the book is the illustrations—a wealth of drawings, models, and photographs.

269. SZAFER, T. Przemysław.
Współczesna architektura polska. Contemporary Polish architecture. Warszawa, Arkady, 1988. 243 p. illus. (part color), plans, ports. NA1455.P6S935 1988

Bibliography: p. 233–235.
"A forty-year anthology" which includes excerpts from writings of the architects and descriptions of the illustrations in Polish, English, and Russian.

Biographical sketches on the architects.

Gives a review of architectural accomplishments in a forty-year period. In addition to drawings, provides eight hundred illustrations. Includes photographs of architects.

270. WISŁOCKA, Izabella.
Awangardowa architektura polska, 1918–1939. [Polish avant-garde architecture, 1918–1939] Warszawa, Arkady, 1968. 289 p. illus., map. NA1191.W5
    Bibliography: p. 259–73.

Part I deals with the origin of modern European architectural thought (Le Corbusier, Mies van der Rohe, van Doesburg, Malewicz). Part II concerns its development in Poland in constructions and projects. An important book in the field of Polish architecture of the period.

III. Sculpture

✳

271. ABAKANOWICZ, Magdalena.
Magdalena Abakanowicz: Museum of Contemporary Art, Chicago. New York, Abbeville Press, 1982. 188 p. illus. (part color). N7255.P63A232 1982

Exhibition held at Museum of Contemporary Art, Chicago, and the Chicago Public Library Cultural Center, Nov. 6, 1982 through Jan. 2, 1983, and other museums.

Bibliography: p. 172–86.

The sculptor, who works on a monumental scale—almost exclusively in fiber—is represented in this text in all phases of her work. Its evolution is traced from the free-form tapestries called "Abakan" to three-dimensional figural and abstract forms that express the human condition. A brief verbal self-portrait, and quotations from the artist that accompany many of the 152 illustrations, are poignant and reveal that nature is the foundation of her work. An excellent publication on an artist of major dimensions.

272. ABAKANOWICZ, Magdalena.
Magdalena Abakanowicz. Textile Strukturen und Konstruktionen. Environments. 29. Marz bis 28. Mai 1972. Düsseldorf, Kunstverein für die Rheinlande und Westfalen, 1972. 33 leaves (chiefly illustrations). N7255.P63A23

Edited by Karl Heinz Hering.

273. BADOWSKI, Ryszard.
Tajemnica bursztynowej komnaty. [The mystery of the Hall of amber] Warszawa, Wydawnictwo Radia i Telewizji, 1976. 202 p. illus. DK651.P93818

Bibliographic references.

Friedrich Wilhelm I of Prussia presented to Peter the Great—on the latter's visit to Potsdam in 1716—the gift of a hall made of amber. It was eventually installed at Tsarskoe Selo, but was later removed during World War II. Four photographs of the hall as it appeared at Tsarskoe Selo are included. The book recounts its removal, hiding, and subsequent loss. Its whereabouts are unknown.

The magnificent sculptured amber panels were carved by artists from Gdańsk, probably designed by Andreas Schlueter, and executed by Ernest Schacht and Gotfryd Turow. It was, however, originally started by master Gotfryd Wolffram from Copenhagen.

274. CERCHA, Stanisław, *and* Feliks Kopera.
Nadworny rzeźbiarz króla Zygmunta Starego Giovanni Cini z Sieny i jego dzieła w Polsce. [Court sculptor of King Sigismund the Old, Giovanni Cini of Sienna and his works in Poland] Kraków, J. Czernecki, 1916. 120 p. illus. NB623.C47C4

Bibliographic references.

Reconstruction of Giovanni Cini's life and work, based on extensive archival documents (1507?–1564) consisting of testaments, contracts through which his collaborators in architecture and sculpture are known, house purchases, and payments for work. The uniformity of design and execution in the Sigismund Chapel on the Wawel shows the authority of a single designer. In the years 1518 to 1529 Cini was responsible for the grotesque relief and free-standing sculpture, decoration of the cupola for the main altar in the cathedral, and the baldachim of the tomb of King Władysław Jagiełło. Returning from Italy in 1531, he undertook numerous independent commissions.

275. CHRZANOWSKI, Tadeusz.
Rzeźba lat 1560–1650 na Śląsku Opolskim. [Sculpture from the years 1560–1650 in Opole Silesia] Warszawa, Państwowe Wydawnictwo Naukowe, 1974. 176 p. 157 illus. NB955.P62O662

Summary in German and Russian.

Bibliographic references.

A survey that includes the sculptors and patrons, as well as discussion of the form and content of the sculptures. Geographic areas covered include Brzeg-Legnica, Nysa, Koźle, Raciborz, and Opole.

276. Cmentarz Powązkowski w Warszawie. [The Powązki Cemetery in Warsaw] Warszawa, Krajowa Agencja Wydawnicza, 1984. 367 p. illus. DK4641.C54C57 1984

❁

Collective work by Jerzy Waldorff, and others.

Bibliography: p. 333.

A vade mecum to one of the most famous nineteenth-century cemeteries in Europe. Fourteen ground plans and fifty photographic illustrations of funerary monuments, some from the twentieth century. Chapters on the history of the cemetery, on the artistic value of the monuments, and on outstanding monuments. Indices to persons by name and by profession, and to artists who executed the tombs.

277. DETTLOFF, Szczęsny.
Wit Stosz. Wrocław, Zakład Narodowy im. Ossolińskich, 1961. 2 v. illus., facsims. NB588.S8D49

Conclusions summarized in French and German in vol. 1.

Bibliography: v. 1, p. 268–76.

Text evenly divided between works from the two centers of Wit Stosz's creative life, Nuremberg and Kraków. Extended analysis of the Kraków altar. References to Kraków sculpture known only from documents. About one hundred reproductions of free-standing sculpture, reliefs, and paintings executed by Stwosz, in addition to the well-known monuments.

278. DOBROWOLSKI, Tadeusz.
Rzeźba neoklasyczna i romantyczna w Polsce; ze studiów nad importem włoskim i świadomoscią estetyczną. [Neoclassical and Romantic sculpture in Poland; Studies on Italian importation and esthetic awareness] Wrocław, Zakład Narodowy im. Ossolińskich,

1974. 216 p. [60] leaves of plates, illus. NB955.P6D62

Bibliographic references.

A study chiefly of Antonio Canova (1757–1822) and Bertel Thorvaldsen (1768–1844)—their Polish patronage, work executed for Poland, and their followers whose careers flourished under Polih commissions. Canova's patrons included King Stanisław August, Elżbieta Czartoryska-Lubomirska of Łańcut, Jan Feliks Tarnowski of Dzików and his wife Waleria, Michał Ludwik Pac, and others. All of Canova's extant works in Poland are accounted for, and models at Passagno are identified. Thorvaldsen's important Polish works are treated similarly; the monument of Włodzimierz Potocki; the Cathedral of Kraków, 1830; the equestrian statue of Prince Józef Poniatowski, Warsaw, 1828, 1830; and the Copernicus Monument, Warsaw, 1827, 1830.

279. GLICENSTEIN, Henryk.
Glicenstein. [By] Jean Cassou. New York, Crown Publishers, 1958. 12, [8] p. of plates. NB237.G55C293

Bibliography.

Insightful essay on Polish-born sculptor of intense, massive, expressionist human forms favored by Rodin in 1906. Thirty-seven sculptures and nineteen drawings are reproduced. Glicenstein settled in the United States in 1928, and lived there until his death in 1942.

280. GRODZISKA-OZÓG, Karolina.
Cmentarz Rakowicki w Krakowie. [The Rakowice Cemetery in Kraków] 2d rev. ed. Kraków, Wydawnictwo Literackie, 1987. 223 p. illus.,

plans. DK4731.C64G76 1987

Bibliography: p. 167–170.

Based on archival material, this work provides a history of the cemetery and a list with information on about three thousand persons who were buried there between 1803 and 1939, including their birth and death dates, professions or positions, and short biographies.

Also includes seventy-six illustrations of funerary chapels, monuments, and tombstones.

281. JAKIMOWICZ, Andrzej.
Polska rzeźba współczesna. [Polish contemporary sculpture] Warszawa, Wydawnictwo Sztuka, 1956. 23 p. 47 plates. NB691.J3

Forty-seven works by thirty-five artists are reproduced, beginning with four sculptures by Xawery Dunikowski, and Alina Szapocznikow's expressive sculpture, First Love, now in the Musée d'Art Moderne in Paris. Among notable or interesting sculptures of women are Anna Pietrowiec's sculpture of Maria Konopnicka and Stanisław Horno-Popławski's Żniwiarka (Harvestress). Other works are by Ludwika Nitschowa, Jacek Puget, Franciszek Strynkiewicz, Natan Rappaport, Alfons Karny, Alfred Wiśniewski, and others.

282. KACZMARZYK, Dariusz.
Rzeźba polska od XVI do początku XX wieku. [Polish sculpture from the sixteenth to the beginning of the twentieth century] Warszawa, Muzeum Narodowe w Warszawie, 1973. 148 p. ports. NB955.P6K32

Bibliography: p. 11–14.

The first published catalog of holdings in the National Museum in Warsaw;

although it lists 549 sculptures, not all are reproduced. Most of the sculptures are busts. Included is a list of names of persons represented in the portraits, and also biographies of the artists.

283. KACZMARZYK, Dariusz.
Straty wojenne Polski w dziedzinie rzeźby. [Losses of Polish sculpture in the War] Warszawa, 1958. 240 p. 206 plates. (Ministerstwo Kultury i Sztuki. Prace i Materiały Biura Rewindykacji i Odszkodowań, no. 14) NB691.K3

Preface and list of plates also in English.

Bibliographies.

One thousand and six objects are listed but, to paraphrase the author, an assessment of the total loss is almost impossible because of its immensity. For each piece, the author provides a description, date of origin, artist or workshop, where it was located, and date it was removed or destroyed. Part A consists of Polish sculpture—Romanesque and Gothic accounting for 600 pieces, Renaissance for 17, Baroque, Roccoco, and classicist for 152, and modern for 137. Part B consists of foreign sculpture including a mobile by Alexander Calder c. 1920, four important works by B. Thorwaldsen, and works by Giambologna and Antonio Rosselino.

284. KALINOWSKI, Konstanty.
Rzeźba barokowa na Śląsku. [Baroque sculpture in Silesia] Warszawa, Państwowe Wydawnictwo Naukowe, 1986. 371 p. illus. (part color). NB955.P62S555 1986

Summary in German.

Bibliographic references.

A comprehensive and profound study of the period 1650 to 1780. Treats subjects such as sculptural workshops of the great cloisters, the ornamentation and compositional schems of altars, Italian and Bohemian sculptors, and the sculptural milieu of Wrocław. Presents an overall view of the epochal expressive qualities of the art. The 376 illustrations are unequal to this great production.

[28]. KARPOWICZ, Mariusz.
Barok w Polsce. [The Baroque in Poland] Warszawa, Arkady, 1988. 338 p. 262 illus., 30 drawings, 24 color plates. DLC

Comments to illustrations: p. 277–316.

Bibliography: p. 325

The author traces the beginning of the Baroque in Poland to the architectural style of the Jesuits Church in Nieśwież, on which construction started in 1582. Discusses other churches in the Baroque style. Of the secular architecture, the royal palace in Warsaw (1599–1619) is seen as the most interesting. Two chapels, those of the Boim Family in Lwów, and St. Kazimir in Wilno Cathedral, are picked as the most beautiful examples of the Baroque in Poland. Good reproductions of paintings and sculp tures of the period.

[32]. Katalog zabytków sztuki w Polsce.
[Catalog of art monuments in Poland] Vols. I–IX, 1953–1982; Seria nowa. [New Series] vol. 1 + Warszawa, Polska Akademia Nauk, Inst Sztuki, 1977 + illus. maps. N6991.K36

This topographical catalog records buildings of architectural significance, exterior and interior furnishings and decorations, paintings, sculpture, sacral goldsmithery, and vestments.

Each volume of the original series of the Katalog zabytków sztuki w Polsce covers one province (województwo) and consists of numerous sections (zeszyty) published on various dates. In 1977, a new series of this catalog was instituted, based on the reorganized administrative divisions of the country. Originally, there were seventeen provinces, now there are forty-nine. The new series does not duplicate the original, but covers territories not previously included in the original series.

Each section includes an index of names and an up-to-date list of volumes and sections published, as well as places covered. Some sections contain hundreds of good, small photographs.

285. KĘBŁOWSKI, Janusz.
Nagrobki gotyckie na Śląsku. [Gothic sepulchral monuments in Silesia] Poznań, Uniwersytet im. Adama Mickiewicza w Poznaniu, 1969. 211 p. illus. (Wydział Filozoficzno-Historyczny. Seria Historii Sztuki, no. 2) NB1596.S5K4

Summary in German.

Bibliographic references.

286. KĘBŁOWSKI, Janusz.
Renesansowa rzeźba na Śląsku 1500–1560. [Renaissance sculpture in Silesia 1500–1560] Poznań, Państwowe Wydawnictwo Naukowe, 1967. 301 p. illus. (Poznańskie Towarzystwo Przyjaciół Nauk. Prace Komisji Historii Sztuki, vol. 8, pt. 1) NA1191.P6

Summary in German.

Describes numerous objects, such as tomb monuments, memorial portraits, pillars, epitaphs, etc., and traces their patronage.

287. KĘPIŃSKI, Zdzisław.

Wit Stwosz. Warszawa, Auriga, 1981. 136 p. of text, 128 illus., 20 color plates, 191 black and white plates (including 10 copper engraving plates). NB588.S8K39 1981

Bibliography: p. 129–34.

Comprehensive monograph that features the Marian altar, Kraków, and discusses contemporaneously executed works as well as later accomplishments such as the St. Roch figure—now in S. Maria Annunziata, Florence. Sculpture, paintings, drawings, and engravings by the artist in abundant illustrations.

288. KIRSTEIN, Lincoln.

Elie Nadelman. New York, Eakins Press, 1973. 358 p. illus. NB237.N23K57

Bibliography and exhibitions compiled by Ellen Grand, p. 321–41.

Bibliography: p. 260–63.

Definitive monograph by a critic of brilliant perception and knowledge. Includes a poetically evocative foreword, a study of the sculptor's life and work, statements by the artist, writings about the artist by André Gide (1909) and Gertrude Stein (1927)—among others—the draft of a catalogue raisonné of Nadelman's sculpture, drawings and prints, and 215 plates. Designed by Martino Mardersteig and printed at the Stamperia Valdonega, Verona, Italy. Copy 22 of 75 copies signed by the author; includes an original drypoint by the artist.

289. KIRSTEIN, Lincoln.

The sculpture of Elie Nadelman. New York, Museum of Modern Art, in collaboration with the Institute of Contemporary Art, Boston, and the Baltimore Museum of Art, 1948. 64 p. illus., port. NB699.N3K5

Brilliant exposition of the art of Elie Nadelman (1882–1946) who, with the twin stylistic references of heroic classicism and West European folk art, achieved his goal of sculptural harmony of form.

290. KOPERA, Feliks.

Jan Maria Padovano. *In* Polska Akademia Umiejętności. Prace Komisji Historji Sztuki, vol. 7, no. 2, 1938, p. 219–63. illus. N6991.P633 v. 7 folio

Bibliographic references.

Lesser-known works of the sculptor (c. 1493–1574): tombs of Bishops Tomicki, Gamrat, and Maciejowski in the cathedral of Kraków; several children's tombs; tombs of the Tarnowski family in Tarnów; and a ciborium in St. Mary's Church, Kraków.

291. KOSSAKOWSKA-SZANAJCA, Zofia.

August Zamoyski. Warszawa, Arkady, 1974. 165 p. illus. NB955.P63Z355

A biographical study of the sculptor August Zamoyski (1896–1970), with some discussion of his aesthetics. Studied in Berlin and Munich (1916–1917), where he was associated with the "Bunt" group that also exhibited in Poznań. In this period he designed scenery and costumes. Peripatetic thereafter, he went to the U.S. in 1920, to Paris in 1924, yet maintained a workshop in Zakopane until 1927, after which he worked in Warsaw. In 1930 he was

again in Paris; spent the years 1940–1955 in Brazil where he organized a school. He interrupted this sojourn, however, for a brief trip to New York where he had a studio on 10th Street. He settled in France in 1955, returned to Poland in 1956 and again from 1963 to 1964. A catalogue raisonné of 133 works of sculpture divided into four parts: "Pre-Formist," "Formist Period," "Return to Nature," and "New Expressionism." List of exhibitions and 113 plates.

292. KOTKOWSKA-BAREJA, Hanna.

Polish contemporary sculpture. Warsaw, Interpress, 1974. 154 p. illus. NB955.P6K6713

Translation by Krystyna Kęplicz of *Polska rzeźba współczesna.*

A lucid and readable short history of developments in Polish sculpture since 1945. The works of the artists are represented in good photographs, and a brief statement by each accompanies his or her portrait. These sculptors are all so talented that individual recognition here would be meaningless and unfair. What can be pointed out is that, of the thirty-two artists, five are women: Wanda Czełkowska, Ludmiła Stehnowa, Alina Szapocznikow, Magdalena Więcek, and Barbara Zbrożyna.

293. KOTULA, Adam, *and* Piotr Krakowski.

Rzeźba współczesna. [Modern sculpture] Warszawa, Wydawnictwo Artystyczne i Filmowe, 1980. 411 p. illus. (part color). NB198.K673

Bibliography: p. 393–95.

Interesting for placing Polish sculptors against the background of Euro-

Virgin and Child from Krużlowa, early fifteenth century. Limewood figure, painted, height 118 cm. From the Parish Church of Krużlowa (Nowy Sącz district). Currenty in the Czartoryski Collection, National Museum, Kraków, this sculpture has been exhibited in France, England, and the United States. Bronisław Rogaliński photo from *Cracow, City of Museums; the Most Beautiful Works of Art from Seven Museums*. Warsaw, Arkady, 1976

pean and American trends: Henryk Wiciński, Maria Jarema, and Marta Par compared to Brançusi and Arp; Tatlin and Rodchenko versus K. Mieduniecki; post-World War II Expressionism and the work of A. Szapocznikow and B. Chromy.

[36]. KOZAKIEWICZ, Stefan, *and* Stanisław Lorentz.

Poland. *In* Encyclopedia of world art. Vol. 11. New York, McGraw-Hill, 1966. p. 376–414. N31.E4833

Bibliography.

A rather authoritative, comprehensive, detailed, clear, and engaging presentation of Polish art and architecture in English. Arranged in two main sections: "Cultural and Artistic Periods" and "Monumental Centers." The first section provides an exposition of architecture and building, painting, and sculpture, each to the degree appropriate for the period. The second section is arranged by provinces (województwo), then by cites within each province. It gives the urban history, and lists important buildings and their architects, and the buildings' contents and surrounding areas, for each historically and artistically significant city. There is a bibliography on each of the cities.

[38]. KOZAKIEWICZOWA, Helena, *and* Stefan Kozakiewicz.

The Renaissance in Poland. Warsaw, Arkady, 1976. 329 p. illus. (part color), map. N7255.P6K6613

Translation by Doreen Heaton Potworowska of *Renesans w Polsce.*

Bibliography: p. 323–25.

An outstanding album for the English-language reader. In an excellent English translation, 252 fine

black and white photographs and eight plates in color are magisterially discussed. The authors call attention to works of art rarely illustrated and details generally overlooked. Lengthy essays trace developments from 1500 to 1640. Contains numerous drawings of plans and a map of all sites mentioned. Reproductions show the most beautiful Renaissance buildings, such as the Town Hall in Poznań (converted from the Gothic style, 1500–1560) by the architect Giovanni Battista Quadro from Lugano. Another Town Hall, built during the years 1570 to 1572 and well preserved, is in Brzeg (Silesia), by the architect Giacomo Pario from Como; also, the Cloth Hall (Sukiennice) in Kraków with its attica. The magnificent Sigismund Chapel in the Wawel Cathedral by the architect Bartolomeo Berrecci, and the Wawel Royal Castle with courtyard galleries, are reproduced in great detail. An abundance of illustrations of paintings, tapestries, tombs, and sculptures, among them—the tomb of Bishop A. Zebrzydowski at Wawel by Jan Michałowicz.*

[39]. KOZAKIEWICZOWA, Helena.

Renesans i manieryzm w Polsce. [The Renaissance and Mannerism in Poland] Warszawa, Auriga, 1978. 173 p. illus. (part color). N7255.P6K65

A brief history of what was principally architectural and sculptural expression, illustrated by fine photographs of infrequently reproduced monuments, such as the tomb of the Mazovian knights, 1526 to 1528 (figs. 13–14), the Castle gateway at Brzeg, 1551 to 1553 (fig. 74), and the tomb of the Firlej family, c. 1600, in Bejsce (figs. 96–97).

294. KRAJEWSKA, Monika.
Time of stones. Warsaw, Interpress, 1983. 164 p. (mostly illus.).
DS135.P6K68 1983
Introduction by Anna Kamieńska.
Translated from Polish by Krystyna Kęplicz.
Published also in Polish, German, and French.
Tombstones from Jewish cemeteries in Poland. The tombstones are embellished with epitaphic symbols. Many tombstones are in Renaissance, Baroque, and Rococo styles.

[41.] Krakowscy malarze,
rzeźbiarze i graficy w 40 lecie Polski Ludowej, lipiec-sierpień 1985. [Cracovian painters, sculptors and printmakers on the fortieth anniversary of Peoples' Poland [exhibition catalog] July–August 1985] Kraków, Urząd miasta Krakowa, Biuro Wystaw Artystycznych, 1985. 1 vol. illus.
N7255.P62K777 1985
Edited by Joanna Radzikowska.
Photographs by Krzysztof Rzepecki.
Includes paintings, sculptures, and prints by Polish artists. Addresses of the artists are given as well as a list of the most important events in the visual arts in Kraków from 1945 to 1985, arranged chronologically.

295. KUNA, Henryk.
Henryk Kuna. Warszawa, Arkady, 1959. 42 p. 59 p. illus.
NB699.K85W3
By Mieczysław Wallis.
Bibliography: p. 38.
Kuna (1879–1945), a student of K. Laszczka at the Kraków Academy of Art, went to Paris in 1903 where he came under the influence of Rodin. On a second trip to Paris, the artist changed his style and became a member of the RYTM group. That group included such painters as Eugeniusz Żak, Wacław Borowski, Ludomir Ślendziński, Roman Kramsztyk, Władysław Skoczylas, and Tymon Niesiołowski. From 1932 to 1939 Kuna was a professor at the Wilno University Art Department. A sculptor whose expressive creations are mostly in the classical style, Kuna worked in wood, stone, marble, and bronze. He won the competition for the bronze monument of Mickiewicz in Wilno. The work on the monument was nearly completed before it was destroyed during World War II.

296. LANGSNER, Jules.
Modern art in Poland. The legacy and the revival. Art International, vol. 5, no. 7. Zurich, J. Fitzsimmons, 1961, p. 22–29. illus. N1.A1A7
Provides a penetrating review of twentieth-century Polish sculpture and painting. Discusses various artists' groups and trends in their development. Concludes with a list of his choices for the most gifted modern painters, in which he includes Tadeusz Kantor (b. 1915), Jan Lebenstein (b. 1930), Bronisław Kierzkowski (b. 1924), Stefan Gierowski (b. 1925), and Wojciech Fangor. Twenty-six photographs of modern Polish artists, sculptures, and paintings.

297. LOSSOW, Hubertus.
Der Marienaltar in der Elisabethkirche zu Breslau; Ein Hauptwerk schlesischer Spätgotik. *In* Jahrbuch der preussischen Kunstsammlungen, vol. 16, pt. 3, 1939, p. 127–40. 9 illus. N3.J2 v. 16
Bibliographic references.
Examines the altarpiece in the Church of St. Elizabeth, Wrocław, of sculpted reliefs, free-standing figures, and eight painted scenes on the shutters and wings. In the center is the Annunciation; above is the Coronation of the Virgin, below are busts of saints in the predella. The style shows the influence of Wit Stwosz and Martin Schongauer.

[176]. ŁOZIŃSKI, Władysław.
Sztuka lwowska w XVI i XVII wieku. Architektura i rzeźba. [The art of Lwów in the sixteenth and seventeenth centuries. Architecture and sculpture] Lwów, H. Altenberg, 1901. 228 p. illus. NA3571.P62L84
Buildings characterized by marked plastic qualities, built by architects native to Lwów as well as Italians and Germans. Many arresting examples, such as the gateway to the Arsenal (fig. 34), and Boim's Chapel, exterior and dome (figs. 76–77). Four chapters each on architecture and sculpture. An old-fashioned book recommended for its subject matter; the text has 103 illustrations.

298. Marian Wnuk. Wystawa rzeźby zorganizowana w 10 rocznicę śmierci Profesora Mariana Wnuka. [Exhibition of sculpture organized on the tenth anniversary of the death of Professor Marian Wnuk] Warszawa, "Zachęta," styczeń–luty 1978. Warszawa, Centralne Biuro Wystaw Artystycznych, 1978. 2 vols. illus.
NB955.P63W582 1978

The exhibit catalog treats not only the sculptures of Marian Wnuk, but also the artwork of forty-nine of his students.

299. MEINERT, Gunther.
Jakob Beinhart, ein schlesischer Bildhauer und Maler der Spätgotik. *In Jahrbuch der preussischen Kunstsammlungen,* vol. 17, pt. 4, 1939, p. 217–36. 11 illus. N3.J2 v. 17

The career of Jakob Beinhart (c. 1460–1525)—contemporary of Dürer—a sculptor and painter, who was active principally in Wrocław (Breslau), but also in Gorlice (Gorlitz) and Świdnica (Schweidnitz).

300. MICIŃSKA, Anna.
Władysław Hasior. Warszawa, Arkady, 1983. 118 p. illus. (part color). N7255.P63H3735 1983
Summary in English.
Bibliography: p. 111–14.

Władysław Hasior (b. 1928) received his art education in Zakopane and at the Warsaw Academy of Art; he also traveled and studied in France. A sculptor of numerous outdoor monuments, Hasior in 1971 won the prize (1st class) of the Ministry of Culture and Art for his outstanding artistic accomplishments.

301. MISSIĄG-BOCHEŃSKA, Anna.
Głowy Wawelskie. [Heads from the Wawel Castle [ceiling]] Kraków, Państwowy Instytut Wydawniczy, 1953. 23 p. NA7764.K7M5

On the ceiling of the Sala Poselska [Representatives' Room] of Wawel Castle are thirty carved heads, which are here illustrated in sixty views.

They were probably sculpted by Sebastian Tauerbach with the help of Hans Schnyczer (Snycerz). Both sculptors were citizens of Kraków, where Hans opened his own workshop in 1533.

302. NADELMAN, Elie.
The sculpture and drawings of Elie Nadelman, 1882–1946: [an exhibition organized by the Whitney Museum of American Art; text by John I.H. Baur] New York, Whitney Museum, 1975. 119 p. illus. NB237.N23B38
Exhibition held at the Whitney Museum of American Art, New York, Sept. 23–Nov. 30, 1975 and the Hirshhorn Museum and Sculpture Garden, Smithsonian Institution, Washington, D.C., Dec. 18, 1975–Feb. 15, 1976.

Essay with reproductions of 103 works of sculpture and thirty drawings. Chronology and stylistic evolution of early works elucidated by Althena T. Spear.

303. Naive Kunst aus Polen:
Skulpturen, Bilder, Reliefs aus der Sammlung Orth. Kunsthalle Nürnberg in der Norishalle 25.10.1980 bis 27.1.1981. Nürnberg, Die Kunsthalle, 1980. 110 p. illus. (part color). N7255.P6N28 1980
Catalog edited by Barbara Wally, Wolfgang Horn, Curt Heigl.
Biographies of artists by Hans Joachim and Chirstina Orth.

Selection of works of great freshness and charm. Biographies of sixty-two artists, and a catalog of their sculpture in the exhibition.

304. NICIEJA, Stanisław S.
Cmentarz Łyczakowski we Lwowie w latach 1786–1986. [The Łyczaków Cemetery in Lwów in the years 1786–1986] 2d rev. ed. Wrocław, Zakład Narodowy im. Ossolińskich, 1989. 447 p. illus. DK508.95.L86N53 1989
Bibliography: p. 399–405.

A history of the multi-denominational cemetery, its numerous artistic tombstones, sepulchral monuments, and reliefs; erected in memory of citizens of Lwów.

[55]. Obóz koncentracyjny Oświęcim w twórczości artystycznej. [The Oświęcim concentration camp in art] 2d ed.
Oświęcim, Wydawnictwo Państwowego Muzeum, 1961–62. 4 v. in 1. illus. (part fold.). N7255.P6O26 1961
Text by Kazimierz Smoleń.
Text in Polish, English, French, German, and Russian.
Contents: Vol. 1–3. Malarstwo [Painting]—v. 4.Rzeźba. [Sculpture].

The first volume (xviii, 79 p.) reproduces drawings in coal by Jerzy Adam Brandhuber; the second (xxii, 40 p.), drawings and a woodcut by Mieczysław Kościelniak; and the third (iii, 61 p.), drawings by Maria Hiszpańska-Neumann, Janina Tollik, Franciszek Jaźwiecki, Tadeusz Myszkowski, Jerzy Potrzebowski, and Władysław Siwek. The fourth volume (74 p.) presents photographs of sculptures by Mieczysław Stobierski, Hanna Raynoch, Tadeusz Myszkowski, Vida Jocić, Hubert van Lith, and G.W. Mizandari. All the artists were professionals, and all were prisoners at Oświęcim. Their works

*reveal the daily experiences of hunger,
exhaustion, torture, and death. Eleven
penetrating portraits by Franciszek
Jaźwiecki were drawn from life at the
camp.*

305. OSĘKA, Andrzej, *and* Wojciech Skrodzki.

Contemporary Polish sculpture.
Warsaw, Arkady, 1978. 156
p. 135 illus., 11 color plates.
NB955.P608313 1978

Translation by Krystyna
Kęplicz of *Współczesna rzeźba
polska.*

*A brief history of Polish sculpture
that concentrates on the 1960s and
1970s. Some paragraphs are devoted
to twentieth-century movements such
as the Formist group, which provided
the significant leap into modernism
during the years 1917 to 1919.
Post-World War II English sculpture
ture was an important influence. The
authors did not intend a balanced
presentation, giving instead their
assessments. Alina Szapocznikow,
from the generation of the 1950s, is
appropriately allotted two pages of
text and twelve plates. "Schools" or
"types" covered are the Atelier at
Mogielnica (Barbara and Franciszek
Strynkiewicz); "Artists of the
Coast," especially the art school of
Gdańsk; sculptors of war memorials,
such as Franciszek Duszenko,
Adam Haupt, and Franciszek
Strynkiewicz, who created the Memorial
to the Victims of Treblinka;
"Dadaism of the 1960s," with
Władysław Hasior; and "Structure
and Space of the mid-1960s" by—
among others—Jerzy Jarnuszkiewicz
and his students. Thirty-two sculptors
working according to various aesthetics
are represented in good photographs,
and in brief statements that accompany
their photographs.*

306. Przegląd rzeźby polskiej

1944–1974 w XXX-lecie Polskiej
Rzeczypospolitej Ludowej. [A
review of Polish sculpture 1944–
1974 on the thirtieth anniversary
of the Polish Peoples' Republic]
Warszawa, Ministerstwo Kultury
i Sztuki, Związek Polskich
Artystów Plastyków, 1974.
81 p. 216 p. of plates, illus.
NB955.P6P79 1974

By: Lech Grabowski, Rajmund
Gruszczyński, Eugeniusz
Kawenczyński, and Hanna
Kotkowska.

*The exhibition was held in six cities
and was divided by sculptural type:
Polish people in sculpture (Lublin),
contemporary portraits (Radom),
relief sculpture (Katowice), medals
(Rzeszów), small-scale sculpture
(Poznań), and plein-air sculpture
(Opole). Among the many works of
interest are those by the following
women: Barbara Bieniulis-
Strynkiewicz, Wiktoria Czechowska-
Antoniewska, Hanna Danilewicz,
Zofia Demkowska, Anna Dębska,
Maria Gorełówna, Anna
Kamieńska-Łapińska, Barbara Lis-
Romańczuk, Maria Maliszewska,
Teresa Michałowska, Janina
Mirecka, Irena Molin-Sowa, Irena
Nadachowska, Angelina Petrucco,
Anna Pietrowiec, Ludmiła
Stehnowa, Zofia Woźna, and Barbara
Zbrożyna.*

307. Rzeźba pomnikowa i

monumentalna w Polsce
Ludowej [wystawa] styczeń 1971.
[Memorial sculptural monuments
and sculpture for monuments in
the Polish Peoples Republic (an
exhibition) January 1971]
Wrocław, Muzeum Architektury,
1971. 1 vol. unpaged. illus.
NB755.P6R95

Sponsored by Ministerstwo
Kultury i Sztuki, Związek
Polskich Artystów Plastyków.

Catalog by Maria Matusińska
and Barbara Mitschein.

*Fifty-seven sculptural monuments
commissioned to commemorate events
during the Nazi occupation. Among
them are: the Warsaw Ghetto, 1948,
by Natan Rappaport; Heroes of the
Lublin Ghetto, 1963, by Bogumił
Zagajewski; Heroes of Warsaw,
1964, by Marian Konieczny; the
concentration camp at Treblinka,
1964, and the Westerplatte, 1966, by
Franciszek Duszenko; Majdanek,
1967, by Wiktor Tołkin; and
Victory at Gołdap, 1970, by
Tadeusz Łodziana. Biographies of
seventy-three sculptors, including those
who executed sculpture for other
monuments.*

308. SKUBISZEWSKI, Piotr.

Rzeźba nagrobna Wita
Stwosza. [The funerary monument
ment in the work of Wit Stwosz]
Warszawa, Państwowy Instytut
Wydawniczy, 1957. 120 p. 162
tables of illus. NB588.S8S55

*Three tombs and one epitaph: the
tomb of King Kazimierz Jagiełło,
in the Cathedral on the Wawel,
Kraków; the tomb of Bishop Piotr of
Bnin, in Włocławek; the tomb
of Bishop Zbigniew Oleśnicki, in
Gniezno; and the epitaph of Filip
Kallimach (Callimachus
Buonacorsi), in the Dominican
Church, Kraków. The first three were
executed in Poland, the last was
stylistically tied to Polish works.
Copious, excellent illustrations.*

309. STOSS, Veit.

Ołtarz Krakowski. [The
Kraków altar] Warszawa, Auriga,

1964. 30 p. 160 plates (21 color). NA5697.S8 1964 folio

Also available in English, see next item.

310. STOSS, Veit.
The Cracow altar. Warsaw, Auriga, 1966. 21 p. 163 plates (22 color). NA5697.K783 folio

Editorial Committee: Szczęsny Dettloff, Tadeusz Dobrowolski, Józef Edward Dutkiewicz, and others.

Translation by Hilda Andrews-Rusiecka of *Ottarz krakowski.*

Honoring the largest Gothic altarpiece in Europe, and Stoss's most important work, this commentary takes into account the climate of contradictions within which it was executed—artistic idealism vs. artistic realism amid conflicting social, economic, regional, and cultural forces. Gives the background of art production in Kraków. Makes brief mention of collaborators. Shows keen appreciation of the artist's psychological understanding. A fine introduction to the subject. Excellent illustrations.

311. SZAPOCZNIKOW, Alina.
Alina Szapocznikow, 1926–1973. Tumeurs, herbier. [Postcript by] Pierre Restany. Paris, Musée d'art moderne de la ville de Paris, 1973. 24 p. illus. NB955.P63S92

The title "Tumeurs, herbier" conveys the qualities of organic growth, both fatal and benign, in these final works of the gifted sculptor. As perceptively stated in the postscript, she was a passionate observer of the human phenomenon who had the gift of great sculptors: that of integrating the idea with the material. Eighteen photographs of the artist and her work, and a chronology of exhibitions.

312. Sztuka polska po 1945 roku.
[Polish art after 1945] Warszawa, Państwowe Wydawnictwo Naukowe, 1987. 404 p. illus. DLC

Materiały Sesji Stowarzyszenia Historyków Sztuki. Warszawa, listopad 1984. [Reports from the Meeting of the Association of Art Historians. Warsaw, November 1984]

Dedicated to the memory of Juliusz Starzyński.

Edited by Teresa Hrankowska.

Over twenty-five papers, loosely organized around such topics as sculpture [A. Król, "Open form: The first modern conception of sculpture in Polish art"; I. Grzesiuk-Olszewska, "Competitions for the design of monuments: Oświęcim and the Heroes of Warsaw as an example of the controversy between creativity and commission"], painting ["The Painting of Socialist Realism in Poland" between 1948 and 1956, by Jerzy Ilkosz], post-modernism [see especially T.S. Jaroszewski, "Against the grain"], the role of museums [Z. Zygulski, "Art versus Museum"], and a review of art literature in Poland during the forty-year postwar period [by Andrzej K. Olszewski].

313. SZULC, Eugeniusz.
Cmentarz Ewangelicko-Augsburski w Warszawie. Zmarli i ich rodziny. [The Lutheran Cemetery in Warsaw. The deceased and their families] Warszawa, Państwowy Instytut Wydawniczy, 1989. 730 p. illus. DK4641.C49S98 1989

Bibliography: p. 631–645.

Provides a history of the Lutheran population—primiarily from Warsaw, but from other parts of Poland as well—through the 644 selective biographies of those buried in the cemetery. The painters Zygmunt Vogel, Wojciech Gerson, and Franciszek Ksawery Lampi, as well as the architect Szymon Bogumił Zug, along with many other artists, are buried in this cemetery. Many of the monuments are of high artistic quality.

314. SZYDŁOWSKI, Tadeusz.
Le Retable de Notre-Dame a Cracovie. Avec une introduction de Pierre Francastel. Paris, Les Belles Lettres, 1935. xx, 46 p. 80 plates, plan. (Institut français de Varsovie, 3) NA5691.S95

Album of eighty photographs made following restoration in the early 1930s, when the original polychromy was discovered. Reproductions in heliotype. The introduction traces stylistic influences evident in the work of Wit Stwosz (Veit Stoss) when executing the altar—from the Danube Valley style of the 1470s to a Flemish component. The text covers style and iconography in depth.

315. Veit Stoss; die Vorträge des Nürnberger Symposions.
Herausgegeben vom Germanischen Nationalmuseum Nürnberg und vom Zentralinstitut für Kunstgeschichte München. München, Deutscher Kunstverlag, 1985. 355 p. illus. NB588.S8V44 1985

Edited by Rainer Kahsnitz.

Bibliography: p. 297–338, compiled by Eduard Isphording.

Contributions by five Polish scholars to mark the 450th anniversary of the artist's death (1533): Kraków archival material bearing on Stoss's origins; overview of Polish research on his Kraków career; Stoss's influence in Central and Eastern Europe; and, by a German scholar, political and economic interdependence of Nuremberg and Kraków in Stoss's lifetime.

See review by Paul Crossley in Burlington Magazine, *vol. 128, June 1986, p. 428–29.*

316. ZAMOYSKI, August.

Au-delà du formisme. Lausanne, Éditions L'Age d'homme, 1975. 197 p. 4 levaes of plates, illus. (Ecrits sur l'art, no. 4) NB955.P63Z352

Précédé de portrait d'un artiste par Hélène Zamoyska.

Four articulate and passionate essays by the sculptor August Zamoyski (d. 1970), written between 1946 and 1960. In "Beyond Form," "The Passion of Forming (Shaping)," "On Sculpture," and "Art and Substance," Zamoyski includes his aesthetic objectives, working methods, techniques, choice of material as well as autobiographical passages and wide-ranging reflections. These essays are preceded by a "Portrait of the Artist" by his widow, which is forthright, vigorous, and sensitive, and are followed by a recollection by Witold Mieczysławski. Two photographs of the artist's studio, and six photographs of sculptures.

317. ŻARNECKI, Jerzy.

Renaissance sculpture in Poland: Padovano and Michałowicz. Burlington Magazine, vol. 86, no. 502, January 1945, p. 10–17. 10 illus. N1.B95 v. 86

Renaissance sculptors were summoned to Poland from northern Italy, the Poles having been "guided by some happy instinct" to go to original stylistic sources. G.M. Padovano, who arrived c. 1529, was the most extraodinary of the sculptors/ architects. The author discusses his tombs and Andrea Sansovino's influences upon Padovano's style. Also an assessment of the art of Michałowicz, the outstanding contemporary Polish practitioner of monumental sculpture.

IV. Painting

❀

318. DOBROWOLSKI, Tadeusz.
Malarstwo polskie ostatnich dwustu lat. [Polish painting of the last two hundred years] Wrocław, Zakład Narodowy im. Ossolińskich, 1976. 232 p. 200 illus. 48 color plates. ND955.P6D57

Deliberates fully on the currents of romanticism, historicism, and symbolism, that shaped European—and especially Polish—painting from the late eighteenth century. Reproductions, forty-eight in color and two hundred in black and white, of many extraordinary, little-known nineteenth- and early twentieth-century paintings. Contemporary examples less well chosen.

319. DOBROWOLSKI, Tadeusz.
Nowoczesne malarstwo polskie. [Modern Polish painting] Wrocław, Zakład Narodowy im. Ossolińskich, 1957–64. 3 vols. illus. (part color). ND955.P6D6
   Bibliography: v. 3, p. 449–74.
   Lists of illustrations also in French.

A most impressive work in terms of its range and the variety of issues investigated. Volume I surveys the history of Polish painting from 1764 to about 1990, classified as the Period of Enlightenment, and then examines the nineteenth century, which the author divides into three parts. The following samples of topics covered convey the flavor and textual richness: painters of ornamental decor, such as J.B. Plersch; portrait painting by J.C. Lampi and J. Grassi; paintings by Norblin and modern realism; the romanticism of P. Michałowski; the training of the artist; representatives of the old classicism and miniaturists (in the period 1880–1833); and the ideology supporting historicism in painting. Volume II begins with the second half of the nineteenth century, treating the major painters of historicism and romanticism—Matejko, Grottger, Brandt, Gottlieb—and the realists as represented by M. Gierymski, Chełmoński, and Gerson. The next section covers Młoda Polska, including Symbolism and Secession, followed by an examination of older contemporaries—J. Fałat, J. Malczewski, J. Mehoffer, F. Ruszczyc—as seen against the more progressive movement of Młoda Polska. Volume III deals with the twentieth century, beginning with W. Weiss, Matejko's youngest pupil, and touches on many intriguing subjects, such as the influences of Wyspiański and regional themes, the Group Five, and the continuing fate of Secession. Next is a section on the period 1914 to 1939, with the Formists versus the Expressionists of Poznań and the Bunt group, and the avant-garde groups of Blok and Praesens. A short section on art after World War II, dealing with socialist realism, completes the book. A wealth of illustrations throughout—over one thousand altogether—which, whatever their shortcomings in printing quality, afford a rich pictorial panorama of the material.

320. DOBRZENIECKI, Tadeusz, and others.
Sztuka sakralna w Polsce; malarstwo. [Sacral art in Poland; painting] Warszawa, Ars Christiana, 1958. 366 p. mostly illus. (part color). N7956.D6 folio
   Catalog of works: p. 335–67.

Covers the range from manuscript illumination of the early twelfth century to painting of the mid-twentieth century, with emphasis on the strongest, i.e., the Gothic period. Nearly one-half of the illustrated objects date before 1600.

321. GĘBAROWICZ, Mieczysław.
Początki malarstwa historycznego w Polsce. [The beginnings of history painting in Poland] Wrocław, Zakład Narodowy im. Ossolińskich, 1981. 194 p. illus. ND955.P6G42
   Sponsored by the Polish Academy of Sciences, Art Institute.
   Summary and list of illustrations in French.

History painting as a subject that went beyond formal, aesthetic consid-

*erations. Among its purposes was the
exaltation of the merits of a living
person for contemporaries and for
posterity. The earliest such paintings
in Poland date from the sixteenth
century and were executed mainly by
German artists influenced by German
and Polish cartographic and battle
schema. Discusses a fascinating group
of paintings commemorating a link
between Poland and Russia: the
ceremonies attendant upon the marriage of Maryna Mniszek and
Dimitry the Pretender in the first
decade of the seventeenth century. A
work of research of the highest
interest.*

322. Ikona w Polsce i jej przeobrażenia. L'Icone en
Pologne et ses metamorphoses.
Katalog wystawy. Catalogue de
l'exposition. Warszawa,
Państwowe Muzeum
Etnograficzne, 1967. 8 leaves, 16
tables, color illus. N8189.P6I38
   Edited by Stanisław
Szymański.

*A brief introduction touches on
historical events that determined new
centers of painting and new forms.
Poland on the frontier between
Roman and Orthodox traditions.
From acheiropoietos to idealistic to
realistic images, chosen for exhibition
for their high aesthetic quality.*

323. JASIEŃSKI, Feliks, and Adam Łada Cybulski.
Sztuka polska. L'art polonais.
Peinture. Sześćdziesiąt pięć
reprodukcyj dzieł
najwybitniejszych przedstawicieli
malarstwa polskiego. Lwów, H.
Altenberg, 1904. 65 leaves, illus.,
ports., 68 mounted plates (part
color). ND691.J3 folio

*Sixty-five reproductions representative
of the most famous Polish paintings.
Plates arranged in no apparent order
except the approximately chronological one by artist's birth. Famous
painters include Juliusz Kossak
(1824–1899), Józef Chełmoński
(1850–1914), and Leon
Wyczółkowski (1825–1936).
Guard sheets with portraits and
biographies. Cover by Józef Mehoffer
(1903).*

324. JORDANOWSKI, Stanisław.
Vademecum malarstwa
polskiego. [A handbook of Polish painting] New York, Bicen-
tennial Publishing Corp., 1988.
270 p. 113 illus. 32 color illus.
ND955.P6J67

*A compendium of paintings by Polish
artists in collections in the United
States. The author includes biographies of about three hundred
painters and provides information on
the locations of their works. Numerous paintings by these artists are in
art collections in Poland.*

325. KĘPIŃSKI, Zdzisław.
Impresjonizm polski. [Polish
Impressionism] Warszawa,
Arkady, 1961. 53 p. 27 black and
white illus., 24 color illus.
DK691.K4 folio
   Summary and list of illustra-
tions in English, French, and
German.
   Bibliography: p. 29–30.
*Valuable as a compilation on Polish
artists who painted in the impression-
ist style, and for extended summaries
in English, French, and German of
the style's history in Poland.*
   *The twenty-four paintings repro-
duced in color are the works of
Aleksander Gierymski (1851–*

*1901), Władysław Podkowiński
(1866–1895), Józef Pankiewicz
(1866–1940), Leon Wyczółkowski
(1852–1936), Władysław Ślewiński
(1854–1918), Olga Boznańska
(1865–1940), Józef Mehoffer
(1869–1946), Jan Stanisławski
(1860–1906), and Wojciech Weiss
(1875–1950).*

326. KŁOSIŃSKA, Janina.
Ikony. [Icons] Kraków,
Muzeum Nardowe, 1973. 312 p.
illus. (part color). (Muzeum
Narodowe w Krakowie. Katalog
zbiorów, vol. 1) N8186.P7K724
   Summary in French.
   Bibliographic references.

*Largest number of icons from the
Carpathian region are unified by
style; their iconography, technique.*

   *First detailed catalog of an impor-
tant collection that was begun in
1884–85, within six years of the
founding of the National Gallery,
Kraków. Part I consists of scholarly
entries on 45 icons arranged by
subject. Part II covers 216 icons
arranged by place of origin, the largest
group from the Carpathian mountain
region, others from Russia, Romania,
Macedonia, Greece, and Dalmatia.*

327. KOPERA, Feliks.
Dzieje malarstwa w Polsce. [A
history of painting in Poland]
Kraków, Drukarnia Narodowa,
1925–1929, 3 v. illus. (part color)
facsims., ports. ND691.K64
   Bibliographic references.
   Vol. 1: Średniowieczne
malarstwo w Polsce. [Painting
of the Middle Ages in Poland]
250 p.

*Emphasis on manuscript illumination
(three chapters) and on stained glass.
Also discusses wall paintings of the*

fourteenth and fifteenth century. Abundant illustrations: more than two hundred figures and twenty-four plates.

Vol. 2: Malarstwo w Polsce od XVI do XVIII wieku. (Renesans, Barok, Rokoko) [Painting in Poland from the XVI to the XVIII centuries (Renaissance, Baroque, Rococo)] 345 p.

Unconventional emphases: manuscript illuminations, including examples from the British Museum, the Bodleian, and the Hermitage; woodcuts and engravings, such as the Crucifixion by H.B. Grien for a Kraków missal (1510); fresco and panel paintings with a discussion of Hans Süss von Kulmbach; portraits, miniatures, and even a silhouette, from foreign collections as well (Florence, Nuremberg, Munich).

Vol. 3: Malarstwo w Polsce XIX i XX wieku. [Painting in Poland in the nineteenth twentieth century] 572 p.

Dependent upon unorthodox materials for argument: watercolors, drawings, etchings, miniatures; and unorthodox sources: the Victoria and Albert Museum and private collections.

328. Malarstwo Polski

południowo-wschodniej 1900–1980. Wystawa. [The painting of southeastern Poland 1900–1980. An exhibition] Rzeszów, Biuro Wystaw Artystycznych, 1982. 253 p. illus. ND955.P6M29 1982

Edited by Wiesław Banach, et al.

Covers twelve cities, including Przemyśl, Rzeszów, Sandomierz, Sanok, and Tarnów. A history of styles pursued in each city, the artists' organizations, exhibitions, patrons,

and the growth of private collections. Biographical sketches of 120 artists, among them J. Malczewski (b. 1854 in Radom). Over one hundred poorly reproduced illustrations.

329. Malarstwo Polskie: Gotyk; Renesans; Wczesny Manieryzm. [Polish painting: Gothic; Renaissance; Early Mannerism] Warszawa, Auriga, 1961. 349 p. illus. (part color). ND955.P6M3 v. 1

By Michał Walicki.
Bibliography: p. 52–56.

The subject is better treated elsewhere—both pictorially and textually—by this same author and others. The 220 black-and white and 12 color reproductions are accompanied by discussions of the plates and a short introduction.

330. Malarstwo polskie: Manieryzm. Barok. [Polish painting: Mannerism. The Baroque] Warszawa, Auriga, 1971. 435 p. illus. (part color). ND955.P6M3 v. 2

Introduction by Michał Walicki and Władysław Tomkiewicz.
Catalog by Andrzej Ryszkiewicz.

A scholarly catalog accompanying 251 plates (fifteen in color) that represent many fabulous, scarcely known paintings.

331. Malarstwo polskie między wojnami 1918–1939. [Polish painting between the wars 1918–1939] Warszawa, Auriga, 1982. 391 p. 225 color illus. ND955.P6P63 1982

By Joanna Pollakówna.

Biographical sketches of the artists by Wanda M. Rudzińska.
Summary in German.
Bibliographic references.

Among 225 paintings selected by the author, the most interesting ones are those by M. Jarema, A. Michalak, L. Sleńdziński, R.K. Witkowski, and J. Zamoyski.

332. Malarstwo polskie: Modernizm. [Polish painting: Modernism] Warszawa, Auriga, 1977. 354 p. illus. (part color). ND955.P6M3, v. 4

Introduction by Wiesław Juszczak.
Biographical notes and catalog by Maria Liczbińska.

The originality of this volume is immediately apparent from the frontispiece, which shows a Polish-costumed muse of the painter J. Malczewski. Discriminating choices in the other 216 plates, of which eighty-eight are excellent color reproductions.

333. Malarstwo polskie: Oświecenie, Klasycyzm, Romantyzm. [Polish painting: The Enlightenment, Classicism, Romanticism] Warszawa, Auriga, 1976. 303 p. illus. (part color). ND955.P6N3 v. 3

Historical outline by Stefan Kozakiewicz.
Bibliography: p. 254.
Catalog by Anna Gradowska and others.

A long introductory essay and a brief catalog to accompany 158 plates, sixteen of which are in color. The emphasis is on lesser-known artists, the stars (Bacciarelli, Bellotto) having been subjects of numerous monographic studies.

**334. MORAWIŃSKA,
Agnieszka.**
Polish painting, 15th to 20th
century. Warszawa, Auriga, 1984.
68 p. 160 p. of plates, color illus.
ND955.P6M67 1984
    Translated from the Polish by
Bogna Piotrowska.
    Bibliographic references.
*A straightforward, clear, and reliable
history of style in Polish painting
from the late 1200s to 1980. Main
currents are outlined; the nineteenth
century—the period in which the
author specializes—is presented in
greater detail. The author's artistic
taste and judgment is evident in the
stimulating choice of illustrations.
Dr. Morawińska is the curator of
paintings at the National Museum of
Art, Warsaw.*

335. Polaków portret własny.
[Polish self-portraits] Warszawa,
Arkady, 1983–86. 2 v. illus. (part
color). N7614.P6P65 1983
    Collective work edited by
Marek Rostworowski.
    Bibliographic references.
    Vol. 1: Illustrations; v. 2: Text.
*An outstanding compilation, imagina-
tively chosen with a very wide range of
subjects and sources, from fourteenth-
century manuscripts and tombs, to
medieval sacred subjects with donors,
to a splendid sixteenth-century metal
relief of mourners. Works of art of
the highest quality, largely unknown,
from all periods. Portraits and genre
subjects up to the 1970s. A checklist
of 760 works in the exhibition. A
detailed catalog of the 393 works
reproduced.*

336. PORĘBSKI, Mieczysław.
Malowane dzieje. [Painted
events] Warszawa, Państwowe

Wydawnictwo Naukowe, 1961.
226 p. illus. ND691.P6
    Bibliographic references.
*A treasure trove for scholars of
nineteenth-century historicism of
little-known painting, prints, and
illustrations. J.P. Norblin is the
subject of the first section: in the first
part, as a painter of historical
anecdote, such as the* Election of
Piast as King; *in the second part,
as a painter of contemporary events,
such as the* Enactment of the
Constitution of 3d May. *The
second section treats Norblin's pupils
and followers, such as A. Orlowski
and his insurrection themes and F.
Smuglewicz and his prints. Book
illustrations and the decorations of the
Bishop's palace, Kraków, adorn the
second half of the section. Followed by
sections on romantic views of history
and on Jan Matejko's paintings.
Examples throughout taken from the
illustrated literature.*

337. RYSZKIEWICZ, Andrzej.
Francusko-polskie związki
artystyczne w kręgu J.L. Davida.
[French-Polish artistic relations
in the circle of J.L. David]
Warszawa, Wydawnictwa
Artystyczne i Filmowe, 1967. 232
p. illus. ports. ND553.D26R9
    Bibliographic references: p.
173–211.
*Jacques-Louis David's influence on
some Polish artists, his and his
students' portraits of Polish sitters,
and David's equestrian portrait of
Stanisław Kostka Potocki (1781),
considered one of his best.*

338. RYSZKIEWICZ, Andrzej.
Zbieracze i obrazy. [Collectors
and paintings] Warszawa,
Państwowe Wydawnictwo

Naukowe, 1972. 326 p. illus.
ports. N7445.8.P7R97
    Bibliographic references.
*Part one: Collectors of art:
Aleksander Chodkiewicz (1776–
1838); Józef K. Ossoliński (1764–
1838) who provided the first public
gallery in Warsaw; Ignacy Korwin
Milewski (1846–1922); Henryk
Hirszel, Warsaw lithographer, print
dealer and, from 1850, paintings
dealer. Part two: foreign artists in
relation to Polish subjects and collections: Antoine Pesne (d. 1757);
Stanisław August Poniatowski as
portrayed by such French painters as
Louis Tocque (1696–1772) and
Marie-Elisabeth-Louise Vigée-
Lebrun (1755–1842); portraits of
Poles by Anton Graff (1736–
1813); and pictures in Polish
collections by Wilhelm Schadow
(1788–1862). Numerous
documentary citations.*

339. SZYMAŃSKI, Stanisław.
Wystroje malarskie kościołów
drewnianych. [Painted decorations of wooden churches]
Warszawa, Instytut Wydawniczy
Pax, 1970. 321 p. illus. (part
color). ND2812.P6S9
    Summary in French.
    Bibliography: p. 305–308.
*Over two hundred sites, dating from
the mid-1400s to the nineteenth
century, have been recovered. Some
ceilings and walls were designed as an
ensemble, some were designed separately. Covers techniques, colors, types
(architectural, narrative, ornamental), and sources and influences.*

340. WAŁEK, Janusz.
Dzieje Polski w malarstwie i
poezji. [Polish history in paintings and poetry] Warszawa,

Interpress, 1987. 311 p. illus. (part color).

Edited by Ewa Trzeciak.

Janusz Tazbir, history consultant.

Also published in English, German, and French editions.

A compilation of over one hundred paintings and other works of art which picture historical events and portray key figures. As may be expected, the nineteenth-century history painters are the primary sources. Examples are A. Lesser, The death of Wanda; *P. Michałowski,* The entrance of Bolesław Chrobry in Kiev *(1018); W. Gerson,* Casimir the Great and the Jews; *J. Simmler,* The oath of Queen Jadwiga *(taken in 1387); and J. Suchodolski,* The death of Cyprian Godebski near Raszyn *(1809). Few examples are drawn from earlier periods: a panel (c. 1500) representing the* Punishment of unfaithful wives; *fourteenth-century miniature paintings showing the* Battle near Legnica *in 1241 against the invasion of the Tatars; Łukasz Ewert's the* Triumphal procession of Casimir Jagiełło after the Victory at Malbork *(1460); and a painting from a diary of A. Boote representing the* Battle near Oliwa, *1627.*

341. WAŁEK, Janusz.

A history of Poland in painting. Warsaw, Interpress, 1988. 174 p. illus. (part color), ports. ND955.P6W3 1988

Translated from the Polish by Katarzyna Zawadzka.

342. WALLIS, Mieczysław.

Autoportrety artystów polskich. [Self-portraits by Polish artists] Warszawa, Wydawnictwa Artystyczne i Filmowe, 1966. 280 p. illus., ports. N7608.W3

Bibliographic references.

From medieval pseudo-portraits, to Hans von Kulmbach, to ingeniously sought-out seventeenth- and eighteenth-century portraits, many of which are readily accessible. Numerous modern examples. The arrangement is by century, then by artist; women are included.

343. Warsaw. Muzeum Narodowe. Galeria Sztuki Polskiej. [Gallery of Polish art] Warszawa, Arkady, 1960–71. 6 vols. illus. some color. ND691.W337

Each volume contains twelve reproductions of paintings, ranging from the fourteenth century (panel paintings) to the twentieth century (interwar period), that are in the Polish National Museum in Warsaw.

344. Warsaw. Muzeum Narodowe w Warszawie. Galeria Sztuki Polskiej. Malarstwo polskie od XVI [i.e. szesnastego] do początku XX [i.e. dwudziestego] wieku; katalog. [Polish painting from the sixteenth to the early twentieth century; a catalog] 2d rev. ed. Warszawa, Muzeum Narodowe, 1975. 465 p. illus. ports. ND955.P6W345 1975

A collective work prepared under the supervision of Stefan Kozakiewicz and Krystyna Sroczyńska.

Bibliography: p. 12.

About 250 artists listed alphabetically, along with their biographies, and 1,230 reproduced paintings. No index. The first edition was published in 1962.

345. Warsaw. Muzeum Narodowe w Warszawie. Galeria Sztuki Polskiej. Miniatury polskie od XVII [i.e. siedemnastego] do XX [i.e. dwudziestego] wieku. [Polish miniatures from the seventeenth to the twentieth century] Warszawa, 1978. 113 p. 60 leaves of plates, 227 miniatures, illus. ND1337.P7W37 1978

Bibliography: p. 17–22.

Catalog of the collection prepared by Halina Kamińska-Krassowska.

A scholarly compendium, mainly of portraits (227 of them), published and reproduced for the first time, of historically important persons, sometimes in an informal guise (T. Kościuszko, nos. 134–35, for instance), or by unexpected artists (S. Chlebowski, painter to Sultan Abdul Aziz, Constantinople, from 1864, no. 22). Biographies of artists, including D. Chodowiecki and A. Orłowski, and sitters. Half of the original collection was lost during World War II.

346. Warsaw. Muzeum Narodowe w Warszawie. Galeria Sztuki Polskiej. La peinture polonaise du XVIe au début du XXe siècle. Catalogue. Varsovie, 1979. 539. p. illus., ports. ND955.P6W345 1979

Edited by Krystyna Sroczyńska.

Translated by Maria Cieszewska.

Bibliography: p 39–52.

Approximately two hundred artists, arranged alphabetically. Informative biographies and discussions of paintings, 1,200 of which are illustrated. Summary; historical introduction.

347. Warsaw. Muzeum Narodowe w Warszawie.
Malarstwo. [The National Museum in Warsaw. Paintings] Warszawa, Arkady, 1984. 70 p. 168 plates of illus. (part color). N3160.A542 1984

History of the collection by Stanisław Lorentz.

Catalog by Tadeusz Dobrzeniecki and others.

Exceptionally fine reproductions of recently conserved paintings. Most are in color. Polish and Flemish Gothic masterpieces are introduced; an important triptych by Maerten van Heemskerck, paintings by Giovanni Battista Cima da Conegliano, Botticelli, Paris Bordone, Gaspare Diziani, and Jean Baptiste Greuze. Half of the pictures are by Polish nineteenth- and twentieth-century artists.

348. Wilanów, Poland.
Pałac. Portrety osobistości polskich znajdujące się w pokojach i w Galerii Pałacu w Wilanowie. Katalog. [Portraits of Polish personalities in the rooms and in the Gallery of the Palace of Wilanów. Catalog] Warszawa, Muzeum Narodowe w Warszawie, 1967. 396 p. illus., ports. N7508.W5

Edited by Stefan Kozakiewicz, et al.

Bibliographic references.

A scholarly catalog of paintings, busts, and medals, arranged alphabetically by sitter. For each artist a brief biography, a description of the work of art, bibliography, and critique of style. Separate section on the kings and queens of Poland.

349. WRÓBLEWSKA, Kamila.
Malarstwo Warmii i Mazur od XV do XIX wieku. [Painting of Warmia and the Mazury region from the fifteenth to the nineteenth century] Olsztyn, Pojezierze, 1978. 55, [6] p. 101 leaves of plates, illus. (part color). ND955.P62W378

Summary in English and German.

Bibliography: p. 50–51.

An introduction to the art of a region that was divided between Catholic and Protestant, the former allied to the painting of Southern Italy, Spain, and Flanders; the latter linked to Germany. In the seventeenth century, both regions were under the influence of Dutch portraiture.

350. AMEISENOWA, Zofia.
Cztery polskie rękopisy iluminowane z lat 1524–1528 w zbiorzch obcych. [Four Polish illuminated manuscripts from the years 1524 to 1528 in foreign collections] Kraków, Uniwersytet Jagielloński, 1967. 95 p. 64 illus. ND3363.A1A44 1967

English summary: p. 79–88.

Title also in Latin.

Prayer books executed by the Krakowian miniaturist Stanisław Samostrzelnik for King Sigismund I, his Queen Bona Sforza, Chancellor Krzysztof Szydłowiecki, and Chancellor Olbracht Gasztołd are now in the British Library, Bodleian, and in Milan and Munich, respectively. Relies on the customary pictorial sources of Dürer, Housebook Master, Altdorfer, and others. A "Purgatory" deriving from Dürer's prayer book for Emperor Maximilian, points to a journey to Vienna. Borders in native Gothic tradition, in Italian Renaissance style, and Flem-ish naturalism. Mystical reformist spirit marks the printings.

351. AMEISENOWA, Zofia.
Kodeks Baltazara Behema. [The Codex of Baltazar Behem] Warszawa, Auriga, 1961. 47 p. 60 plates of illus. (part color). ND3399.C47A65

Bibliographic references.

Twenty-six miniatures painted in Kraków about 1505. Eighteen represent tradesmen and their occupations: tailor, baker, mural painter, cobbler, goldsmith, potter, among other. Seven represent coats of arms of guilds, such as saddlers and wheelwrights. The coats of arms of Kraków on another leaf. The miniatures accompany statutes of the guilds (twelve of the projected twenty-five executed) written by Behem, secretary and notary of the Kraków City government. The witty and genial illustrations are of highest interest for their portrayal of city life, interiors, and costumes. In the collection of the Jagiellonian University Library, Kraków.

352. AMEISENOWA, Zofia.
Les principaux manuscrits a peintures de la Bibliothèque Jagiellonienne de Cracovie. Paris, 1933. 119 p. xvi plates (including facsims.). (Bulletin de la Société française de reproductions de manuscrits à peintures, no. 17) ND3345.P16 no. 17

Holdings of the Jagiellonian University Library: fourteen illuminated manuscripts and eighty-six fragments (leaves, initial letters). The earliest manuscript is Paduan or Bolognese, circa 1200. Another is a Czech chronicle of 1531. The Behem codex is included. A concordance between the manuscripts and the twenty-six plates is on p. 119.

[320]. DOBRZENIECKI, Tadeusz, *and* others.
Sztuka sakralna w Polsce; malarstwo. [Sacral art in Poland; painting] Warszawa, Ars Christiana, 1958. 366 p. mostly illus. (part color). N7956.D6 folio

Catalog of works: p. 335–67.

Covers the range from manuscript illumination of the early twelfth century to painting of the mid-twentieth century, with emphasis on the strongest, i.e., the Gothic period. Nearly one-half of the illustrated objects date before 1600.

353. ESTREICHER, Karol.
Minjatury Kodeksu Bema oraz ich treść obyczajowa. [Miniatures of the Behem Codex and their documentary content] Rocznik Krakowski, vol. 24, 1933, p. 199–244. illus. (part color). DB879.K8R58 v. 24

Summary in English.
Bibliographic references.

In the twenty-five depictions of artisans and trades there are moralizing and critical components along with references to guild regulations and prohibitions. A fool, personifying sin, appears in the coat of arms of the glove makers guild. He embraces a woman who views him through her fingers, an idiomatic reference to making allowances.

[21]. GIEYSZTOR, Aleksander, Michał, Walicki, *and* Jan Zachwatowicz.
Sztuka polska przedromańska i romańska do schyłku XIII wieku. [Polish pre-Romanesque and Romanesque art before the end of the thirteenth century] Warszawa, Państwowe Wydawnictwo Naukowe, 1971.

914 p. illus. (part color), leaves of plates. (Dzieje Sztuki Polskiej, vol. 1, part 1–2) N7255.P6G53 v. 1

Sponsored by the Art Institute of the Polish Academy of Sciences.

Bibliography (p. 796–839) and catalog by Maria Pietrusińska.

List of illustrations in English and Russian.

A sumptuous scholarly publication that begins with artifacts of the early Middle Ages, town planning, and architectural sculpture. There is an extensive section on manuscript illumination, book bindings, and ecclesiastical and courtly objects of art. Excellent reproductions. English translation of the table of contents and a twenty-one-page list of illustrations on over twelve hundred black and white plates, plus eight in color.

Of the significant works of art that have survived from the period before the end of the thirteenth century, virtually every one has been included here.

354. Iluminatorstwo polskie.
[Illumination in Poland] *In* Encyklopedia wiedzy o książce. Wrocław, Zakład Narodowy im. Ossolińskich, 1971. p. 927–41. Z1006.E575

Edited by Stanisława Sawicka.
Bibliography.

355. JAROSŁAWIECKA-Gąsiorowska, Maria.
Les principaux manuscrits à peintures du Musée des Princes Czartoryski à Cracovie. Paris, 1935. 2 v. (Bulletin de la Société française de reproductions de manuscrits à peintures, no. 18) ND3345.P16 no. 18

Vol. 1: Text. 203 p.; v. 2: 48 plates.

Bibliographic references in v. 1.

Describes thirty-six magnificent manuscripts with all scholarly probity. Thirty Western manuscripts (originating in France, the Low Countries, Germany, and Poland) dating from the eleventh to the late sixteenth century. Six oriental manuscripts (Persian, Turkish, Indian). Concordances between manuscripts and illustrations on pp. 199–203.

356. KOPERA, Feliks, *and* Leonard Lepszy.
Iluminowane rękopisy księgozbiorów. OO. Dominikanów i OO. Karmelitów w Krakowie. [Illuminated manuscripts from the collections of the Dominican and the Carmelite Fathers in Kraków] Kraków, Polska Akademia Umiejętności, 1926. 85 p. illus., facsims. (Zabytki sztuki w Polsce, 2) Z6621.P7Z3

Scholarly presentation of thirty-nine psalters, antiphonaries, and graduals—several of extraordinary quality—with dates ranging from circa 1390 to the eighteenth century. Their sixteenth- and seventeenth-century bindings are discussed and illustrated.

[327]. KOPERA, Feliks.
Dzieje malarstwa w Polsce. [A history of painting in Poland] Kraków, Drukarnia Narodowa, 1925–1929, 3 v. illus. (part color) facsims., ports. ND691.K64

Bibliographic references.
Vol. 1: Średniowieczne malarstwo w Polsce. [Painting of the Middle Ages in Poland] 250 p.

Manuscript Illumination

Emphasis on manuscript illumination (three chapters) and on stained glass. Also discusses wall paintings of the fourteenth and fifteenth century. Abundant illustrations: more than two hundred figures and twenty-four plates.

Vol. 2: Malarstwo w Polsce od XVI do XVIII wieku. (Renesans, Barok, Rokoko) [Painting in Poland from the XVI to the XVIII centuries (Renaissance, Baroque, Rococo)] 345 p.

Unconventional emphases: manuscript illuminations, including examples from the British Museum, the Bodleian, and the Hermitage: woodcuts and engravings, such as the Crucifixion by H.B. Grien for a Kraków missal (1510); fresco and panel paintings with a discussion of Hans Süss von Kulmbach; portraits, miniatures, and even a silhouette, from foreign collections as well (Florence, Nuremberg, Munich).

Vol. 3: Malarstwo w Polsce XIX i XX wieku. [Painting in Poland in the nineteenth and twentieth centuries] 572 p.

Dependent upon unorthodox materials for argument: watercolors, drawings, etchings, miniatures; and unorthodox sources: the Victoria and Albert Museum and private collections.

357. Kraków. Uniwersytet Jagielloński. Biblioteka. Rękopisy i pierwodruki iluminowane Biblioteki Jagiellońskiej. [Illuminated manuscripts and early printed books in the Jagiellonian Library] Wrocław, Zakład Narodowy im. Ossolińskich, 1958. 233 p. (154) p. of facsims., 12 mounted color illus. ND3177.K7K75 folio

By Zofia Ameisenowa.
Bibliography: p. 228–31.
Catalog of 215 items of Italian, French, Czech, Polish, and other origin, from the mid-twelfth through the sixteenth century. Complete scholarly apparatus. Numerous appendices such as provenances, scribes, copyists, authors, artists, repositories of related materials, and detailed iconography. A publication of highest importance. Among the manuscripts is the famous Codex Picturatus Balthasaris Behem (c. 1505) consisting of 372 leaves, illustrated with 26 multi-colored miniatures.

358. MARS, Anna Maria.
Polish miniature painters in the first half of the sixteenth century. The Burlington Magazine, vol. 86, Jan. 1945. Polish number, p. 17–20. N1.B95 v. 86
Concentrates on Stanisław Mogiła (b. about 1480, d. about 1540, a Cistercian monk and master of a prolific workshop of miniature painting near Kraków. His "Crucifixion" in the Liber Pontificalis of Erasmus Ciołek is a touchstone for attributing other early works. Analyzes the style of four prayer books (British Library, Bodleian, Munich, Ambrosiana) and discusses other signed works as well as workshop production.

359. MIODOŃSKA, Barbara.
Iluminacje krakowskich rękopisów z I. połowy w. XV w Archiwum Kapituły Metropolitalnej na Wawelu. [Illumination of Kraków manuscripts from the first half of the 15th century in the collection of the Archives of the Metropolitan

Curia at Wawel Castle] Kraków, Ministerstwo Kultury i Sztuki; Zarząd Muzeów i Ochrony Zabytków, 1967. 170 p. illus., color plates. ND3235.P62K76
Summary in French.
Bibliographic references.
A group of manuscripts, cohesive in style, made for the clergy of the Cathedral of Wawel. Executed from about 1400 to 1430, they range from those influenced by a pervasive Czech style, to an angular style. An outstanding scholarly work.

360. MIODOŃSKA, Barbara.
Iluminator Mszału Jasnogórskiego i Pontifikału Erazma Ciołka. [An illuminator of the Jasna Góra Missal and the Pontifical of Erazm Ciołek] Rozprawy i Sprawozdania Muzeum Narodowego w Krakowie, vol. 9, 1967, p. 51–77. illus. AM101.K7432
Summary in French.
Bibliographic references.

361. MIODOŃSKA, Barbara.
Miniatury Stanisława Samostrzelnika. [Miniatures by Stanisław Samostrzelnik] Warszawa, Wydawnictwa Artystyczne i Filmowe, "Auriga" Oficyna Wydawnicza, 1983. 138 p. color illus. ND3235.P63S36 1983
Bibliography: p. 28–29.
Also called Stanislaus Claratumbensis, and Stanisław from Kraków, or Pietor de Mogiła, Stanisław Samostrzelnik (c. 1480–1541) was chiefly a miniature painter who combined the best painterly tradition of Kraków with new Renaissance forms. Thirty illuminations reproduced from Books of Hours,

missals, and antiphons in the British Library, Bodleian, Ambrosiana, as well as Polish libraries. A scholarly study that includes the artist's wall and panel paintings (sixteen reproductions).

362. MIODOŃSKA, Barbara.

Rex Regum i Rex Poloniae w dekoracji malarskiej Graduału Jana Olbrachta i Pontifikału Erazma Ciołka. Rex Regum and Rex Poloniae in illuminated manuscripts: The Gradual of King Jan Olbracht and the Pontifical of Erazm Ciołek. Kraków, Muzeum Narodowe w Krakowie, 1979. 238 p. 156 illus. facsims. ND3389.4.K72M56

Z Zagadnień ikonografii władzy królewskiej w sztuce polskiej wieku XVI.

Some problems in the iconography of the King's power in Polish sixteenth-century art.

Summary in English.

Bibliographic references.

363. PIEŃKOWSKA, Hanna.

Średniowieczna pracownia miniatorska w Krakowie. [Medieval workshop of miniature painting in Kraków] Rocznik Krakowski, vol. 32, part 2, 1951, p. 45–58. 14 p. of illus. DB879.K8R58 v. 32

Examines a group of six antiphonaries in the Church of Corpus Christi (Kraków). Characterizes and individualizes their style (strong chiaroscuro, sentient color), and attributes both script and illuminations to Simon, a monk of the Order of Regular Canons and prior and presbyter of the Church of Corpus Christi, who died in 1422.

364. POTKOWSKI, Edward.

Książka rękopiśmienna w kulturze Polski średniowiecznej. [The manuscript book in Polish medieval culture] Warszawa, Ludowa Spółdzielnia Wydawnicza, 1984. 301 p. illus. Z8.P6P67 1948

Bibliography: p. 237–60.

This is the first detailed synthesis of the role of the manuscript book in the Polish cultural life of the fourteenth and fifteenth century. It is a thoroughly researched study, largely of primary but also secondary sources. It deals principally with the function of writing and the centers of literacy. Only Chapter 3 considers production of the manuscript book and the organization of the painters-illuminators and binders. A moderate number of illustrations in color.

365. PRZYBYSZEWSKI, Bolesław.

Stanisław Samostrzelnik. Biuletyn Historii Sztuki, vol. 13, no. 2–3, 1951, p. 47–87. illus. N6.B5 v. 13

Bibliographic references.

The greatest Polish Renaissance painter, specializing in miniatures, decorated Books of Hours for King Zygmunt I and Queen Bona Sforza. Samostrzelnik was a Cistercian and served his chief patron, Chancellor Krzysztof Szydłowiecki, as chaplain and court painter for some two decades. About 1530, he executed a history of the family, painting full-length, full-page portraits, ten of which are extant. One of his outstanding works is The Lives of the Gniezno Archbishops, *commissioned by the Bishop of Kraków, Piotr Tomicki. At his monastery, Samostrzelnik executed frescoes of the Cistercian Fathers at Mogiła.*

366. SAWICKA, Stanisława.

Nieznany krakowski rękopis iluminowany z początku XVI wieku. [An unknown Cracovian illuminated manuscript from the beginning of the sixteenth century] Studia Renesansowe, vol. 2, 1957, p. 5–90. 65 figs. 1 plate (color). N6991.S87 v. 2

Summary in French and Russian.

A Missale Romanorum *in the collection of the Fathers of St. Paul the Hermit, Jasna Góra, Częstochowa. Its calendar of saints venerated in Poland proves its Polish origin. Executed at the apogee of miniature painting in Kraków, it is embellished by two miniatures and nineteen historiated initials. Author traces its correspondences with other works and suggests King Sigismund I (1506–1548) as its donor.*

367. SAWICKA, Stanisława.

Les principaux manuscrits à peintures de la Bibliothèque Nationale de Varsovie, du Chateaux Royal et des bibliothèques des Zamoyski à Varsovie, du Seminaire de Płock et du Chapître de Gniezno. Paris, 1938. ix, 319 p. 49 plates, facsims. (Bulletin de la Société française de reproductions de manuscrits à peintures, année 19) ND3345.P16 no. 19

Bibliographies.

By the foremost scholar of illuminated manuscripts in Poland, an exhaustive presentation of thirty-eight examples dating from the mid-eleventh century. Two tables, p. 296–319, have concordances with the forty-eight excellent plates: one table lists manuscripts by number, one by name. Each manuscript has at least one illustration.

The king kneeling in prayer before Mary and the Child, one of forty-seven miniatures from the Gradual of King Jan Olbracht. Completed in 1506 after his death, the three-volume gradual was a gift from the king to the Cathedral at Wawel in Kraków, where it still remains. From *Rex Regum i Rex Poloniae w dekoracji malarskiej Graduału Jana Olbrachta*. Kraków, Muzeum Narodowe, 1979

In her addendum to this book ("Les pertes des collections polonaises dans le domaine des manuscrits eluminés." Scriptorum, XV 1961, p. 300–302), the author updates information, accounting for quite a few manuscripts. Some were recovered in Poland and some were returned by the Soviets who had seized them from the Nazis.

369. WINKLER, Friedrich.
Der Krakauer Behaim-Codex. Berlin, Deutscher Verein für Kunstwissenschaft, 1941. 124 p. illus. (part color) 38 plates.
Codex picturatus Balthasaris Behem.
Bibliography: p. 100.
Color reproductions of twenty miniatures of tradesmen and their craft, and guild coats of arms, executed in Kraków about 1505. Seven miniatures, including a Crucifixion, are in black and white. Two leaves of text show foliated borders. Reproductions in nearly original size. Illuminations accompany guild statutes written by Balthazar Behem, Kraków city government secretary and notary. Manuscript in the Japiellonian University Library, Kraków. Stylistic comparison to the Pontifical of Bishop Ciołek (Czartoryski Museum) and also to prints by Dürer and the Master MZ. Reproduced in color and black and white.

368. SAWICKA, Stanisława.
Straty wojenne zbiorów polskich w dziedzinie rękopisów iluminowanych. [Losses during the war from Polish collections of illuminated manuscripts] Warszawa, Ministerstwo Kultury i Sztuki, 1952. 97 p. illus. 130 plates (Prace i Materiały Biura Rewindykacji i Odszkodowań, no. 10) ND3175.S3
Bibliography: p. 78–79.
Detailed scholarly descriptions of 218 codices lost from nineteen institutions whose collectors' marks are reproduced. Illustrations in 130 plates of manuscripts dating from the eleventh century.

370. FLIK, Józef.
Toruńskie protrety mieszczańskie drugiej połowy XVI wieku z Muzeum w Toruniu. [Toruń burghers' portraits of the second half of the sixteenth century in the Toruń Museum] Toruń, 1982. 130 p. 26 plates. ND1324.P62F55 1982

Summary in English, French, and Russian.

Bibliography: p. 121–25.

Media determine not only pictorial appearance but, together with technological examination, make possible hypotheses regarding the origins of a portrait. That of Mikołaj Kopernik (Copernicus), which has no counterpart among works of Polish origin, may have been executed in England by a Netherlandish master, perhaps Marcus Gheeraert or Johann de Critz.

371. GADOMSKI, Jerzy.
Gotyckie malarstwo tablicowe Małopolski, 1420–1470. [Gothic panel painting from Małopolska, 1420–1470] Warszawa, Państwowe Wydawnictwo Naukowe, 1981. 165 p. 174 p. of plates, illus. (part color). ND955.P62M34 1981

Summary in German and Russian.

Bibliography: p. 136–42.
Bibliographic references.

A scholarly study divided into three parts: commissions and subject matter; the artists and their workshops, with proposed reconstructions of the altarpieces; the works discussed in terms of style and chronology. Erudition not well served by poor quality of reproductions.

372. GIEYSZTOR, Aleksander.
Lassitude du Gothique? Reflets de l'iconoclasme Hussite en Pologne au XVe siècle. *In* Ars auro prior: studia Ioanni Białostocki sexagenario dicata. p. 223–26. N7442.B5 1981

Reviews the infrequent iconophobia in Western art: Bernard of Clairvaux, Savonarola, and the Hussites in Bohemia in the fourteenth and fifteenth century, whose ideas were transplanted to Poland in the fifteenth century.

373. GOETEL-KOPFF, Maria.
Tryptyk Wawelski Michała Lancza z Kitzingen. [A triptych in the Wawel by Michał Lancz of Kitzingen] Studia Renesansowe, vol. 2, 1957, p. 91–133. 23 figs. N6991. S87 v. 2

Summary in French and Russian.

Bibliographic references.

The most monumental extant work (dated 1521) from the painter's Polish period. He is little known in Poland and Germany. The date of his death is known from the archives of Kraków to be 1523. He became a citizen of Kraków in 1507. An eclectic artist who may have worked in Dürer's workshop, he also borrowed from the engravings of Israel van Mechenem. For a bio-bibliography on Lancz (Lantcz) see Słownik artystów polskich. *Vol. 4, 1986, p. 431–33. (N7255.P6S59)*

374. Gotyckie malarstwo ścienne w Polsce. [Gothic wall painting in Poland] Poznań, Uniwersytet im. Adama Mickiewicza w Poznaniu, 1984. 535 p. illus. map. (Seria Historii sztuki, no. 17) ND2812.P6G68 1984

Essays by Jerzy Domasłowski, Alicja Karłowska-Kamzowa, Marian Kornecki, Helena Malkiewiczówna.

Summary in German.
Bibliography: p. 175–92.
Bibliographic references.

A unique monograph on the subject. The outcome of investigations by a team of scholars working within the borders of present-day Poland. They have recorded what is preserved and diagrammatically reconstructed what existed. History of the genre in Poland, with reference to manuscript illumination and panel painting. The production of Polish and foreign workshops is differentiated. Extensive table arranged according to regions, cities and towns, buildings, date of the paintings, subjects, state of preservation, and bibliography.

375. GRZYBOWSKA, Teresa.
Andrzej Stech malarz gdański. [Andrzej Stech, Gdańsk painter] Warszawa, Państwowe Wydawnictwo Naukowe, 1979. 187 p. illus., ports. ND955.P63S7934 1979

Summary in Russian and English.

Bibliography: p. 171–78.
Bibliographic references.

Born in Słupsk, Stech died about 1697 in Gdańsk, where he made his career as a painter of portraits, religious subjects, and still lifes. In his religious paintings he was influenced chiefly by Rubens, whose work he studied in engravings. His portraits, however, are his greatest achievement, among them that of the Gdańsk astronomer Johannes Hevelius (Oxford, Bodleian Library). He made drawings to illustrate Hevelius' books, such as Machinae coelestis *(Gdańsk, 1673), which has thirty-nine engravings. He introduced Dutch still-life painting into Gdańsk. Catalog of paintings, drawings, and prints after his designs.*

376. KARPOWICZ, Mariusz.
Działalność artystyczna Michelangela Palloniego w

Polsce. [The artistic activity of Michelangelo Palloni in Poland] Warszawa, Państwowe Wydawnictwo Naukowe, 1967. 163p. illus. ND623.P19K3

Summary in English: p. 160–63.

Bibliographic references.

Michelangelo Palloni, Tuscan-born painter, pupil of B. Franceschini in Florence and Ciro Ferri in Rome, was spiritual heir to Pietro da Cortona. His entire career (1677–1708) centered on Poland where he decorated churches and palaces. Chronological list of works (p. 86–90). A scholarly study that places the artist in the aesthetic and pictorial currents of his day. Analyses of achievements in Poland. Good English summary.

377. KARPOWICZ, Mariusz.

Jerzy Eleuter Siemiginowski, malarz polskiego baroku. [Jerzy Eleuter Siemiginowski, painter of the Polish Baroque] Wrocław, Zakład Narodowy im. Ossolińskich, 1974. 205 p. 48 leaves of plates, illus. (part color). ND955.P63E444

Summary in English.
Bibliographic references.

A painter (1660–1711) who studied in Rome, returning to Poland in 1684. Active at the Court of King Jan Sobieski as portraitist and decorator of the palace at Wilanów.

[38]. KOZAKIEWICZOWA, Helena, *and* Stefan Kozakiewicz.

The Renaissance in Poland. Warsaw, Arkady, 1976. 329 p. illus. (part color), map. N7255.P6K6613

Translation by Doreen Heaton

Potworowska of *Renesans w Polsce.*

Bibliography: p. 323–25.

An outstanding album for the English-language reader. In an excellent English translation, 252 fine black and white photographs and eight plates in color are magisterially discussed. The authors call attention to works of art rarely illustrated and details generally overlooked. Lengthy essays trace developments from 1500 to 1640. Contains numerous drawings of plans and a map of all sites mentioned. Reproductions show the most beautiful Renaissance buildings, such as the Town Hall in Poznań (converted from the Gothic style, 1550–1560) by the architect Giovanni Battista Quadro from Lugano. Another Town Hall, built during the years 1570 to 1572 and well preserved, is in Brzeg (Silesia), by the architect Giacomo Pario from Como; also, the Cloth Hall (Sukiennice) in Kraków with its attica. The magnificent Sigismund Chapel in the Wawel Cathedral by the architect Bartolomeo Berrecci, and the Wawel Royal Castle with courtyard galleries, are reproduced in great detail. An abundance of illustrations of paintings, tapestries, tombs, and sculptures, among them—the tomb of Bishop A. Zebrzydowski at Wawel by Jan Michałowicz.

378. LABUDA, Adam S.

Malarstwo tablicowe w Gdańsku w 2 poł. XV w. [Panel painting in Gdańsk in the second half of the fifteenth century] Warszawa, Państwowe Wydawnictwo Naukowe, 1979. 253 p. 64 leaves of plates, illus. (part color). ND955.P62G354

Summary in German and Russian.

Bibliography: p. 220–25.
Bibliographic references.

Provides a historic and socio-artistic framework. Traces the paintings' beginnings and divides them into three stylistic groups: the Western group, and Gdańsk A and B. A scholarly catalog of twenty-four works with numerous pictorial comparisons, albeit in poor reproductions.

379. MACHARSKA, Maria.

Ze studiów nad rolą grafiki w polskim malarstwie okresu manieryzmu i wczesnego Baroku (Obrazy w kościołach Wielkopolski oraz w Kolegiacie Łowickiej). [Studies on the role of prints in Polish painting in the Mannerist and Early Baroque periods (Paintings in the churches of Great Poland and in the Collegiate Church of Łowicz).] Folia Historiae Artium, vol. 11, 1975. p. 139–65. illus. N6.F6 v. 11

Summary in French.
Bibliographic references.

For seven paintings by Mateusz Kossior, dating from 1570 to 1600, and three unassigned paintings (c. 1672), the author adduces mainly Netherlandish but also two Italian printed sources: Jan and Raphael Sadeler after M. de Vos and P. Candid; A. Collaert and S. à Bolswert after Stradanus and E. Quellinus; G. Britto and G. Ghisi, and a Netherlandish engraver after Barocci.

[329]. Malarstwo Polskie:

Gotyk; Renesans; Wczesny Manieryzm. [Polish painting: Gothic; Renaissance; Early Mannerism] Warszawa, Auriga, 1961.

349 p. illus. (part color).
ND955.P6M3 v. 1

By Michał Walicki.

Bibliography: p. 52–56.

The subject is better treated else-
where—both pictorially and textu-
ally—by this same author and others.
The 220 black-and white and 12
color reproductions are accompanied
by discussions of the plates and a short
introduction.

[330]. Malarstwo polskie:
Manieryzm. Barok. [Polish painting: Mannerism. The Baroque]
Warszawa, Auriga, 1971. 435 p.
illus. (part color). ND955.P6M3
v. 2

Introduction by Michał
Walicki and Władysław
Tomkiewicz.

Catalog by Andrzej
Ryszkiewicz.

A scholarly catalog accompanying
251 plates (fifteen in color) that
represent many scarcely known
paintings.

**380. MICHAŁOWSKA-OTTO,
Maria.**
Gotyckie malarstwo tablicowe
w Polsce. [Gothic panel painting
in Poland] Warszawa, Arkady,
1982. 14 p. of plates (part color).
ND955.P6O87 1982

Contains reproductions of 50
paintings on wood panels.

Bibliography.

A scholarly introduction to paintings
of the highest quality of the period
1310–1510.

381. MICHALSKI, Sergiusz.
Gdańsk als Auserwählte
Christengemeinschaft. *In Ars*
auro prior Ioanni Bialostocki

sexagenario dicata. p. 509–16.
3 illus. N7442.B5 1981

The iconography of the Apotheosis
of Gdańsk, *painted by Isaak van der*
Blocke (1606–1608) and installed
on the ceiling in the Gdańsk Town
Hall.

**382. Muzeum Narodowe we
Wrocławiu.** Śląskie malarstwo
gotyckie. [Silesian Gothic paint-
ing] Wrocław, 1986. 100 p. illus.,
19 color plates. ND955.P62S57
1986

By Anna Ziomecka.

Introduction by Mariusz
Hermansdorfer.

Text in Polish, German, and
English.

Bibliographic references.

**383. RÓŻYCKA-BRYZEK,
Anna.**
Bizantyńsko-ruskie malowidła
w kaplicy Zamku Lubelskiego.
[The Byzantine-Russian wall
paintings in the chapel of Lublin
Castle] Warszawa, Państwowe
Wydawnictwo Naukowe, 1983.
175 p. illus. (part color).
ND2812.P63L847 1983

Summary in English and Russian.

Bibliographic references.
Bibliography: p. 154–64.

Executed in 1418 during the reign of
King Władysław Jagiełło, who was
raised in Wilno in an atmosphere of
Russian culture, and who commis-
sioned a number of church decorations.
Here, in a Gothic structure, are
Russian Orthodox wall paintings
serving as a setting for the Roman
liturgy. Includes a discussion of
iconography (Old Testament, Saints,
an ideal equestrian portrait of the
King), and style.

384. TOMKIEWICZ, Władysław.
La peinture venetienne en
Pologne
dans la premiere moitié du
XVIIe
siècle. *In* Venezia e la Polonia nei
secoli dal XVII al XIX. Venezia,
Istituto per la Collaborazione
Culturale, 1965,
p. 53–64. 10 illus. NX371.P6V4

Edited by Luigi Cini.

In the middle of the sixteenth century,
two Venetian painters were active in
Poland: Giovanni Battista Ferro and
Petrus Venetus. Carlo Ridolfi, Delle
Meraviglie dell'Arte ... *provided*
notices on overtures by King
Sigismund III to Aliense who sent
paintings to Kraków (1595–1598)
and his chief assistant, T. Dollabella.
Accounts of canvases by Palma
Giovane and Domenico Tintoretto.

385. WALICKI, Michał.
La peinture d'autels et retables
en Pologne au temps des
Jagellons. Paris, Société
d'éditions "Les Belles lettres,"
1937. xvi p. 1., 46 p. 66 plates.
ND691.W3 folio

Issued in portfolio.

Bibliographic footnotes.

A scholarly presentation of approxi-
mately thirty altar paintings and
retables from the early fifteenth to the
second quarter of the sixteenth
century. In these mostly unpublished
works the author defines the Polish
manner of painting which was
influenced by international currents—
Flemish, Burgundian, East European
and Byzantine, among others. He
affirms the importance of prints and
miniatures (Master of the Playing
Cards, Master of the Amsterdam
Cabinet) in the diffusion of forms.

**Gothic. Renaissance.
Mannerism. Baroque**

386. WOLFF-ŁOZIŃSKA, Barbara.

Malowidła stropów polskich 1 połowy XVI w. Dekoracje roślinne i kasetowe. [Polish ceiling paintings in the first half of the sixteenth century. Floriated and coffered decorations] Warszawa, Państwowe Wydawnictwo Naukowe, 1971. 244 p. illus. ND2812.P6W6

Part I traces the evolution of Gothic floriated and figured polychrome design, then examines churches in three areas of Małopolska and Silesia, concentrating on decorative compositions and their sources, especially the graphic inspiration. Part II examines rosette-centered cofferings, and surveys paintings in seven locations. Symbolism of this type of decoration, and new forms after 1550 are considered. Generously illustrated.

387. BATOWSKI, Zygmunt.

Aleksander Kucharski. Warszawa, Towarzystwo Naukowe Warszawskie, 1948. 41 p. 9 portraits. (Prace z Historii Sztuki, vol. 3, pt. 1) 4ND-148

Bibliographic references.

Born in Warsaw in 1741, Aleksander Kucharski died in Paris in 1819. He had gone to Paris about 1760, and trained there under Vien and Vanloo. Portraiture was his strength; he was painter to the Prince of Condé, and painted many royal and noble personages, French, Polish, and others. For example, the Empress Catherine of Russia was one of his subjects. Much of his work is lost. Among his most famous portraits is an unfinished, life-size, half-length pastel of Marie Antoinette drawn in 1791. A second portrait of her while she was in prison is known only from a poor copy.

388. BATOWSKI, Zygmunt.

Jean Pillement na dworze Stanisława Augusta. Warszawa, Towarzystwo Naukowe Warszawskie, 1936. 40 p. illus. 16 plates. (Prace z historji sztuki, 2) ND553.P525B3

"Jean Pillement à la cour de Stanilas Auguste (resumé)": p. 38–40.

Documentary evidence of the Polish sojourn of Pillement. The artist arrived before the Spring of 1765 and remained until 1767 to decorate the palaces at Warsaw and Ujazdów. Nineteen drawings and paintings in Polish collections and related works elsewhere are reproduced.

389. BATOWSKI, Zygmunt.

Malarki Stanisława Augusta. [Women painters of Stanisław August] Wrocław, Zakład Narodowy im. Ossolińskich, 1951. 71 p. ports.

Summary in French.
Bibliographical references.
Introduction by Stanisław Lorentz.

An excellent work discussing portraits by eight women painters. Among them are Anna Rajecka (c. 1760–1832), Weronika Paszkowska (1766–1842), Anna Charczewska (1762–1806), Fryderyka Bacciarelli (1733–1812) and her two daughters, and Marie-Elisabeth-Louise Vigée-Lebrun (1755–1842), one of the greatest woman painters.

390. BATOWSKI, Zygmunt.

Marcello Bacciarelli. Okres pierwszy: lata 1731–1765/66. [Marcello Bacciarelli. The earliest period: the years 1731–1765/66] Biuletyn Historii Sztuki, vol. 13, no. 4, 1951, p. 75–96. illus., port. N6.B5 v. 13

Marcello Bacciarelli was a renowned portraitist in his early career. Born in Rome in 1731, he worked in Dresden as a painter and draftsman for prints (at the behest of K.H. von Heinecken, director of the Royal Gallery). Came to Warsaw in 1756, painting first for King August III, later acting as superintendent of art for Stanisław August as Charles Le Brun did for Louis XIV. Batowski died before completing this essay.

391. Bellotto, Bernardo, *called* Canaletto. Drezno i Warszawa w twórczości Bernarda Bellotta Canaletta. Katalog. [Dresden and Warsaw in the art of Bernardo Bellotto, called Canaletto. Catalog (of the exhibition)] Warszawa, Muzeum Narodowe w Warszawie, 1964. 243 p. chiefly illus. ND623.B43D7

The exhibition prepared jointly by the museums of art in Dresden and Warsaw.

Bibliography: p. 97–103.

Dresden and Warsaw shared a monarch, Federick August II of Saxony, who was August III of Poland during Bellotto's two periods of painting in Dresden, 1747 to 1758 and 1761 to 1766. Bellotto settled in Warsaw in 1767, having been appointed court painter by the successor to August III, King Stanisław August Poniatowski. Catalog by Stefan Kozakiewicz, of twenty-five views of Warsaw, two historical paintings, two equestrian subjects, two drawings of attire, and a ceiling design for the lost decorations at Castle Ujazdów. All illustrated with numerous details.

392. Bellotto, Bernardo, *called* Canaletto. Canaletto, the painter of Warsaw. By Mieczysław

❋

Wallis. Warszawa, Państwowy Instytut Wydawniczy, 1954. 37 p. 121 plates (part color). ND623.B43W312

A popular account of selected pictures, among them some twenty-six views of Warsaw and its environs, that place the subject of Warsaw in cultural and political context. Describes details of city life with quotations from Polish and foreign authors. Biography of the painter. As for the illustrations, which are a muddy black and white in this printing, the revised 1983 Polish-language edition should be consulted.

393. DOBROWOLSKI, Tadeusz.

Polskie malarstwo portretowe. Ze studiów nad sztuką epoki Sarmatyzmu. [Polish portrait painting. Studies in the art of the Sarmatian period] Kraków, Polska Akademia Umiejętności, 1948. 239 p. 187 portraits. ND1324.P6D6

Summary in French.

Analyzes a class of eighteenth-century portraits that were painted from a traditional, nationalistic viewpoint (Sarmatian) that is readily identifiable from the style, pose, and attire.

May be supplemented with a work by the Russian scholar Larisa Ivanovna Tananaeva:

Sarmatskii portret; iz istorii polskogo portreta epokhi barokko. [The Sarmatian portrait; from the history of Polish portraiture of the Baroque period] Moskva, Nauka, 1979. 303 p. illus. (part color). ND1324.P63T36

Bibliographic references.

Scholarly work with good illustrations.

394. KĘPIŃSKA, Alicja.

Jan Piotr Norblin. Wrocław, Zakład Narodowy im. Ossolińskich, 1978. 94 p. 184 illus., ports. N7255.P63N6735 1978

Bibliographic notes.

Jean-Pierre Norblin de la Gourdaine (1745–1830) is seen here in his capacity as the prolific draftsman. The essay places him in pictorial and historical context. Illustrations compare him to influences (Rembrandt) and contemporaries (Fragonard). Norblin came to Poland in 1774, recorded the battles of 1791 to 1794—including a wounded Kościuszko—and the Enactment of the Third of May Constitution.

395. KOZAKIEWICZ, Stefan.

Bernardo Bellotto. London, Elek, 1972. 2 v. illus. (part color). ND623.B43K5913 1972

Vol. 1: Text; v. 2: Catalog.

Translated from the German by Mary Whittall.

Bibliography: v. 1, p. 243–64.

In a prodigious catalogue raisonné, the author lays before the reader the life and work of Bernardo Bellotto (1721–1780), from the early Venetian city views he painted and etched under the influence of his uncle Antonio Canale (called Canaletto), through the evolution and maturation of his art, first in Dresden at the court of Frederick August II of Saxony (August III of Poland), where he stayed from 1747 to 1758, and to which he also returned for a five-year stay in the 1760s. The interim years from 1759 to 1761 he spent in Vienna and Munich at the courts of Maria Theresa and the Elector of Bavaria. In his final years, from 1767 until his death in 1780, he

worked in Warsaw as court painter to King Stanisław August Poniatowski.

Bellotto painted twenty-six views of Warsaw and its environs, twenty-four of which are now assembled (one having been lost around 1795, another during World War II). All the paintings that Bellotto executed for the king in the last ten years of his life, which included historical subjects and equestrian genre paintings, are known and datable from an extant document.

Volume 1 contains a comprehensive study of views by Bellotto and such contemporaries as Piranesi, and data on Bellotto's interior decorations in Poland. Volume 2 cuts a wide swath, covering not only all the artist's authentic paintings and etchings, but also a great number of replicas and attributed works.

Bellotto pained post-medieval Warsaw in so realistic a style that his paintings served to provide documentary evidence when the city was rebuilt after World War II.

[333]. Malarstwo polskie:

Oświecenie, Klasycyzm, Romantyzm. [Polish painting: The Enlightenment, Classicism, Romanticism] Warszawa, Auriga, 1976. 303 p. illus. (part color). ND955.P6N3 v. 3

Historical outline by Stefan Kozakiewicz.

Bibliography: p. 254.

Catalog by Anna Gradowska and others.

A long introductory essay and a brief catalog to accompany 158 plates, sixteen of which are in color. The emphasis is on lesser-known artists, the stars (Bacciarelli, Bellotto) having been subjects of numerous monographic studies.

Enlightenment. Romanticism

396. MICHAŁOWSKI, Piotr.
Piotr Michałowski. Warschau, Auriga, 1960. 79 p. 312 plates, 12 color plates. ND699.M5S5

By Jerzy Sienkiewicz, Jerzy Zanoziński, and Janusz Michałowski.

In German.

A true representative of Romanticism in Polish painting, Piotr Michałowski (1800–1855) was influenced by Theodore Géricault and other French painters. His extensive oeuvre favored military subjects—especially cavalry and portraits of soldiers—and genre scenes. Over three hundred fine reproductions of oil paintings, water colors, and drawings, including portraits of his family and friends.

[334]. MORAWIŃSKA, Agnieszka.
Polish painting, 15th to 20th century. Warszawa, Auriga, 1984. 68 p. 160 p. of plates, color illus. ND955.P6M67 1984

Translated from the Polish by Bogna Piotrowska.

Bibliographic references.

A straightforward, clear, and reliable history of style in Polish painting from the late 1200s to 1980. Main currents are outlined; the nineteenth century—the period in which the author specializes—is presented in greater detail. The author's artistic taste and judgment is evident in the stimulating choice of illustrations. Dr. Morawińska is the curator of paintings at the National Museum of Art, Warsaw.

397. NELKEN, Halina.
Alexander Orłowski. The works of a great Polish painter in American collections. Polish review, vol. 21, no. 3, 1976, p.

195–206. 4 illus. DK4010.P64, v. 21

A probing exposition of the art of the painter-lithographer Alexander Orłowski (1777–1832), and a biographical account of him and his teacher, Jean Pierre Norblin, with whom he founded the Polish School of realistic genre painting. The title is a misnomer, there being only cursory references to collections (principally the Dietrich Collection, New Hamsphire).

398. OSTROWSKI, Jan K.
Piotr Michałowski. Warszawa, Krajowa Agencja Wydawnicza, 1985. 167 p. illus. (part color). ND955.P63M536 1985

Bibliography: p. 166.

Piotr Michałowski (1800–1855) was a prolific and gifted artist who painted military and equestrian subjects and portraits, in the style of Géricault and Delacroix. An exceptionally well-produced book having 124 reproductions of his oils, watercolors, and sketches. An account of his career and critical reception; contains some of his letters and documents.

399. RUSZCZYCÓWNA, Janina.
Portrety polskie Józefa Grassiego. [Polish portraits painted by Józef Grassi] Biuletyn Historii Sztuki, vol. 16, no. 2, 1954, p. 262–69. illus., ports. N6.B5 v. 16

A native of Vienna, Józef Grassi (1758–1838) painted in Poland from 1791 to 1795. His best known subjects were Tadeusz Kościuszko and Prince Józef Poniatowski. Many of his sitters were members of the Polish Patriotic Society. He also painted

portraits of aristocratic women, including Tekla Jabłonowska, Ludwika Lubomirska, and Anetka Tyszkiewiczówna.

400. SROCZYŃSKA, Krystyna.
Antoni Brodowski 1784–1832; życie i dzieło. [Antoni Brodowski 1784–1832; his life and work] Warszawa, Muzeum Narodowe w Warszawie, 1985. 119 p. illus. (part color). ND1329.B757S67 1985

Summary also in French.
Bibliographic references.

Brodowski was the most eminent Polish painter of classical subjects and one of the country's finest nineteenth-century portraitists. He trained in Paris in the circle of Jacques-Louis David, then introduced French classicism into Poland. The subjects of his psychologically rendered portraits were mainly intellectuals from the sphere of literature and academia. Biographical outline, scholarly catalog with seventy-five paintings plus miniatures, water-colors, and drawings, and thirteen rejected works.

401. SZYMAŃSKI, Stanisław.
Sylwester August Miryś. Wrocław, Zakład Narodowy im. Ossolińskich, 1964. 153 p., 154 illus. ND699.M527S9

Summary in French.
Bibliography: p. 99–101.
Bibliographic references.

An important study of the painter Sylwester August Miryś, born c. 1700 in France or Scotland, who lived in Rome, and worked in Poland from 1730 until his death in 1790. He painted portraits of the Polish aristocracy, including the Jabłonowskis, Lubomirskis, Sapiehas, Bishop Ignacy Krasicki, and the Branickis of Białystok.

✻

Miryś painted the portrait of Tomasz Kajetan Węgierski (now at the National Museum in Kraków), a young Polish poet who traveled to the newly independent America in 1783. Węgierski not only recorded his observations but also speculated about the future of the young nation. In his letter to John Dickinson (then President of the Council of the State of Pennsylvania), Węgierski raised such questions as whether Congress would be able to gain the respect due the representatives of the highest authority, indispensable in any republic; and whether America could exist without a navy to foster commerce and protect its shores.

Miryś also painted murals on religious themes. Only a portion of his oeuvres survived.

402. WALLIS, Mieczysław.

Canaletto malarz Warszawy. [Canaletto, the painter of Warsaw] Wyd. 7, zmienione. Warszawa, Auriga, 1983. 36 p. color illus. 112 p. of plates. ND623.B43W3 1983

Bibliography: p. 38.

Text essentially that of the 1954 English-language edition. The few changes do not add to the subject. Color illustrations are of the same pictures and details as in the 1954 edition, apart from a small number of additional plates.

403. ZANOZIŃSKI, Jerzy.

Piotr Michałowski; życie i twórczość, 1800–1855. [Piotr Michałowski; his life and work, 1800–1855] Wrocław, Zakład Narodowy im. Ossolińskich, 1965. 103 p. 83 plates (part color). ND699.M5Z3

Summary in French and English.

Bibliography: p. 94–99.

Military subjects captured the artistic imagination of Piotr Michałowski (1800–1855). After the uprising of 1831, he fled to Paris where he enrolled in the studio of Nicolas Charlet. Influenced also by Théodore Géricault, and inspired by old masters, especially Velazquez. True representative of Romanticism in Polish painting. Famous for cavalry and other equestrian subjects.

404. ADAMOWICZ, Tadeusz.

Witraże fryburgskie Józefa Mehoffera. [The Fribourg stained glass windows of Józef Mehoffer] Wrocław, Zakład Narodowy im. Ossolińskich, 1982. 178 p. illus. (part color). (Studia z Historii Sztuki, vol. 33) NK5398.M36A84 1982

Summary, list of illustrations, and table of contents also in French.

Bibliographic references.

An excellent study of the monumental project in the Cathedral of Fribourg (Switzerland). Sixteen windows of the nave executed during the years 1895–1918; five great presbytery windows completed between 1918 and 1934. Discusses the artist's education and its bearing on the work; lists a chronology of the design; and presents a stylistic and iconographical analysis of the compositions. Reproductions of preliminary figure drawings and designs. Eight color plates of the cartoons. Floor plan of the installation.

405. Album de l'art polonais.

Paris, I. Lapina, 1913. 2 leaves, 29 p. 50 color plates. ND691.A7 folio

Issued in portfolio.

Introduction in French and Polish in parallel columns.

Each plate accompanied by guard sheet with descriptive letterpress in Polish and French.

Fifty consummate paintings by eminent history and landscape painters from Jan Matejko (1838–1893) to artists who matured around 1900 (Kazimierz Sichulski, Vlastimil Hofmann, and others). Each picture perceptively criticized. Biographical details. Reproductions of superior quality. A prolix history of Polish painting from its origin.

406. Album jubileuszowe, Grunwald; szkic historyczny.

[Jubilee album, Grunwald; an historical sketch] Poznań, Nakładem Z. Rzepeckiego, 1910. 12 p. 344 p. illus., color plates, ports. (part color), maps. DK420.B7

Prepared by Jasław z Bratkowa [pseud].

Valuable for its contents, the old-fashioned printing notwithstanding. Commemorates the 500th anniversary of the Battle of Grunwald (Tannenberg) when the Poles and Lithuanians defeated the Teutonic Knights. Paintings and drawings by Jan Styka (1858–1925) and Tadeusz Styka (b. 1889), including a diorama. Photographs of the site, map of the region, the castles, and coats of arms of the participants.

407. BLUMÓWNA, Helena.

Stanisław Wyspiański. Warszawa, Auriga, 1969. ND699.W9B6 folio

Biography and creative development of Stanisław Wyspiański (1869–1907) explicated in terms of correspondence

Saint Mary's coronation. Panel from the stained glass window in the Dominican Church in Kraków. From Feliks Kopera's *Dzieje malarstwa w Polsce.* **Vol. 1. Kraków, 1925**

and of illustrated works; 19 plates in color, 147 plates in black and white, 19 figures. Splendid reproductions with emphasis on portraits.

[318]. DOBROWOLSKI, Tadeusz.
Malarstwo polskie ostatnich dwustu lat. [Polish painting of the last two hundred years] Wrocław, Zakład Narodowy im. Ossolińskich, 1976. 232 p. 200 illus. 48 color plates. ND955.P6D57

Deliberates fully on the currents of romanticism, historicism, and symbolism that shaped European—and especially Polish—painting from the late eighteenth century. Reproductions, forty-eight in color and two hundred in

black and white, of many extraordinary, little-known nineteenth- and early twentieth-century paintings. Contemporary examples less well chosen.

408. DUŻYK, Józef.
Siemiradzki; opowieść biograficzna. [Siemiradzki; a biographical account] Warszawa, Ludowa Spółdzielnia Wydawnicza, 1986. 613 p. [96] p. of plates, illus. ND955.PG3S5434 1986

Bibliography: p. 572–81.

Henryk Siemiradzki (1843–1902) was a graduate of the St. Petersburg Academy of Fine Arts, studied at the Munich Academy under K. Piloty, and eventually settled in Rome in 1872, although he frequently returned to Poland. He exhibited in Poland, Russia, Rome, Berlin, London, Paris, and Melbourne. His paintings were primarily scenes from antiquity and lives of the early Christians, but also included pastorals, landscapes, and historical subjects. Siemiradzki's notable work in the decorative arts is exemplified by the curtains he created for the municipal theaters of Kraków (1896) and Lwów (1900).

409. Ferdynand Ruszczyc, życie i dzieło. [Ferdynand Ruszczyc, his life and work] Wilno, Księgarnia św. Wojciecha, 1939. 470 p. illus. (part color). ND699.R87A44

Title also in French.

Collective work edited by Jan Bułhak, Jerzy Hoppen, Mieczysław Limanowski, Marjan Morelowski, and Ludwik Szweykowski.

Ferdynand Ruszczyc (1870–1936), an artist of European orientation who situated himself in the cultural and political milieu of his native Wilno. Landscape painter, graphic designer (book illustrations, posters, postage stamps), and designer for the theater. Extended French summary.

A commemorative volume.

410. GIERYMSKI, Aleksander.

Aleksander Gierymski.
Warsaw, Auriga, 1971. 44 p., 24 color plates, 188 black and white plates. ND955.P63G5313 folio
By Juliusz Starzyński.

Aleksander Gierymski (1850–1901) was raised on the realist art of the Munich Academy of the late 1860s. His landscapes, genre, and naturalistic recreations of historical, costumed genre were in opposition to the symbolism of Jan Matejko and the Kraków School. He remained independent, although aware, of impressionist and post-impressionist painting.

While living in Warsaw, Gierymski found his genre subjects among the poor in the Jewish ghetto and in the Vistula (Wisła) districts. His realistic paintings included such works as the "Vistula Quarter," "Jewess with Lemons," and "Day of Trumpets," the somber holy Day of Yom Kippur (the Day of Atonement). Gierymski's nocturnal city scenes contributed to the rise in colorism and luminist art in Poland. Exhibited in Vienna and Berlin, he won the gold medal at the Munich exhibition in 1890, and was decorated with the Order of Francis Joseph at the Polish Art Exhibit (Lwów, Lvov) in 1894.

411. GRZYBOWSKA, Teresa.

The Pseudojapanese in "Young Poland" Art. *In Artibus et Historiae, no. 11 (VI), 1985, p.*

137–46. illus., ports.
NX1.A1A77 no. 11
Bibliographic references.

May be consulted for the illustrated works of art; the naively assessed social and aesthetic background should be passed over. Polish artists are said to have encountered Nipponism in the 1880s and 1890s in Paris, Munich, and St. Petersburg. Among the few to visit Japan directly were J. Fałat and K. Frycz. The chief figure for the spread of Nipponism in Poland was the critic and art collector Feliks Jasieński.

412. JAKIMOWICZ, Andrzej.

Jacek Malczewski. Warszawa, Auriga, 1974. 26 p. 92 leaves of plates, illus. (part color). ND955.P63M332 1974
Bibliographic references.

Malczewski (1854–1929), the great luminary of the Młoda Polska movement, is introduced with reference to the symbolism—fauns and satyrs, muses, medusa, water—that appears in his portraits, landscapes, and allegories. Twenty-two color plates and 136 in black and white illustrate his genius.

413. JAWORSKA, Władysława.

Władysław Ślewiński, 1854–1918; wystawa monograficzna. Warszawa, Muzeum Narodowe w Warszawie, 1983. 122 p. (260) p. of plates, illus. (part color). ND955.P63S5552 1983
Exhibition catalog; text in English, French, and Polish.
Bibliography: p. 47.

Paul Gauguin and members of the Pont-Aven school had a strong influence on Ślewiński's artistic career. Born in Poland, Ślewiński spent many years in Paris, and also in

Brittany, where he died in 1918. His paintings: landscapes, seascapes, portraits, and still lifes are characterized by sharp contours and a simplicity bordering on ascetism.

414. KĘPIŃSKI, Zdzisław.

Stanisław Wyspiański.
Warszawa, Krajowa Agencja Wydawnicza, 1984. 227 p. illus. (part color). ND955.P63W9438 1984
Bibliographic references.

Stanisław Wyspiański (1869–1907), seen at his most brilliantly creative. Thematically arranged text deals with the curtain for the Słowacki Theater in Kraków, preparatory sketches, etc., for stained glass windows (Lwów, Kraków), drawings for the Iliad, and other subjects. Numerous color reproductions of stained glass and pastels demonstrate his extraordinary sense of color. Comparisons throughout to contemporaries: Gaugin, Rodin, Redon, Mucha.

415. Kolor w malarstwie

polskim 19 i 20 wieku. Katalog wystawy. [Color in Polish painting of the nineteenth and twentieth centuries. Exhibition catalog] Muzeum Narodowe w Poznaniu, czerwiec-październik 1978. Poznań, Muzeum Narodowe, 1978. 113 p. 68 plates (part color). ND955.P6K64
Collective work edited by Maria Berdyszakowa.
Bibliographic references.

The authors trace the history of impressionism and colorism in Poland. Biographical notes included on eighty-five artists.

416. LIGOCKI, Alfred.

Józef Chełmoński. Warszawa,

Krajowa Agencja Wydawnicza, 1983. 103 p., illus. (part color). ND955.P63C4734 1983

Bibliographic references.

Chełmoński (1849–1914), who was deeply in tune with nature and worked with great facility, made lyrical paintings of the Polish landscape. At times he painted in the realistic style, at other times in the romantic and impressionist styles. Many equestrian and rural subjects. His famous painting "Kuropatwy" [Patridges] was awarded an Ehrendiplom at the International Art Exhibition in Berlin in 1891. Excellent reproductions. A chronology of his life.

417. MAKOWIECKI, Tadeusz.

Poeta-malarz; studium o Stanisławie Wyspiańskim. [Poet-painter; a study of Stanisław Wyspiański] Warszawa, Państwowy Instytut Wydawniczy, 1969. 289 p. illus. (part color), ports. ND699.W9M3 1969

Bibliographic references.

Discusses subjects such as Stanisław Wyspiański's illustrations interpreting Tasso, Ariosto, Homer, and others; literary influences on his paintings; and foreign pictorial influences (Delacroix, Burne-Jones, Munch). A serious work of art history that suffers from poor reproductions.

[332]. Malarstwo polskie:

Modernizm. [Polish painting: Modernism] Warszawa, Auriga, 1977. 354 p. illus. (part color). ND955.P6M3 v. 4

Introduction by Wiesław Juszczak.

Biographical notes and catalog by Maria Liczbińska.

The originality of this volume is immediately apparent from the frontispiece, which shows a Polish-costumed muse of the painter J. Malczewski. Discriminating choices in the other 216 plates, of which eighty-eight are excellent color reproductions.

418. MALCZEWSKI, Jacek.

Malczewski: [Ausstellung] Württembergischer Kunstverein Stuttgart, 3. April–1. Juni 1980; Kunsthalle zu Kiel und Schleswig-Holsteinischer Kunstverein in Verbindung mit der Stadt Kiel, 20. Juni–24. August 1980; Wilhelm-Lehmbruck-Museum der Stadt Duisburg, 7. September–12. Oktober 1980, in Zusammenarbeit mit dem Muzeum Narodowe, Poznań. Stuttgart, Württembergischer Kunstverein, 1980. 211 p. illus. (part color). ND955.P63M332 1980

Bibliography: p. 209–11.

Catalog by Agnieszka Ławniczakowa.

Essays on the great symbolist painter Jacek Malczewski (1854–1929) by A. Ławniczakowa, T. Osterwold, J.C. Jensen: Formation and expression, with comparisons to L. Corinth, M. Klinger, and A. Böcklin. Catalog of 121 works. Biographical outline with photographs of the artist, his family and friends.

419. MALINOWSKI, Jerzy.

Julian Fałat. Warszawa, Krajowa Agencja Wydawnicza, 1985. 128 p. illus. (part color). ND955.P63F356 1985

Bibliography: p. 100.

Chronology of Fałat's life and career.

Reminiscent of Winslow Homer in his fresh vision and gift for color, the watercolors and oils of Julian Fałat (1853–1929) are here especially well reproduced. The vigorous, naturalistic landscapes notwithstanding, his art is touched by art nouveau characteristics and fashion, in the style of Tissot.

420. MASŁOWSKI, Maciej.

Juliusz Kossak. Warszawa, Wydawnictwa Artystyczne i Filmowe, 1985. 51 p. 116 illus. (part color). N7255.P63K672

Includes the equestrian paintings of Juliusz Kossak (1824–1899), whether they are portraits, hunting scenes, horse fairs, or historic cavalry battles.

Among more recent scholarly publications is Kazimierz Olszański's Juliusz Kossak. Wrocław, Zakład Narodowy im. Ossolińskich, 1988. More than 150 plates, some in color. Reproductions of the artist's large canvases depicting Jan III Sobieski entering Vienna in 1683, "Sobieski on Kahlenberg," "The Election of King Jan Kazimierz," and some other history paintings. Juliusz Kossak was well known also as a book illustrator; he illustrated A. Mickiewicz' Konrad Wallenrod and Grażyna, and H. Sienkiewicz' Ogniem i mieczem. After he settled in Kraków in 1870, Kossak's paintings reflected his interest in the life of the Kraków region, its people, and their folklore.

Drawings, water colors, and lithographs well reproduced.

421. MATEJKO, Jan.

Jan Matejko. Warszawa, Arkady, 1962. 29 p. 234 plates (20 color). ND699.M3S73 folio

Introduction by Juliusz Starzyński.

Introduction to Jan Matejko (1838–1893), the incomparable Polish painter of profoundly patriotic, historical subjects. The illustrations—preponderantly of details of the vast canvases, and of preparatory drawings—disclose the artist's enormous facility as a draftsman and painter.

422. MEHOFFER, Józef.

Józef Mehoffer; katalog wystawy zbiorowej. [Józef Mehoffer; catalog of an exhibition of collected works] Kraków, Muzeum Narodowe w Krakowie, 1964. 190 p. 80 illus. ND699.M34T6

Introduction by Helena Blum.
Bibliography: p. 213–35.

Catalog of 457 works: paintings, including studies; cartoons for stained glass windows; decorative projects and cartoons; drawings and watercolors; prints (in dry point, etching, engraving, verni mous, lithography); scenic design. List of portrait subjects. Modest illustrations that nevertheless convey the superior gifts of the artist.

[334]. MORAWIŃSKA, Agnieszka.

Polish painting, 15th to 20th century. Warszawa, Auriga, 1984. 68 p. 160 p. of plates, color illus. ND955.P6M67 1984

Translated from the Polish by Bogna Piotrowska.

Bibliographic references.

A straightfoward, clear, and reliable history of style in Polish painting from the late 1200s to 1980. Main currents are outlined; the nineteenth century—the period in which the author specializes—is presented in greater detail. The author's artistic taste and judgment is evident in the stimulating choice of illustrations.

Dr. Morawińska is the curator of paintings at the National Museum of Art, Warsaw.

423. Muzeum Narodowe w Poznaniu. Jacek Malczewski. Katalog wystawy monograficznej. [Jacek Malczewski. Catalog of the exhibition] Poznań, 1968. 241 p. illus. ND955.P63M322 1968

Edited by Agnieszka Ławniczakowa.

Summary in English.
Bibliography: p. 230–41.

Valuable chronology on Jacek Malczewski (1854–1929). Chronology of life and work; catalog of 355 items in oils, drawings, and watercolors; index of portrait subjects; list of exhibitions.

424. NELKEN, Halina.

Stanisław Wyspiański. Warszawa, Arkady, 1958. 33 p. 35 illus. (part color), plates, ports. ND699.W9N4

The illustrations of Stanisław Wyspiański's work concentrate on the portraits of this great colorist, who was close in style to Oskar Kokoschka. Some rare sketches are reproduced alongside better known sheets.

425. New York. Metropolitan Museum of Art. Nineteenth-century Polish Paintings. A loan exhibition, February 16 to March 19, 1944, under the auspices of His Excellency, Jan Ciechanowski, Ambassador of Poland, with the assistance of the Polish Information Center. Arranged by Bolesław Mastal. New York, The Metropolitan Museum of Art, 1944. 42 p. illus. DLC

Foreword by Horace H.F. Jayne.

Among the paintings exhibited are the canvases of Piotr Michałowski, Jan Matejko, Artur Grottger, Józef Brandt, Julian Fałat, Włodzimierz Tetmajer, and Alfred Wierusz-Kowalski.

426. Nineteenth-century Polish painting. [An exhibition catalog] Warsaw, National Museum in Warsaw; New York, National Academy of Design, 1988. 180 p. 85 plates (part color). DLC

Agnieszka Morawińska, coordinator of the exhibition.
Bibliography: p. 173–78.

The works of forty-five painters are represented in the catalog, from Marcello Bacciarelli's portrait of King Stanislaus Augustus to Marcin Zaleski's canvas depicting the fighting near the Arsenal on Długa Street at the beginning of the November 1830 insurrection in Warsaw. Also included are four paintings by Piotr Michałowski, and works by Antoni Brodowski, Jan Matejko, Maurycy Gottlieb, Anna Billińska-Bohdanowicz, and others.

427. Panorama Racławicka.

The Panorama of the Battle of Racławice. Panorama der Schlact bei Racławice. Warszawa, Interpress, 1981. 1 leaf. 12 color illus. DK4344.R3P36 1981 folio

Text in Polish, English, and German.

Commemorating the battle of 4 April 1794 waged by the Polish army, under the command of Tadeusz Kościuszko, against the Russian forces. The painting was executed at the centenary of the Insurrection by Jan Styka and Wojciech Kossak.

First exhibited in Lwów, where it remained until 1946. Restored after being damaged during the war, the canvas now hangs in Wrocław.

428. Polnische Malerei von 1830 bis 1914. [24. Juni–20. August 1978. Kunsthalle zu Kiel, 7. September bis 29. Oktober 1978, Württembergischer Kunstverein, Stuttgart, 12. November 1978 bis 8. Januar 1979, von-der-Heydt-Museum der Stadt Wuppertal] Organisation, Muzeum Narodowe in Warszawa. Herausgegeben von Jens Christian Jensen. Köln, DuMont, 1978. 277 p. illus. (part color). ND955.P6P64

Bibliographic references.

Ten brief essays in Part I address the Polish self-image and self-portrait, Polish realism as a dialogue between the concept of art and of native land, and other aspects of the painting of the period. Part II has biographies of the forty artists represented, and a catalog of the exhibition prepared by Agnieszka Morawińska, with the assistance of the staff of the Gallery of Polish Painting at the National Museum, Warsaw. Discerning, exemplary selection is evident, despite the reduced size of the reproductions.

429. POTOCKI, Antoni.
Grottger. Lwów, Księgarnia Altenberga; Warszawa, E. Wende, 1907. 236 p. plates (part color). ND699.G74P6

Bibliographic references: p. 213–21.

Artur Grottger (1837–1867) was one of Poland's quintessential history painters. Inspired by his country's tragic political events, he created such famous series as "Warszawa," "Lithuania," "Polonia," and "War." *Highly precocious, and exhibiting beautiful pictorial invention, his work encompassed mystical allegories as well as verisimilar portraiture. He studied in Kraków, Vienna, and Munich, and also in Italy, where classical sources such as Raphael influenced him. A prolific artist, he died in France at the age of thirty.*

430. PUCIATA-PAWŁOWSKA, Jadwiga.
Jacek Malczewski. Wrocław, Zakład Narodowy im. Ossolińskich, 1968. 335 p. 330 illus. (part color). ND699.M282P8

Bibliographic references.

A leading European symbolist painter, Jacek Malczewski (1854–1929) was an artist of extraordinary productivity and power. The text is arranged by themes, such as Christ and the Madonna, angels and chimeras, and Thanatos. A prolific portrait painter. The reproductions are wholly inadequate to his genius.

431. PUCIATA PAWŁOWSKA, Jadwiga. Maksymilian Antoni Piotrowski (1813–1875). Studia Pomorskie, vol. 2, Wrocław, 1957, p. 432–531. illus. port. N6876.P56W3

Summary in French and Russian.

Bibliographic references.

Born in Bydgoszcz, the painter Maksymilian Antoni Piotrowski, began his training in 1833 in Berlin and completed it in Düsseldorf, where he came under the influence of Wilhelm Schadow. In Rome from 1842, he was drawn to Friedrich Overbeck, founder of the Nazarenes. He returned to Poland at the end of the 1840s and was caught up in the revolutionary currents. Appointed to the Academy of Fine Arts, Königsberg, he lived there for the remainder of his life. The major collection of his paintings is in Bydgoszcz. Realistic and idealistic currents flow in his paintings, one of his chief works being a subject of national heroism, The last moments of Wanda (National Museum, Kraków).

432. RUTKOWSKI, Tadeusz.
Rok 1863 w malarstwie polskim. [The year 1863 in Polish painting] Lwów, Altenberg, 1918. 7 p. 63 plates. ND691.R8

Commemorates the 1863 uprising against Russian domination. Paintings by twenty-four artists, including Artur Grottger (1837–1867), Maksymilian Gierymski (1847–1874), and Jacek Malczewski (1854–1929).

433. SIMMLER, Józef.
Józef Simmler 1823–1868; katalog wystawy monograficznej. [Józef Simmler 1823–1868; exhibition catalog] Muzeum Narodowe w Warszawie. Warszawa, Muzeum Narodowe, 1979. 129 p. 50 leaves of plates, illus. (part color). ND1329.S55A4 1979

Exhibition catalog by Tadeusz S. Jaroszewski and Elżbieta Charazińska.

Bibliography.

Józef Simmler was born in Warsaw to a family of cabinet makers that had emigrated from Switzerland to Poland in the eighteenth century. Simmler was educated in Warsaw and attended the Dresden Academy of Arts, but it was his two-year stay in

*Paris, where he became acquainted
with the work of Paul Delaroche,
that played an important role in his
career. He painted mainly portraits
and religious scenes. The famous
portrait of his wife, Julia (1863), is
in the collections of the National
Museum in Warsaw.*

434. STARZYŃSKI, Juliusz.
L'inspiration de l'art vénetien
dans la peinture polonaise des
XIXe et XXe siècles. *In* Venezia
e la Polonia nei secoli dal XVII al
XIX. Edited by Luigi Cini.
Venezia, Istituto per la
Collaborazione Culturale, 1965,
p. 105–19. 17 illus. NX371.P6V4
*Venetian Renaissance colorism, espe-
cially that of Titian and Veronese,
was important to such nineteenth-
century Polish painters as Wojciech
Stattler (1800–1875), Henryk
Rodakowski (1823–1894), Jan
Matejko (1838–1893), and
Aleksander Gierymski
(1850–1901).*

435. STĘPIEŃ, Halina.
Malarstwo Maksymiliana
Gierymskiego. [Paintings of
Maksymilian Gierymski]
Wrocław, Zakład Narodowy im.
Ossolińskich, 1979. 256 p. 174
illus. (part color).
ND955.P63G547
Summary and list of illustrations in English.
Bibliography: p. 159–62.
*An eminent painter, Maksymilian
Gierymski (1847–1874) was
trained in Warsaw, and had a
prolonged residence in Munich, then
the international arts center, where he
was exposed to the French Barbizon
school. He created the Polish school of
historical and landscape genre painting. Catalog of 308 paintings,*
*drawings, watercolors, illustrations,
and sketchbooks.*

[81]. Stowarzyszenie
Historyków Sztuki. Sztuka
XIX wieku w Polsce. Naród—
Miasto. [The art of the nine-
teenth century in Poland. The
nation—the city] Warszawa,
Państwowe Wydawnictwo
Naukowe, 1979. 272 p. illus.
N7255.P6S8 1979
Materiały Sesji Stowarzyszenia
Historyków Sztuki, Poznań,
grudzień 1977.
Bibliographic references.
*Fourteen essays selected from the
many papers delivered at a session of
the Association of Art Historians
held in Poznań in December 1977.
The theme of the session was the
history of art during the period of the
partitions. An essay by Maria Janion
discusses "The Romantic artist and
the national 'sacrum'." History
painting is represented by an essay on
Jan Matejko's three canvases collectively entitled "The Allegory of
Poland" that discusses "Father
Skarga's Sermon," "Rejtan at the
Warsaw Sejm in 1773," and "Poland shackled." "Residential architecture of the Warsaw grande bourgeoisie," "capitalist architecture in
Łódź," and "The 'National
Historism' of the years 1919–1929
as an expression of romantic thought"
are some of the other essay titles.*

436. Symbolism in Polish
painting 1890–1914. Detroit,
Detroit Institute of Arts, 1984.
163 p. illus. (part color).
ND955.P6S9 1984
Polish Symbolism by
Agnieszka Morawińska, p. 13–
14.

The book is published in
conjunction with the exhibition
"Symbolism in Polish painting
1890–1914," presented at the
Detroit Institute of Arts, July
30–September 23, 1984.
Bibliography: p. 161–63.
*A substantive and nuanced study
on a subject heretofore unknown to
English-speaking readers. A deeply
creative period in Polish art sprang
from national strongholds of landscape
and hearth that were invested with
states of the soul. The works of
twenty artists in paintings and
drawings, including Stanisław
Wyspiański, Józef Mehoffer, and
Jacek Malczewski. Excellent reproductions in color and black and white.*

437. Sztuka polska. Zbiór
plansz facsimiljowych według
dzieł artystów współczesnych.
Wydał J. Mortkowicz. [Polish
art. A collection of facsimile
plates after the works of
contemporary artists. Published
by J. Mortkowicz] Warszawa,
Kraków, Towarzystwo
Wydawnicze, 1927. The Editorial
Society, London, Paris, New
York, 1927–28. Part I–V.
N6991.M6 folio
*Fine full-color reproductions of
twenty-three paintings and drawings:
Part I, four plates of J. Pankiewicz;
Part II, two plates each of W.
Skoczylas and W. Weiss; Part III,
two plates of M. Kisling ("Man with
a Pipe," "Still life") and three of
E. Żak; Part IV, five plates of L.
Wyczółkowski; Part V, five plates
of drawings by Pankiewicz, T.
Pruszkowski, Weiss, Wyczółkowski,
and Żak (the latter's "Portrait of a
girl" in the style of Lucien Freud
avant la lettre).*

❀

438. TRETER, Mieczysław.
Matejko; osobowość artysty,
twórczość, forma i styl. [Matejko;
the artist's personality, creativity,
form and style] Lwów,
Książnica-Atlas, 1939. 685 p.
illus., color plates, ports.
ND699.M3T7

Summary in French.
Bibliography: p. 558–80.
Contains 385 figures and 40
plates.

*A monumental study befitting the
immense creativity of Jan Matejko
(1838–1893). By far the most
important Polish painter of historical
and patriotic subjects, Matejko's
dramatic power reveals itself fully in
scenes of battle and tumult. His
vigorous, stately portraits are sometimes less realistic and introspective
than histrionic. A book with useful
apparatus such as chronological outline, list of pupils, tables of contemporary native and foreign painters,
and extracts from European critical
opinions.*

**439. Warsaw. Muzeum
Narodowe.** Stanisław Lentz,
1861–1920. Katalog wystawy
monograficznej. [Stanisław
Lentz, 1861–1920. Catalog of an
exhibition] Warszawa, Muzeum
Narodowe, 1976. 95 p. [50]
leaves of plates, illus. (part
color). N7255.P63L36537

Collective work edited by Lija
Skalska-Miecik.

Bibliographic references.
*One of a series of exhibitions of
modern artists, mainly in Warsaw.
A vivid portraitist, Stanisław Lentz
painted subjects who were important
in the social and cultural life of the
period. Biography in outline. Catalog,
with full bibliographies, of 88
canvases in the exhibition, 130 lost*

*paintings, 48 drawings, and 20
portraits in lithography; also a list of
drawings reproduced in periodicals.*

**440. Warszawska "Cyganeria"
malarska.** Grupa Marcina
Olszyńskiego. [Warsaw
Bohemian group of painters. The
Circle of Marcin Olszyński]
Wrocław, Zakład Narodowy im.
Ossolińskich, 1955. 420 p. illus.,
ports. (Źrodła do dziejów sztuki
polskiej, vol. 8) N7255.P6Z76
v. 8

Edited by Stefan Kozakiewicz
and Andrzej Ryszkiewicz.

*Albums and correspondence that
illuminate the life of Marcin
Olszyński (1829–1904) and his
artistic circle. Oil sketches, watercolors, drawings, photographs, prints,
manuscript notes, and* cartes de
visite *assembled by the artist between
circa 1850 and the early 1870s testify
to the upper bourgeois Bohemian life
led in Warsaw, Western Europe, and
Russia by Wojciech Gerson (1831–
1901), Edward Petzold (1829–
1888), Henryk Pillati (1832–
1894), and others. Correspondence
into the 1890s. Marked throughout
by high humor.*

441. WIERCIŃSKA, Janina.
Andriolli. Opowieść
biograficzna. [Andriolli. A biographical account] Warszawa,
Ludowa Spółdzielnia
Wydawnicza, 1981. 461 p. 105
illus., port. N7255.P63A6438

Bibliography: p. 457–61.
*The political activism of Elwiro
Andriolli (1836–1893) shaped his
life. Born in Wilno, he chose to live in
London and Paris as a young
expatriate, but then, in the late
1860s and early 1870s, had to spend
time in Russia, and also studied in*

*Rome. He eventually settled down to a
successful life as a recognized artist in
Warsaw. He chose historical subject
matter for his art, and also gained
respect as a landscape artist and book
illustrator.*

**442. WIERZCHOWSKA,
Wiesława.**
Władysław Podkowiński.
Warszawa, Krajowa Agencja
Wydawnicza RSW Prasa-
Książka-Ruch, 1981. 106 p. illus.
(part color). ND955.P63P59538

Bibliography: p. 103.
Chronology of Podkowiński's
artistic career.

*Władysław Podkowiński
(1866–1895), together with Józef
Pankiewicz, studied in Warsaw, St.
Petersburg, and Paris, where he
became fascinated by impressionism.
His landscapes and portraits reflect
his belief in its principles. He later
produced works promoting Polish
Symbolism. Much controversy
arose over his oil painting Szał
("Ecstasy," 1894), depicting a
naked woman on a huge horse-beast.
It was acclaimed by younger artists
as a profound example of Polish
Symbolism.*

*Podkowiński died in poverty at the
age of twenty-nine. Most of his
canvases, including Szał, are in the
Warsaw National Museum; others
are in the museums of Kraków and
Poznań.*

443. WYSPIAŃSKI, Stanisław.
Dzieła Malarskie. [The painted
works] Bydgoszcz, Instytut
Wydawniczy "Biblioteka
Polska," 1925. 131 p. illus., plates
(part color), ports. ND699.W9P8
folio

Text by Stanisław

Przybyszewski and Tadeusz
Żuk-Skarszewski.

Indexes by Stanisław Swierz.
Summary in French.

*The authors celebrate all aspects
of the artist's visual creativity.
Wyspiański (1869–1907) contributed new forms to each genre in which
he worked, including furniture design,
ornamental metal work, theater costume, architectural design, and book
illustration. Table of 554 paintings,
prints, and sculptures, arranged chronologically by project.*

444. ZANOZIŃSKI, Jerzy.

Aleksander Kotsis, 1836–1877.
Warszawa, Państwowy Instytut
Wydawniczy, 1953. 32 p., 94
black and white and 4 color
plates. ND955.P63K739 1953

*Kotsis, in his many emotion-filled
landscapes, portrays poor, suffering
village inhabitants whose love for the
countryside in the Kraków and Tatra
foothill regions matched his own. He
mitigated the deep sadness and tragedy
of his painting with his use of soft
colors, often creating a sense of
calmness. His early artistic activity is
represented by "Rekrutacja w
Galicji" [The draft of men in
Galicia]. Painted in 1866 and
exhibited in Poland, the work documents the recruitment of 1866, when
Galicia was obliged to provide a
contingent of soldiers for Austria's
war against Prussia. "Ostatnia
chudoba" [The last possession]—
exhibited in Kraków, 1870—depicts
a poor village family whose last
possession, the family goat, is being
sold to pay debts.*

445. ABERDAM, Alfred.

Alfred Aberdam, 1894–1963.
[Exposition], Petit Palais,
Genève, 11 mars–5 avril 1970.

[Catalogue] Genève, Petit Palais,
1970. 59 p. illus. (part color).
ND955.P63A23

*Reproductions of forty-four of the
eighty paintings exhibited by the
Lwów-born painter and sculptor, who
lived in Paris from 1923 to 1960.
Apart from a 1922 "Self-portrait,"
and a 1938 "Still Life," all
paintings after the late 1940s are of
abstract, diaphanous, buoyant,
luminist forms on dark backgrounds.*

446. L'Avanguardia Polacca
1910–1978: S.I. Witkiewicz,
construttivismo, artisti
contemporanei. Roma, Palazzo
delle Esposizioni, 27 gennaio–4
marzo 1979. Milano, Electa
Editrice, 1979. 173 p., illus.
N7255.P6W482 1979

Bibliographies.
Exhibition catalog edited by
Ryszard Stanislawski, et al.
Translated from the Polish by
Jadwiga Kruger and Luigi
Barbaro.

*Divided into four chapters, the first
one deals with S.I. Witkiewicz
(1885–1939), a surrealist painter,
dramatist, philosopher, and novelist;
the second with the Polish
Constructivists, who included outstanding women, such as K. Kobro,
M. Nicz-Borowiak, T. Żarnower,
and the works of W. Strzemiński
that astonishingly presaged contemporary developments (pl. II, fig. 62);
chapter 3 deals with H. Stażewski's
vital works of 1961–78; and chapter
4 treats ten contemporaries who work
in the conceptual, serialist, and
minimalist modes.*

447. BANACH, Andrzej.

Nikifor. Warszawa,
Wydawnictwo Arkady, 1984. 183

p. illus. (part color).
ND2035.P63N5433 1983

*Biography and Stylistic analysis of
Poland's clearly loved naive painter,
Nikifor (about 1895–1968). Water
colors in excellent reproductions.*

448. BIEGAS, Boleslas.

Boleslas Biegas. Exposition 15
octobre–9 novembre 1974.
Galerie J.C. Gaubert. Paris,
Galerie J.C. Gaubert, 1974. 68 p.
illus. ND955.P63B52

*Photo of the artist, Boleslas Biegas,
born 1877, and thirty-three undated
paintings, including the cover, reproduced with expository statements by
Guillaume Appolinaire and others.
Style reminiscent of A. Böcklin—to
whom one painting is dedicated—and
the art deco style of Erte.*

449. BLATTER, Janet, *and*
Sybil Milton.

Art of the Holocaust. New
York, The Rutledge Press, 1981.
272 p. illus. N7417.6.B59 1981
Bibliography: p. 270–72.

*Searingly painful and deeply moving
works of art from the Nazi ghettos
and concentration camps in Poland,
1939–45. Drawings and paintings
made at the time. Biographies of 158
artists, Jews and Christians, Poles
and other nationalities. Three hundred
fifty-nine reproductions of works by
many gifted artists, such as Xawery
Dunikowski, Maria Hiszpańska-
Neumann, Mieczysław Kościelniak,
Lea Lilienblum, Gela Seksztein, and
Szymon Szerman.*

450. BLUMÓWNA, Helena.

Hanna Rudzka-Cybisowa.
Warszawa, RSW "Prasa-Książka-
Ruch," 1975. 65 p. color illus.
ND955.P63R832
Bibliography: p. 63

Paintings by the gifted colorist, born 1897, whose artistic ties are to Bonnard, Vuillard, and Matisse. Twenty reproductions in color and black and white. An account of her career.

451. BLUMÓWNA, Helena.
Pronaszko. Warszawa, Arkady, 1958. 80 p. 89 plates (part color), illus. ND699.P74B5
Bibliographic references.
Zbigniew Pronaszko (1885–1958), painter, sculptor, and scenographer, was one of the founders of the Formist group (around 1917); later, his paintings show the influence of the Colorist movement, and color played an important role in his work for the rest of his life. Reproduced are portraits of his wife, brother Andrzej, famous actor Ludwik Solski, sculptor Xawery Dunikowski, and many still lifes and landscapes.

452. COSTANZA, Mary S.
The living witness. Art in the concentration camps and ghettos. New York, The Free Press, a Division of Macmillan Publishing Co., 1982. xxv, 196 p. illus. N7417.6.C67 1982
Bibliographic references.
Visual documents of pain, horror, and tragedy. Circumstances under which the art was made are recounted by survivors, sometimes in notes left behind. About one hundred unnumbered reproductions. Artists included are Sara Gliksman-Faitlovitz, Franciszek Jaźwiecki, Roman Kramsztyk, Halina Ołomucki, and Józef Szajna.

453. CYBIS, Jan.
Jan Cybis; katalog wystawy, Warszawa, luty–marzec 1965. [Jan Cybis; catalog of an exhibi-

tion held in Warsaw, February–March 1965] Warszawa, 1965. 72 p. 32 color plates.
ND699.C93A47
Prepared under the direction of Jerzy Zanoziński, by Halina Piperkowa, et al.
In Polish and French.
Bibliographies.

454. CYBIS, Jan.
Jan Cybis, notatki malarskie: dzienniki, 1954–1966. [Jan Cybis, his notes on painting; diaries, 1954–1966] Warszawa, Państwowy Instytut Wydawniczy, 1980. 449 p. 38 p. of plates, illus. (part color), ports. ND955.P6C9 1980
Selected by Dominik Horodyński.

455. DŁUBAK, Zbigniew.
Zbigniew Dłubak, prace z lat 1945–1980. Works from 1945–1980. Muzeum Narodowe we Wrocławiu, luty–marzec 1981. February–March 1981. [Exhibition] Wrocław, Muzeum Narodowe we Wrocławiu, 1981. 107 p. illus. port.
N7255.P63D482 1981
Introduction by Adam Sobota in Polish and English.
Bibliography: p. 100–102.
A painter and photographer, Dłubak (b. 1921) came under the direct influence, in 1947, of the Polish analytic constructivists Władysław Strzemiński and Henryk Stażewski. An outcome of their theory has been a two-tiered production: art serving its social function, and experimental art; or, social realism alongside—eventually—conceptual art. More recently, using photography, the artist has sought to desymbolize old myths. His theoretical speculations are

quoted. Included is a biography, a list of significant events in his creative life, and a list of exhibitions. Approximately one hundred illustrations—only one in color—show the artist and his work.

[319]. DOBROWOLSKI, Tadeusz.
Nowoczesne malarstwo polskie. [Modern Polish painting] Wrocław, Zakład Narodowy im. Ossolińskich, 1957–64. 3 vols. illus. (part color). ND955.P6D6
Bibliography: v. 3, p. 449–74.
Lists of illustrations also in French.
A most impressive work in terms of its range and the variety of issues investigated. Volume I surveys the history of Polish painting from 1764 to about 1900, classified as the Period of Enlightenment, and then examines the nineteenth century, which the author divides into three parts. The following samples of topics covered convey the flavor and textual richness: painters of ornamental decor, such as J.B. Plersch; portrait painting by J.C. Lampi and J. Grassi; paintings by Norblin and modern realism; the romanticism of P. Michałowski; the training of the artist; representatives of the old classicism and miniaturists (in the period 1800–1833); and the ideology supporting historicism in painting. Volume II begins with the second half of the nineteenth century, treating the major painters of historicism and romanticism—Matejko, Grottger, Brandt, Gottlieb—and the realists as represented by M. Gierymski, Chełmoński, and Gerson. The next section covers Młoda Polska, including Symbolism and Secession, followed by an examination of older contemporaries—J.Fałat, J. Malczewski, J. Mehoffer,

F. Ruszczyc—as seen against the more progressive movement of Młoda Polska. Volume III deals with the twentieth century, beginning with W. Weiss, Matejko's youngest pupil, and touches on many intriguing subjects, such as the influences of Wyspiański and regional themes, the Group Five, and the continuing fate of Secession. Next is a section on the period 1914 to 1939 with the Formists versus the Expressionists of Poznań and the Bunt group, and the avant-garde groups of Blok and Praesens. A short section on art after World War II, dealing with socialist realism, completes the book. A wealth of illustrations throughout—over one thousand altogether—which, whatever their shortcomings in printing quality, afford a rich pictorial panorama of the material.

456. DOMINIK, Tadeusz.
Jan Cybis. Warszawa, Wydawnictwo Arkady, 1985. 150 p. illus. (some color). ND955.P63C833 1985

Bibliography: p. 152–55.

Jan Cybis (1897–1972) was a Colorist—a spiritual descendant of Edouard Vuillard and other Post-Impressionists. Includes a chronological catalog of works, a list of his own publications, and a schedule of exhibitions.

457. Grupa Realistów. W kręgu realizmu. XI [i.e., Jedenasta] Krajowa Wystawa Prac, Warszawa, Zachęta, grudzień 1976–styczeń 1977. [The Realists Group. In the grip of realism. The Eleventh Polish Exhibition in Art] Warszawa, "Zachęta," December 1976– January 1977] Warszawa, Centralne Biuro

Wystaw Artystycznych, 1977. [102] p., illus. N7255.P6G8 1977

Sponsored by the Ministry of Culture and Art, and the Polish Visual Arts Association.

Catalog edited by Barbara Mitschein.

Eighty artists participated in this exhibition, in which 367 works were shown. Barbara Zbrożyna and Adam Myjak, whose sculptures express past tragic experience; the portrait painter Kazimierz Poczmański; the landscape painter Magdalena Spasowicz; and draftsman and printmaker Eugeniusz Stec.

[22]. GRYGLEWICZ, Tomasz.
Groteska w sztuce polskiej XX wieku. [The grotesque in Polish twentieth-century art] Kraków, Wydawnictwo Literackie, 1984. 190 p. 56 p. of plates, illus. N7255.P6G83 1984

Bibliographic references.

The grotesque is traced from the Domus Aurea to Polish art of the 1970s. Different facets of the subject are examined, from lyrical and expressionistic grotesquerie, to the avant-garde. Among the many artists included are two who were active around 1900, Leon Chwistek and Witold Wojtkiewicz, and two moderns, Stefan Żechowski and Bronisław Linke.

458. HERMANSDORFER, Mariusz.
Alfons Mazurkiewicz. Wrocław, Biuro Wystaw Artystycznych, 1976. 109 p. illus. ND955.P63M3962 1976

Catalog of the exhibition held at the Galeria Sztuki Współczesnej "Awangarda," Wrocław, December 1976– January 1977.

Introduction in Polish and English.

Bibliographic references.

Mazurkiewicz (1922–1975) painted architectural landscapes of naive simplicity. His colorist paintings—essentially non-objective—give the appearance of tufts of grass or ostrich feathers. He belonged to the Wrocław group of artists, exhibited mostly in that city, and was a faculty member of its Higher School of Art.

459. JAKIMOWICZ, Irena.
Witkacy, the painter. Warszawa, Auriga, Wydawnicaw Artystyczne i Filmowe, 1987. 22 p., 206 color illus. N7255.P63W47213 1987

Translated from the Polish by Ewa Krasińska.

Bibliography: p. 18.
"Stanisław Ignacy Witkiewicz."

Also available in Polish and German.

Witkacy (Stanisław Ignacy Witkiewicz, 1885–1939) was a painter whose style ran from Symbolism and Art Nouveau to Surrealism, with consistently vigorous artistic expression. His work is reproduced here in 206 color plates, along with a short introduction to his art, a list of his theoretical writings, and a list of his exhibitions.

460. JAREMA, Joseph.
Jarema. [Publié par] Marie Sperling et Christian Leprette. Preface de Pierre Courthion. Paris, Imprimerie Union, 1978. 203 p. (24 leaves of color plates), illus. ND955.P6J32 1978

Text by Michel Seuphor, François Gachot, Jacques

Lepage, Joseph Czapski, Pierre Courthion, et al.

Bibliography: p. 201.

Józef Jarema, born in 1900 in the province of Lwów, died in 1974 in Munich. He was a painter, sculptor, weaver, and playwright who recognized his coloristic gifts at an early age. Essays trace his life and work from Paris and Italy in 1924–30 to his return to Kraków and Warsaw, and the resumption of his career after 1946 in Italy and France. Photographs of the artist, his friends, and associates. His sister, Maria Jarema, born 1908, is the well-known sculptress and painter.

461. JAWORSKA, Janina.

"Nie wszystek umrę."
Twórczość plastyczna Polaków w hitlerowskich więzieniach i obozach koncentracyjnych, 1939–1945.["Not all of me shall die." The creative visual arts of Poles in Nazi prisons and concentration camps, 1939–1945] Warszawa, Książka i Wiedza, 1975. 392 p. 622 illus. (part color), ports. N7255.P6J36

Bibliographic references.

One of the best books of its kind: comprehensive, detailed, and extensively illustrated. Anguished documents, mostly portraits, that acutely capture the great suffering in recurring scenes of cruel everyday life. Artists listed according to the prisons and camps in which they were incarcerated. Ninety-six who were professional artists are given extended biographical notices.

462. JAWORSKA, Władysława.

Tadeusz Makowski, polski malarz w Paryżu. [Tadeusz Makowski, Polish painter in Paris] Wrocław, Zakład

Narodowy im. Ossolińskich, 1976. 162 p. 62 leaves of plates, illus. (part color). ND955.P63M3125

Bibliography: p. 147–54.

Full-scale study of the painter Makowski (1882–1932), who was influenced by Puvis de Chavannes and Cubism, and adopted a spare and naive style. Works in oil and watercolor; also drawings and prints. Documentation: correspondence, literary fragments, reviews, and casual references.

463. KANTOR, Tadeusz.

Tadeusz Kantor.
Metamorphoses. Paris, Chêne/Hachette, 1982. 141 p. illus. NX571.P64K362 1982

Born in 1915, Kantor went through an evolution in his art, from metaphoric, surrealistic compositions to abstract art—especially tachism—which he adopted during his stay in France.

464. KĘPIŃSKA, Alicja.

Nowa sztuka, sztuka polska w latach 1945–1978. [The new art. Polish art in the years 1945–1978] Warszawa, Auriga, 1981. 279 p. illus. (part color). N7255.P6K46

Bibliographic references.

Intellectual and aesthetic context, as demonstrated by chapters on the polyphonic model of art of the 1960s and "Space and Light: parameters of the new sensibility." Well-chosen, interesting illustrations: 183 in black and white, fifteen in color.

[325]. KĘPIŃSKI, Zdzisław.

Impresjonism polski. [Polish Impressionism] Warszawa, Arkady, 1961. 53 p. 27 black and

white illus., 24 color illus. DK691.K4 folio

Summary and list of illustrations in English, French, and German.

Bibliography: p. 29–30.

Valuable as a compilation on Polish artists who painted in the impressionist style, and for extended summaries in English, French, and German of the style's history in Poland.

The twenty-four paintings reproduced in color are the works of Aleksander Gierymski (1851–1901), Władysław Podkowiński (1866–1895), Józef Pankiewicz (1866–1940), Leon Wyczółkowski (1852–1936), Władysław Ślewiński (1854–1918), Olga Boznańska (1865–1940), Józef Mehoffer (1869–1946), Jan Stanisławski (1860–1906), and Wojciech Weiss (1875–1950).

465. KĘPIŃSKI, Zdzisław.

Piotr Potworowski. Warszawa, Arkady, 1978. 46 p. 77 illus. (part color). ND955.P63P634

The painter Piotr Potworowski (d. 1962), a greatly gifted colorist whose sensibility was paired with a powerful pictorial intuition, trained in Paris in the 1930s and traveled extensively throughout Europe and North Africa. He spent the war years in London, and then returned to Poland. His works are in most of the Polish museums. Fine color reproductions.

466. KOBZDEJ, Aleksander.

Katalog wystawy Aleksandra Kobzdeja, Poznań 1969. [Exhibition catalog of work by Aleksander Kobzdej] Poznań, Muzeum Narodowe w Poznaniu, 1969. 183 p. plates (part color), port. N7255.P63K6

Biographical notes on the painter by Maria Berdyszakowa. Bibliographies.

The artist (1920–1972) here exhibits his coloristic, impressionist, and abstract art of 1961–68. Catalog of seventy-nine paintings. A biographical outline mentions his work in the style of Socialist Realism, his participation in the design of distinguished monuments to heroism (Gdynia, Bydgoszcz), and his famous painting Give me a brick.

[415]. Kolor w malarstwie polskim 19 i 20 wieku. Katalog wystawy. [Color in Polish painting of the nineteenth and twentieth centuries. Exhibition catalog] Muzeum Narodowe w Poznaniu, czerwiec-październik 1978. Poznań, Muzeum Narodowe, 1978. 113 p. 68 plates (part color). ND955.P6K64

Collective work edited by Maria Berdyszakowa.

Bibliographic references.

The authors trace the history of impressionism and colorism in Poland. Biographical notes included on eighty-five artists.

467. KOWALSKA, Bożena.
Polska awangarda malarska, 1945–1970. Szanse i mity. [The Polish avant-garde, 1945–1970. Fortune and myths] Warszawa, Państwowe Wydawnictwo Naukowe, 1975. 242 p. illus. (part color).

Summary in English and Russian.

Bibliography: p. 193–219.

A searching and intellectually challenging argument, rendered in excellent English translation, regarding the place of Polish painting in

West European and American pictorial expression. Argues convincingly for phases of autonomous Polish expression that are "more profound, fuller, and richer than elsewhere."

468. KOWALSKA, Bożena.
Polska awangarda malarska, 1945–1980. Szanse i mity. [Polish avant-garde painting, 1945–1980. Fortune and myths] 2d rev. and enl. edition. Warszawa, Państwowe Wydawnictwo Naukowe, 1988. 384 p. [108] plates, facsims., ports. N7255.P6K642

Bibliography: p. 313–50.

Summary in English.

A chronology and analysis of the transformation in Polish painting during the thirty-five year period. Ranges from the counter-exhibition by "Group 55" at the Desa Salon in the Old Town of Warsaw (1955) to ritual art, short avant-garde films, and visual theater. Among the artists included are Tadeusz Kantor, Jonasz Stern, Henry Stażewski, Zbigniew Dłubak, Maria Jarema, Władysław Hasior, Tadeusz Brzozowski, Jerzy Nowosielski, Roman Opałka, Magdalena Abakanowicz, Józef Szajna, and Jerzy Grotowski.

469. Kraków. Muzeum Narodowe w Krakowie. Olga Boznańska (1865–1940). Wystawa zbiorowa. [Collective exhibition] Kraków, Muzeum Narodowe w Krakowie, 1960. 84 p. 56 plates. ND 699.B69K7

Bibliography: p. 77–80.

Catalog compiled by Helena Blumówna, Zofia Tobiaszowa, and Zofia Kucielska.

Olga Boznańska studied in Kraków and Munich, with K. Kricheldorf and W. Dürr, then opened her own studio

in Munich in 1889. In Paris—her permanent home, beginning in 1898—her studio was a center for Polish cultural life. She was a member of the "Sztuka" Society of Polish Artists and the Société Nationale des Beaux-Arts. Fascinated by Velázquez and Goya, her work centered on portraits, but also included still lifes and landscapes, painted almost exclusively on cardboard. A catalog of 172 paintings, but only fifty-six are reproduced.

[41]. Krakowscy malarze, rzeźbiarze i graficy w 40 lecie Polski Ludowej, lipiec-sierpień 1985. [Cracovian painters, sculptors and printmakers on the fortieth anniversary of Peoples' Poland [exhibition catalog] July–August 1985] Kraków, Urząd miasta Krakowa, Biuro Wystaw Artystycznych, 1985. 1 vol. illus. N7255. P62K777 1985

Edited by Joanna Radzikowska.

Photogaphs by Krzysztof Rzepecki.

Includes paintings, sculptures, and prints by Polish artists. Addresses of the artists are given as well as a list of the most important events in the visual arts in Kraków from 1945 to 1985, arranged chronologically.

[296]. LANGSNER, Jules.
Modern art in Poland. The legacy and the revival. Art International, vol. 5, no. 7. Zurich, J. Fitzsimmons, 1961, p. 22–29. illus. N1.A1A7

Provides a penetrating review of twentieth-century Polish sculpture and painting. Discusses various artists' groups and trends in their development. Concludes with a list of his choices for the most gifted modern painters, in which he includes Tadeusz Kantor (b. 1915), Jan Lebenstein (b. 1930), Bronisław Kierzkowski (b. 1924), Stefan Gierowski (b. 1925), and Wojciech Fangor. Twenty-six photographs of modern Polish artists, sculptures, and paintings.

470. LEMPICKA, Tamara de.
Tamara de Lempicka. Introduzione di Giancarlo Marmori; Con di diario di Aelis Mazoyer governante di Gabriele d'Annunzio a cura di Piero Chiara e Federico Roncoroni. Parma, F.M. Ricci, 1977. 155 p. 63 illus. (part color). ND955.P63L457 folio

Lempicka (1906–1980) was a portraitist of considerable pictorial invention and psychological insight who channeled a romantic temperament into artistic expression. Thirty-three full-page and eight quarter-page reproductions in color of portraits and figure studies. The text gives biographical data: trained in Paris by Maurice Denis, she was influenced by André Lhote. Many paintings cited by title, but not reproduced.

471. LIGOCKI, Alfred.
Józef Pankiewicz. Warszawa, RSW Prasa-Książka-Ruch, 1973. 102 p. illus. (part color). ND955.P63P375

Bibliography: p. 97.
Chronology of Pankiewicz's artistic career.

Józef Pankiewicz (1866–1940) who studied painting in Warsaw and in St. Petersburg (1885–1886), later traveled extensively to France, Italy, Holland, Belgium, England, Germany, and Austria. In 1906, he became professor at the Kraków Academy of Fine Arts. From 1914

to 1919 he lived in Spain. He exhibited his work in Paris in 1922, 1927, and 1929, and spent the remainder of his life there. He was awarded the French Legion of Honor in 1928.

Influenced initially by Aleksander Gierymski, he eventually abandoned realism and became an Impressionist. He then moved in the direction of Symbolism, and later returned to an emphasis on color. Pankiewicz was important in the development of colorism; his works include primarily landscapes, still lifes, and portraits.

472. LUDOMIR Sleńdziński.
Pamiętnik wystawy. [Ludomir Śleńdziński. Memento of an exhibition] Warszawa, Muzeum Narodowe w Warszawie, 1977. 280 p. illus. ND955.P6S5534 1977

A collective work.
Introduction by Stanisław Lorentz.

A descriptive list of seventy-five paintings—dating mainly from the 1970s—by the distinguished portrait painter Ludomir Sleńdziński (1889–1980) that supplements the catalog published on the occasion of his exhibition in 1973 at the National Museum, Warsaw. In addition to an essay on the substance and form of his creativity (he matured as a classical realist in the 1920s), there is a study on other visual artists in Wilno in the years 1920 to 1939, illustrating the strength of that school of painting, and a study on Sleńdziński; contributions to the illustrated trade quarterly Południe.

[47]. ŁUKASZEWICZ, Piotr, and Jerzy Malinowski.
Ekspresjonizm w sztuce polskiej. [Expressionism in Pol-

ish art] Wrocław, Muzeum Narodowe we Wrocławiu, 1980. 100 p. 100 black and white illus., and 6 color plates. N7255.P6L814

Exhibition catalog.
Summary in English.
Bibliography: p. 52–54.

The exhibition included paintings executed between 1912 and 1937. The catalog lists over 600 works, of which 206 are reproduced. Traces the history of the movement and foreign artists' influences, and provides a chronology of the activities of the Polish Expressionists.

473. ŁUKASZEWICZ, Piotr.
Zrzeszenie artystów plastyków ARTES 1929–1935. [Association of visual art artists ARTES 1929–1935] Wrocław, Zakład Narodowy im. Ossolińskich, 1975. 197 p. illus., ports. (Studia z historii sztuki, vol. 24) N7255.P6L82

Edited by Zofia Dillenius.
Bibliographic references.
Includes a chronicle of activities of the Association.
Summary, list of artists and their reproduced works, and table of contents in French.

The short-lived movement of visual artists was related to surrealism and cubism. This revised doctoral dissertation—submitted at the Art Institute of the Polish Academy of Sciences (Warsaw)—describes the art movement and its association ARTES, which was begun in Lwów in 1929 by the artists Jerzy Janisch (1901–1962), Aleksander Krzywobłocki (b. 1901), and Mieczysław Wysocki (b. 1899).

[328]. Malarstwo Polski południowo-wschodniej 1900–1980. Wystawa. [The painting of souteastern Poland 1900–1980. An exhibition] Rzeszów, Biuro Wystaw Artystycznych, 1982, 253 p. illus. ND955.P6M29 1982

Edited by Wiesław Banach, et al.

Covers twelve cities, including Przemyśl, Rzeszów, Sandomierz, Sanok, and Tarnów. A history of styles pursued in each city, the artists' organizations, exhibitions, patrons, and the growth of private collections. Biographical sketches of 120 artists, among them J. Malczewski (b. 1854 in Radom). Over one hundred poorly reproduced illustrations.

[331]. Malarstwo polskie między wojnami 1918–1939.

[Polish painting pbetween the wars 1918–1939] Warszawa, Auriga, 1982. 391 p. 225 color illus. ND955.P6P63 1982

By Joanna Pollakówna.

Biographical sketches of the artists by Wanda M. Rudzińska.

Summary in German.

Bibliographic references.

Among 225 paintings selected by the author, the most interesting ones are those by M. Jarema, A Michalak, L. Sleńdziński, R.K. Witkowski, and J. Zamoyski.

474. Malarze z kręgu Tadeusza Pruszkowskiego, Bractwo św. Łukasza; Szkoła Warszawska; Loża Wolnomularska; Grupa Czwarta. [Painters in the Circle of Tadeusz Pruszkowski. The Brotherhood of St. Luke; the School of Warsaw; the Free Masons Lodge; The Fourth Group] (exhibition) Muzeum Narodowe w Warszawie, Wrzesień-październik 1978. Warszawa, 1978. 67 p. illus. N7255.P6M35 1978

Honoring Tadeusz Pruszkowski, the pre-1939 educator at the Academy of Fine Arts, Warsaw; an exhibition by more than forty painters with recent realist and neo-realist artistic tendencies. An account of pre-World War II aesthetic currents.

[422]. MEHOFFER, Józef.

Józef Mehoffer; katalog wystawy zbiorowej. [Józef Mehoffer; catalog of an exhibition of collected works] Kraków, Muzeum Narodowe w Krakowie, 1964. 190 p. 80 illus. ND699.M34T6

Introduction by Helena Blum. Bibliography: p. 213–35.

Catalog of 457 works: paintings, including studies; cartoons for stained glass windows; decorative projects and cartoons; drawings and watercolors; prints (in dry point, etching, engraving, verni mous, lithography); scenic design. List of portrait subjects. Modest illustrations that nevertheless convey the superior gifts of the artist.

475. Mieczysław Szczuka.

Warszawa, Wydawnictwa Artystyczne i Filmowe, 1965. 192 p. illus. N7255.P63S9536 1965

Authors: Anatol Stern and Mieczysław Berman.

Summary in Russian, French, English, and German.

A pioneer of constructivism in Poland, Mieczysław Szczuka (1898–1927) was a force in modern painting and applied graphic art. Claiming architecture to be the synthesis of all the arts, Szczuka created sculpture including mobiles, paintings, drawings, and was the first Polish exponent of collage and photomontage. Co-founder of the group and periodical "Blok"

(1923/24). Many reproductions of his applied graphics.

476. New York. Museum of Modern Art. 15 [i.e., fifteen] Polish painters. [Exhibition catalog] Garden City, N.Y., Distributed by Doubleday, 1961. 64 p., illus. ND691.N52

By Peter Selz.

Paintings dating between 1955 and 1961 that have maintained their vitality and high interest. Insightful choices from collections in the United States, Montreal, London, Paris, and Poland. The painters represented include Henry Stażewski, Tadeusz Kantor, Tadeusz Brzozowski, Teresa Rudowicz, Wojciech Fangor, Stefan Gierowski, Tadeusz Dominik, Teresa Pągowska, Jerzy Nowosielski, Bronisław Kierzkowski, Aleksander Kobzdej, Jan Lebenstein, Piotr Potworowski, Jerzy Tchórzewski, and Marian Warzecha.

[55]. Obóz koncentracyjny Oświęcim w twórczości artystycznej. [The Oświęcim concentration camp in art] 2d ed. Oświęcim, Wydawnictwo Państwowego Muzeum, 1961–62. 4 v. in 1. illus. (part fold.). N7255.P6O26 1961

Text by Kazimierz Smoleń.

Text in Polish, English, French, German, and Russian.

Contents: Vol. 1–3. Malarstwo [Painting]—v. 4. Rzeźba. [Sculpture].

The first volume (xviii, 79 p.) reproduces drawings in coal by Jerzy Adam Brandhuber; the second (xxii, 40 p.), drawings and a woodcut by Mieczysław Kościelniak; and the third (iii, 61 p.), drawings by Maria Hiszpańska-Neumann, Janina

Tollik, Franciszek Jaźwiecki, Tadeusz Myszkowski, Jerzy Potrzebowski, and Władysław Siwek. The fourth volume (74 p.) presents photographs of sculptures by Mieczysław Stobierski, Hanna Raynoch, Tadeusz Myszkowski, Vida Jocić, Hubert van Lith, and G.W. Mizandari. All the artists were professionals, and all were prisoners at Oświęcim. Their works reveal the daily experiences of hunger, exhaustion, torture, and death. Eleven penetrating portraits by Franciszek Jaźwiecki were drawn from life at the camp.

477. Ogólnopolska Wystawa Malarstwa i Grafiki, 1st.

Warsaw, 1986. 1. [i.e. Pierwsza] Ogólnopolska Wystawa Malarstwa i Grafiki członków Związku Polskich Artystów Malarzy i Grafików. Marzec 1986 Warszawa "Zachęta." [The First National Exhibition of Paintings and Prints by the members of the Association of Polish Painters and Printmakers. March 1986 Warsaw, "Zachęta." Warszawa, Zachęta, 1986. 346 p. illus. N7255.P6O335 1986

Exhibition catalog edited by Alicja Goduń and Artur Palasiewicz.

The illustrations are arranged alphabetically by artists' surnames, thus creating awkward juxtapositions. The 368 works are keyed to biographical sketches.

478. OKOŃSKA, Alicja.

Malarki polskie. [Polish women painters] Warszawa, Nasza Księgarnia, 1976. 262 p. illus., ports. ND955.P604

Bibliographic references.

Biographies of nine modern painters, the oldest born 1837, the youngest, 1894. The latter, Zofia Lubańska-Stryjeńska, is celebrated for her art deco renderings of costumes and dances. Another recognized talent is Anna Bilińska-Bohdanowicz (1857–1983). Others deserve fame. Reproductions of self-portraits and other works—regrettably in a poor printing.

479. OLSZAŃSKI, Kazimierz.

Wojciech Kossak. 3d enlarged ed. Wrocław, Zakład Narodowy im. Ossolińskich, 1982. 79 p. 208 p. of plates, illus. (part color). ND955.P63K696 1982

Summary and description of illustrations in English.

Bibliographic references.

Wojciech Kossak (1856–1942) was a prodigiously creative painter with a facile brush. He produced mainly battle scenes recreating past Polish glories. At a time of political decline. these works nourished patriotic sentiments.

Highly esteemed by his European and Polish contemporaries, Kossak painted portraits of many well-known personalities (Generals J. Pershing, F. Foch, M. Weygand) as well as members of high society. A substantial publication with many fine color illustrations appropriate to the heroic subject matter. Included are 321 reproductions of the artist's work.

480. Picasso w Polsce. [Picasso in Poland] Praca zbiorowa pod redakcją Mieczysława Bibrowskiego. Kraków, Wydawnictwo Literackie, 1979. 296 p. illus. (part color). N6853.P5P53

Collective work edited by Mieczysław Bibrowski.

Summary in English, French, and Russian.

Originates from Picasso's visit to Poland, 25 August–6 September 1948. Recollections by participants on various aspects of the occasion. Essay on Picasso's influence on Polish art, theater, and literature. Catalog and reproductions of drawings, prints, and ceramics in Polish public collections (twenty ceramics, gift of Picasso; ten prints, gift of D.H. Kahnweiler). Reproduces drawings by Picasso made during the sojourn.

[63]. POLLAKÓWNA, Joanna.

Formiści. [The Formists] Wrocław, Zakład Narodowy im. Ossolińskich, 1972. 199 p. illus (Studia z Historii Sztuki, vol. 14) N7255.P6P64

Sponsored by the Polska Akademia Nauk, Instytut Sztuki.

Summary in French.

Bibliographic references.

Pollakówna's work is one of the first on Formiści (the Formists) to provide a broad picture of that short-lived movement. The first use of the name Formists to denote the group was at the second exhibition of Polish Expressionists, in August 1918. The following year an exhibition of Formist art was held in Warsaw. Especially notable among the Formists were Stanisław Ignacy Witkiewicz, Leon Chwistek, Tytus Czyżewski, Zbigniew Pronaszko, and Andrzej Pronaszko.

[67]. Polskie życie artystyczne w latach 1915–1939. [Polish artistic life in the years 1915–1939] Wrocław, Zakład Narodowy im. Ossolińskich, 1974. 738 p. illus. N7255.P6P677

Sponsored by the Art Institute of the Polish Academy of Sciences.

Collective work edited by Aleksander Wojciechowski. Bibliographies.

More than half the volume is devoted to a chronology of the major artistic events throughout the country and Polish art events abroad (United States, United Kingdom, France, Germany, Latin America). Covers competitions, with names of submitting artists, exhibitions and their participants, dedications of monuments, publications of illustrated books, and theatrical productions of artistic significance. Special chapters on architecture, art education, and artists' organizations. The editors are sensitive to the participation of women in the arts. Numerous photographs.

481. PORĘBSKI, Mieczysław.
Les avant-gardes. Artibus et historiae, no. 10, 1984, p. 147–64. illus. NX1.A1A77 no. 10
Bibliographic references.

In a discussion of the theories and doctrines of the twentieth-century avant-garde, Stanisław Ignacy Witkiewicz is seen as an artist who viewed his calling as a real social and moral choice, in contrast to Władysław Strzemiński and Katarzyna Kobro, who sought a utopian language where art and actual space were undivided.

[70]. Presences polonaises.
Witkiewicz, Constructivisme, les contemporains: L'art vivant autour du Musée de Łódź. Centre Georges Pompidou, 23 juin–26 septembre, 1983. [Exhibition catalog] Paris, Le Centre, 1983. 335

p. illus. (part color).
NX571.P6P74 1983
Exhibition catalog.

A French tribute to the Museum of Art in Łódź, which was inaugurated in 1931 and is among the first museums of modern art in Europe, and to the multidisciplinary exponents of modern art movements: Stanisław Ignacy Witkiewicz, visual artist, dramatist, writer, originator of "Czysta Forma" (Pure Form), and his contemporary Bruno Schulz; the many practitioners of Constructivism, also in architecture, and of Futurism. Modern conceptual visual artists, writers, dramatists, composers. Biographies, oeuvres catalogs, collection of the Łódź Museum. An important investigation and analysis of modern art in Poland.

482. RADAJEWSKI, Adam.
Józef Mehoffer. Warszawa, Krajowa Agencja Wydawnicza RSW Prasa-Książka-Ruch, 1976. 126 p. illus. (part color).
ND955.P63M473
Bibliography: p. 121.

A publication worthy of the great talent of Józef Mehoffer (1869–1946). Fine color reproductions convey his luxuriant color in interior subjects, in portraits, and especially in the cartoons for stained glass windows. One major commission was the windows at the Cathedral of Fribourg (Switzerland). Earlier windows at the cathedrals of Wawel and Płock.

483. RUSZCZYC, Ferdynand.
Ferdynand Ruszczyc, 1870–1963 [i.e. 1936]; katalog. Warszawa, Muzeum Narodowe, 1964. 164 p. plates, port.
ND699.R87R8

Edited by Janina Ruszczycówna.

Summary in French and Russian.

Bibliography: p. 27–33.

Catalog by Irena Kołoszyńska and others.

The authors sought to write a catalogue raisonné, but admit to gaps. Prolific production of the artist who worked mainly in Wilno. Divided into sketches and oil paintings; drawings; and prints (book covers, title pages, vignettes). Illustrations are inadequate.

484. 17 [i.e., Seventeen] Polish painters. Exhibition circulated by the D'Arcy Galleries. New York, 1966–67. 111 p. (chiefly illus.) ports. ND955.P6S4

Exhibition organized by the Desa Gallery, Warsaw, Poland.

Translation by Krzysztof Klinger.

Painters wo achieved a mature style after World War II; representative examples in the range of international styles of the late 1940s to 1960s.

485. SLEŃDZIŃSKI, Ludomir.
Katalog wystawy malarstwa i rzeźby Ludomira Śleńdzińskiego. [Catalog of an exhibition of painting and sculpture by Ludomir Sleńdziński] Białystok, Muzeum Okręgowe, 1972. 97 p. illus. ND955.P63S55

Catalog prepared by Irena Kołoszyńska.

Bibliography: p. 24–27.

486. Tre pionérer for Polsk Avant-Garde: [Władysław Strzemiński, Katarzyna Kobro, Henryk Stażewski;] med et appendix om Franciska Clausen. Three pioneers of the Polish

Avant-Garde; including an appendix on Franciska Clausen. Odense, Fyns Kunstmuseum, 1985. 136 p. illus. (part color). N7255.P6T73 1985

Catalog of the exhibition edited by Lise-Lotte Blom.

In Danish and English.

Bibliographies.

Exhibition held June 8–August 31, 1985 at Fyns Kunstmuseum, Odense.

487. WEISS, Wojciech.

Wojciech Weiss 1875–1850. Wystawa monograficzna. [Wojciech Weiss 1875–1950. An exhibition] Muzeum Narodowe w Poznaniu, Czerwiec-Wrzesień 1977. Poznań, 1977. 386 p. illus. ND955.P63W442 1977

Introduction by Agnieszka Ławniczakowa.

Chronology of life and work by Jerzy Nowakowski.

Bibliography: p. 153–63.

Painter, sculptor, printmaker formed by the Polish Art Nouveau (Młoda Polska), of which Kraków was the pictorial and literary cradle. Influence of E. Munch through S. Przybyszewski. Weiss's "psychic naturalism" gave way to a "middle class Arcadia." Chronology of his life and work, and a catalogue raisonné. Good English summaries.

488. W kręgu "Chimery."

Sztuka i literatura polskiego modernizmu. [In the circle of "Chimera." Art and literature of Polish modernism] Katalog-pamiętnik wystawy, 25.IX.1979 r.–30.V.1980 r. Warszawa, Muzeum Literatury im. Adama Mickiewicza w Warszawie, 1980. 166 p. 79 p. of plates, illus. NX571.P6W2 1980

Summary in French.

Bibliographic references.

Catalog by Mirosława Puchalska and Wojciech Chmurzyński.

Catalog of an exhibition commemorating the periodical Chimera, *published in Warsaw 1901–1907. The contributing visual artists represented the Polish manifestations of art nouveau (Młoda Polska): Okuń, Mehoffer, Krzyżanowski, Wojtkiewicz, and others. A complete list is included. Among the literary protagonists were Leśmian, Przybyszewski, and Reymont.*

489. Władysław Strzemiński in memoriam. Łódź, PP "Sztuka Polska" Oddział w Łodzi, 1988. 190 p. illus (part color). N7255.P63S7938 1988

Edited by Janusz Zagrodzki.

Bibliography: p. 190.

Five sketches of remembrances by Strzemiński's friends, essays by nine artists about his work and theories of art, good reproductions of his paintings and drawings, and a collection of his selected writings.

[106]. WŁODARCZYK, Wojciech.

Socrealizm. Sztuka polska w latach 1950–1954. [Socialist realism. Polish art during the years 1950–1954] Paris, Libella, 1986. 135 p. 12 illus. (Historia i terazniejszosc, 11) N7255.P6W57 1986

Looks at socialist realism as a worldwide phenomenon. Examines its theory and sources under headings such as "Tradition" and "Mysticism of Architecture." Then looks at

applications (as in the Academy of Fine Arts, Warsaw). The third section is titled "Irreconcilable Strategies." A scholarly work that draws together politics, visual arts, architecture, and literature.*

490. WOJCIECHOWSKI, Aleksander.

Młode malarstwo polskie 1944–1974. [Painting of the young Polish generation 1944–1974] Wrocław, Zakład Narodowy im. Ossolińskich, 1975. 162 p. illus. (part color). N7255.P6W6

Bibliographic references.

Traces developments since 1946 in the visual arts, often comparing a particular impetus with the equivalent French situation. Among the artists included in this study are Felicjan Szczęsny Kowarski, Maria Jarema, Andrzej Wróblewski, Marek Włodarski, Tadeusz Brzozowski, Jerzy Nowosielski, Andrzej Kobzdej, Tadeusz Kantor, Jerzy Wolff, Henryk Stażewski, Artur Nacht-Sambrowski, and Roman Opałka.

491. ZANOZIŃSKI, Jerzy.

Contemporary Polish painting. Warsaw, Arkady, 1975. 140 p. color illus. ND955.P6Z25

Sixty-three painters, the oldest born in 1875, the youngest having matured in the 1950s, selected to represent all of Poland's artistic communities, and all trends over the past thirty years. Biographical sketches and essays that accompany the reproductions of their paintings characterize the painters' evolution as artists. All paintings in the collection of the National Museum, Warsaw.

V. Prints

V. Prints

❀

[5.] BANACH, Jerzy.
Ikonografia Wawelu.
[Iconography of the Wawel]
Kraków, 1977. 2 v. illus (Źródła
do dziejów Wawelu, vol. 9,
parts 1 and 2)
DK4735.W3Z76 v. 9
> Summary in French in v. 2.
> Bibliography references.

*In vol 1, panoramas and long views of
the buildings from various vantage
points. In vol. 2, the buildings and
interiors in detail. A work of great
interest that assembles and describes
the subject matter of prints, drawings,
watercolors, and photographs, from
the sixteenth to the nineteenth century.
Full scholarly apparatus. A delightful compendium.*

492. BIAŁOSTOCKI, Jan.
W. pracowniach dawnych
grafików. [In the workshops of
old master printmakers]
Warszawa, Arkady, 1957. 125 p.
illus. NE400.B5
> Bibliography: p. 118–22.

*An abbreviated history of printmak-
ing in Poland. The illustrations for
the chapter on Polish printmaking
include the printer's mark of
Stanislaus Polonus, circa 1500;
landscape etching by Bogdan
Lubieniecki (1653–1729) in the
Dutch style; Michał Płoński
(1778–1812), working in a
Rembrandt-cum-Rowlandson style;
and the lithographer Jan Feliks
Piwarski (1795–1859). Other illustrations are of techniques: engraving,
represented by J. Falck's portrait of
Frederick III of Denmark, and a*

*printing workshop, in a drawing by
D. Chodowiecki.*

**493. BÓBR, Maciej, *and*
Krzysztof Kruzel.**
Katalog rycin Biblioteki
Polskiej Akademii Nauk w
Krakowie. Szkoła niemiecka XV
i XVI w. [Catalog of prints in the
Library of the Polish Academy of
Sciences in Kraków. The Ger-
man school of the fifteenth and
sixteenth century] Wrocław,
Zakład Narodowy im.
Ossolińskich, 1987. 180 p. 48 p.
of illus. NE651.B58 1987
> Edited by Maria Macharska.
> Summary in French.
> Bibliography: p. 148–49.

*Formed from the eighteenth-century
Moszyński collection and a collection
assembled in the nineteenth century at
the Bibliothèque Polonaise in Paris
that was then transferred to Poland in
1931. Eight hundred eighteen prints
that include not only the major
artists, such as Schongauer, Dürer,
Altdorfer, and Baldung, but also
extremely obscure artists such as
Wenzel von Olmutz, G. Zehender,
Hans Leinberger, and the Monogramists MZ and ASG. Twenty-two
pages on watermarks. Only minimal
cataloging data.*

[252.] CEMPLA, Józef.
Wawel. Katedra Królewska.
[Wawel. The Royal Cathedral]
Kraków, "Starodruk," 1957. 6 p.
16 plates of drawings.
NA5691.C4 folio

*Sixteen drawings by Józef Cempla,
fifteen of which are in pencil, one in
charcoal. Most are on paper that is
tinted yellow, with white highlights
reserved.*

494. CHODOWIECKI, Daniel.
Daniel Chodowiecki.
Warszawa, Sztuka, 1953. 16 p. of
text, 40 plates of illus.
NC251.C5A4 1953
> Introduction by A.
Ryszkiewicz.
> Bibliography: p. 13.
> Portfolio prepared by Wacław
Zawadzki.

*Presents a list of works by the artist
on Polish subjects: portraits, nos.
1–13; drawings, including those that
were executed in prints by others, nos.
14–76; prints by the artist, nos.
77–111, with Engelmann references.
Forty plates, of which twenty-six
reproduce drawings selected from
those made on the journey from Berlin
to Gdańsk, 1773; eight plates of
Polish history; five portraits; and a
sheet of sketches from life, including
one of a man playing a violin while
seated on a large dog.*

495. CHODOWIECKI, Daniel N.
Von Berlin nach Danzig, eine
Kunstlerfahrt im Jahre 1773.
Leipzig, Insel-verlag, 1923. 94 p.
port., 83 plates on 22 leaves.
NC1145.C3 1923
> Edited by Wolfgang von
Oettingen.

*Eighty-three plates of reproductions
of selected drawings, recording the*

artist's journey from Berlin to Gdańsk, such as crossing the Odra River on a raft with his horse, but mainly views of the streets of Gdańsk, interiors of houses of the high bourgeoisie, including the artist himself drawing portraits and sketches of notable citizens. Valuable for the authenticity of its representations.

496. CHOJECKA, Ewa.

Krakowska grafika kalendarzowa i astronomiczna XVI wieku. [Printed illustrations in calendars and astronomical treatises in Kraków in the sixteenth century] Studia Renesansowe, vol. 3, 1963, p. 319–482. illus. N6991.S87

Summary in French and Russian.

Bibliographic references.

Exhaustive study with copious reproductions of illustrations of celestial phenomena, intended for both popular and scientific consumption. Kraków was central because of the large number of presses and the importance of mathematics and science at the University. Subjects of the illustrations were the labors of the months, personifications of the planets, and geometrical representations of planetary movements. Among the sources were Hans Sebald Beham, Leipzig printers, and Hartmann Schedl's Nuremberg Chronicle.

497. Grafika i rysunki polskie w zbiorach polskich. [Polish prints and drawings in Polish collections] Warszawa, Arkady, 1977. 130 p. 148 illus. (part color). NE735.P6G68

Edited by Maria Mrozińska and Stanisława Sawicka.

Introduction by Alina Chyczewska.

Summary and list of illustrations in French.

Bibliographies.

Prints and drawings by widely known artists along with works by artists virtually unknown to non-Polish historians of art. Among many works placed in the context of European art history are those by T.B. Lubieniecki (1654–1718?), J. Wall (1754–1798), Z. Vogel (1764–1826), P. Michałowski (1800–1891), A.T. Kwiatkowski (1809–1891), B. Zaleski (1819–1880), and J. Chełmoński (1849–1914).

498. GROTTGER, Artur.

Cykle I–IV: Warszawa, Polonia, Lithuania, Wojna. [Cycles I–IV: Warsaw, Polonia, Lithuania, War] Warszawa, H. Altenberg, 1908. 16 p. 34 illus. ND699.G74A43 folio

Cycles I–III with an introduction by Antoni Potocki; Cycle IV introduced by Tadeusz Pini.

Artur Grottger (1837–1867) concentrated his deeply felt patriotism and his power of pictorial drama in these drawings that illustrate, symbolize, and allegorize politics and war in Poland in the 1860s. Crayon drawings with the addition of watercolor in Cycle IV, reproduced on yellow paper.

499. GROTTGER, Artur.

Pozostałe nieznane prace świętej pamięci Artura Grottgera, zebrane i wydane przez jego siostrę. [Works by Artur Grottger, collected and published after the artist's death by his sister] Wiedeń, M. Perles, 1894. 20 plates (in portfolio). ND699.G74A45 folio

Ten portfolios containing twenty heliogravures after drawings in chalk

and wash. Subjects include patriotic and moralizing stories and portraits (Poland as a Crucifixus; Departure for war and return; Mickiewicz; self-portrait when young).

500. GRZENIEWSKI, Ludwik B.

Warszawa Aleksandra Gierymskiego. [The Warsaw of Aleksander Gierymski] Warszawa, Państwowy Instytut Wydawniczy, 1973. 68 p., illus. NC312.P63G534

Life in the city and its environs in the 1880s, drawn by the artist for reproduction in periodicals. Sixty illustrations and notes are important to the history of nineteenth-century wood engraving; included are names of draftsmen who transferred the artist's drawing to the wood blocks, the wood engravers, the wood engraving shops, and the periodicals and dates of publication.

501. HEYDUK, Bronisław.

Dahlbergh w Polsce. Dziennik i ryciny szwedzkie z dziejów "Potopu" 1656–1657. [Dahlbergh in Poland. Diary and Swedish illustrations relating to the history of "The Deluge" (Swedish-Polish War) 1656–1657] Wstęp Adama Przybosia. Wrocław, Zakład Narodowy im. Ossolińskich, 1971. 205 p. illus., port. DL725.D33H49

Dziennik Eryka Dahlbergha: 57–74 (Polish translation of Erik Jonson Dahlberg's *Dagbok*, 1625–1699).

Bibliography: p. 75–76.

Erik Dahlbergh (1625–1703), Swedish soldier and military engineer in the service of King Charles X Gustav, was stationed in Poland from 1656 to 1657, where he made innumerable drawings of great detail and precision, from life, of battles (at Warsaw, July 1656), castle sieges, and city views (Gdańsk, Kraków). The work is in the tradition of Jacques Callot. One hundred ten plates of etchings, after the drawings, by Willem Swidde, Noël Cochin, L. Perelle, and others. Text deals with biography and history, giving little account of the publication of the prints.

502. Inspiracje sztuką Japonii
w malarstwie i grafice polskich modernistów. Katalog. [The inspiration of Japanese art in the painting and prints of modern Polish artists; a catalog] Kielce, Muzeum Narodowe w Kielcach, 1981. 124 p. illus. N7255.P6I57 1981

By Zofia Alberowa and Łukasz Kossowski.

Summaries in English.
Bibliography: p. 79–81.

Japanese woodcuts brought to Poland from Paris in the 1880s and 1890s by F. Jasieński (1862–1901). Exhibition tracing the subject matter, technique, and compositional style these prints fostered in Polish art.

503. IWANOYKO, Eugeniusz.
Jeremiasz Falck Polonus; ze studiów nad grafiką polską XVII w. [Jeremiasz Falck Polonus; studies on Polish prints of the seventeenth century] Poznań, Poznańskie Towarzystwo Przyjaciół Nauk, 1952. 56 p. plates, illus. (Prace Komisji Historii Sztuki, vol. 2, no. 3) NA1191.P6 v. 2, no. 3 NE735.P6

Summary in French.
Bibliographic references.

A peripatetic engraver born in Gdańsk, probably in 1610, Falck

was active in Paris, Stockholm, Amsterdam, Hamburg, and in Danish cities as well as in his own native city, where he died in 1677. This is a scholarly study of the subjects and style of the engraver to the court of Queen Christina of Sweden. He also worked with the engravers of the Rubens school on the Gallery of the Reynst brothers. Falck is important in Polish culture as a portraitist.

In a wide-ranging critique of the book, published in Biuletyn Historii Sztuki, *vol. 16, no. 1, 1954, p. 175–90, Maria Mrozińska makes a substantial contribution to the study of Falck and seventeenth-century engraving. She discusses the relationship of Falck to J. Ziarnko, Hieronymus David, J. Callot, and other contemporaries. She takes issue with Iwanoyko's interpretation of Falck's engraving style and makes corrections and additions.*

504. JAKRZEWSKA-Śnieżko, Zofia.
Gdańsk w dawnych rycinach. [Gdańsk in old etchings] Wrocław, Zakład Narodowy im. Ossolińskich, 1977. 143 p. chiefly illus. NE2143.J34

Summary in English.
Bibliography: p. 139.

More than fifty panoramic city views, and particulars of the port, markets, city gates, and important buildings, such as the astronomical observatory of Jan Hevelius; from Braun and Hogenberg (1573) to the eighteenth century. Poorly reproduced prints, with legends invariably trimmed off. The etchings are in the Library of the Polish Academy of Sciences in Gdańsk.

505. KAEMMERER, Ludwig J.
Chodowiecki. Bielefeld und

Leipzig, Velhagen & Klasing, 1897. [5]–131 p. illus., ports. NE654.C5K3 Rare Bk Coll. Rosenwald Collection

Reproductions of drawings and paintings by Daniel Chodowiecki (1726–1801) of his family. Eight drawings from the sketchbook of his journey from Berlin to Gdańsk, 1773.

506. Katalog rysunków z Gabinetu Rycin Biblioteki Uniwersyteckiej w Warszawie.
[Catalog of drawings from the Print Room of the Warsaw University Library] Warszawa, Państwowe Wydawnictwo Naukowe, 1967–69. 2 v. illus. (Biblioteka Muzealnictwa i Ochrony Zabytków, Series A, vols. 4 and 5) AM70.P6B5, v. 4, 5

Vol. 1: Varsaviana. Rysunki architektoniczne, dekoracyjne, plany i widoki z XVIII i XIX wieku. [Varsaviana. Drawings of architecture and decoration, plans and views of the eighteenth and nineteenth century] 385 p.

V. 2: Miejscowości różne. Rysunki architektoniczne, dekoracyjne, plany i widoki z XVIII i XIX wieku. [Various locations. Drawings of architecture and decoration, plans and views of the eighteenth and nineteenth century] 379 p.

The core of the collection is the abundant and splendid material gathered by King Stanisław August Poniatowski (died 1798) which was acquired for the University Library in 1818. Part 1 of the scholarly catalog, prepared by Teresa Sulerzyska, Stanisława Sawicka, and Jadwiga Trenklerówna, consists of 1,394 items. Undertaken in large part for the monarch, they consist of building projects, including urban plans, churches and chapels, palaces and other residences, academies, monuments, and architectural decorations (triumphal arches, festivals). Part 2, prepared by Teresa Sulerzyska, catalogs nearly one thousand items—projects in Poland arranged topographically, and some designs for foreign locations (Tsarskoe Selo, Versailles). Indexes by person, place name, and by building type. Two hundred fourteen inadequate illustrations.

[394]. KĘPIŃSKA, Alicja.
Jan Piotr Norblin. Wrocław, Zakład Narodowy im. Ossolińskich, 1978. 94 p. 184 illus., ports. N7255.P63N6735 1978
   Bibliographic notes.
Jean-Pierre Norblin de la Gourdaine (1745–1830) is seen here in his capacity as the prolific draftsman. The essay places him in pictorial and historical context. Illustrations compare him to influences (Rembrandt) and contemporaries (Fragonard). Norblin came to Poland in 1774, recorded the battles of 1791 to 1794—including a wounded Kościuszko—and the Enactment of the Third of May Constitution.

507. KOBIELSKI, Dobrosław.
Pejzaże dawnej Warszawy. [Landscapes of old Warsaw] Warszawa, Wydawnictwo Artystyczno-Graficzne, 1974. 258 p. illus. (part color). DK651.W243K6 1974
   Summary in English.
   Bibliography: p. 238–39.
Prospects of the city, views of the streets, buildings, markets, shops, and other sites, in sixteenth- and seventeenth-century woodcuts, etchings, and paintings, but mostly in nineteenth-

century engravings and lithographs. These are juxtaposed with modern photographs of the same sites. Works of art are not particularized beyond artist, subject, medium, and date. Each illustration is described in a paragraph.

508. KOBIELSKI, Dobrosław.
Widoki dawnej Warszawy. [Views of old Warsaw] Wyd. 3. Warszawa, Krajowa Agencja Wydawnicza, 1984. 155 [i.e., 310], xxviii p. illus. (part color). DK4624.K63 1984
   Summary in English.
   Bibliography: p. 157–58.
Buildings, streets, prospects in old representations are juxtaposed with photographs of the same buildings, streets, prospects. Among early views are Braun and Hogenberg (1618) and an oil painting on canvas by Christian Melich, c. 1620. In this third edition, the representations are large and legible.

509. KURKOWA, Alicja.
Grafika illustracyjna gdańskich druków okolicznościowych XVII wieku. [Engravings illustrating ephemera printed in Gdańsk in the seventeenth century] Wrocław, Zakład Narodowy im. Ossolińskich, 1979. 251 p. illus., facsims., ports. NE735.P6K87 1979
   Summary in English and Russian.
   Bibliography: p. 230–36.
Pictorial emblems, coats of arms, portraits illustrating epithalamia, songs, political prints, funeral sermons. List of foreign artists active in Gdańsk and their dates (e.g. Abraham Bloeteling, 1683; Gerard Edelinck, 1683–1700). The distinctive bourgeois climate produced an

atmosphere favorable to the flowering of this art. An original and important study.

510. LEHRS, Max.
Veit Stoss. *In his* Geschichte und kritischer Katalog des Deutschen, Niederlandischen und Französischen Kupperstichs im XV. Jahrhundert. Vol. 8. Wien, Gessellschaft für vervielfaltigende Kunst, 1932. p. 241–70, plates in part containing reproductions of the engravings, p. 233–35. NE1450.L5 folio
Historiography on the artist as printmaker, and an analysis of his style. Catalogue raisonné of the ten engravings, six of which are reproduced.

511. MATEJKO, Jan.
Jan Matejko. Warszawa, Arkady, 1962. 29 p. 234 plates (20 color). ND699.M3S73 folio
   Introduction by Juliusz Starzyński.
Introduction to Jan Matejko (1838–1893), incomparable Polish painter of profoundly patriotic historical subjects. Illustrations, preponderantly of details of the vast canvases and of preparatory drawings, disclose the artist's enormous facility as draftsman.

512. MUNTZ, Jean-Henri.
Jana Henryka Muntza podróże malownicze po Polsce i Ukrainie (1781–1783). Les voyages pittoresques de Jean-Henri Muntz en Pologne et en Ukraine (1781–1783). Warszawa, Wydawnictwo Uniwersytetu Warszawskiego, 1982. 354 p. illus. DK4050.M86 1982
   Album from the collection of drawings in the Warsaw Univer-

sity Library prepared by Elżbieta Budzińska.

Summary in French. Some descriptions in French.

Bibliographic references.

One hundred twenty-six landscape and six costume drawings; descriptions of the views executed by an Alsatian painter, engineer, and architect who traveled in the service of Prince Stanisław Poniatowski, nephew of King Stanisław August Poniatowski.

513. Norblin de la Gourdaine, Jean P. Sejmiki w rysunkach J.P. Norblina. [Local diets in drawings by J.P. Norblin] Warszawa, Arkady, 1958. 29 p., 49 plates. NC1157.N6K4

By Alicja Kępińska.

Bibliographic references.

Invaluable documents of political and social genre executed in the last quarter of the eighteenth century, which perk up seventeenth century realism with eighteenth century buoyancy. Biographical essay.

514. OLSZEWSKI, Andrzej K. Pierwowzory graficzne późnogotyckiej sztuki małopolskiej. [Graphic models for Late Gothic art in Małopolska] Wrocław, Zakład Narodowy im. Ossolińskich, 1975. 240 p. illus. (Studia z Historii Sztuki, vol. 23) N7255.P62M346

Summary, list of illustrations, and table of contents in English.

Bibliography: p. 170–75.

Engravings and woodcuts as models for sculpture, panel painting, and illuminated manuscripts. Figural representations of Master ES, Master of

the Playing Cards, M. Schongauer, Dürer, H. Schäufelein, and Hans Sebald Beham, adapted c. 1400–1550. Considers the question of how essential these models were for the development of art in Little Poland (Małopolska).

515. PASZKIEWICZ, Mieczysław. Tematyka polska w twórczości Stefano della Belli. [Polish themes in the art of Stefano della Bella] Rocznik Historii Sztuki, vol. 14, 1984, p. 187–261; v. 15, 1985, p. 55–128. illus. N9.6.R58 v. 14, 15

Summary in English.

Bibliographic references.

A comprehensive search of Stefano della Bella's prints and drawings for Polish subjects. Most works falling into this category were inspired by two actual historic occasions, each involving an entry into a major city by Polish dignitaries. The first, occuring in Rome in 1633, was the entry of the Polish envoys, led by Chancellor Jerzy Ossoliński, to see Pope Urban VIII. This event was recorded on six etched plates. Numerous related drawings are extant: sketchbooks in the Uffizi and the Albertina, sheets at the Pierpont Morgan Library, the Seilern collection (Courtauld Institute), Louvre, Berlin-Dahlem, etc. The second occasion, occurring in Paris in 1645, was the entry of the Polish delegation to contract the marriage of Marie Louise de Gonzaga to Władysław IV. In the British Museum, fourteen sheets of drawings survive. The author corrects De Vesme's misidentifications, and describes Stefano's technical innovation used in late plates of Polish subjects.

516. Polskie kolekcjonerstwo grafiki i rysunku. [Collecting prints and drawings in Poland] (Polskie zbiory graficzne.) [Polish graphic arts collections] Warsawa, Arkady, 1980. 218 p. NE735.P6P64

Edited by Maria Mrozińska and Stanisława Sawicka.

Bibliography: p. 214–15.

Bibliographic references.

Summary in French.

Describes holdings of prints, some foreign, in forty-six collections in nineteen cities and towns, and traces the history of the collections. The oldest is the collection of King Stanisław August Poniatowski.

517. Portrety i sceny polskie w sztychach Falcka i Hondiusza. [Polish portraits and scenes in etchings of Falck and Hondius] Wrocław, Zakład Narodowy im. Ossolińskich, 1955. 14 p. 52 plates, illus. (mostly portraits). (Biblioteka gdańska. Seria graficzna, no. 4) DD901.D29B5 no. 4

By Zofia Jakrzewska, Irena Fabiani-Madeyska, and Marian Pelczar.

Bibliography: p. 13–14.

Jeremiasz Falck (Gdańsk, 1610–1677) and Wilhelm Hondius (The Hague, after 1597–Gdańsk, 1652), engravers of high artistry, known for their documentary works. Brief introduction to the portraits (fifteen portraits by Hondius, twenty-one portraits by Falck): the ceremonial procession staged on the occasion of the arrival and entry into Gdańsk of Queen Ludovica Maria Gonzaga, 1646; the transportation and erection of the column of King Zygmunt, Warsaw, 1646; and dramatic scences in the Wieliczka salt mines.

518. ROSIŃSKI, Zygmunt.
Spis miedziorytow polskich obejmujacy przeważnie portrety polskich osobistośći oraz widoki miast polskich i mapki geograficzne z 16., 17., 18., i 19. wieku w zbiorze Zygmunta Rosińskiego. [A list of copper engravings including portraits of prominent Poles, views of Polish cities, as well as geographic maps from the 16th, 17th, 18th, and 19th centuries in the collection of Zygmunt Rosiński] Poznań, 1918. 16s p. illus., ports. NE676.P6R6

Portraits arranged alphabetically by sitter, the subjects and the artists dating from the sixteenth to the nineteenth century. City views and maps arranged by name of the printmaker. Important for the list of early maps and for the 106 illustrations of rarely reproduced portraits, such as those by P. Drevet (Augustus II), Cesare Vicellio (Henri III), and J. Falck.

519. RUSZCZYCÓWNA, Janina.
Konstytucja 3 maja 1791 r. w grafice XVIII wieku. [The constitution of the 3 May 1791 in eighteenth-century prints] Biuletyn Historii Sztuki, vol. 17, no. 2, 1955, p. 234–49. N6.B5 v. 17

At the end of the eighteenth century, the great works of certain painters were those commemorating historical events. In France, it was David. In America, John Trumbull's major work was his painting of the Declaration of Independence (painted between 1786 and 1794).

In Warsaw of the 1790s, the Polish constitution was commemorated by such painters as F. Smuglewicz, J. Chrzciciel Lampie, G. Taubert, and

others such as K. Groll and F. John. *The most noble image is the print by J. Leski after J.P. Norblin showing the Sejm [Congress] assembled in the Royal Castle, Warsaw, on 3 May, 1791.*

520. SAWICKA, Stanisława.
Jan Ziarnko, a Polish painter-etcher of the first quarter of the 17th century. The Print collector's quarterly, vol. 23, no. 1, 1936, p. 278–301. illus. NE1.P7 v. 23

Ziarnko (c. 1575–before 1630) was a draftsman and etcher of great ability whose earliest extant work is an engraving (1596) of a diploma in his natal city of Lwów. He trained as a painter in Italy and was active in Paris from 1605 to 1629. His subjects represent and reflect events in the reigns of Henri IV and Louis XIII. He etched and supplied drawings to be reproduced by other printmakers such as Claude Mellan and the publisher Jean Le Clerc.

521. SAWICKA, Stanisława.
Jan Ziarnko, peintre-graveur Polonais et son activité à Paris au premier quart du XVIIe siècle. La France et la Pologne dans leurs relations artistiques, vol. 1, no. 2–3, Paris, Bibliothèque Polonaise, 1938, p. 103–257. illus. N6991.F7

"Catalogue raisonné de l'oeuvre grave": p. 152–86.

Jan Ziarnko (born about 1575 in Lwów, died in Paris before 1630), was an etcher and engraver who was active in Paris by 1608. Only thirty-five prints by his hand are extant, but more than one hundred prints are attributable to his designs (executed by Claude Mellan and others). His subjects were festivals

(two plates of the Carousel held in 1612 on the Place Royale for the engagements of Louis XIII to Anne of Austria, and of Philip of Spain to Elizabeth of France), allegories, portraits, city views, book illustrations. The most authoritative on the artist, with a catalogue raisonné.

522. SAWICKA, Stanisława.
Ryciny Wita Stwosza. [The engravings of Wit Stwosz] Warszawa, Wydawnictwo Sztuka, 1957. 62 p. 51 plates of illus. NE654.S72S3

Summary in French.
Bibliographic references.

Engravings stylistically datable to 1477–1489, the years the artist was at work on the altarpiece in Kraków. Six impressions have the watermark of paper used in Kraków between 1480 and 1490. Four impressions from Polish collections lost in World War II. The artist differs from M. Schongauer, Master ES, and other frequently cited associations. Rather, he is related to Jan Polak and N. Gerhaert. The author sees the character of the forms as models for sculpture, cites contemporary sculptural adaptations, and reproduces several paintings and one drawing by Stwosz.

523. SIENKIEWICZ, Jerzy.
Rysunek polski od Oświecenia do Młodej Polski. [Polish drawing from the Enlightenment to Młoda Polska] Warszawa, Arkady, 1970. 410 p. illus. (part color). NC312.P6S5

Catalog of Janusz Derwojed.

A scholarly catalog of 338 drawings with biographical data on the artists. The drawings, by 118 artists, are reproduced in black and white, with six plates in color.

Very good drawings, little known outside Poland; equal in quality and variety to those in European art centers.

The artists include M.E. Andriolli, M. Bacciarelli, J. Brandt, J. Brodowski, J. Fałat, W. Gerson, J. Chełmoński, A. and M. Gierymski, A. Grottger, J. Malczewski, J. Matejko, P. Michałowski, C.K. Norwid, A. Orłowski, H. Rodakowski, L. Wyczółkowski, and S. Wyspiański.

524. SROCZYŃSKA, Krystyna.

Zygmunt Vogel, rysownik gabinetowy Stanisława Augusta. [Zygmunt Vogel, limner of the Cabinet of Stanisław August] Wrocław, Zakład Narodowy im. Ossolińskich, 1969. 265 p. illus., map. NC269.V58S65

Sponsored by the Art Institute of the Polish Academy of Sciences.

Bibliographic references.

The first monographic study of the view painter Zygmunt Vogel (1764–1826) who recorded architectural and archaeological monuments and scenery in the Kingdom. Catalog of over three hundred paintings and drawings; prints by him including ten lithographs (1821–1825), and after his designs. Archival documents.

525. STOSS, Veit.

Veit Stoss; Nachbildungen seiner Kupferstiche, 13 Tafeln in Kupferstiefatzung, hrsg. von Engelbert Baumeister. Berlin, B. Cassirer, 1913. 6 p. 13 plates. (Graphische Gesellschaft, XVII Veröffentlichung). NE654.S7A3 folio

"Verzeichnis der Kupferstiche": p. 5–6.

Catalogue raisonné of ten engravings, three reproduced in two states, citing watermarks and all impressions known to the author. In Munich, one impression from each plate. Facsimile reproductions of extraordinary fidelity. The two-page introduction stresses their painterly quality.

526. SUCHODOLSKA, Maria.

Realistyczny-obraz wsi polskiej w twórczości Jana Piotra Norblina. [A realist picture of Polish village life in the works of Jan Piotr Norblin] Biuletyn Historii Sztuki, vol. 13, no. 4, 1951, p. 97–123. illus. N6.B5 v. 13

Bibliographic references.

Influenced by Rembrandt in his genre subjects and drawing style, Norblin's sustained realism is a consequence of his life studies. A prolific draftsman, he liked peasant subjects and rural landscapes. A set of his "Costumes Polonais" was published in 1804.

527. TURNAU, Irena.

Kultura materialna Oświecenia w rycinach Daniela Chodowieckiego. [Material culture illustrated in the drawings of Daniel Chodowiecki] Wrocław, Zakład Narodowy im. Ossolińskich, 1968. 132 p. [168] p. of illus. (Źródła do historii kultury materialnej) NE1212.C45T8

Summary in German.
Bibliographic references.

Prints by and after Daniel Chodowiecki, featuring Polish subjects (e.g., nos. 105, 118, 123, 126, 134, representing a hospital, a coach mired in a swamp, an elegant sleigh) or subjects represented by drawings of his in Polish collections (nos. 11, 70, 115, 117, and others).

528. WELLISZ, Leopold.

Felix Stanislas Jasiński, graveur: Sa vie et son oeuvre. Avec une étude sur les procédés techniques de F. Jasiński, par Thadée Cieślewski fils. Paris, G. Van Oest, 1934. 195 p. illus., ports., facsims., diagr. NE678.J3W4

Bibliography: p. 187.

A printmaker of great virtuosity, Felix Stanislas Jasiński (1862–1901) made reproductive etchings (seventy-one prints after S. Botticelli, pre-Raphaelites such as E. Burne-Jones and D.G. Rossetti, and E. Meissonier), and original prints (etchings, aquatints, woodcuts). Catalog of works and valuable appendices such as listings of his French, English, Polish, and American print publishers. Reproductions of progress proofs, and portraits of the artist by his friend, Félix Vallotton.

529. WIDACKA, Hanna.

Fryderyk Krzysztof i Adolf Fryderyk Dietrichowie. [Fryderyk Krzysztof and Adolf Fryderyk Dietrich] Wystawa monograficzna ze zbiorów warszawskich. [An exhibition of items from Warsaw collections] Warszawa, Biblioteka Narodowa, 1977. 101 p. illus., ports. NE735.P6D532 1977

Bibliographic references.

These were printmakers of leading importance for their depiction of city life, buildings, and monuments in the nineteenth century. The father, Fryderyk Krzysztof, was born in Franconia in 1779 and died in Łódz. Active in Warsaw from 1817. Adolf Fryderyk (1817–1860) was the oldest son. They executed woodcuts, etchings, aquatints, and lithographs.

Prints and Drawings, c. 1474–c. 1900

*A scholarly catalog with, unfortu-
nately, the poorest reproductions.*

530. WIDACKA, Hanna.
Ikonografia Króla Stanisława
Augusta w grafice XVIII wieku.
[The iconography of King
Stanisław August in eighteenth-
century prints] Rocznik Historii
Sztuki, vol. 15, 1985, p. 163–220.
illus., ports. N9.6.R58 v. 15
   Summary in English.
   Bibliographic references.
*King Stanisław August (1732–
1798) used the publicity his portraits
afforded to consolidate his rule, to gain
popularity, and to assuage his vanity.
An official iconography nourished the
first objective (mezzotints by Philip
Haid and Johann Martin Will). The
author discusses the most famous
portrait types, including medals and
engraved gems, and their distribution
through engravings. Some painted
portraits are known only through
engravings (by B. de Folino after M.
Bacciarelli, 1778). Raphael Morghen
made a print after the sculpture of
Domenico Cardelli representing the
King in antique guise.*

531. WIDACKA, Hanna.
Jan III Sobieski w grafice
XVII i XVIII wieku. [Jan III
Sobieski in prints of the seven-
teenth and eighteenth centuries]
Warszawa, Państwowe
Wydawnictwo Naukowe, 1987.
176 p. 136 p. of plates, illus.
N7592.3.W53 1987
   Summary in French and Ger-
man.
   Bibliographic references.
*A scholarly catalog of 194 portraits
of King Jan III Sobieski (1624–
1697), and related subjects, arranged
by date of the prints' execution,
ranging from 1673 to 1795. Print-*

*makers include Romeyn de Hooghe
and Jacob von Sandrart. Subjects
include his catafalque in Rome, the
Church of St. Stanisław, 1696,
etched by P. Santo and F. Bartoli. A
brief overview links the portraits
iconographically to the pictorial context (by combining reminiscences, for
example).*

532. WITKE-JEŻEWSKI,
Dominik. Pamietnik wystawy
starych rycin polskich ze zbioru
Dominika Witke-Jeżewskiego
urządzonej staraniem
Towarzystwa Opieki nad
Zabytkami Przeszłości w r. 1914.
[A souvenir catalog of the
exhibition of old Polish prints
from the collection of Dominik
Witke-Jeżewski, organized in
1914 by the Society for the
Preservation of Ancient Docu-
ments] Warszawa, 1914. 143 p.
illus. NE735.P6W5
   Introduction by Józef
Weyssenhoff.

*A print collection of great artistic
and historical interest. Over one
thousand prints from all periods,
approximately fifty being reproduced.
Sheets of the greatest rarity are
illustrated, perhaps uniquely. A
Monument to Judaism, aquatint
by A.F. Dietrich; J. Ziarnko's great
Carrousel on the Place Royale,
1612; several views of the buildings at
Puławy, etched by C.A. Richter;
portraits of Polish subjects, such as J.
Zamoyski by A. Oleszczyński, 1856,
as well as portraits of contemporaries
by J. Falck and W. Hondius.*

533. WYNEN, Arnulf.
Daniel Chodowiecki, Johann
Karl Schultz. Zwei Danziger
Künstler. Ausstellung anlässlich
des Danziger Treffens 1965 in

Stuttgart. Stuttgart, 1965. 31 p.
illus. NC251.C5W9
*Chodowiecki (1726–1801), is repre-
sented by a selection of ninety-nine
prints and thirty-six drawings—
seven of which are reproduced—from
his profuse oeuvre. Schultz (1801–
1875), who painted and etched views
of Gdańsk, is represented by five
etchings reproduced from a set first
issued between 1855 and 1867 (a
second set was issued in 1872).*

534. ZIARNKO, Jan.
Grafika Jana Ziarnki.
Przewodnik po wystawie
czasowej w zbiorach
Czartoryskich Muzeum
Narodowego w Krakowie. [The
prints of Jan Ziarnko. A guide to
the temporary exhibition in the
Czartoryski collection, National
Museum, Kraków] Kraków,
1966. 11, 16 p. chiefly illus.
NE678.Z5R6
   Edited by Władysława
Rothowa.

*Reduced reproductions of thirteen
etchings, including a frontispiece.*

535. ŻYWIRSKA, Maria.
Saliny Wielickie w sztychach
Wilhelma Hondiusa. [The
Wieliczka salt mines in the engravings of Wilhelm Hondius]
Biuletyn Historii Sztuki, vol. 16,
no. 4, 1954, p. 420–32. illus.
N6.B5 v. 16
*Engravings by Wilhelm Hondius (c.
1597–1652) of the great cavernous,
candlelit spaces in the Wieliczka salt
mines. The set consists of four plates,
three of which are oblong interior
views of the mines (figs. 2, 7, 12);
the fourth (fig. 16) is a rectangular
above-ground view combined with a
map of the region. Published in 1645*

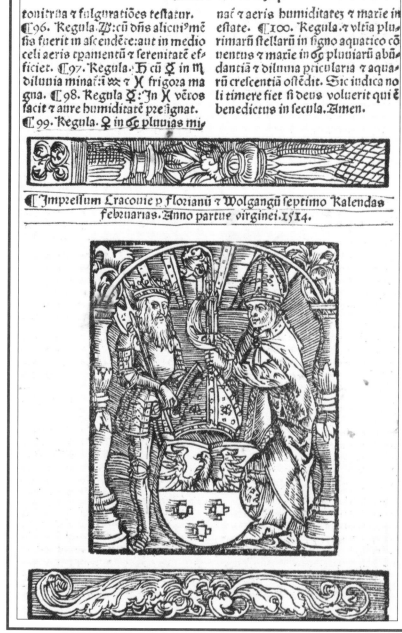

Colophon from the book by Joannes Glogoviensis (Jan Głogowczyk) *Tractatus preclarissimus in judiciis astrorum de mutationibus aeris,* **printed in Kraków by Florian Ungler and Wolfgang Lern in 1514. A fine example cf early printing in Poland, it is also one of the earliest works on weather forecasting to appear in print. The author, a native of Silesia, was professor of mathematics and astronomy at Kraków University and was one of the teachers of Nicolaus Copernicus. Library of Congress, Rare Book and Special Collections Division**

in Gdańsk. *The plates are described, and the inscriptions given, in full; the images are based on the geometric measurements of Marcin German. The representations of technology take their place among such treatises as G. Agricola's* De re metallica *(1580), and W. Rożdżeński (Kraków, 1612).*

536. BANACH, Andrzej.
Warszawa Cieślewskiego Syna. [Warsaw by Cieślewski the Younger] Warszawa, Wydawnictwa Artystyczne i Filmowe, 1962. 271 p. illus. NE678.C5B3
Biography of the artist Tadeusz Cieślewski the Younger. More than fifty reproductions of his wood engravings of Warsaw cityscapes— some real, some imaginary. Gifted in the invention of strong, dramatic compositions on a small scale (has executed many ex libris). List of all 431 works between 1923 and 1944.

537. BIAŁOSTOCKI, Jan.
Poland. *In* Who's who in graphic art. An illustrated book of reference of the world's leading graphic designers, illustrations, typographers and cartoonists. Edited by Walter Amstutz. Zurich, Amstutz & Herdeg Graphic Press, 1962. p. 380–400. illus. NC45.W5
Selected works of eighteen artists reproduced in miniature, with curriculum vitae and a portrait of each artist. Preceded by an overview of the history and development of Polish graphic arts, from the prominent art nouveau painter Stanisław Wyspiański to the achievements of current artists in quality children's book illustrations. In English, French, and German.

❁

538. Biblioteka Narodowa (Poland). Wiktor Zbigniew Langner: Retrospektywna wystawa grafiki. Katalog. [Wiktor Zbigniew Langner: Retrospective exhibition of prints. Catalog] Warszawa, Biblioteka Narodowa, 1981. 90 p. 77 p. of plates, illus. NE735.P6B52 1981

Bibliography: p. 28–29.

Catalog prepared by Alicja Zendara.

A printmaker, born in 1906, whose work is rooted in the ornamental woodcuts of the 1920s but evolved into the abstractions of the 1960s. Catalog of 586 works from 1932 to 1981, including many ex libris.

539. BLUM, Helena.
Józef Pankiewicz. Grafika. [Józef Pankiewicz. Prints.] Warszawa, Arkady, 1958. 16 p. 24 leaves of illus. NC269.P34B5 folio

An account of the career of the painter-printmaker Józef Pankiewicz (1866–1942). His subjects originated mainly from his travels in France and Italy. His most prolific period was between 1899 and 1908. He worked in etching and drypoint, as well as in aquatint and engraving.

540. BLUM, Helena.
Twórczość Władysława Skoczylasa (1883–1934). [The work of Władysław Skoczylas (1883–1934)] Nike, vol. 1, 1937, p. 87–117. illus. N6.N6 v. 1

Summary in French.

The principal Polish wood engraver, who created powerful three-dimensional portraits and illustrated Polish subjects, along with other subjects of general interest.

541. CZERMAŃSKI, Zdzisław.
Józef Piłsudski w 13 planszach. [Józef Piłsudski in thirteen plates] 2d ed. Warszawa, J. Przeworski, 1935. ports. (in portfolio). DK440.5.P5C8 1935

Portrait drawings of Józef Piłsudski (1867–1935), the Commander-in-Chief of the Polish army and Chief of State, representing him between 1914 and 1935. Photo-offset reproductions of pencil drawings about 1935.

542. Exhibition of Polish graphic art. Exposition de l'art graphique polonais. Warsaw, Sztuka, 1955. illus. NE735.P6E93

In English and French.

Introduction by Jan Białostocki.

A succinct summary of the best of traditional realism, which formed stylistically before 1939. Woodcuts were particularly expressive in the work of W. Skoczylas, E. Bartłomiejczyk, S. Ostoja-Chrostowski, and others.

543. GÓRSKA, Hanna, *and* Eryk Lipiński.
Z dziejów karykatury polskiej. [From the history of Polish caricature] Warszawa, Wiedza Powszechna, 1977. 366 p. illus. NC1660.P6G67

Bibliography: p. 339–42.

Beginning with medieval grotesques and historical rarities, such as versos of playing cards etched by Jan Rusten after 1848, the authors concentrate on twentieth-century works.

544. Grafica polacca contemporanea dal dopoguerra al 1986; a cura di Alina Kaczyńska e Vanni Scheiwiller, prefazione di Giulio Carlo Argan. Milano, Libri Scheiwiller, 1986. 128 p. illus. NE735.P6G66 1986

Bibliography: p. 123–28.

Catalog of the exhibition of Polish modern prints held in Milan from December 18, 1986 to January 25, 1987. Polish artists lauded for their faithfulness to authentic standards of printmaking craftsmanship. Each of forty-eight artists represented by a single work; among them are: Halina Chrostowska, Roman Cieślewicz, Stanisław Fijałkowski, Józef Gielniak, Maria Jarema, Jerzy Panek, Krystyna Piotrowska, and Jacek Waltoś.

545. Grafika Polska około roku 1990. Katalog. [Polish prints around 1900. A catalog.] Kraków, Muzeum Narodowe w Krakowie, 1968. 71 p. 24 p. of illus. 2 color plates. NE735.P6G7

Catalog of the exhibition by Zofia Kucielska and Zofia Tobiaszowa.

Summary in French.

Bibliography: p. 67–72.

A period of great fecundity in Polish art. Reproductions in severely reduced format preclude a fair assessment of some eminent prints, such as F. Jansiński's The Golden Staircase after E. Burne-Jones, Józef Mehoffer's Head of a Woman, and Wanda Komorowska's Study of a Woman.

546. Grafika z krakowskiej Akademii Sztuk Pięknych.
Prints from the Kraków Academy of Fine Arts. [Exhibition catalog] Kraków, Biuro Wystaw Artystycznych w Krakowie, 1986. 1 vol. illus. NE735.P6G74 1986

Edited by Tomasz Gryglewicz.
In Polish and English.
Photographs by Adam
Wierzba.

*Works of ninety-two artists, former
students of the Kraków Academy of
Fine Arts, are exhibited in chronological order by artists' birth dates.
At the older end of the range, the
artists and their works are Leon
Wyczółkowski (1852–1936)—
a landscape and the portrait of a
fisherman (soft varnish); Jan
Stanisławski (1860–1907)—a
color lithograph of St. Mark's church
in Venice and a wood engraving of a
landscape (Poplars); and Józef
Pankiewicz (1866–1940)—a landscape of the Pinsk Canal in dry point
and a self-portrait. At the youngest
end, Jacek Walusiak (b. 1957)
shows his two lithographs: "From the
Gospel according to Matthew" and
"Family of lizards."*

*Preceding the brief biographies of
the artists and the photographs of
their works is a short history of the
study of prints at the Kraków
Academy of Fine Arts by
Franciszek Bunsch and Tomasz
Gryglewicz.*

547. Gravura polaca
contemporânea. Lisboa,
Funda.a.o Calouste Gulbenkian,
1981. 83 p. in various pagings.
illus. NE735.P6G76 1981

Catalog of an exhibition held
in the Funda.a.o Calouste
Gulbenkian, Lisbon, Portugal.

Exhibition of Polish twentieth-
century prints.

In Portuguese.

*Thirty-seven printmakers, each repre-
sented by a single print. Discerning
choice of participants, who show
works of high imagination and
artistry.*

548. GROŃSKA, Maria.
Nowoczesny drzeworyt polski
(do 1945 roku). [Modern Polish
wood engraving (to 1945)]
Wrocław, Zakład Narodowy im.
Ossolińskich, 1971. 510 p. illus.
(part color). NE1171.P6G7.

Summary in English.

Bibliography: p. 465–[477].

*The author presents a history of
modern Polish wood engraving, from
its beginnings and early development
(1913–1918)—associated with
Władysław Skoczylas and such gifted
between-the-wars artists as Tadeusz
Cieślewski, Jr., Tadeusz Kulisiewicz,
and Stefan Mrożewski—to the wood
engraving work done in World War
II officer prisoner-of-war camps.*

*Inspired by the way of life in the
Tatra mountains, Skoczylas in his
early wood engravings recreated religious scenes and scenes from the lives
of brigands. Later, in 1925, he began
the influential Association of Graphic
Artists (Ryt), which included some
of the finest pre-World War II
graphic artists. Important contributions were also made by Edmund
Bartłomiejczyk, who called for an end
to the distinction between artistic and
applied graphic art, and Stanisław
Chrostowski, an exceptional graphic
artist and book designer. Among
other noteworthy groups were the
Society of Graphic Artists in Lwów,
and "Bunt" (Revolt) and "Zdrój"
(The Fountain) in Poznań.*

*Biographies of over two hundred
artists.*

549. GROŃSKA, Maria.
Tadeusz Cieślewski syn.
[Tadeusz Cieślewski the Youn-
ger] Wrocław, Zakład Narodowy
im. Issolińskich, 1962. 214 p. 85
illus. (part color). NE678.C5G7

Bibliography: p. 210–14.

*Born in 1895, Cieślewski died in the
Warsaw Uprising in 1944. He was
a graphic artist who worked in
woodcut, wood engraving, and etching.
Made views of Warsaw and Gdańsk,
some composite and imaginary, and
Italian cityscapes. Works of charm
and wit on a small scale, as in the ex
libris format. Author of Drzeworyt
w książce, tece i na ścianie
(Warsaw, 1923).*

*Catalogue raisonné of his pro-
duction.*

550. GROŃSKA, Maria.
Władysław Skoczylas.
Wrocław, Zakład Narodowy im.
Ossolińskich, 1966. 106 p. illus.,
ports. NE678.S55G7

Bibliography: p. 66.

*A traditional wood engraver who
found subject matter in the life around
him and in landscapes. Worked in a
realistic style and in the art deco style
of the 1930s.*

551. JAKIMOWICZ, Irena.
Współczesna grafika polska.
[Contemporary Polish graphic
art] Warszawa, Arkady, 1975. 251
p. illus. (part color).
NE735.P6J34

Bibliography: p. 249–52.

552. JAKIMOWICZ, Irena.
Contemporary Polish graphic
art. With 40 reproductions in
color and 132 in black and white.
Warsaw, Arkady, 1975. 206 p.
illus. (part color).
NE735.P6J3413

Translation by Edward
Rothert of *Współczesna grafika
polska.*

Available also in German.

*Printmakers' mainly aesthetic orien-
tations stressed in a synoptic and
somewhat superficial introduction.*

Survey of printmaking in Poland since 1945, from a period of social realism to the watershed years (c. 1955), when printmakers began to participate in the major artistic issues that have engaged them ever since. Representative illustrations in large format of the eighty-one artists, with biographical data furnished for each.

553. KALISZAN, Jósef.
The Warsaw Ghetto. Drawings by Józef Kaliszan. Compiled and edited by Czesław Z. Banasiewicz. New York, Thomas Yoseloff, 1968 [?]. 111 p. mostly illus. N6999.K3B3

In forty drawings, the artist (born in 1927) recollects the suffering and sadism which the Jews endured under the Nazis. Since 1945, the artist has worked principally as a sculptor, but also as a designer for the theater and as a printmaker.

[228]. KIRSTEIN, Lincoln.
Elie Nadelman. New York, Eakins Press, 1973. 358 p. illus. NB237.N23K57
    Bibliography and exhibitions compiled by Ellen Grand, p. 321–41.
    Bibliography: p. 260–63.
Definitive monograph by a critic of brilliant perception and knowledge. Includes a poetically evocative foreword, a study of the sculptor's life and work, statements by the artist, writings about the artist by André Gide (1909) and Gertrude Stein (1927)—among others—the draft of a catalogue raisonné of Nadelman's sculpture, drawings and prints, and 215 plates. Designed by Martino Mardersteig and printed at the Stamperia Valdonega, Verona, Italy. Copy 22 of 75 copies signed

by the author; includes an original drypoint by the artist.

554. Xawery [i.e. Ksawery] Dunikowski i polscy artyści w obozie koncentracyjnym Auschwitz w latach 1940–1945. Rysunki, obrazy, rzeźby. [Xawery Dunikowski and Polish artists in the concentration camp of Auschwitz in the years 1940–1945. Drawings, pictures, sculpture] Wystawa, styczeń–kwiecień 1985. [Exhibition held January–April 1985] Warszawa, Muzeum Narodowe, 1985. 96 p. 120 p. of plates, illus. (part color). N7255.P63D852 1985
    Bibliographies.
    Catalog by Aleksandra Kodurowa.
Tragic and deeply moving works of art. Many harrowing and sorrowful portraits. Drawings of events and conditions in camp life.

555. KUCIELSKA, Zofia, *and* Jerzy Malinowski.
Ekspresjonizm w grafice polskiej. Expressionnisme dans la gravure polonaise. VI Międzynarodowe Biennale Grafiki w Krakowie. VIe Biennale Internationale de la Gravure à Cracovie. Katalog wystawy 1976. Catalogue de l'exposition 1976. Kraków, Muzeum Narodowe w Krakowie, 1976. 70 p. 72 illus. NE735.P6K8
Artists whose pictorial forms, sometimes taken from primitive art, are marked by vigorous simplifications, color contrasts, and figural deformations. Polish counterparts to E. Munch, O. Redon, J. Ensor, and German Expressionists. Over one hundred artists, most of whom were born around 1900 or earlier, including

W. Weiss (1875–1950), Bruno Schulz (1892–1942), and Maria Jarema (1908–1958).

556. KULISIEWICZ, Tadeusz.
Warsaw, 1945, in drawings. Warsaw, Czytelnik, 1947. 6 p. 32 plates. NC1157.K8A59 folio
A devastated Warsaw at the end of World War II, as it appeared in drawings by Tadeusz Kulisiewicz, one of the most important graphic artists of the two decades between the wars. Technically, the character of the broad pen line, halting and irregular at the edges, and the brush-applied black ink and brush-applied washes, convey perfectly the smoke and rubble.

557. KULISIEWICZ, Tadeusz.
Zeichnungen zur Inszenierung des Berliner Ensembles Bertold Brecht: Der kaukasische Kreidekreis. Berlin, Henschelverlag, 1956. 11 p. 72 p. of illus. NC1157.K8A595
Seventy-two drawings of the characters and scenes in Bertold Brecht's The Caucasian Chalk Circle *as staged by the Berliner Ensemble. Drawings in pen and ink derivative of Picasso's classicist style.*

558. LOEWIG, Roger.
Roger Loewig, rysunki i grafiki. Wystawa daru dla Muzeum Narodowego. Warszawa. 1. XII. 1986–15. I. 1987. Roger Loewig, Handzeichnungen und Graphik. Ausstellung der Schenkung für das Nationalmuseum. Warszawa, C. Troike-Loewig i R. Loewig, and Muzeum Narodowe, 1987. 130 p. illus. (part color). N6889.5.L64A4 1987
    In Polish and German.

Bibliography: p. 128.

Supplement: "Roger Loewig, rysunki" inserted at end.

Loewig, who was born in 1930 in Lower Silesia, has drawn recollections of war and strife in a surrealist and symbolist mode. Legends and verses accompany his drawings and prints in the manner of Paul Klee and others. Catalog of 136 drawings and fifteen soft ground etchings; nearly all reproduced.

559. Małe formy grafiki.

Polska-Łódź '87. [Small-format prints Poland-Łódź '87] Łódź, Biuro Wystaw Artystycznych, 1987. 225 p. chiefly illus. NE491.M35 1987

Preface also in English.

Exhibition catalog by Michał Kuna.

An internationally juried exhibition in Łódź of international participants working in all print media, including lithography, linocut, silk screen, and mezzotint, in a small format not exceeding—and usually less than—ten inches on either side. Over seven hundred prints reproduced, the vast majority being very strong and arresting statements.

560. Międzynarodowe Biennale Grafiki, 5th, Kraków, 1974. 5

[i.e. Piąte Międzynarodowe Biennale Grafiki; Katalog wystawy. Grafiki w Krakowie 1945–1974. V Biennale Internationale de la Gravure. Catalogue de l'exposition. L'art graphique à Cracovie 1945–1974. Kraków, Muzeum Narodowe, 1974. 72 p. 37 leaves of plates, illus. NE735.P6M53 1974

A brief synopsis of trends by Helena Blum. In the late 1940s, monotypes

and etchings were preferred for the freedom they offered. Since then, all techniques have been found viable as, for example, typography with seriography. Printmaking now used as an expressive medium on a par with painting and sculpture. One print by each of the seventy-two participants is reproduced.

561. Międzynarodowe Biennale Grafiki, 7th, Kraków, 1978.

Ilustracja/figuracja: katalog wystawy-Illustration/figuration: catalogue de l'exposition. Muzeum Narodowe w Krakowie, VII Międzynarodowe Biennale Grafiki w Krakowie. Kraków, 1978. 68 p. 119 plates. NC989.P6M53 1978

Text in French and Polish.

Catalog by Barbara Ochmańska-Jodłowksa and Andrzej Zabrowski.

A catalog of 694 works from 1800 to 1970, of which 119 are illustrated. Poor quality of the reproductions and unclear typography make for difficult reading however interesting the material. Rare works include lithographs of an Indian temple and Persepolis tomb, 1818, by J.P. Lelewel and an aquatint of the Arsenal, Warsaw, 1819, by J.F. Piwarski.

562. MITZNER, Laryssa, and Andrzej Rudziński.

eds. Graphic arts of contemporary Poland. Warszawa, Wydawnictwo Artystyczno-Graficzne, 1954. 3 p. 32 plates. NE675.M5 folio

Work of conservative, figural artists reproduced.

563. MROZOWSKA, Alina, and Tadeusz Majda.

Rysunki o tematyce tureckiej z

kolekcji króla Stanisława Augusta w Gabinecie Rycin Biblioteki Uniwersyteckiej w Warszawie. [Drawings on Turkish themes from the collection of king Stanislaus Augustus in the archives of drawings of the Warsaw University Library] Warszawa, Wydawnictwo Uniwersytetu Warszawskiego, 1978. 79 p. illus. NC87.W37 1973 v. 2.

Drawings by F.A. Lohrmann (c. 1735–after 1793), J.C. Kamsetzer (1750–1795), and others depicting life in Constantinople, its buildings, events at court, the coronation of the Sultan, the audiences of the English, Dutch, and Venetian ambassadors, etc. All fifty-one illustrations are described, but there is no numerical correlation between the catalog and the plates.

564. MUSZANKA, Danuta.

Karykatury Kazimierza Sichulskiego. [The caricatures of Kazimierz Sichulski] Wrocław, Zakład Narodowy im. Ossolińskich, 1970. 198 p. illus. NC1670.S56M8

Bibliography: p. 184–87.

Bibliographic references.

A major portraitist, comparable in psychology and style to Henri de Toulouse-Lautrec and Oskar Kokoschka, and often forthrightly caricaturial. Born in 1879, he died in 1942. Sitters were artists, intellectuals, politicians, and theatrical personages. Works by forerunners and contemporaries also reproduced among the 250 illustrations.

565. Muzeum Narodowe we Wrocławiu. Gabinet Grafiki.

Katalog zbiorów Gabinetu

Grafiki. [Catalog of the collection of the Print Department (of the National Museum in Wrocław)] Wrocław, Muzeum Narodowe, 1983+ NE735.P6M87 1983

Vol. 1: Grafika polska w latach 1901–1939. [Polish prints, 1901–1939] Prepared by Irena Rylska. 240 p. illus.

Summary in English.
Bibliography: vol. 1, p. 38–42.
Bibliographic references.
Short biographies of artists.

A catalog of 819 works representing the best from the schools of Lwów and Kraków; few prints from the schools of Warsaw and Poznań, none from Wilno. The poor quality of the reproductions fails to do justice to some interesting work.

566. NADELMAN, Elie.
Elie Nadelman drawings, by Lincoln Kirstein. New York, Hacker Art Books, 1970. 53 p. illus., 58 plates. NC312.P63N3

Reprint of 1949 ed.

A penetrating account of the sculptor's aesthetic. The author perceives the artist's humanity in her subtle abstractions, in contrast to cerebral Cubism. Catalog of fifty-eight drawings, which are illustrated. Comparisons to Seurat; influences of Picasso, Modigliani, and Brancuşi are suggested.

[55]. Obóz koncentracyjny Oświęcim w twórczości artystycznej. [The Oświęcim concentration camp in art] 2d ed. Oświęcim, Wydawnictwo Państwowego Muzeum, 1961–62. 4 v. in 1. illus. (part fold.). N7255.P6O26 1961

Text by Kazimierz Smoleń.
Text in Polish, English, French, German, and Russian.

Contents: Vol. 1–3. Marlarstwo [Painting]—v. 4. Rzeźba. [Sculpture].

The first volume (xviii, 79 p.) reproduces drawings in coal by Jerzy Adam Brandhuber; the second (xxii, 40 p.), drawings and a woodcut by Mieczysław Kościelniak; and the third (iii, 61 p.), drawings by Maria Hiszpańska-Neumann, Janina Tollik, Franciszek Jaźwiecki, Tadeusz Myszkowski, Jerzy Potrzebowski, and Władysław Siwek. The fourth volume (74 p.) presents photographs of sculptures by Mieczysław Stobierski, Hanna Raynoch, Tadeusz Myszkowski, Vida Jocic, Hubert van Lith, and G.W. Mizandari. All the artists were professionals, and all were prisoners at Oświęcim. Their works reveal the daily experiences of hunger, exhaustion, torture, and death. Eleven penetrating portraits by Franciszek Jaźwiecki were drawn from life at the camp.

567. Ogólnopolska Wystawa Grafiki, 7th, Warsaw, 1975. VII [i.e. Siódma] Ogólnopolska Wystawa Grafiki. [The seventh Polish National Exhibition of prints] Styczeń–luty 1975, "Zachęta." Katalog. [January–February, 1975. Warsaw, "Zachęta." Catalog] Warszawa, 1976. 132 p. illus. NE735.P6O35 1976

Introduction by Irena Jakimowicz in English, French, and Russian.

The theme of the national exhibition corresponds to the theme adopted by UNESCO for the given year. This Seventh National Exhibition was organized in honor of the "Women's Year," with prizes awarded in two categories.

Provides an overview of the traditions of graphic art in Poland, emphasizing the organizations (Graphic Art Lovers Society, the Warsaw School of Fine Arts, Black and White) and influential artists (Wit Stwosz, Władysław Skoczylas, Tadeusz Cieślewski, Jr.). Important competitions and exhibitions included the Henryk Grohman competitions (1911, 1914), the Mobile Exhibition of Graphic Art (1922), the Kraków Biennale of Graphic Art (1960–1964)—after 1966 renamed the International Biennale of Graphic Art—and the National Exhibition of the Works of Young Graphic Artists.

568. Ogólnopolska Wystawa Grafiki, 8th, Warsaw, 1978. VIII [i.e. Ósma] Ogólnopolska Wystawa Grafiki: luty-marzec 1978, Warszawa "Zachęta." [The eighth Polish National Exhibition of prints February-March 1978, Warsaw "Zachęta"] Warszawa, Centralne Biuro Wystaw Artystycznych, 1977. 82 p. illus. NE735.P6O35 1978

Introduction in Polish, Russian, English, and French.

Cursory review of national exhibitions of Polish printmakers since 1911. Photographs of the 125 artists participating in the current show. Lists, covering the period 1973 to 1975, of international print shows in Poland, of Polish artists participating in international shows abroad, and of Polish art exhibitions abroad.

[477]. Ogólnopolska wystawa Malarstwa i Grafiki, lst. Warsaw, 1986. 1. [i.e. Pierwsza] Ogólnopolska Wystawa Malarstwa i Grafiki członków Związku Polskich Artystów

Malarzy i Grafików. Marzec 1986 Warszawa "Zachęta." [The First National Exhibition of Paintings and Prints by the members of the Association of Polish Painters and Printmakers. March 1986 Warsaw, "Zachęta." Warszawa, Zachęta, 1986. 346 p. illus. N7255.P60 335 1986

Exhibition catalog edited by Alicja Goduń and Artur Palasiewicz.

The illustrations an arranged alphabetically by artists' surnames, thus creating awkward juxtapositions. The 368 works are keyed to biographical sketches.

569. PIWOCKI, Ksawery.
Polish graphic arts and posters. Warszawa, Drukarnia im. Rewolucji Październikowej, 1966. 100 p. plates. NE676.P6P5

Translated from the Polish by Maria Paczyńska.

Valuable for the short historical survey in English of modern Polish book illustration and single-sheet prints; forty-one works illustrated, but all date from the early 1960s.

570. Rzeszów. Museum Okręgowe w Rzeszowie. Alina Kalczyńska; wystawa grafiki, luty 1976. [Alina Kalczyńska; Exhibition of prints, February 1976] Rzeszów, 1978. 20. p. illus. NE735.P6R94 1978

Bibliography: p. 8.

Kalczyńska, a printmaker of elegance and wit specializing in woodcuts, has made many ex libris. The catalog itself is a work of art. Very well documented (lists of exhibitions, collections), but it is vexing to find only two examples of the artist's work.

571. SICHULSKI, Kazimierz.
Karykatury współczesne: legiony-politycy-literaci-malarze-aktorzy. [Contemporary caricatures: the military-politicians-writers-painters-actors] Kraków, Księgarnia J. Czerneckiego, 1918. 38 p. 32 plates, illus. NC1325.S5

Penetrating, yet good-humored, satires by a draftsman of great skill and wit, Kazimierz Sichulski (1879–1942). He studied in Vienna and Kraków, and was a professor at the Art Academy in Kraków.

572. SITKOWSKA, Maryla.
Andrzej Jurkiewicz, 1907–1967. Warszawa, listopad–grudzień 1980. [Andrzej Jurkiewicz, 1907–1967. Warsaw, November–December 1980. (An exhibition)] Warszawa, Muzeum Narodowe w Warszawie, Galeria Sztuki Współczesnej, 1980. 84 p. 72 p. of plates, illus. (part color). NE735.P6J877 1980

Bibliography: p. 35–37.
Catalog by Maryla Sitkowska.

Jurkiewicz was a printmaker, draftsman, painter, and educator at the Academy of Fine Arts in Kraków. Biographical outline, list of exhibitions and of the artist's writings. Catalog of his works: 354 prints, 243 drawings, 79 paintings.

573. STOPKA, Andrzej.
Komedia ludzka Andrzeja Stopki. [The human comedy of Andrzej Stopka] Kraków, Wydawnictwo Literackie, 1985. 137 p. chiefly illus. NC1670.S77A4 1985

Edited by Henryk Vogler.

Stopka (1904–1973) was a caricaturist of genial wit and distinctive

artistry. Over one hundred portraits of his contemporaries, presented with technical variety—painters, poets, writers, critics, actors, directors. Biography and photographs of Stopka.

574. SZANCER, Jan Marcin.
Rysunki, ilustracje, scenografia z lat 1945–1965. [Drawings, illustrations, scenography from 1945–1965] Warszawa, "Zachęta," listopad 1965. [Catalog of the exhibition] Warszawa, Centralne Biuro Wystaw Artystycznych, 1965. unpaged. illus. NC1157.S9M3

Catalog edited by Maria Matusińska.

Thirty-four drawings from the years 1945 to 1965, captioned autobiographically by Szancer. List of his designs and costumes for the theater, television, and film for the same years. Also lists of the books he illustrated, but without specific data on techniques, publishers, or dates. These include Gulliver's Travels, *Pushkin's* Eugene Onegin, *Hans Christian Andersen,* Pinocchio, *E.T.A. Hoffmann's* Nutcracker, *and Polish authors such as M. Konopnicka. An illustrator of great wit and charm.*

575. SZYK, Artur.
The new order. Introduction by Roger W. Straus, Jr. New York, G.P. Putnam's Sons, 1941. 4 p. 38 plates (part color). NC1670.S9

"A current history book."

Incisive satires on the Axis powers: the Nazis, Italian Fascists, the Japanese, and the Vichy government. Reproductions of nine pen-and-watercolor drawings in color, thirty in black and white. Artur Szyk, famous for his miniature paintings, technically akin to medieval illumination, is represented here in a broader style. His conceptions are in the rich Polish satirical tradition.

576. WARCHAŁOWSKI, Jerzy.
Tadeusz Kulisiewicz. Ein polnischer Holzschnittkünstler. Gutenberg-Jahrbuch, vol. 5, 1931, Meinz, p. 310–20. illus. Z1008.G98 v. 5

Tadeusz Kulisiewicz (b. 1899), a sophisticated graphic artist trained in Poznań and Warsaw, found subjects for his woodcuts in the town of Szlembark.

577. Warsaw. Muzeum Narodowe w Warszawie.
Współczesne rysunki obce w zbiorach Muzeum Narodowego w Warszawie. [Contemporary foreign drawings in the collections of the National Museum in Warsaw] Warszawa, Muzeum Narodowe, 1982. 67 p. 172 p. of plates. NC27.P7W375 1982

578. Warszawa w karykaturze.
[Warsaw in caricature] Warszawa, Państwowe Wydawnictwo Naukowe, 1983. 382 p. illus. NC1660.P6W37 1983
  Selection and texts by Eryk Lipiński.
  Brief biographies of 86 artists.

A book of drawings of wit, charm, and artistry, that date from the early nineteenth century to the present. It includes drawings by the compiler himself on subjects such as characteristic types of people, housing, transportation, parks, and culture. Among well-known fellow artists-caricaturists he has included are Jerzy Zaruba

(1891–1971), Arkadiusz Mucharski (1855–1899), and Maja Berezowska (1898–1978).

579. WEISS, Wojciech.
Grafika Wojciecha Weissa; techniki artystyczne, monotypie, grafika użytkowa. Katalog wystawowy. [The graphic work of Wojciech Weiss; artistic techniques, monotypes, applied graphics. Exhibition catalog] Kraków, październik 1975. Kraków, Muzeum Narodowe, 1975. 58, 34 p. illus. NE735.P6W38
  Summary in French.

An artist who worked in styles that reflect art nouveau, Degas's monotypes, and even constructivism. A useful checklist of graphic work, but with inadequate illustrations.

580. WIERZCHOWSKA, Wiesława.
Współczesny rysunek polski. [The contemporary Polish drawing] Warszawa, Auriga, 1982. 203 p. chiefly illus. (part color). NC312.P6W53 1982
  Summary in English.
  Bibliographic references.

Reproductions of 236 works by sixty-six artists, for whom professional data, including addresses, are given. A brief, cogent essay in English translation appraises the drawing "scene" in Poland since 1945, with emphasis on the 1960s and 1970s. Among the artists surveyed are Tadeusz Kulisiewicz, Barbara Jonscher, Halina Chrostowska-Piotrowicz, Jan Młodożeniec, Ryszard Otręba, Aleksander Kobzdej, Izabella Gustowska, Andrzej Pietsch, Jacek Waltos, and Tadeusz Kantor.

581. WITZ, Ignacy, *and* Jerzy Zaruba.
50 [i.e., pięćdziesiąt] lat karykatury polskiej, 1900–1950. [Fifty years of Polish caricature, 1900–1950] Warszawa, Arkady, 1961. 61 p. 296 illus., 9 color plates. NC1576.W5

A brief history of Polish caricature, an art form that dates back only to the early nineteenth century. In Kraków, especially during the years 1860 to 1880, it was nurtured in cafes such as Jama Michalikowa. The locale then shifted to Warsaw, where the art also flourished through periodicals, such as Sowizdrzał. Over ninety artists are listed alphabetically, with biographical notes. The 296 illustrations are arranged chronologically: from anticlerical and antiestablishment satires of the early decades to antifascist satires of the 1930s and the years of World War II.

582. WRÓBLEWSKA, Danuta.
Polska grafika współczesna; grafika warsztatowa, plakat, grafika książkowa, grafika prasowa. [Polish contemporary graphics: fine prints, posters, book illustrations, book jackets] Warszawa, Interpress, 1983. 34 p. 154 p. of plates, illus. (part color). NE735.P6W7 1983

An interesting selection, though the cramped layout shows a lack of sensitivity for the individual object.

583. WRÓBLEWSKA, Danuta.
Polish contemporary graphic art: studio graphic, the poster, book design, press design. Warsaw, Interpress, 1988. 35, [155] p. of plates, illus. (part color). DLC

"Spacer" [The Promenade], a drawing by Daniel Chodowiecki included in his album "Von Berlin nach Danzig. Eine Künstlerfahrt im Jahre 1773." From Fryderyk Schultz, *Podróże Inflantczyka z Rygi do Warszawy i po Polsce w latach* 1791–1793. Warszawa, Czytelnik, 1956

Translation of *Polska grafika współczesna: grafika warsztatowa, plakat, grafika książkowa, grafika prasowa.*

584. Zeichnungen fünfzehn polnischer Künstler. Drawings of fifteen Polish artists. [An exhibition catalog] Leverkusen, Städtisches Museum, 1978. 110 p. chiefly illus. NC312.P6Z44

Exhibition held Sept. 15–Oct. 29, 1978 at the Städtisches Museum, Leverkusen, Schloss Morsbroich, and organized by the Muzeum Sztuki, Łódź.

Catalog by Janusz Głowacki.

In English and German.

Included in this group of artists are the former students of Władysław Strzemiński from the University of Łódź: Stanisław Fijałkowski,

Danuta Kula-Przyboś, Antoni Starczewski, and Andrzej Strumiłło, as well as artists from schools of fine arts in Kraków, Wrocław, and Warsaw. All these artists achieved recognition in their own field— painting, the graphic arts, photography, or drawing. Exhibition held in Poland and abroad.

585. ANDRIOLLI, Michał E. Elviro Michele Andriolli illustratore e pittore (1836–1893). Trento, 1978. 120 p. illus. (Collana artisti trentini, 60) N7255.P63A642 1978

Edited by Stanisław Szymański.

Introduction by Riccardo Maroni.

Bibliography: p. 59–64.

Born in Wilno, studied in Moscow and Rome. As a book illustrator, he is probably best known for the illustrations he did for Adam Mickiewicz's Pan Tadeusz, *the 1882 and 1889 editions. He was also a history painter and landscape artist.*

586. BAJDOR, Alicja, *and* Halina Natuniewicz. Pan Tadeusz w ilustracjach. [Illustrations for Pan Tadeusz] Gdańsk, Krajowa Agencja Wydawnicza, 1984. 259 p. illus. (part color). NC989.P6B28 1984

To illustrate the verses of the twelve chapters of the classic by Adam Mickiewicz, Pan Tadeusz, *or The last journey to Lithuania—a history of the landed gentry in the years 1811 and 1812—the authors selected corresponding illustrations drawn from nineteenth- and twentieth- century editions. Illustrations from the first edition, Paris, 1834, are also reproduced.*

587. BANACH, Andrzej.
Polska książka ilustrowana
1800–1900. [The Polish illustrated book 1800–1900] Kraków, Wydawnictwo Literackie, 1959. 508 p. illus. NC989.P6B3
Bibliography: p. 405–71.

Abundant reproductions illustrate sections of the volume covering subjects such as romantic lithography, costume books in the style of Biedermeier, landscape in illustration, the nineteenth-century portrait, and children's books. Provides an extensive list of the most important illustrated editions of books.

[537]. BIAŁOSTOCKI, Jan.
Poland. *In* Who's who in graphic art. An illustrated book of reference of the world's leading graphic designers, illustrators, typographers and cartoonists. Edited by Walter Amstutz. Zurich, Amstutz & Herdeg Graphic Pree, 1962. p. 380–400. illus. NC45.W5

Selected works of eighteen artists reproduced in miniature, with curriculum vitae and a portrait of each artist. Preceded by an overview of the history and development of Polish graphic arts, from the prominent art nouveau painter Stanisław Wyspiański to the achievements of current artists in creating quality children's book illustrations. In English, French, and German.

588. DRUŻYCKI, Jerzy.
Det moderne polske exlibris = Das moderne polnische Exlibris = L'Exlibris moderne polonais = The modern Polish book-plate. Frederikshavn, Exlibristen, 1974. 105 p. illus. (Det europaeiske exlibris efter 1950, vol. 1) (Exlibris publika-tion, no. 100) Z993.E86 v. 1 Rare Book Coll.
In Danish, English, French, and German.
Bibliography: p. 103–05.

Book plates are a traditional format for Polish artists. At present this art form is encouraged at art schools, and production is fostered by exhibitions, and by art collectors. Thirty-four artists are represented; short biographies and numerous examples of their art reproduced; several original plates are tipped in.

589. ENGELMANN, Wilhelm.
Daniel Chodowiecki's sämtliche Kupferstiche. Leipzig, Engelmann, 1857. u. 1906. lxii, 543, 148 p. illus. NE654.C5E63

Daniel Chodowiecki (1726–1801) was a prodigious etcher of book, almanac, and calendar illustrations and portraits. This detailed catalogue raisonné, arranged chronologically (1758–1800), contains 950 entries —most with multiple prints. Chodowiecki illustrated Shakespeare, Goethe, J.C. Lavater, and J.J. Rousseau, among others. Worked mainly in Berlin. Some Polish subjects (e.g., no. 138), including family portraits.

590. GRONOWSKI, Tadeusz.
Tadeusz Gronowski. Grafika książkowa 1918–1978. [Tadeusz Gronowski. Book illustration 1918–1978] [Exhibition catalog] Wrocław, Grudzień 1978– Styczeń 1979. Wrocław, Muzeum Narodowe we Wrocławiu, 1979. 26 p., 11 leaves of plates, ports. NC989.P62G768 1979
Introduction in Polish and French by Jan Białostocki.
Catalog by Teresa Pieniążek.
Bibliography.

Catalog of 144 illustrations for books, periodicals, and posters. The elegant style, developed around the time of World War I, is of a deceptive delicacy. The breadth of the artist's talent showed itself in his inventive graphics of the 1930s.

591. Ilustratorstwo w Polsce.
[Book illustration in Poland] *In* Encyklopedia wiedzy o książce. Wrocław, Zakład Narodowy im. Ossolińskich, 1971. p. 966–80. Z1006.E575
Edited by Irena Dunikowska.
Bibliographic references.

592 LAM, Stanisław.
Książka wytworna. Rzecz o estetyce druku. [The refined book: the aesthetics of printing] Warszawa, Władysław Lazarski, 1922. 123 p. illus. Z276.L2

Reproduces numerous title pages from Polish books and periodicals, and samples of fine printing.

593. L'illustration du livre et la littérature au XVIIIe siècle en France et en Pologne. Actes du Colloque organisé par l'Institut de Littérature Polonaise et le Centre de Civilisation Fran.aise de l'Université de Varsovie (Novembre 1975). Varsovie, Editions de l'Université de Varsovie, 1982. 320 p. 41 p. of plates, illus. (Les Cahiers de Varsovie, 9) NC980.I45 1982

Zdzisław Libera, editor of this issue.

Bibliographic references.

Among the fifteen papers in the volume, one discusses publications that glorify King Stanisław Leszczyński in Lorraine (1737–1766), who was a noted patron of architecture and

❀

art; another discusses illustrations, notably those by Charles Eisen for B. and Sz. Zimorowicz's Les bucoliques polonaises *(1788)*, those by J.P. Norblin for J. Krasicki's La Souriade, *and those by various illustrators for Polish sentimental novels, circa 1800.*

594. Librorum in Polonia editorum deliciae czyli wdzięk i urok polskiej książki. [... or, the charm and fascination of the Polish book] Warszawa, Wydawnictwa Artystyczne i Filmowe, 1974. 31 p. 109 leaves of plates, facsims. (part color). Z163.L5

Text by Jan Zygmunt Jakubowski, Alodia Gryczowa.
Bibliographic references.

The high-sounding subtitle notwithstanding, a scholarly selection of more than one hundred reproductions, from the earliest Polish imprint of 1474 to the present. The excellent reproductions include nine incunabula leaves and twenty-seven—mostly illustrated—sixteenth-century leaves. Many notable in nineteenth- and twentieth-century selections. Issued on the quincentenary of printing in Poland.

595. Ogólnopolska Wystawa Grafiki Książkowej, maj 1967. [Katalog] [An all-Polish exhibition of book illustration (Catalog)] Warszawa, Związek Polskich Artystów Plastyków, Centralne Biuro Wystaw Artystycznych, 1967. 1 v. (unpaged) illus. NE735.P6O34

Edited by Ada Potocka.

This modestly produced book features some witty and imaginative book covers as well as illustrations.

596. 500 [i.e., pięćset] lat drukarstwa w Krakowie. [Five hundred years of printing in Kraków] Katalog wystawy. Kraków, Muzeum Narodowe, 1974. 158 p. illus. Z164.K8P53

An exhibit organized by the Jagiellonian University Library and the Historical Museum of Kraków.

Summary in French.

Concentrates on the early years of printing, when Kraków was the center of the nation's cultural, political, and scholarly life. Essays touch on outstanding books through the centuries. The earliest printing from movable type dates from 1474. In the sixteenth century, Erasmus and Calvinist authors are published as well as a Polish grammar for Germans. Numerous reproductions of figured title pages, illustrations, and printers' devices—although on a reduced scale. No information on illustrators is provided.

[569]. PIWOCKI, Ksawery. Polish graphic arts and posters. Warszawa, Drukarnia im. Rewolucji Październikowej, 1966. 100 p. plates. NE676.P6P5

Translated from the Polish by Maria Paczyńska.

Valuable for the short historical survey in English of modern Polish book illustration and single-sheet prints; forty-one works illustrated, but all date from the early 1960s.

597. Polska ilustracja książkowa. Polish book illustrations. Warszawa, Wydawnictwo Artystyczne i Filmowe, 1964. 164 p. illus. (part color), ports. NC989.P6P6

Edited by Michał Bylina, Józef Czerwiński, and Roman Tomaszewski.

Polish, English, French, and German.

Over eighty illustrators, active at the time this book was published. Each artist is represented by several works and a brief biography. Polish book illustrations reflect the contemporary painting styles found, for the most part, in highly sophisticated works of art.

598. RYSZKIEWICZ, Andrzej. Exlibris polski. [Polish exlibris] Warszawa, Wydawnictwo Artystyczno-graficzne RSW "Prasa," 1959. 140 p. illus. 10 plates. Z994.P6R9

Bibliography: p. 149

Includes book plates of seventy-one artists.

599. SKIERKOWSKA, Elżbieta. Wyspiański, artysta książki. [Wyspiański, artist of the book] Wrocław Zakład Narodowy im. Ossolińskich, *1960.* 205 p. illus. (Książki o książce) NC269.W9S5

Some background—especially art nouveau illustration—is given for Wyspianski's major work, the illustrations for Homer's Iliad.

600. SOCHA, Gabriela. Andriolli i rozwój drzeworytu w Polsce. [Andriolli and the development of wood engraving in Poland] Wrocław, Zakład Narodowy im. Ossolińskich, 1988. 278 p. illus., port. (Książki o książce) NE1171.P6S63

Bibliography: p. 270–72.

Michał Elwiro Andriolli (1836–1893), an illustrator of books, exerted a strong influence on the art of drawing and wood engraving in

Poland. The author discusses techniques of engraving, lithography, and xylography used by the artists who worked with Andriolli. A list of the artists is included, as is a list of books illustrated by Andriolli.

601. SZYK, Arthur.

Arthur Szyk: illuminator (1894–1951). A selection of his works, November 1974–February 1975. [Exhibition Catalog] New York, Yeshiva University Museum, 1974. 11 leaves. illus. ND3039.S98A4

Miniatures from the collections of the Jewish Museum, the Metropolitan Museum, Galerie Sumers, two private collections, and the sponsoring institution. Six illustrations, including a self-portrait, and plates of The Statute of Kalisz, The Holidays, War Cartoons, *and* The Haggadah.

The Statute of Kalisz, *the legal document granting rights to Polish Jewry, is considered to be Szyk's finest work of illustration.*

The Statute *is the subject of an article by Joseph P. Ansell, "Art against prejudice: Arthur Szyk's Statute of Kalisz,"* D A P A. The Journal of Decorative and Propaganda Arts, *Fall 1989. Color illustrations.*

602. THEMERSON, Stefan.

Jankel Adler, an artist seen from one of many possible angles. London, Gaberbocchus Press, 1948. 31 p. illus. ND699.A3T5 Rare Book Coll.

The destiny of Jankel Adler (1895–1949) as a visual artist is symbolized by a green lizard in this fantastic tale. Copy 191 of 400 copies printed by the Gaberbocchus Press, signed by the author and the artist, and

illustrated with reproductions of twelve drawings made by the artist for this book.

603. Under the star of fantasy.

Graphic art in Polish books for children. Warsaw, Krajowa Agencja Wydawnicza, 1977. 71 p. chiefly illus. (part in color). NC989.P6U53

The work of twenty-three artists is reproduced, demonstrating once again the high artistic quality of book illustration in Poland.

604. UNIECHOWSKI, Antoni.

Antoni Uniechowski. [Exhibition] Warszawa, "Zachęta," kwiecień 1974. Warszawa, Centralne Biuro Wystaw Artystycznych, 1974 [42] p. illus. NC989.P62U54

Sponsored by the Ministerstwo Kultury i Sztuki and Związek Polskich Artystów Plastyków.

Introduction in Polish and French by Jerzy Abacki.

List of publications illustrated by Uniechowski.

Antoni Uniechowski (b. 1903 in Wilno), draftsman and painter, studied in Warsaw from 1923 to 1930 at the Academy of Art. He created posters and illustrated many books, including V. Hugo's Les Misérables *(1956 Polish ed.) and numerous other works of classic French literature translated into Polish, as well as works by Polish writers, such as I. Krasicki, H. Sienkiewicz, and B. Prus (Głowacki). Uniechowski exhibited in Denmark, Sweden, Yugoslavia, and Poland, and was the recipient of numerous awards.*

605. WALLIS, Mieczysław.

Zofja Stryjeńska jako

ilustratorka. [Zofia Stryjeńska as an illustrator] Sztuki Piękne, vol. 4, 1927–28, p. 173–87. illus. N6.S9 v. 4

Discusses illustrations of the classics and folklore executed by the artist in the charming and decorative style of the 1920s. She frequently employed the motifs of peasant costumes as in Kolędy *(Christmas Carols), published in Warsaw in 1926.*

606. WIERCIŃSKA, Janina.

Sztuka i książka. [Art and the book] Warszawa, Państwowe Wydawnictwo Naukowe, 1986, 222 p. 120 p. of plates, 286 illus. (part color). NC977.W53 1986
Summary in English
Bibliographic references.

Reviews the historiography of Polish book illustration that began in 1895 during a period of experimental typography (S. Wyspiański) and purposeful illustrative achievement (Z. Przesmycki). The word "illustration" was in English usage from the early nineteenth century, in Polish usage from about 1844. Chapters on influential artists: Antoni Zaleski (1824–1885), and Antoni Kamieński (1860–1933).

607. Zbiór odcisków

drzeworytów w różnych dziełach polskich w XVI i XVII wieku odbitych a teraz w Bibliotece Uniwersytetu Jagiellońskiego zachowanych. Recueil de gravures sur bois imprimées dans divers ouvrages plonais au seizième et au dix-septième siècle, dont les planches sont conservées à la Bibliothèque de l'Université de Jagellon. Kraków, W drukarni Uniwersyteckiej, 1849. 10 p. of text. 2,816 illus. Kraków, Krajowa Agencja Wydawnicza,

1985 (reprint). NE1171.P6B5 folio

Reproduction of over two thousand woodcuts used to illustrate books printed in Kraków in the sixteenth and seventeenth century. Many blocks are of German origin, and earlier printing, such as nos. 184–248, after Jost Amman, and nos. 149–172, after H. Schaufelein. The latter blocks, cut in 1539, were used only in 1594 in Kraków. Such detailed information is not invariably provided. The book also contains many other blocks of Polish origin such as nos. 845–855, The Dialogues of King Salomon with Marcolphe (1521), nos. 1046–1124, The Nest of Virtue (Gniazdo cnoty, by Bartosz Paprocki—one of the earliest armorials of the knights of the Polish-Lithuanian Commonwealth—printed in 1578), nos. 1160–1212, Chronica Polonorum by Maciej from Miechów printed in 1521 by Wietor, and reprinted in 1554 and 1565.

608. Bibliothèque Forney.
Catalogue des affiches polonaises. 2d ed. Paris, Société des amis de la Bibliothèque Forney, 1980. 209 p. illus. NC1807.P6B5 1980

Cover title: Affiches polonaises.

Catalog of 1,093 posters in the collection of the Bibliothèque Forney. Arranged alphabetically by artist. Catalog gives dimensions, place and date of publication, designer (if different from executor), and inventory number. Subject index.

609. BOJKO, Szymon.
Polska sztuka plakatu, początki i rozwój do 1939 roku. [The

Polish art of the poster, its beginnings and development to 1939] Warszawa, Wydawnictwo Artystyczno-Graficzne, 1971. 230 p. illus. (part color). NC1807.P6B65

Summary in English.
Bibliographic references.
Biographies of artists by Janina Fijałkowska.

Documents the dynamic and brilliant forerunners of the artistic form in which contemporary Polish artists are preeminent. Discusses Tadeusz Gronowski, whose prolific designs were the single strongest influence on pre-World War II graphics. In the 1930s, this art form reached maturity. Abundantly illustrated. Biographical notes by Janina Fijałkowska. On more than one hundred artists; lists of exhibitions and competitions since 1898.

610. BOJKO, Szymon.
Polski Plakat Współczesny [Wystawa]. The Polish poster today [An exhibition]. Polnische Plakatkunst von Heute. Warszawa, Agencja Autorska, 1972. 107 p. illus. (part color). NC1807.P6B652

Polish, English, and German.

A brief and superficial introduction that relates Polish poster art to contemporary artistic trends. As the reproductions attest, pictorially sophisticated pre-1939 posters had commerical application, the author's high-minded asseverations notwithstanding. List of publishers, schools of applied art, and institutions collecting and sponsoring exhibitions. Fifty-two artists are represented in this catalog, each by three or four reproduced examples of his or her work.

611. CIEŚLEWICZ, Roman.
Plakate. Affiches. Posters. Collages. [Catalog] Heidelberg, Braus, 1984. 184 p. illus. (part color). N7255.P6C542 1984

Catalog of the exhibition held Sept. 30–Nov. 11, 1984 at the Kunsthalle, Darmstadt.

Text by Jean-Christoph Bailly, et al.

Edited by Dorit Marhenke.

Introduction in German, French, and English.

The brief introduction succinctly portrays the character of the artist's creations. It is pure and original fantasy in a surrealistic mode, blending images from the fine arts and photography. Born in 1930 in Lwów, Cieślewicz has lived in Paris since 1963. One of Europe's leading poster artists.

612. Contemporary Polish posters in full color. New York, Dover Publications, 1979. 42 p. (chiefly color illus.). NC1807.P6C66

Selected and introduced by Joseph S. Częstochowski, in co-operation with Janina Fijałkowska.

Forty-six contemporary posters selected from the unique Muzeum Plakatu [Poster Museum] in Wilanów, near Warsaw, for a two-year exhibition that toured the United States in the early 1980s. These works, handsomely reproduced in color on good stock, reveal a new vibrant national force in the graphic arts. Many of the younger poster designers are also active as painters, printmakers, and cinematographers. As Mr. Częstochowski points out in his introduction, "contemporary Polish posters have little to do with

*advertising in the Western sense ...
Rather, [the imagery] is applied to
themes of a social ... or cultural
nature (the circus, national celebrations, education, films, theater perfor-
mances, music and sports events, and
artistic exhibitions). The circus
posters, an ongoing series, are not
related to specific troupes or perfor-
mances."*

**613. FIJAŁKOWSKA, Janina,
and ALICJA Kalinowska.**
Od Młodej Polski do naszych
dni; katalog wystawy plakatu.
[From Młoda Polska to the
present; catalog of an exhibition
of posters] Warszawa, Muzeum
Narodowe w Warszawie, 1966.
165 p. illus. (part color).
NC1807.P6F5

Introduction in French and
Russian.

*Poster art developed in Kraków at the
end of the nineteenth century. It is an
art form inspired by contemporary
theory (William Morris) and pictorial manifestations (Eugène Grasset,
Walter Crane, japonisme). Production moved to Warsaw after World
War I and continues to have wide
pictorial referants. Catalog of 468
posters, of which sixty-four are
illustrated in black and white and
nine in color.*

*An excellent and comprehensive
article in English by Danuta
A. Boczar, "The Polish Poster,"
p. 16–27 in the Spring 1984 issue of
Art Journal [N81.A887],
provides an historical account of the
development of poster art against the
background of the shifting political
situation in Poland during the past
century. Included are photographs of
posters by such artists as Axentovicz
(1898 poster), T. Gronowski (1926
poster), T. Trepkowski (1948*

*poster), W. Zakrzewski (1955
poster), H. Tomaszewski (1959
poster), M. Urbaniec (his 1970
Mona Lisa circus poster), a 1976
poster by W. Swierzy, and others.*

614. KOWALSKI, Tadeusz, ed.
Polski plakat filmowy. [The
Polish film poster] Warszawa,
Filmowa Agencja Wydawnicza,
1957. 18 p. 141 p. of illus.
NC1810.K64

Introduction by Jan Lenica.
Texts in Polish, French, Russian, and English.

*Posters by forty-nine artists which
typify the production of a decade
(1946–56). No particulars given
other than the names of the artists
and titles of the works.*

**615. Kraków. Akademia Sztuk
Pięknych.** Biblioteka Główna.
Plakat do roku 1939 ze zbiorów
Biblioteki Głównej Akademii
Sztuk Pięknych w Krakowie.
[The poster to the year 1939
from the collections of the Main
Library of the Academy of Fine
Arts in Kraków] [An exhibition
catalog] Kraków, 1972. n.p. illus.
NC1827.P7K724

Edited by Irena Konopka.
Introduction by Janina
Więckowska-Lazar.

*Principally Polish posters of high
artistry from about 1900. Classic
styles well represented: Karol Frycz,
no. 57; Henryk Kunzek, nos.
68–69; Ivo Seremet, no. 205. Other
strong images whose creators are
unidentified: nos. 61, 163, 202.*

616. LENICA, Jan.
Jan Lenica. Catalogue conçu à
l'occasion de l'exposition
consacrée à Jan Lenica par le

Centre Georges Pompidou du 2
avril au 26 mai 1980, au
promemoir de la mezzanine.
Paris, Centre national d'art et de
culture Georges Pompidou, 1980.
96 p. illus. (part color).
N7255.P63L362 1980

Filmography: p. 72–95.

*"Sous la direction de Jean-Loup
Passek; textes de Robert Benayoun,
R.-J. Moulin, Jean-Loup Passek et
Jan Lenica."*

617. LENICA, Jan.
Jan Lenica, Plakat- und
Filmkunst. Ausstellung. [Berlin]
Frölich & Kaufmann, 1981. 190
p. illus. (part color), ports.
NC1850.L38A4 1981

Edited by Margareta
Gorschenek, Heinz-Jürgen
Kristahn and Annamaria
Rucktäschel.

*Mainly full-color reproductions of
113 posters for films, theater, opera,
and travel, commissioned in Poland,
France, and Germany. Catalog with
data on publishers and printers. Stills
from six animated films, including
one made at the Carpenter Center,
Harvard. Expository essays on the
pictorial and intellectual foundations
and meaning of Lenica's art.*

618. Muzeum w Wilanowie.
Das polnische Plakat von 1892
bis Heute; aus den Sammlungen
des Plakatmuseums Wilanów.
Berlin u. d. Nationalmuseums
Warschau, Hochschule der
Künste Berlin. Münster-
schwarzach, Vier-Türme-Verlag,
1980. 192 p. illus. (part color).
NC1807.P6M86 1980

Edited by Anna Rutkiewicz, et
al.

Bibliography: p. 190–92.

❀

Consists mainly of three hundred color reproductions of posters with a descriptive entry for each and biographical sketches of more than one hundred artists. Six short essays, such as "Structure, aesthetic, and semiotics of the Polish poster."

[569]. PIWOCKI, Ksawery.
Polish graphic arts and posters. Warszawa, Drukarnia im. Rewolucji Październikowej, 1966. 100 p. plates. NE676.P6P5
Translated from the Polish by Maria Paczyńska.

Valuable for the short historical survey in English of modern Polish book illustration and single-sheet prints; forty-one works illustrated, but all date from the early 1960s.

619. Plakat polski 1970–1978.
[The Polish poster 1970–1978] Warszawa, Krajowa Agencja Wydawnicza RSW Prasa, Książka, Ruch, 1979. 207 p. 411 illus. (part color). NC1807.P6P55 1979

Edited by Zdzisław Schubert. Introduction in Polish and English.

Jan Młodożeniec, Roman Cieślewicz, Karol Śliwka, Waldemar Świerzy, Jan Lenica, Franciszek Starowieyski, and Józef Mroszczak are among the artists whose posters are reproduced.

620. Polnische Plakate der Nachkriegszeit. Catalog of the exhibition held March–May 1985 in Munich. Munich, 1985. 87 p. illus. (part color). NC1807.P6P65 1985
Edited by Hans Wichmann. Biographies of artists.

Works by fifty-nine artists. Of 104 illustrations, nineteen are of the famous "Cyrk" (Circus) series, the latest dated 1980.

621. Polski plakat polityczny.
[The Polish political poster] Warszawa, Krajowa Agencja Wydawnicza, 1980. 2 p. of text.

96 leaves of color illus. DK4436.P67 1980
Edited by Antoni Cetnarowski.

Posters dating from the 1950s are concentrated in the 1970s. A brief introduction addresses the persuasive power of the poster in directing national thought toward building socialism. Issued on the occasion of the Eighth Congress of the Polish United Workers' Party.

622. SZEMBERG, Henryk, ed.
Polish poster. Warszawa, Wydawnictwo Artystyczno-Graficzne RSW Prasa, 1957. 187 p. chiefly illus. (part color), ports. NC1810.S93

Photographs and biographical sketches of thirty-one artists, the eldest born before 1900, others born in the 1920s and 1930s. Each represented by a generous number of illustrations. Subjects frequently political, although designs for theaters, cinemas, and books are also included.

Posters

"Husarz"—Polish cavalryman
serving in "Husaria," by Piotr
Michałowski (1800–1850). From

Polska Mapa Administracyjna
[Adminisitrative map of Poland].
Warszawa, Państwowe
Przedsiębiorstwo Wydawnictw
Kartograficznych, 1979. Library of
Congress, Geography and Map
Division

A tailor's shop. Scene from *Codex
picturatus Balthasaris Behem*, the
illuminated code of Kraków city
guild statutes written around 1505
by Balthazar Behem, secretary of
the Kraków city government. The
manuscript is in the Jagiellonian
University Library, Kraków.
From Friedrich Winkler's *Der
Krakauer Behaim-Codex*. Berlin,
1941

Vidi aquam. ℣ Qui apud te est fons vite alla. Et ℣ dne exaudi oratiōm mea. dns.

Deus tuus oremus. Robora spiritu totius corporis ecclie scificatū et retribu cōserua i noua familie pxpre scificationis tieria quam dedisti ut corpe et mente renouati in vnitate fidei feruētes tibi domino seruire mereami. Per xpm. Ad processionē ℟ Veni spiritus alme. ℣ Loquebat varijs linguis apli alleluia. Oratio

Omps sempiterne deus q paschale sacramentum quadragintā dierum voluisti misterio contineri pra pei intercessionez omim sctorum tuorum ut tientiam facta dispositio lin triarū diuisione ad vnitā cōfessionez tui nominis celesti munere cōmittatur. Per xpm. In reuersione pnitus bta nobis gaudia ℣ Confirma hoc deus quod opatus es in nobis alla. Oro. Deus qui sacramētis festinitatis hodierne vni

uersam tuam ecclia in omni gente et natione scificas intercedentibus omnibus sctis tuis in totā in dei latitudinē spiritus tui dona diffunde. Per xpm. Lictor.

Spiritus domini repleuit replenit orbem terrarum alleluia et hoc quod continet omnia scientiam habet vocis alla alla alla. Ps. Confirma hoc deus quod opatus es in nobis a templo sancto quod est in iherusalem. Oro.

Deus qui hodierna die corda fidelium sancti spiritus illustratione docuisti da nobis in eodem spiritu recta sapere et de eius semper consolatione gaudere. Per eiusdem. Lectio actuū apolorum

"The scene before a bear hunt in
Nieśwież, 1892," by Julian Fałat
(1853–1929), is typical of that
painter's Polish impressionist
hunting scenes and winter
landscapes. From *Sztuka polska;
malarstwo*. Lwów, Altenberg,
1904.

Stańczyk, painted by Jan Matejko
in 1862 (oil on canvas, 88 × 120
cm). National Museum, Warsaw.
In this scene Stańczyk, who was
royal jester to King Sigismund I,
has the features of Matejko
himself, and is depicted during
the ball held at Wawel Castle,
engrossed in his thoughts and
deeply concerned about the fate of
Poland after learning of the Polish
army's defeat at Smolensk in 1514
during the war with Muscovy.
From *Galeria sztuki polskiej*.
Warszawa, Arkady, 1961

The City Hall in Poznań, one of the most beautiful buildings in Poland, was converted in 1550–60 from a Gothic into a Renaissance structure by the architect Giovanni Battista Quadro of Lugano. Partially destroyed during World War II, it was later interior of its great hall testifies to the obvious pride of the burghers in their love of art—and also to their wealth. Photo by E. Kupiecki from *Renesans i manieryzm w Polsce*, by Helena Kozakiewiczowa. Warszawa, Auriga, 1978

Lady with an Ermine, by Leonardo da Vinci, oil on walnut panel (53.4 × 39.3 cm). Painted around 1480–1490 during Leonardo's stay at the court of Lodovico Sforza, Duke of Milan, the portrait is thought to be of Cecilia Gallerani, a lady of the court and Sforza's mistress. The painting was acquired in Italy around 1800 by Prince Adam Jerzy Czartoryski (1770–1861) and is in the Czartoryski Collections at the National Museum in Kraków. Photo by Kraków photographer Konrad Pollesch.

Jan Matejko, self-portrait painted
in 1892, the year before the artist's
death. Oil on canvas (160 × 110
cm.) in the collections of the
National Museum, Warsaw.
Photo by Zbigniew Kamykowski
from J. M. Michałowski's book
Jan Matejko. Warszawa, Arkady,
1979

"The Encounter" of two wealthy
country girls and their mother
with a poor young orphan
shepherdess, painted by
Aleksander Kotsis (1836–1877).
This prolific painter, whose works
hang in art museums throughout
Poland, often depicted the life of
the very poor in Kraków and the
Tatra foothills. From the original
painting in the collection of Dr.
and Mrs. Thomas Lesnik of
Norwich, Connecticut

View of Wawel Castle. Color
lithograph from *Album
Jubileuszowe Grunwald*. Poznań,
Z. Rzepecki, 1910

Death of St. Adalbert (Wojciech). Detail from the bronze door of Gniezno Cathedral, executed in the second half of the twelfth century by an unknown engraver. Saint Adalbert, Bishop of Prague, a monk of the Benedictine Abbey of Saints Alexius and Boniface in Rome, devoted the last part of his life to missionary work among the heathen Prussians on the Baltic coast, where he met his martyr's death. Born to a princely Slavnik dynasty in Bohemia, and friend of Emperor Otto III, St. Adalbert died in 997, was canonized shortly thereafter, and is venerated in Poland as a saint and patron of the Catholic Church. Photo by Mirosław Kopydłowski from *Drzwi Gnieźnieńskie, dokumentacja fotograficzna*, M. Walicki and T. Adamowicz, eds. Wrocław, Zakład Narodowy im. Ossolińskich, 1956

VI. Decorative Arts

✻

623. Artyści plastycy z kręgu "Cepelii." Wystawa Ogólnopolska, Warszawa, "Zachęta," lipiec 1973. [Visual artists from the Cepelia Circle; A nationwide exhibition, Warsaw, "Zachęta," July 1973] Warszawa, Centralne Biuro Wystaw Artystycznych, 1975. Unpaged. Chiefly illus. NK1035.P6A78

Introduction also in English.

Biographical sketches of the artists.

"Visual artists from the Cepelia Circle" was an exhibition of 1,072 works by 185 artists associated with the Cepelia cooperative. Held at Zachęta in July 1973 on the ocassion of the twenty-fifth anniversary of the Cepelia cooperative, the exhibit reflected Cepelia's two types of practitioners: the trained artist and the folk artist. Media included fabric (carpets, clothing, curtains, tapestries), metal, leather, ceramics, wicker, and wood. Weaving prevailed as the strongest of the crafts. Among the many groups represented were the Ład cooperative, the Zakopane Model Workshops, and the Imago-Artists cooperative.

624. BOCHNAK, Adam, *and* Kazimierz Buczkowski. Decorative arts in Poland. Warsaw, Arkady, 1972. 331 p. plates. NK1035.P6B613

Translation by Paul Crossley and Marek Latyński of *Rzemiosło artystyczne w Polsce.*

Extraordinarily fine metalwork, glass, textile, and ceramic objects dating from the Gothic, Renaissance, and Baroque periods. Other examples are from the Romanesque period and the eighteenth through the twentieth century. Scholarly introductions to each period. The authors include both religious and secular art, draw comparisons with other East European art, and point out foreign influences. Prominent contemporary artists, schools, and cooperatives are enumerated within each section. Superior reproductions featuring many details.

625. BOCHNAK, Adam. Eksport z miast pruskich w głąb Polski w zakresie rzemiosła artystycznego. [The export of objects of art from Prussian cities into Poland] Studia Pomorskie, vol. 2, 1957, p. 7–112. illus. N6876.P56W3 v. 2

Summary in French and Russian.

Bibliographic references.

Western Prussia, with its cities of Toruń, Gdańsk, and Elbląg, came under Polish sovereignty in accordance with the Treaty of Toruń (1466) between Poland and the Teutonic Knights. The production of metal art objects flourished in Gdańsk, Toruń, and later Elbląg, from the fourteenth to the eighteenth century. Artists and artisans were drawn there by the high level of culture and the vigorous economy. The clergy of Gniezno and Włocławek were the patrons (chalices, monstrances, reliquaries). Other objects illustrated in the study are sumptuous coffins for kings and other royalty buried in Kraków; bronze doors and candelabra (1590, 1598) furnished by Christophe Oldendorf; and two coffin-shaped reliquaries by Piotr van der Rennen, one in Gniezno (1662), the other in Kraków (1669–1671).

626. BOCHNAK, Adam. Mecenat Zygmunta Starego w zarkresie rzemiosła artstycznego. [The patronage of crafts by King Sigismund I] Studia do dziejów Wawelu, vol. 2, 1961, p. 131–301. illus. NA7764.K7W27 v. 2

Summary in French.

An article of great importance for the breadth of material it covers and the quality of the archival documentation it provides to support the argument. These extensive accounts and inventories offer the means for a detailed insight into the patronage of Sigismund I (reigned 1506–1548) in the decorative arts. He introduced the Italian Renaissance to Poland, yet maintained contacts with Nuremberg. He ordered utensils, jewelry, and harnesses from Hungary. In Kraków he employed the goldsmith Martin Marciniec (1502, 1512) and commissioned an immense bell (1520) from Hans Beham, a Nuremberg founder who settled in Kraków. In 1535, for the occasion of his daughter's wedding to the Elector of Brandenburg, Sigismund I commissioned a silver casket enriched with enamels and precious stones, whose subsequent course to the collection in the Hermitage is then charted. A wealth of information on other large and important commissions is included in the article. The Nuremberg craftsmen supplied many art objects for the Sigismund Chapel in the Wawel Cathedral and for the church on Jasna Góra in Częstochowa.

627. GRABOWSKA, Janina.

Polski bursztyn. [Polish amber] Warszawa, Interpress, 1983. 44 p. 112 p. of color plates, illus. NK6000.G73 1983

Bibliography: p. 42–44.

Photographs by Janina Gardzielewska and Janusz Korpal.

A history of Polish amber. Describes, and illustrates in color, artistic amber objects made in Gdańsk and Królewiec (Königsberg): jewelry, small chests, checkerboards, chess pieces, and medallions. Also describes the establishment of a permanent museum of amber in the castle of Malbork.

Perhaps the most spectacular achievement of amber art was the amber hall, which was made in Gdańsk and given by Frederick Wilhelm of Prussia to Tsar Peter I of Russia (1716).

628. HUML, Irena.

Polska sztuka stosowana XX wieku. [Polish applied art of the twentieth century] Warszawa, Wydawnictwa Artystyczne i Filmowe, 1978. 297 p. illus. (part color). NK1035.P6H85

Summary in English.

Bibliography: p. 282–84.

To deal with the various branches of applied art, the author discusses major figures and groups, as well as their achievements. Interior and furniture design, weaving, ceramics, glass, and metalwork are presented from

their twentieth-century beginnings through the work of Stanisław Witkiewicz and Stanisław Wyspiański to the contemporary work of Magdalena Abakanowicz. Over two hundred illustrations of furniture, textiles, glass, and ceramics— principally as used in interior design (c.1900 through 1974). Contemporary textiles of outstanding interest.

[40]. Kraków. Muzeum Narodowe. L'art à Cracovie

entre 1350 et 1550; exposition organisée à l'occasion du sixième centenaire de la fondation de l'Université Jagellone. Cracovie, 1964. 386 p. 105 plates. N6997.K7K714

Catalog by Maria Kopffowa, et al.

Bibliography: p. 251–72.

Catalog from the exhibition of medieval and Renaissance Polish art, on the 600th anniversary of the founding of the Jagiellonian University, Kraków. A total of 313 entries; covers decorative art from the fifteenth and sixteenth century, ranging from goldsmithery and metalwork to textiles. The lengthy introduction (57 p.) by Maria Kopffowa discusses the history as well as the intellectual and cultural life of Kraków.

629. Ład XXX; wystawa

spółdzielni artystów plastyków. [Ład (Thirty years of existence); exhibition of its artists] Warszawa, Centralne Biuro Wystaw Artystycznych, 1956. 41 p. 64 p. of plates, illus. NK1035.P6L3 1956

Bibliography: p. 22–28.

Anniversary exhibition of a craftsmen's cooperative that originated in 1926 at the Warsaw School of Fine

Arts, and was known for its high-quality products. Selected bibliography and catalog divided between artists working to 1944, and those active between 1945 and 1956.

630. LUDWIKOWSKI, Leszek, and Tadeusz Wroński.

Tradycyjna szopka krakowska. [The traditional crèche of Kraków] Kraków, Krajowa Agencja Wydawnicza, 1978. 52 p. illus. (part color). N8065.L83

Summary in German and English.

Bibliography: p. 44–45.

The Kraków crèches are so richly designed and ornamented because their form is traditionally based on the city's historic buildings. Twenty-four color photographs of outstanding examples. Photographs in black and white of competitions and entries from the 1930s and from the 1950s through the 1970s.

[51]. MAŃKOWSKI, Tadeusz.

Orient w polskiej kulturze artystycznej. [The Orient in Polish artistic culture] Wrocław, Zakład Narodowy im. Ossolińskich, 1959. 255 p. plates, illus. (part color). N7255.P6M36 1959

Summary and table of contents in French.

Bibliographic references.

The influence may be divided between the Byzantine ascendance—from the Middle Ages to the fall of Constantinople in 1453—and the Islamic dominance from that date to the nineteenth century. During the first period, painting in particular, in various media, was charged with Near Eastern styles through Armenian influence. During the second period, rugs, especially, but also fabrics, arms and armor, were imported from Persia by way of Turkey. Polish artists and architects were also active in Turkey and Transylvania.

[52]. MAŃKOWSKI, Tadeusz.
Sztuka Islamu w Polsce w XVII i XVIII wieku. [Islamic art in Poland in the seventeenth and eighteenth centuries] Kraków, Gebethner and Wolff, 1935. 126 p. illus. 40 plates. (Polska Akademia Umiejętności. Wydział Filologiczny. Rozprawy, vol. 64, no. 3) AS142.K85
Bibliographic references.

A study in seven chapters covering topics such as the infiltration of Eastern art, especially Islamic, into Poland, from the Middle Ages to the Baroque, through trade, war, or other mechanisms; Persian carpets collected by Polish kings from Sigismund Augustus to Augustus III; Eastern and Western influences on Polish seventeenth-century weaving; Eastern and Polish sashes; production in Lwów of arms, embroidery, and clothing, with their particular styles and ornamentation.

[54]. Mille ans d'art en Pologne, Petit Palais, Paris, avril–juillet 1969. Paris, Petit Palais, 1969. 1 v. (unpaged) illus., color plates. N6991.M5
Bibliographic references.
Exhibition catalog.
Within the wide chronological span, the widest diversity in materials and quality. Great objects of Gothic sculpture, goldsmithery, ecclesiastical vestments, and Renaissance tapestries. Also portraits and other paintings—Gothic to the present—and decorative arts. A summary catalog.
Reviews in the French press by

André Chastel, Le Monde (May 3, 1969), Pierre du Colombier, L'Amateur de l'Art (April 24, 1969), Pierre Schneider, L'Express (May 26–June 1, 1969), and others.

631. Muzeum w Wilanowie.
Rzemiosło artystyczne i plastyka w zbiorach wilanowskich. Katalog-Przewodnik po Galerii. [Decorative arts and sculpture in the Wilanów Museum. Catalog and guide to the Gallery] Warszawa, Muzeum Narodowe w Warszawie, 1980. 340 p. illus. (Katalog zbiorów artystycznych, 2) NK480.W54M89 1980
Edited by Włodzimierz Baldowski, et al.
Bibliography: p. 15–16.
Arranged by materials: ceramics, including majolica and delftware, and an extensive collection of Meissen; glassware; silver; bronze; arms; furniture; Far Eastern objects; nineteenth-century medals. German, Dutch, English, Russian, Italian, and Polish schools are represented. Well-reproduced illustrations.

[133]. The Old Town and the Royal Castle in Warsaw.
Warsaw, Arkady, 1988. 63 p. of text, 24 illus., 159 color plates, plans. DK4637. S7S7313 1988
Edited by Bożena Wierzbicka.
Translated by Jerzy A. Bałdyga.
Four essays on the history and reconstruction of Warsaw's Old Town and the Royal Castle by Jan Zachwatowicz, Piotr Biegański, Stanisław Lorentz, and Aleksander Gieysztor. Good illustrations of the interior of the castle—its furnishings, sculptures, paintings, clocks, candela-

bra, etc. Also available in Polish, Stare miasto i Zamek Królewski w Warszawie *(1988).*

632. O rzemiośle artystycznym w Polsce. [Decorative arts in Poland] Warszawa, Państwowe Wydawnictwo Naukowe, 1976. 321 p. illus. N7255.P6 O18
Edited by Teresa Hrankowska.
Table of contents in English.
Bibliographic references.
Materiały Sesji Naukowej zorganizowanej przez Oddział Poznański Stowarzyszenia Historyków Sztuki i Muzeum Narodowego w Poznaniu w dniach 22–24 października 1973 przy współudziale Przedsiębiorstwa Państwowego "DESA" Dzieła Sztuki i Antyki.
Fifteen papers presented at the Conference of the Association of Polish Art Historians, Poznań Branch (Poznań, October 22–24, 1973). Topics include the French silver collection in Wilanów; a history of the first porcelain factories in Poland at the end of the eighteenth century; furniture renovation in the Wawel Castle during the reign of Sigismund I (sixteenth century); the embroidery of vestments preserved in the treasury of Jasna Góra; jewels and costumes used by the dukes of Szczecin; and metal work as well as the artistic qualities of arms and armor.

633. Piękno użyteczne.
Ćwierćwiecze Cepelii. [The beauty of useful objects. A quarter century of Cepelia] Warszawa, Zakład Wydawnictw CRS, 1975. 226 p. illus. (part color). NK19.P7C466
Summaries in English, French, and Russian.

Overview

Report on Cepelia (the name is an acronym for the National Organization for Folk and Popular Art). Established in 1949, it coordinates the industry and markets its products. A history of the organization and its interactions with the participating bodies throughout the country. Administration, merchandising, and international fairs are the book's subjects, not the craftsmen.

634. Polonia, arte e cultura dal medioevo all'illuminismo.

Roma, Palazzo Venezia, 23 maggio–22 luglio 1975. Firenze, Centro Di: Scala [1975] 286 p. illus. (art color). N7255.P6P675

Bibliography: p. 284–86.

Exhibition catalog.

The exhibition sponsored by Ministero per i beni culturali e ambientali, Direzione generale delle antichita e belle arti.

A catalog of the exhibition of Polish art, from the thirteenth through the eighteenth century, of the paintings, metalwork (liturgical vessels, crucifixes reliquaries, secular gold objects, arms and armor), tapestries, rugs, and sashes. The exhibition was held in Rome in 1975 under the patronage of the presidents of Italy and Poland.

635. Polska Sztuka Użytkowa w 25-lecie PRL.
[Polish applied art in a quarter century of the Peoples Republic of Poland] Warszawa, Związek Polskich Artystów Plastyków, 1972. unpaged. illus. NK1035.P6P64

Polish applied arts during twenty-five years of the Polish Peoples' Republic was celebrated by a series of national exhibitions held in Poznań, Łódź, Gdańsk, Wrocław, Lublin, and Warsaw in the Spring of 1969. This handbook is based on that series of exhibitions, representing nearly six hundred artists. The work is divided into six sections: planning the exhibitions, unique and commercial textiles, glass and ceramic design, furniture, and interior decoration.

[75]. ROZANOW, Zofia, *and* Ewa Smulikowska.

Skarby kultury na Jasnej Górze. [Cultural treasures at Jasna Góra] 2d rev. ed. Warszawa. Interpress, 1979. 211 p. color illus. N7255.P62C937 1979

Introduction by Władysław Tomkiewicz.

Bibliography: p. 209–10.

Photographs by Jan Michlewski and Janusz Rosikoń.

Also available in the English translation (see next entry).

[76]. ROZANOW, Zofia, *and* Ewa Smulikowska.

The cultural heritage of Jasna Góra. 2d rev. ed. Warsaw, Interpress, 1979. 211 p. color illus. N7255.P62C936 1979

Introduction by Władysław Tomkiewicz.

Translation by Stanisław Tarnowski.

Bibliography: p. 209–11.

Photographs by Jan Michlewski and Janusz Rosikoń.

Art treasures at the Pauline Monastery in Częstochowa. Lavish gifts were bestowed on Jasna Góra by the kings of Poland: croziers and chalices, a reliquary crucifix of 1510, the scepter of the Jagiellonians of 1500, a silver repoussé antependium of the early eighteenth century, and many more. Seventeenth-century paintings of the history of the monastery, including the Hussite attack in 1430, when the picture of the Madonna was slashed.

636. ROŻEK, Michał.

Polskie koronacje i korony. [Polish coronations and crowns] Kraków, Krajowa Agencja Wydawnicza, 1987. 160 p. illus. (part color), ports. DK4131.R69 1987

Bibliography: p. 151–60.

Historical background of the coronations of the kings and queens of Poland, beginning with that of Bolesław Chrobry in 1025. Description of the ceremonies from the fourteenth century onward. History of the coronation insignia and regalia, including their fate in the nineteenth and twentieth century. Archival and printed sources given in the bibliography, although the text is without footnotes. Abundant reproductions of seals, coins, miniatures, prints, drawings; these, however, are inadequately described and repositories are not cited.

637. Skarby Jasnej Góry.

[Treasures of Jasna Góra] Wyd. 2, zmienione i rozszerzone. Warszawa, Interpress, 1983. 223 p. color illus. N7971.P62C977 1983

By Janusz St. Pasierb and Jan Samek.

Bibliography: p. 222–23.

For the English language edition, see next item.

In 192 color plates, reproductions of the great seventeenth- and eighteenth-century interior furnishings of the church, and sixteenth-century illuminated parchment manuscripts. A prodigious number of liturgical objects from the sixteenth and seventeenth century, many reproduced in detail.

638. The Shrine of the Black Madonna at Częstochowa.

Warsaw, Interpress, 1989. 3rd ed.

223 p. color illus. N7971.P62
C976 1989

Text by Janusz S. Pasierb;
captions and bibliography by Jan
Samek.

Translation of *Skarby Jasnej
Góry.*

Bibliography: p. 223–24.

639. Straty wojenne zbiorów
polskich w dziedzinie rzemiosła
artystycznego. [Decorative arts
from Polish collections lost in the
War] Warszawa, Ministerstwo
Kultury i Sztuki, 1953. 2 vols.
illus. (Prace i Materiały Biura
Rewindykacji i Odszkodowań,
no. 12, 13) N6991.S84

Collective work by Benedykt
Tyszkiewicz, Bogusław
Kopydłowski, Maria Markiewicz,
Zdzisław Szulc, Tadeusz
Seweryn, Józef Sandel, and
Mieczysław Chojnacki.

*Vol. I: Glass and ceramics; gold-
smithery; weaving; furniture; musical
instruments. Vol. II: Folk art;
Jewish ceremonial objects; arms. Altogether 1,690 objects, each of which
is described along with a bibliography.
Lists of former owners. The 303
Jewish ceremonial works of art shown
came from fifty-five private owners
and institutions, such as synagogues in
Częstochowa, Gdańsk, Kraków,
Lublin, and Warsaw.*

640. WIĘCKOWSKA, Jolanta.
Chateau de Łańcut. Le bref guide
de la Collection de Musée.
Łańcut, Musée de Łańcut, 1976.
83 p. illus. DK4800.L36W53

Translation by Aleksandra
Żarynowa.

Bibliography: p. 70–71.

*Arranged by order of progression
through the rooms of the palace, the
text sketches in barest outline the*
*history of the building, its architec-
ture, and furnishings and objects that
remain, as well as those that were
dispersed (notably the paintings by F.
Boucher that, until 1944 hung in the
Castle's Salon de Boucher). Outstanding furnishings are identified by
maker (e.g., the "giraffe" piano,
made c. 1810 by C.E. Burger in
Vienna). Index of persons, who
are identified by date, métier, and
production.*

Also available in English: Łańcut
Castle: a brief guide to museum
collections. *Łańcut, 1974. 80 p.
illus. N A 7764.L3 W 5313*

[109] Wzory sztuki
średniowiecznej i z epoki
Odrodzenia po koniec wieku
XVII w dawnej Polsce.
Monuments du Moyen-Age et de
la Renaissance dans l'ancienne
Pologne depuis les temps les plus
reculés jusqu'à la fin du XVII
siècle. Warszawa, Paris, Zakład
Chromolitograficzny M. Fajansa;
Drukarnia J. Ungara, 1853–1858.
2 vols. illus. (part color).
N7255.P6W98 1986
Edited by Alexander Przeździecki
and Edward Rastawiecki.
Text in French and Polish.
Reprinted in 1986 by
Wydawnictwa Artystyczne i
Filmowe.
Originally published in sections
for subscribers.

*The first work that extensively
describes the decorative arts of ancient
Poland, from medieval and Renaissance times through the seventeenth
century.*

**641. Związek Polskich
Artystów Plastyków.** Wystawa
Ogólnopolska tkaniny, ceramiki i
szkła. [Polish national exhibition
of weaving, ceramics, and glass]
Warszawa, Zachęta, kwiecień
1964. Warszawa, Centralne Biuro
Wystaw Artystycznych, [1964]
unpaged. chiefly illus.
NK976.P6Z9
*Exhibition catalog edited by Maria
Matusińska and Barbara Mitschein.*

*Includes reproductions of 140
objects. Essays on weaving, ceramics,
and glass precede the catalog of
reproductions.*

642. ŻYGULSKI, Zdzisław, Jr.
Dzieje polskiego rzemiosła
artystycznego. [A History of
Polish artistic craftsmanship]
Warszawa, Interpress, 1987. 250
p. illus. (part color).
NK1035.P6Z94 1987

Bibliography: p. 238–43.

Photographs by Stanisław
Markowski.

643. ŻYGULSKI, Zdzisław, Jr.
An outline history of Polish
applied art. Warsaw, Interpress,
1987. 263 p., color illus.
NK1035.P6 Z95 1987

Translation from Polish by
Stanisław Tarnowski.

Bibliography: p. 249–56.

*The best text in English on the
Polish decorative arts. The exposition
is long, scholarly, and authoritative,
and rewards the reader's perseverance
despite editorial failure to provide
subheadings and other amenities (such
as cross-references to the plates to
guide the reader). Dividing the subject
into four periods, the author reviews
all the crafts, and describes various
examples of each, beginning with the
most important. As background, he
provides a history of the period,
taking into account economic conditions, political events and their
outcome, and workshop conditions. He*

Overview

gives probably the best discussion in English of the culture of the inward-looking Sarmatian period (chapter 2), and tackles a multitude of other fascinating subjects, such as typonomy, as indicative of early sites of craft production (e.g., złotniki); evidence, in painting, of attire, utensils and vessels, and furniture for a history of the decorative arts; the battle crown of Casimir the Great (c. 1360); and royal burial crowns, scepters, and other insignia excavated in 1973. Nearly two hundred fine color plates.

644. ŻYGULSKI, Zdzisław, Jr.
Odsiecz Wiedeńska 1683. [The relief of Vienna 1683] Kraków, Krajowa Agencja Wydawnicza, 1988. 38 p. 229 illus. (part color), maps, ports. DR536.Z94 1988
   In Polish and English.
   Bibliography.

Divided into eight parts, each of which is richly illustrated. Materials include the decorative arts, carpets, arms and armor, costumes, uniforms, chasubles of Turkish fabric, vestments made from fabrics confiscated at Vienna, Turkish saddles, Polish saddles and accessories, the Karacena armor of King Sobieski, and of Hetman Jabłonowski.

A special section depicts the Vienna trophies and the Grand Viziers' tents. In addition to all these items, there are numerous portraits of notable figures from the period and paintings of contemporary, historical events. Very good photographs.

[271]. ABAKANOWICZ, Magdalena.
Magdalena Abakanowicz: Museum of Contemporary Art, Chicago. New York, Abbeville Press, 1982. 188 p. illus. (part color). N7255.P63A232 1982

Exhibition held at Museum of Contemporary Art, Chicago, and the Chicago Public Library Cultural Center, Nov. 6, 1982 through Jan. 2, 1983, and other museums.
   Bibliography: p. 172–86.
The sculptor, who works on a monumental scale—almost exclusively in fiber—is represented in this text in all phases of her work. Its evolution is traced from the free-form tapestries called "Abakan" to three-dimensional figural and abstract forms that express the human condition. A brief verbal self-portrait, and quotations from the artist that accompany many of the 152 illustrations, are poignant and reveal that nature is the foundation of her work. An excellent publication on an artist of major dimensions.

[272]. ABAKANOWICZ, Magdalena.
Magdalena Abakanowicz. Textile Strukturen und Konstruktionen. Environments. 29. Marz bis 28. Mai 1972. Düsseldorf, Kunstverein für die Rheinlande und Westfalen, 1972. 33 leaves (chiefly illustrations). N7255.P63A23
   Edited by Karl Heinz Hering.

645. Arrasy flamandzkie w Zamku Królewskim na Wawelu. [The Flemish tapestries at the Wawel Royal Castle] Warszawa, Arkady; Antwerp, Fonds Mercator, 1975. 501 p. color illus. ports. NK3071.P63K72 folio
   Edited by Jerzy Szablowski.
   By Anna Missiąg-Bocheńska, Marie Hennel-Bernasikowa, Magdalena Piwocka, Sophie

Schneebal-Perelman, and Adelbrecht
L. J. Van De Walle.
   Bibliography: p. 481–87.
   For English-language edition, 1972, see item 652.

646. GĘBAROWICZ, Mieczysław, *and* Tadeusz Mańkowski.
Arrasy Zygmunta Augusta. [The tapestries of (King) Sigismund Augustus] Rocznik Krakowski, vol. 29, 1937. 220 p. illus. DB879.K8R58 v. 29
   Summary in French.
   Bibliographic references.

A fundamental scholarly study to which Szabłowski et al. (no. 652) pay tribute. King Sigismund Augustus (reigned 1548–1572) owned about 350 tapestries at the time of his death. The research focuses mainly on the Genesis set: comparisons with analogous tapestries elsewhere; workshops where they were executed. Discussion of the eleven copies after various cartoons of the three Kraków series (Stuttgart). Transcriptions of the extensive archival documents.

647. HUML, Irena.
Współczesna tkanina polska. [Contemporary Polish weaving] Warszawa, Arkady, 1989. 244 p. 175 illus. (part color). NK8971.P6H86 1989

Album of artistic Polish weaving of the twentieth century. Well illustrated.

648. MAŃKOWSKI, Tadeusz.
Polskie tkaniny i hafty XVI–XVIII wieku. [Polish weavings and embroideries of the sixteenth to eighteenth centuries] Wrocław, Zakład Narodowy im.

Ossolińskich, 1954. 180 p. illus., color plates. (Studia z dziejów polskiego rzemiosła artystycznego, vol. 2) NK9271.P7M3

Table of contents and list of illustrations also in English, French, German, and Russian.

Bibliographic references.

A rich, historical account studded with detailed knowledge of workshops, techniques, craftsmen, guilds, patrons, fashions, costumes, and ceremonies— at court and in town. Special chapters on tapestry, kilims, woolen carpets, and waist sashes. A chapter on tents particularizes not only their military uses but their fashionable role in courtly amusement. Sixteen good color plates that reproduce the surface texture of the textiles, and over one hundred black and white plates.

649. MARKIEWICZ, Maria.
Z zagadnień polskiego tkactwa renesansowego. [Problems in Polish Renaissance weaving] Studia Renesansowe, vol. 3, 1963. p. 483–520. illus. N6991.S87

Summary in French and Russian.

Bibliographic references.

A limited number of Renaissance woven tapestries survive; archives indicate the extent of losses. Three sets, which the author discusses, embody the favored subjects: the Story of Samson, commissioned by a high Polish-Lithuanian nobleman (d. 1598); the Credo, commissioned by lower-ranking nobility (early seventeenth century); and the virtues of commerce, woven for Gdańsk patricians (c. 1620). Woven silks were introduced in Kraków, Leszno, and Warsaw.

650. Moderne polnische Teppiche. Essen, Museum Folkwang, 1970. 62 p. illus. NK3071.P6M6

Catalog of the exhibition held March 1–April 5, 1970 at the Museum Folkwang in Essen.

Edited by Hanna Kotkowska-Bareja.

Items by twenty-four weavers who work in an abstractly pictorial and highly tactile mode.

651. PIWOCKI, Ksawery, ed. Tkanina polska. [Polish weaving] Warszawa, Arkady, 1959. 108 p. 228 illus. NK8856.P5

Summary in French.
Bibliographies.

Stresses that weaving is a highly developed Polish national form. Essays on the history of Polish textiles to the nineteenth century, on popular specimens, and on double-sided weavings, both historical and modern, but the main emphasis is on contemporary weavers. Many illustrations reproduce the surface texture.

652. SZABLOWSKI, Jerzy.
The Flemish tapestries at Wawel Castle in Cracow. Treasures of King Sigismund Augustus Jagiello. Antwerp, Fonds Mercator, 1972. 501 p. color illus. NK3071.P63K78 folio

Various chapters by Anna Missiąg-Bocheńska, Marie Hennel-Bernasikowa, Magdalena Piwocka, Sophie Schneebal-Perelman, and Adelbrecht L.J. Van De Walle.

Bibliography: p. 481–87.

Also published in French, Flemish, and German. A Polish

edition was published in 1975 (see item 645).

One of the finest books ever published on art in Poland. Three sets of tapestries commissioned by King Sigismund II Augustus (1520–1572) are illustrated in 136 unsurpassed color plates. The text, of appropriate quality, furnishes the cultural and artistic circumstances that led to these commissions. One set consists of eighteen hangings with subjects from Genesis based on designs by Michiel Coxie; another is of forty-four verdures with real and fantastic animals, having antecedents in the work of Joachim Patinir, Pieter Brueghel the Elder, and Mathieu and Hieronymus Cock, among others, and anticipating mannerist landscapes; the third set is made up of sixty-two tapestries with grotesque subjects whose basis in ancient, Italian, and Netherlandish art is explored.

653. SZUMAN, Stefan.
Dawne kilimy w Polsce i na Ukrainie. [Old kilims in Poland and the Ukraine] Poznań, Fiszer i Majewski, 1929. 138 p. 60 plates of illus. (part color). [4NK-17]

Summary in French.
Bibliography: p. 155–56.

The Europeanized rugs are said to have an imprint of Asiatic fantasy, a folk-like charm, and noble and archaic simplicity. Investigates the origins of the kilims, the development of their ornament—especially with reference to oriental influences in Poland and the Ukraine—and the technique of their production, etc. Approximately seventy rugs in the catalog.

654. Tapis de Pologne, Lithuanie, Yougoslavie. Paris,

Editions Arts & Couleurs, 1930. chiefly color illus. NK2842.T3 folio

Edited by Henri Erns.

Ten rugs exhibited in Paris in 1927 at the Musée des Arts Décoratifs. Seven were modern rugs from Zakopane and Warsaw, identified by designer and manufacturer. The other three rugs predated 1900.

655. Tkanina artystyczna w 40-leciu PRL. Katalog wystawy. [Artistic weaving in 40 years of the Polish Peoples Republic. Exhibition catalog] Łódź, Centralne Muzeum Włókiennictwa, 1985. 120 p. illus. (part color). NK3071.P6T43 1985

Prepared by Aleksandra Sowińska and Małgorzata Wróblewska-Markiewicz.

Introduction by Halina Jurga and Norbert Zawisza.

Conservative as well as exploratory styles; 115 weavers, of whom fifteen are men; biographies. Forty black and white illustrations inadequately represent the objects.

656. BANAŚ, Paweł.
Polskie współczesne szkło artystyczne. [Polish contemporary artistic glass] Wrocław, Zakład Narodowy im. Ossolińskich, 1982. 246 p. illus. NK5171.P6B36 1982

Bibliographic references.

A scholarly study of glass of this century in relation to theories of design and developments in style. An account of Polish artists working in the medium; the official organization of the craft; Wrocław and Warsaw as centers of production from 1949 to 1964 and in the 1960s, respectively;

and developments in the 1970s. Well illustrated.

657. CHOJNACKA, Halina.
Fajanse polskie XVIII–XIX wieku. [Polish faience of the eighteenth and nineteenth century] Warszawa, Krajowa Agencja Wydawnicza, 1981. 87 p. illus. NK4305.5.P7C49 1981

These ceramics of great charm were produced in Poland at a time when such manufacture flourished throughout Europe. A history of technical developments in Poland. Mostly pottery but also figures in Chinese and Wedgewood styles and other correspondences.

658. DĄBROWSKA, Maria.
Kafle i piece kaflowe w Polsce do końca XVIII wieku. [Tiles and tile stoves in Poland to the end of the eighteenth century] Wrocław, Zakład Narodowy im. Ossolińskich, 1987. 269p p. [102] p. of plates, illus. (Studia i materiały z historii kultury materialnej, vol. 58) NK4670.7.P55D33 1987

Bibliography: p. 221–32.
English summary.

The author discusses production methods, shapes, decorative patterns, and regional differences in the tiles, from their appearance in the mid-fourteenth century through the eighteenth century.

659. KOŁODZIEJOWA, Bolesława, *and* Zbigniew M. Stadnicki.
Zakłady porcelany Ćmielów. [The Ćmielów porcelain factory] Kraków, Krajowa Agencja Wydawnicza, 1986. 311 p. illus. (part color). NK4210.Z27K65

Summary in English, German, French, and Russian.
Bibliography: p. 48–49.
Photographs by Janusz Podlecki.

History and production of a factory that has been active since 1804. About two hundred illustrations in color reproduce the faience, porcelain, stoneware, and majolica. Tables of names of services and ornamental figures and of the ceramicists who executed them, (1920–1939 and since 1946). Thirty-six earlier marks reproduced.

660. Muzeum Narodowe we Wrocławiu. Polskie współczesne szkło artystyczne. [Contemporary Polish artistic glass] Wrocław, 1979. 158 p. illus. NK5171.P6M8 1979

Summary in English.

An account of modern developments in glass. Biographies of thirty-nine participating artists and a catalog of more than three hundred works. The fine quality of the objects is discernible despite the severly reduced illustrations.

661. PIĄTKIEWICZ-DERENIOWA, Maria.
Kafle wawelskie okresu wczesnego Renesansu. [Wawel stove tiles in the early Renaissance period] Studia do dziejów Wawelu, vol. 2, 1961, p. 303–75. illus. (part color). NA7764.K7W27 v. 2

Summary in French.
Bibliographic references.

These finely executed ceramic stove tiles were found primarily during excavations on the Wawel in 1927 and 1956–57. The author divides them according to the representation:

✽

figural, floral, or architectural. Stylistically, they reflect the transition from Gothic to Renaissance. The author proposes reconstruction of the stoves based on archival documents, representations of stoves in contemporary prints, and surviving stoves in other European collections.

662. PIWKOWSKI, Włodzimierz.
Manufaktura majoliki w Nieborowie. [The manufacture of majolica in Nieborów] *In* Rocznik Muzeum Narodowego w Warszawie. Annuaire du Musée National de Varsovie. No. 29. Warszawa, 1985, p. 369–421. illus. AM101.W3674 no. 29
Summary in French and Russian.
Bibliography: p. 148.
Established in 1881 by Michał Piotr Radziwiłł on his estate of Nieborów, the manufacture existed until 1907, but produced artistic items only during its first stage (until 1886). Among these were vases with pictures of historical scenes, plates with royal portraits and coats of arms of Poland and Lithuania, and clocks, candelabra, chandeliers, etc. Later, it also produced tiles.
Signatures of painters, their names, and marks of the manufacture are provided.

663. Polska porcelana. [Polish porcelain] 2d ed. Wrocław, Zakład Narodowy im. Ossolińskich, 1983. 220 p. illus. (part color). NK4541.P6P6 1983
By Elżbieta Kowecka, et al.
Bibliography: p. 201–202.
Chapters on the history of porcelain manufacture in Poland; on materials, techniques, and organization of production; and on guidelines for collectors. Over one hundred manufacturers'

marks diagramatically reproduced. *Photographically reproduced marks of the porcelain on eight color plates and 209 black and white plates.*

√ 664. Polskie szkło do połowy XIX wieku. [Polish glass to the middle of the nineteenth century] 2d rev. ed. Wrocław, Zakład Narodowy im. Ossolińskich, 1987. 192 p. 120 p. of plates, illus., maps. NK5171.P6P65 1987
Edited by Zofia Kamieńska and Kazimierz Buczkowski.
Summary in French.
Bibliography: p. 185–87.
Covers the importation of glass and its manufacture in Poland from antiquity. Marked production from the Middle Ages onward, especially in Silesia. Includes mirrors and chandeliers as well as stained glass of the Małopolska and Pomeranian regions. Five color, and 160 black and white photographs.

665. STARZEWSKA, Maria.
Polska ceramika artystyczna pierwszej połowy XX wieku. [Polish artistic ceramics of the first half of the twentieth century] Wrocław, Muzeum Śląskie we Wrocławiu, 1952. 114 p. illus. NK4141.P6S8

666. STARZEWSKA, Maria, *and* Maria Jeżewska.
Polski fajans. [Polish faience] Wrocław, Zakład Narodowy im. Ossolińskich, 1978. 138 p. 139 p. of plates, illus., map. NK4305.5.P7S75 1978
Catalog of potteries and their marks from the eighteenth century to the present. Map of sites where faience has been produced. Some good illustrations.

667. BARTKIEWICZ, Magdalena.
Polski ubiór do 1864 roku. [Polish costumes before 1864] Wrocław, Zakład Narodowy im. Ossolińskich, 1979. 146 p. 101 plates, illus. (part color). GT1060.B29
Bibliography: p. 134–38.
Well-illustrated history of national costumes from the thirteenth century until 1864, the romantic period. The study is based on the collections of costumes in Polish ethnographic museums, old illustrative material such as the Behem Codex, and portraits in galleries. While waist sashes, fans, and other accessories are included, costumes of clergy and children are not. Military uniforms are treated marginally. The author believes that military costumes, which are strongly linked to the national tradition, should be treated in a separate study.

668. GUTKOWSKA-RYCHLEWSKA, Maria, *and* Maria Taszycka.
Polskie hafty średniowieczne. Katalog wystawy maj–czerwiec 1967. [Medieval Polish embroidery. Exhibition catalog May–June 1967] Kraków, Muzeum Narodowe w Krakowie, 1967. 84 p. 64 plates. NK9256.G8
Summary and list of illustrations also in French.
Bibliography: p. 21.
A scholarly catalog of sixty-four works. The small-scale, black and white reproductions scarcely hint at the beauty of these interesting fabrics, which were mostly made up into chasubles.

Ceramics, Glassware, Pottery

669. GUTKOWSKA-RYCHLEWSKA, Maria, *and* Maria Taszycka.
Ubiory i akcesoria mody wieku XIX. [Costumes and accessories of the nineteenth century] Kraków, Muzeum Narodowe w Krakowie, 1967. 64 p. tables. GT1060.G8

Table of illustrations also in English.

Mostly women's, but also men's costumes, dating from about 1805 to the 1860s. Manufactured in Poland, except for a few examples from elsewhere in Europe. Accessories include Kashmir shawls and their European imitations, combs, fans, and handbags. Glossary of terms. Catalog of over sixty-four objects to which the small reproductions do not do justice.

670. KNOBLOCH, Mieczysław.
Polska biżuteria. [Polish jewelry] Wrocław, Zakład Narodowy im. Ossolińskich, 1980. 106 p. 129 illus. color plates. NK7371.P6K57

Bibliography: p. 99–101.

Begins the narrative with the tenth century. Compiles gold and silversmiths' marks from the Middle Ages to the eighteenth century. Notices on the craftsmen. A long chapter is devoted to technology, mostly of the twentieth century. Fourteen pieces reproduced in color, 125 examples in black and white; reproductions are mainly unsatisfactory.

671. MAŃKOWSKI, Tadeusz.
Pasy polskie. [Polish waist sashes] Polska Akademia Umiejętności. Prace Komisji Historji Sztuki, vol. 7, no. 2, 1938, p. 101–218. illus. N6991.P633 v. 7 folio

Summary in English.
Bibliographic references.

In the eighteenth century, waist sashes were a requisite of noblemen's attire. The waist sash imitated an article of dress in the Islamic Middle East. The earliest were manufactured in southeastern Poland by Armenians, first on Turkish, then on Persian models. Later, production moved to the Warsaw region. Decorative elements changed to conform to Polish taste, sometimes under French (Lyonnaise) influence. Manufacturing sites, weavers, patrons, and designs are examined.

Among more recent works is Maria Taszycka's Polskie pasy kontuszowe. [Polish waist sashes] Kraków, Wydawnictwo Literackie, 1985. 111 p. illus. (NK8971.P6T28), which describes and reproduces forty-four sashes from the collections of the National Museum in Kraków.

672. MATEJKO, Jan.
Ubiory w Polsce 1200–1795. [Costumes in Poland 1200–1795] Kraków, 1967. 259 p. illus. (part color), ports. GT1060.M33

Summary in English, French, and Russian.

Bibliographic references.

Matejko's costume drawings and watercolors—copied from illuminated manuscripts (e.g., the Codex of Behem), books, paintings, seals, and coins—have served many historians and artists in their work.

Costumes from all social and occupational classes and genders, including royalty, clergy, magnates, peasants, the military, knights, savants, burghers, Jews, students, guild and fraternity members, and women.

673. MIODOŃSKA, Barbara.
Haft gotycki ze scenami Pasji z katedry Wawelskiej (tzw, antependium z Rudawy). [A Gothic embroidery with scenes of the Passion from the Wawel Cathedral (the so-called Antependium from Rudawa)] Folia Historiae Artium, vol. 18, 1982, p. 43–104. 61 figs., 1 color plate. N6.F6 v. 18

Summary in French.
Bibliographic references.

A Franco-Flemish embroidery, one of the most remarkable late Gothic embroideries in Europe, was executed in the years 1410 to 1420, and brought to Poland shortly thereafter. Altered to the antependium form; technique, style, iconography, and history.

674. TASZYCKA, Maria.
Włoskie jedwabne tkaniny odzieżowe w Polsce w pierwszej połowie XVII wieku. [Italian woven silks used for attire in Poland in the first half of the seventeenth century] Wrocław, Zakład Narodowy im. Ossolińskich, 1971. 96 p. 60 plates. NK8971.P6T3

Summary in French.
Bibliography: p. 85–86.

There was an abundance of such material in the Poland of this period. While Western Europeans dressed in the somber Spanish mode, Polish dress was rich in colors. The styles of the designs could be divided into nine groups. Importers were mainly Italian merchants in Kraków. Poor reproductions of interesting pieces.

675. TURNAU, Irena.
Odzież mieszczaństwa warszawskiego w XVIII wieku. [Costumes of the Warsaw

burghers in the eighteenth century] Wrocław, Zakład Narodowy im. Ossolińskich, 1967. 404 p. illus. GT1060.T87

Sponsored by the Institute of Material Culture of the Polish Academy of Sciences.

Summary in French and Russian.

Bibliography: p. 355–65.
Bibliographic references.

676. TURSKA, Krystyna.
Ubiór dworski w Polsce w dobie pierwszych Jagiellonów. [Court costumes in Poland during the region of the first Jagiellons] Wrocław, Zakład Narodowy im. Ossolińskich, 1987. 281 p. illus. GT1755.P7T87 1987

Sponsored by the Polish Academy of Sciences, Institute of Material Culture.

Summary in French.
Bibliographic references.

677. ŻYGULSKI, Zdzisław, Jr., *and* Henryk Wielecki.
Polski mundur wojskowy. [Polish military uniform] Kraków, Krajowa Agencja Wydawnicza, 1988. 417 p. 94 illus (part color), 360 color plates. UC485.P6Z94 1988

Bibliography: p. 404–410.
Description of illustrations in the album in Polish, English, and Russian.

Reproductions of the most characteristic examples of Polish military uniforms worn in Poland and abroad through the centuries, some belonging to famous individuals. The book is a history not only of military uniforms but of Polish armed forces as well. Each uniform is adequately described and information about its location is

provided. The uniforms are housed mainly in five museums: the Polish Army Museum in Warsaw, the National Museum and the Czartoryski Collection in Kraków, the National Museum in Poznań, and the Museum of Polish Arms in Kołobrzeg. Some drawings of uniforms are also reproduced from the rich collection of drawings made by B. Gembarzewski (1872–1941) housed in the National Museum in Warsaw.

678. BOCHNAK, Adam, *and* Julian Pagaczewski.
Polskie rzemiosło artystyczne wieków średnich. [Polish artistic craftsmanship of the Middle Ages] Kraków, Uniwersytet Jagielloński, 1959. 318 p. illus. (Rozprawy i studia, 5) NK1035.P6 B62

Summary in French.
Bibliographic references.

679. BOCHNAK, Adam.
Zabytki złotnictwa późnogotyckiego związane z Kard. Fryderykiem Jagiellończykiem. [Late Gothic goldsmith works connected with Cardinal Fryderyk Jagiełło] Prace Komisji Historii Sztuki, Polska Akademia Umiejętności, vol. 9, Kraków, 1948, p. 1–26. illus. N6991.P633 folio

Summary in French.
Bibliographic references.

Deals with works originating in the late fifteenth and early sixteenth century that were in the possession of, or commissioned by, Cardinal Frederick (Fryderyk) Jagiełło (1468–1503), son of King Kazimierz IV (Casimir IV) Jagiełło (1427–1492). Notable works of goldsmithery include the reliquary of St. Stanislaus, made by

Martin Marciniec, adorned with scenes from the life of St. Stanislaus, Bishop of Kraków (1030–1079). Other important items are the mace of the rector of Kraków University, a gift from Cardinal Fryderyk, and a beautiful, large cross. The reliquary and the mace are in the treasury of the Wawel Cathedral, the cross is in the Gniezno Cathedral.

680. BUJAŃSKA, Jadwiga.
Stare srebra. [Old silver] Kraków, Muzeum Narodowe, 1972. 137 p. 45 plates, illus. 2 p. marks. (Małe katalogi zabytków wybranych, 4) NK7102.5.P6K72

Catalog of forty-five silver objects, dating from the first to the nineteenth century. Among the objects are a nautilus cup with a cover in the shape of a peacock, Polish altar crosses, and processional crosses. Most of the objects come from the Czartoryski collection.

681. CHRZANOWSKI, Tadeusz, *and* Marian Kornecki.
Złotnictwo toruńskie. Studium o wyrobach cechu toruńskiego od wieku XIV do 1832. [Goldsmithery in Toruń. A study of guild production from the fourteenth century to 1832] Warszawa, Państwowe Wydawnictwo Naukowe, 1988. 160 p. 309 illus. (part color). NK7215.C57 1988

Summary in English and German.

Bibliographic references.
A list of goldsmiths and their work.

The earliest record of goldsmithery dates from the second half of the fourteenth century. The authors assign some crosses, chalices, and other liturgical objects to that period. Such

St. Stanisław presents the
kneeling Cardinal Frederick
Jagiełło to the enthroned
Madonna and Child. Epitaph
in memory of the Cardinal
(1468–1503), son of King
Kazimierz Jagiełło
(Jagiellończyk), in the Wawel
Cathedral, 1510. The bronze plate
was made in the renowned
workshop of Vischers in
Nuremberg. From Adam
Bochnak and Kazimierz
Buczkowski, *Decorative Arts in
Poland*. Warsaw, Arkady, 1972

*production flourished until the Refor-
mation, when objects of a secular
nature took precedence. A new
liturgical wave (c. 1580) came with
the Counterreformation and abated
only with the partition of the country
in the eighteenth century. Table of
printers' marks from the sixteenth
century that can be correlated with
artists' name. Techniques of producing
and decorating are described.*

682. DUBROWSKA, Małgorzata, *and* Andrzej Soltan.

Rzemiosło artystyczne
Minterów 1828–1881. [Artistic
craftsmanship of the Minter
family 1828–1881] Warszawa,
Państwowe Wydawnictwo

Naukowe, 1987. 205 p. illus.,
ports. NK7998.F34A4 1987
Bibliography: p. 202–04.

*Karol Fryderyk Minter (1780–
1847), a lithographer from Germany, settled in 1822 in Warsaw,
where he established a shop and a
foundry. Numbered among his early
achievements are a copperplate topo-
graphic map of Poland and numerous
portraits of prominent Polish personalities. In 1828, he opened a
factory consisting of nine shops that
specialized in the production of
lamps, tubs, medallions, children's
toys, statuettes, and many other
objects. His son, Karol Juliusz,
inherited the factory and enlarged its
production. Candelabra, chandeliers*

(one in the Wilanów palace), busts of prominent figures, as well as medallions of various sizes, sarcophagi, gravestones, artistic fountains in Warsaw in the shape of tritons, dolphins, mermaids, and many other objects were produced in the son's foundry. The artists who sculpted the objects were August Kiss (Berlin), Herman Fritsch, Konstanty Hegel, and Leonard Marconi from Warsaw, and a number of other Polish sculptors. Some of the tritons and mermaids can still be seen in Warsaw.

683. GIEYSZTOR, Aleksander.
La porte de bronze à Gniezno. Document de l'histoire de Pologne au XIIe siècle. Roma, Academia Polacca di Scienze e Lettere, 1959. 18 p. 6 illus. (Conferenze, fasc. 4)
NA5697.G5G5
Bibliographic references.

Explicates the historical and political sources of inspiration for the bronze doors, executed in the second half of the twelfth century, that represent the life of St. Adalbert (Wojciech) in eighteen scenes; installed in the cathedral in Gniezno, which at the time was the spiritual capital of Poland.

684. KIRYK, Feliks.
Cechowe rzemiosło metalowe; zarys dziejów do 1939 r. [Guild metal handicraft; an outline of its history prior to 1939] Warszawa, Biuro Wydawnictw K.D.W., 1972. 495 p. 26 leaves of plates. illus. (part color).
NK6471.P62K725
Bibliography: p. 464–68.

Provides a historical introduction to Kraków and the history of its metal

handicraft guilds. Here—from the middle ages to 1939—various shops produced jewelry, religious items, ornamented silver dishes, candelabra, bas reliefs, lanterns, iron doors, fences and gates, window bars, etc. The metal objects were produced for the royal court, Wawel Cathedral and other churches, and Polish magnates and high dignitaries. The significant patronage of Kings Sigismund I and Sigismund Augustus in the sixteenth century encouraged the blossoming of silver and goldsmith art shops in which artists from Germany, Italy, Hungary, and Poland worked.

This study is based on a multitude of archival documents in Kraków. It was issued on the millenium of the existence of metal handicraft in Poland. It includes a name index and an index of guild members registered in 1972 in Kraków. The metal binding with engraved eagles gives the book a unique appearance.

685. KOPYDŁOWSKI, Bogusław.
Polskie kowalstwo architektoniczne. [Polish architectural iron work] Warszawa, Arkady, 1958. 19 p. 262 illus.
NA3950.K6

Locks, gates, iron doors, window grills, etc., from the twelfth to the twentieth century. The nineteen-page introduction is divided into periods: Romanesque, Gothic, Renaissance, Baroque, Rococo, and Classicism. The remainder of the book consists of illustrations arranged in three groups, by subject. Many good reproductions of the artistic objects.

686. LEPSZY, Leonard.
Przemysł złotniczy w Polsce. [The gold industry in Poland] Kraków, Nakładem Muzeum

Przemysłowego, 1933. 358 p. illus. NK7156.L4

Alphabetical list of places where goldsmithery was practiced; history of manufacture at the sites—sometimes extending back to the late Middle Ages. Names of leading goldsmiths. Reproduced marks of numerous shops and goldsmiths. Covers the modern gold industry, as well, with its regulations and markings. Includes both secular and sacral objects.

687. LILEYKO, Halina.
Srebra warszawskie w zbiorach Muzeum Historycznego m. st. Warszawy. [Warsaw silver in the collections of the History Museum of the capital city of Warsaw] Warszawa, Państwowe Wydawnictwo Naukowe, 1979. 103 p. 125 plates of illus.
NK7171.P62W374
Summary in English and French.
Biographic sketches of the silversmiths.
Bibliography: p. 80–81.

One hundred twenty-five objects by sixty silversmiths, representing the style of given workshops and ranging from the eighteenth through the early twentieth century.

688. LILEYKO, Jerzy.
Regalia polskie. [Polish regalia] Warszawa, Krajowa Agencja Wydawnicza, 1987. 153 p. illus. (part color), ports.
CR616.L55 1987
Bibliography: p. 153.
Bibliographic references.

An important publication that discusses the following: the oldest Polish coronation insignia; the symbols of power of the Polish princes; the "ordo coronandi" of the Polish kings; the

Goldsmithery. Metalwork. Arms

so-called "crown of Chrobry"; the Jagged Sword (Szczerbiec); the coronation sword, scepter, apple, and other regalia; other royal crowns; and the royal treasury and its history.

689. MICHALSKA, Janina.
Cyna w dawnych wiekach. Katalog wystawy. [Old pewter. An exhibition catalog] Kraków, Muzeum Narodowe w Krakowie, 1973. 160 p. of text, 78 plates, illus. makers' marks. NK8401.5.P7K725

    Bibliography: p. 152–56.

A loan exhibition of pewter borrowed from seventeen institutions. Historical introduction to pewter fabrication in Poland from antiquity onward, with emphasis on the centers in Silesia, Western Pomerania, and Prussia. Applications, including funerary caskets. Detailed catalog of 250 objects from the fifteenth century to the second half of the nineteenth. Hallmarks of the objects are reproduced.

690. NADOLSKI, Andrzej.
Polska broń, broń biała. [Polish arms, sidearms] Wrocław, Zakład Narodowy im. Ossolińskich, 1974. 167 p. illus. 235 figures, ports. U856.P7N32

    Bibliography: p. 149–55.
    Bibliographic references.

Deals with swords, sabres, cutlasses, daggers, etc., that are characteristic and typical of Polish armory, wherever produced. A history of this subject is, by definition, a Polish military history; in six chapters, from the ninth century to 1945. "Szczerbiec," the Coronation Sword of Polish kings (color plate I, figures 20–21) belonged originally to Boleslaus, Prince of Sandomierz and Mazovia (d. 1248) and was first used in the coronation of Ladislaus

the Short in 1320. References are made to weapon types used by Hungarians, Turks, Russians, Swedes, Teutonic Knights, and others. Eleven plates in color, and twenty-one drawings in the text.

691. NADOLSKI, Andrzej.
Polish arms, sidearms. Wrocław, Zakład Narodowy im. Ossolińskich, 1974. 61 p. illus. 235 figures, ports. U856.P7N3213

    Translation by Maria Abramowiczowa of *Polska broń, broń biała.*

    Bibliography: p. 49.
    Bibliographic references.

The English translation has reduced the original text by two-thirds, but all the illustrations are retained. A lively, highly readable, and scholarly text in a superior translation.

692. REMBOWSKA, Irena.
Gdański cech złotników od XIV do końca XVIII w. [The Gold guild of Gdańsk from the fourteenth to the end of the eighteenth century] Gdańsk, Zakład Narodowy im. Ossolińskich, 1971. 252 p. illus. map. (Studia i materiały do dziejów Gdańska, 4) DD901.D21S8 no. 4

    Summary in French and Russian

    Bibliography: p. 236–42.

A study based on material in the Gdańsk Provincial State Archives and the Library of the Polish Academy of Sciences in Gdańsk. The first part of the book is devoted to the history of the guild, the second to a description of the gold objects. Includes a list of extant gold items made in Gdańsk.

693. Romańskie drzwi Płockie,
1154-ok. 1430–1982. [The

Romanesque doors of circa 1154 of Płock Cathedral. 1430–1982] Płock, Towarzystwo Naukowe Płockie, 1983. 151 p. illus., (part color). NB1287.P56R66 1983

    Summary in English, French, German, and Russian.

    Bibliography: p. 28.

Issued to commemorate the installation of bronze replicas of the Romanesque doors at the Cathedral of Płock. Executed in 1152–1154, perhaps by the Magdeburg Master Riquin working in Płock, the original doors were removed in about 1430 to Novgorod, where they remain. Iconographic and stylistic comparisons to other Romanesque bronze doors. Technical data on the fabrication of the replicas.

694. ROSIŃSKI, Zygmunt.
Spis miedziorytów polskich obejmujący przeważnie portrety polskich osobistości oraz widoki miast polskich i mapki geograficzne z 16., 17., 18., i 19. wieku w zbiorze Zygmunta Rosińskiego. [A list of copper engravings including mostly portraits of prominent Poles and views of Polish cities as well as geographic maps from the sixteenth, seventeenth, eighteenth, and nineteenth century, that are in the collection of Zygmunt Rosiński] Poznań, 1918. 163 p. illus., ports. NE676.P6R6

Portraits arranged alphabetically by sitter, the subjects and the artists date from the sixteenth to the nineteenth century. City views and maps arranged by name of the printmaker. Important for the list of early maps and the 106 illustrations of rarely reproduced portraits such as those by P. Drevet, Cesare Vecellio (Henri III), and J. Falck.

❀

695. SAMEK, Jan.
Polskie złotnictwo. [Polish goldsmithery] Wrocław, Zakład Narodowy im. Ossolińskich Wydawnictwo, 1988. 316 p. 253 illus. (part color). NK7171.P6S26 1988

Summary in English.

A historical study of goldsmithery in Poland, from the tenth through the twentieth century, including such centers of the craft as Kraków, Poznań, and Gdańsk. The study deals with secular as well as Christian and Jewish religious items.

696. SKUBISZEWSKI, Piotr.
The iconography of a Romanesque chalice from Trzemeszno. Journal of the Warburg Courtauld Institutes, vol. 34. London, University of London, 1971. p. 40–64. illus. AS122.L8515

Bibliographic references.

The chalice, dating from the last quarter of the twelfth century, is decorated with twelve scenes from the two Books of Samuel and the Book of Kings. The author explains the significance of the subject matter that is unparalleled for medieval art. He determines the author of the program to have been a south German theologian. The donor was a lady from the reigning Piast dynasty.

697. Studia i materialy do dziejów dawnego uzbrojenia i ubioru wojskowego. [Studies and materials toward a history of early weapons and military uniforms] Vol. 1+ Kraków, Muzeum Narodowe w Krakowie, 1963+ illus. U820.P7S78

Bibliographies.

Articles on all periods—from sixteenth-century body armor to nineteenth-century uniforms—and types; for example, the origins of the Polish general's uniform. Summaries in English or German. Well illustrated with photographs and drawings.

698. SZCZEPKOWSKA-NALIWAJEK, Kinga.
Złotnictwo gotyckie Pomorza Gdańskiego, Ziemi Chełmińskiej i Warmii. [Gothic goldsmithery of Gdańsk Pomerania, Chełmno region, and Warmia [Ermland]] Wrocław, Zakład Narodowy im. Ossolińskich, 1987. 298 p. 358 illus. (Studia z Historii Sztuki, 11) NK7171.P6S93 1987

Summary and list of illustrations in German.

Bibliography: p. 161–73.

This work—a revised doctoral dissertation from Warsaw University—covers the territory of so-called Royal Prussia, the name used in the 1466 treaty of Toruń by which that area was returned to Poland. In the period under discussion—1300–1550—the production of gold, silver-gilt, and silver objects included chalices, altar crosses, monstrances, reliquaries, ciboria, etc. Most of the objects were gifts to churches—some can still be found in their original locations, some are in museums. The catalog includes 185 objects. It is followed by a lengthy essay on the history of goldsmithery in that area.

**699. WALICKI, Michał, *ed.*
Drzwi gnieźnieńskie.**
[The Gniezno (cathedral) doors] Wrocław, Zakład Narodowy im. Ossolińskich, 1956–59. 3 v. illus. NA5697.G5W3

Vol. 3 has subtitle: Dokumentacja fotograficzna. [Photographic documentation]

Summaries and some texts in French and Russian.

Bibliographic references.

Definitive, collected studies by historians, art historians, iconologists, and paleographers, on the bronze doors executed in the twelfth century. Vol. 1: two essays on the promulgation of the St. Adalbert [Wojciech] legend, and the program of the doors as religious ideology and political expression. Three other essays on style, technical problems, and monogram. Vol. 2: two extensive studies on the ideological, iconographic, symbolic, and aesthetic contents. Short essays on the inscriptions uncovered in the restoration of 1955. Vol. 3: 153 photographs of the doors.

700. WŁODARSKA, Barbara.
Cyna. Katalog Zbiorów Muzeum Narodowego w Gdańsku. [Pewter. Catalog of collections at the National Museum in Gdańsk] Gdańsk, Krajowa Agencja Wydawnicza, 1975. 93 p. illus. NK8402.5.P7G388

Text in Polish, English, Russian, and French.

Bibliography: p. 33–34.

Few late Gothic pewter objects are extant, the material often having been melted down and recycled. Mostly objects fabricated in the seventeenth and eighteenth century. Stresses the importance of hallmarks to define makers and composition of alloy. Discusses elements of Pomeranian marks from the sixteenth century onward. The illustrated catalog reproduces hallmarks of the objects.

701. ZERNER, Henri.
Sur Giovanni Jacobo Caraglio. *In* International Congress of the History of Art, 22d. Budapest,

1969. Actes du XXII Congrès International d'histoire de l'art. Évolution générale et developpements régionaux en histoire de l'art. Budapest, Akadémiai Kiadó. Vol. 1, 1972, p. 691–95. N21.I585 1969 v. 1

Focuses on Caraglio's career in Poland (settled in 1539, died in 1565) where he worked as goldsmith, gem cutter, medalist, and architect for King Sigismund and Queen Bona Sforza, then for Sigismund Augustus. Mentions various extant works including a mounted sardonyx portrait of Bona in the Metropolitan Museum, New York. A portrait of the artist by Paris Bordone, then in a private collection, is now at the Wawel Castle.

702. ŻYGULSKI, Zdzisław, Jr.

Broń w dawnej Polsce na tle uzbrojenia Europy i Bliskiego Wschodu. [Weapons in Old Poland compared to arms and armor of Europe and the Near East] Warszawa, Państwowe Wydawnictwo Naukowe, 1975. 335 p. illus. (part color). U820.P7Z93

Bibliographic references.

A state-of-the-art volume in terms of scholarship and book production. First, the author surveys the collections in Austria, Germany, Great Britain, France, Italy, and elsewhere. He then divides the material of eight centuries—from the Middle Ages to the 1700s—into four periods. For each period, he covers items such as swords, helmets, armor, equestrian equipment, and others, in Western Europe, the Near East, and Poland. The iconography of the material of each period is discussed. Eight plates in color include the armor of the winged Hussar cavalry (c. 1700);

377 plates in black and white, twelve plates of figures, and over one hundred diagrams.

703. ŻYGULSKI, Zdzisław, Jr.

Stara broń w polskich zbiorach. [Old arms and armor in Polish collections] 2d rev. ed. Warszawa, Krajowa Agencja Wydawnicza, 1984. 274 p. color illus. NK6671.P6Z94 1984

Bibliography: p. 273–76.

Contents: I. Broń Polska. [Polish armor]; II. Broń obca w rękach polskich. [Foreign arms and armor in Poland]; III. Broń zachodnio-Europejska nabyta w XIX i XX wieku. [West European arms and armor acquired in the nineteenth and twentieth centuries]; IV. Broń wschodnia nabyta w XIX i XX wieku. [Eastern arms and armor acquired in the nineteenth and twentieth centuries].

The author includes swords, helmets, equestrian equipment, armor, sabers, and maces. Each item is fully described and the provenance is given; 274 fine color illustrations. The arms and armor come from the Museum of the Polish Army (Warsaw), the National Museum in Kraków, the State Collections of Art at Wawel, the National Museum in Poznań and the Kórnik Library, the Pauline Monastery at Jasna Góra in Częstochowa, and the Museum of Malbork Castle.

704. GOSTWICKA, Janina.

Dawne meble polskie. [Polish antique furniture] Warszawa, Arkady, 1965. 108 p. 139 illus., 6 color plates. NK2576.G6

Summary in French.
Bibliography: p. 82–86.

A history of Polish furniture styles and their sources from storage chests of the twelfth and thirteenth centuries, to a Renaissance cradle, and a desk by J.H. Riesener (1769) for King Stanislaw August Poniatowski, through a large group of Biedermeier pieces. Renaissance furniture is also illustrated by etchings from Tomasz Treter, Theatrum virtutum D. Stanislai Hossi (1588) that show the furnished interiors of Wawel Castle.

705. MASZKOWSKA, Bożena.

Z dziejów polskiego meblarstwa okresu Oświecenia. [History of Polish furniture from the period of the Enlightenment] Wrocław, Zakład Narodowy im. Ossolińskich, 1956. 109 p. 118 plates. (Studia z dziejów polskiego rzemiosła artystycznego, vol. 1) NK2575.M3

Bibliographic references.

Covers the period 1750–1800. Part 1 deals with the production centers—Warsaw, Gdańsk, and Kolbuszowa. Part 2 is on the design, taste, and markets, all with reference to styles in Western Europe—France, England, Saxony, and Holland. Catalog of 104 illustrated works, some of Polish manufacture, some imported.

Numerous drawings of furniture were made by Daniel Chodowiecki on his journey from Berlin to Gdańsk in 1773. They are depicted in publications entered under entry numbers 494 and 495.

706. REHOROWSKI, Marian.

Meble gdańskie XVII i XVIII stulecia. [Gdańsk furniture of the seventeenth and eighteenth centuries] Rocznik Gdański, vol.

17/18, 1958–59, p. 93–129. illus.
DD901.D2R6

Summary in English and Russian.

Bibliographic references.

Traces the popularity of furniture made in Gdańsk during the Baroque and Rococo periods and its use in Poland's homes. Mentions the craftsmanship of Dutch artists, such as John Vredeman de Vries, the van dem Blocke family, and Antony van Opbergen, who worked in Gdańsk, and the work of Polish artists John Strakowski and Andrew Karfycz. Using oak and walnut, they manufactured clocks, chests, tables, presses, mirrors, and wardrobes.

707. SIENICKI, Stefan.

Meble Kolbuszowskie. [Furniture made in Kolbuszowa] Warszawa, Instytut Wydawniczy Biblioteka Polska, 1936. 158 p. illus. 52 tables. (Biblioteka Zakładu Architektury Polskiej i Historji Sztuki Politechniki Warszawskiej, vol. 5) NK2576.S5 v. 5

Summary in French.
Bibliography: p. 139–41.
List of archival sources.

A scholarly work covering the eighteenth and beginning of the nineteenth century; based on archival material and on samples of artistic furniture from Kolbuszowa (in Rzeszów province)—desks, sideboards, chests, tables, cabinets, and a wardrobe— in late Baroque, Neo-classical, and Biedermeier styles.

The author examines furniture from private collections, including those of Count Jerzy Tyszkiewicz (the owner of the Kolbuszowa estate) and Count Franciszek Potocki (Kraków).

708. TŁOCZEK, Ignacy.

Polskie snycerstwo. [Polish wood carving] Wrocław, Zakład Narodowy im. Ossolińskich, 1984. 134 p. 96 p. of plates, illus. NK9771.P6T56 1984

Bibliography: p. 120–22.

An undiscriminating study that lumps together sculpture and furniture of all periods. Interesting, nevertheless, for the extraordinary objects reproduced—Baroque organs and neo-Gothic doorways, for example.

Furniture

VII. Folk Art

✻

709. Atlas polskich strojów ludowych. [Atlas of Polish folk costumes] Lublin, Polskie Towarzystwo Ludoznawcze, 1949–1960. 18 vols. illus. (part color). GT1060.A8

Summary in English, French, or Russian.

The monographic series is divided into five parts that correspond to the major geographical-historical regions of Poland. Each part is subdivided into ethnic regions. Highly authoritative studies by various authors. Liberally illustrated by photographs and drawings of entire costumes and details, diagrams, and maps.

710. CZARNECKA, Irena. Polska sztuka ludowa. [Folk art in Poland] Warszawa, Polonia, 1958. 234 p. illus. (part color). NK1035.P6C9 folio

Introduction by Tadeusz Delimat.

Exceptional for photographs of leather and metalwork, costumes and textiles (embroideries and weavings), and interiors featuring painted stoves. Also furniture, pottery, and cut paper.

Also published in French, English, and German. The English language edition is temporarily not available in the Library of Congress.

711. Dawne meble ludowe północnej Polski. [Antique folk furniture from northern Poland] Toruń, Muzeum Etnograficzne w Toruniu, 1976. 74 p. plates, illus. (part color). NK2635.P7D38

Summary in English and Russian.

Eighteenth- and nineteenth-century chests, chairs, tables, wardrobes, and sideboards—painted, carved, and inlaid—in nineteen good color illustrations, plus many in black and white. A repertory of carved chair backs. List of eleven northern Polish museums collecting folk furniture.

712. FRYŚ-PIETRASZKOWA, Ewa, Anna Kunczyńska-Iracka, *and* Marian Pokropek. Sztuka ludowa w Polsce. [Folk art in Poland] Warszawa, Arkady, 1988. 338 p. illus. (part color). NK1035.P6F79 1988

Bibliography: p. 302–21.

The text is divided into chapters on architecture, interior decorations, wood carving, ceramics, metal works, sculpture, paintings, and the art connected with customs and celebrations. Bibliography includes books and articles from Polska Sztuka Ludowa [Polish folk art], a scholarly periodical published since 1947; 453 illustrations are adequately described on thirty-one pages.

713. GÓRALOWA, Danuta. Warmińska rzeźba ludowa. [Folk sculpture of Warmia] Olsztyn, Wydawnictwo Pojezierze, 1979. 188 p. illus. NK9771.P6G67

Summary in English, German, and Russian.

Bibliography: p. 188.

Wooden sculpture of the eighteenth and nineteenth century, inspired by Gothic and Baroque art. Illustrated in forty-nine photographs.

714. GRABOWSKI, Józef. Dawna polska rzeźba ludowa. [Old Polish folk sculpture] Warszawa, Auriga, 1968. 37 p. 192 plates of illus. (part color). N7956.G68 folio

Folk sculptures in readily available wood, devoted exclusively to sacred subjects, the earliest example illustrated dating from 1647. Excellent reproductions in color and in black and white. Scholarly appraisal and catalog.

715. GRABOWSKI, Józef. Ludowe obrazy drzeworytnicze. [Folk pictures in woodcut] Warszawa, Pax, 1970. 250 p. illus. NE958.3.P7G7

Bibliographic references.

Discusses the regional styles, techniques, and iconography of various works. These are illustrated in 123 plates, four of which are in color, and forty-seven figures in the text.

716. GRABOWSKI, Józef. Sztuka ludowa: formy i regiony w Polsce. [Folk art: forms and regions in Poland] Warszawa, Arkady, 1967. 520 p. illus. NK976.P6G7

Summary and lists of illustrations in English and Russian.

Bibliography: p. 446–47.

The twelve chapters correspond to twelve regions. This division allows quantitative and qualitative comparisons among the regions in the different

*branches of folk art. Weaving is
carried out all over the country
whereas painted tiles are confined to
certain regions. Timber architecture is
formally the most powerful. The
latter half of the nineteenth and the
early twentieth century was the most
vigorous period for folk art in
Poland.*

717. Haft i zdobienie stroju ludowego. [Embroidery and the embellishment of folk costumes] Warszawa, Sztuka, 1955. 71 p. 163 plates (24 color). NK9271.P7H3

Edited by Ewa Maszyńska.
Foreword by Kazimierz
Pietkiewicz.
Introduction by Zofia
Czasznicka and Jadwiga Nowak.
Bibliography: p. 23.

*Treats folk costumes from eight
regions, and illustrates the use of
embroidery and lace on various parts
of the attire. Seventy-four diagrams of
needlework.*

718. JACKOWSKI, Aleksander, and Jadwiga Jarnuszkiewicz. Folk art of Poland. Warsaw, Arkady, 1968. 476 p. chiefly illus. NK1035.P6J3213

Translation by Marek Latyński
of *Sztuka ludu polskiego.*

*A scintillating book thanks to 521
splendid photographs over thirty of
which are in color, representing
shrines, sculpted groups and individual
saints' figures, creches, woodcuts,
paintings, cut paper, tiles, architecture, furniture, utensils, baskets,
ceramics, textiles, and costumes. Each
object is carefully described.*

719. KIESZKOWSKI, Jerzy. Zwięzły katalog wystawy Dawnych Drzeworytów

Ludowych zebranych i wydanych
przez Zygmunta Łazarskiego.
[Companion catalog to the exhi-
bition of Old Folk Woodcuts
collected and published by
Zygmunt Łazarski] Warszawa,
Wł. Łazarski, 1921. 39 p.
NE1171.P6K5

*A descriptive catalog accompanying
an exhibition of sixty-six Old Folk
Woodcuts, assembled by Zygmunt
Łazarski (see entry 722).*

720. Kraków. Muzeum Etnograficzne. Polska grafika ludowa [wystawa]. Kraków 1970. Gravure populaire polonaise. Kraków, 1970. 250 p. chiefly illus. NE958.3.P7K72 1970

Bibliography: p. 53–54.
Catalog prepared by
Aleksandra Jacher-Tyszkowa and
Wiesława Otto-Weissowa.

*An exhibition, organized on the
occasion of the Third International
Biennale of Prints, of 287 items
assembled from museums, libraries,
archives, and private collectors, which
include traditional Polish woodcuts,
mostly of a religious character.*

721. KROH, Antoni. Współczesna rzeźba ludowa Karpat Polskich. [Contemporary folk sculpture of the Polish Carpathian region] Wrocław, Zakład Narodowy im. Ossolińskich, 1979. 136 p. 99 illus. NK9771.P6K76

Summary in English.
Bibliography: p. 111–17.
Biographical notes on the
artists.

*In the 1960s and 1970s the author
researched a regenerated tradition that
is being supported by the authorities
through competitions, purchases, and
publicity.*

722. ŁAZARSKI, Zygmunt. Teka drzeworytów ludowych dawnych. [A portfolio of Old Folk Woodcuts] Warszawa, Wł. Łazarski, 1921. 1 p. (leaf) 66 plates (part color). NE1171.P6L3 folio

*Portfolio of sixty-six woodcuts.
Nearly two-thirds of these, originating in the north of Poland, were
executed by Lithuanian, Polish, German, and Belorussian artists; the
remaining third, from eastern Poland,
were executed by Polish and perhaps
Belorussian artists. The woodcuts,
often free adaptations of high art,
were used to embellish modest dwell-
ings and furnishings. By custom, they
were seldom signed.*

723. Muzeum im. Władysława Orkana w Rabce. Katalog zbiorów sztuki w Muzeum im. Władysława Orkana w Rabce. [Catalog of the art collection in the Władysław Orkan Museum in Rabka] Rabka, 1977. 274 p. 212 plates, illus., maps. N7255.P6M893 1977

Introduction and catalog by
Teresa Jabłońska.
Bibliographic references.

*This ethnographic museum, founded in
1936, is devoted to the Gorce, Beskid
Wyspowy, and northern Podhale
regions. Established in the name of
the first outstanding writer and poet
of the Podhale area (Władysław
Orkan, 1875–1930), its holdings
represent all areas of folk art and
culture, including one of the largest
Polish collections of folk sculpture
and painting on glass, canvas, and
paper.*

*The catalog of 459 works is
arranged by technique: sculpture,
painting (on glass and on all other
materials), and prints. Under each*

technique, the arrangement is iconographic: Madonna, Christ, God the Father, Saints. A scholarly presentation that includes an index to places of origin of the works.

724. OLĘDZKI, Jacek.
Sztuka Kurpiów. [Art of the Kurp region] Wrocław, Zakład Narodowy im. Ossolińskich, 1970. 77 p. 150 plates of illus. NK1035.P62K87

Bibliography: p. 67.

List of illustrations in Polish and English.

Popular artistic traditions of the region that lies on the right bank of the river Narew, in Mazowia, in northeastern Poland. Its figural and ornamental wood carvings, textiles, ironwork, clay, cut paper, woven straw, are illustrated.

725. POKROPEK, Marian.
Guide to folk art and folklore in Poland. Warsaw, Arkady, 1980. 269 p. 36 p. of plates, illus., maps. NK1035.P6P6

The guide is arranged according to significant ethnographic places (2,500 localities) that are keyed to good maps. The buildings, shrines, museums, and artists (including performing artists) are mentioned under each place name. Nearly four hundred illustrations. Informative and easy to use.

726. REINFUSS, Roman, *and* Jan ŚWIDERSKI.
Sztuka ludowa w Polsce. [Folk art in Poland] Kraków, Wydawnictwo Literackie, 1960. 174 p. illus. NK976.P6R4

Especially noteworthy among the object classes shown in the more than two hundred illustrations is the carved and painted furniture. Most folk arts

are represented: buildings, woodcarvings, weaving, laces, costumes, paintings on paper and glass, and pottery.

727. REINFUSS, Roman.
Garnarstwo ludowe. [Folk pottery] Warszawa, Wydawnictwo Sztuka, 1955. 96 p. illus., 47 plates. NK4112.P6R4

Bibliographic references.

An historical outline of folk pottery in Poland as well as modern forms, manufacture, and marketing. Nearly one hundred reproductions of pieces noteworthy for form and decoration.

728. REINFUSS, Roman.
Ludowe kowalstwo artystyczne w Polsce. [Artistic folk ironwork in Poland] Wrocław, Zakład Narodowy im. Ossolińskich, 1983. 288 p. 246 illus. NK8271.P6R44 1983

Summary in German.

Bibliographic references.

Techniques, workshops, patterns, and their application to shop signs, weather vanes, candelabra, door hinges and locks, gates, and ornamentation for wagons. Within the text, 131 figures, plus 245 separate illustrations.

729. REINFUSS, Roman.
Meblarstwo ludowe w Polsce. [Folk furniture in Poland] Wroclaw, Zaklad Narodowy im. Ossolińksich, 1977. 300 p. 181 illus. (part color). TT194.R44

Summary in German.

Bibliographic references: p. 244–80.

Carved and painted chests, benches, chairs, beds, and cradles that are decoratively and mechanically ingenious. Numerous diagrammatic repre

sentations as well as photographs of interiors.

730. RUSZEL, Krzysztof.
Motyw pracy w twórczości ludowej. Katalog konkursu i wystawy. [The motif of work in folk art. Catalog of the competition and exhibitional Rzeszów, Museum Okręgowe w Rzeszowie, 1978. 75 p., 52 illus. NK1035.P6R87 1978

Ingenuous folk art thrives even among younger artists. Biographies of more than fifty participants.

731. RUSZEL, Krzysztof.
Tematy ludowe w akwarelach, rysunkach i grafice XIX i pocz. XX wieku. [Folk themes in watercolors, drawings, and prints of the nineteenth and early twentieth century] Katalog wystawy ze zbiorów Muzeum Okręgowego w Rzeszowie. [An exhibition catalog from the collections of the Regional Museum in Rzeszów] Rzeszów, 1976. 74 p. illus. N7255.P6R87

Studies of costumes ranging from important ethnographical documents, as by L. Łepkowski (b. 1829) to ornamental works, as by P.L. Debucourt after J.P. Norblin (1745–1830), of which thirty-two plates are described.

A catalog of the exhibition.

732. SCHAUSS, Hans-Joachim.
Contemporary Polish folk artists. New York, Hippocrene Books, 1987. 208 p. illus. (part color), ports. NK1035.P6S3 1987

Translation from the German by Dorothy Jaesschke.

Twenty-four artists are featured; each is depicted in a photograph. Inter views with each artist present the sources of their inspiration and the story of their careers. The flavor of the personalities is retained. The author provides his own impressions of the artists, the circumstances in which they live, and the characteristics of their work. Fine reproductions.

[138]. SEWERYN, Tadeusz.
Kapliczki i krzyże prydrożne w Polsce. [Roadside chapels and crosses in Poland] Warszawa, Instytut wydawniczy PAX, 1958. illus. NA4875.S4
Bibliographic references.

Presents the history and tradition of placing shrines and crosses along roadsides. Nearly four hundred illustrations of work done entirely by local villagers. Discusses the rich variety of wooden shrines—and occasional stone shrines—with the figures of Christ and saints also sculptured in wood. These were usually placed inside the shrines but, at times, above crosses. Some shrines were linked to legends, others were created as an act of thanksgiving, or as a prayer for help or forgiveness, while still others were erected to honor the dead, including those killed in battle.

733. SEWERYN, Tadeusz.
Ludowa grafika staropolska. [Folk art of old Poland] Polska Sztuka Ludowa, vol. 7, no. 4–5, 1953, p. 201–44. illus. NK7.P6, v. 7

Emblematic, mainly fantastic animals, and scenes of country life executed in woodcuts by anonymous folk artists; used as book illustrations in the sixteenth and seventeenth centuries.

734. SEWERYN, Tadeusz.
Polskie malarstwo ludowe.

[Folk painting in Poland] Kraków, Muzeum Etnograficzne, 1937. 114 p. illus. (part color). (Wydawnictwa Muzeum Etnograficznego w Krakowie, no. 10) ND691.S4
Summary in French.

Examines popular painting according to the same categories as those applied to high art: aesthetic and psychological; social and iconographic; and others.

SEWERYN, Tadeusz.
Staropolska grafika ludowa. [Old Polish folk prints] Warszawa, Sztuka, 1956. 205 p. 157 illus. NE676.P6S4
Bibliographic references.

Mostly anonymous sixteenth- and seventeenth-century works: copies after Hans Holbein, illustrated fables, technological handbooks, playing cards, and sacred motifs.

736. SKOCZYLAS, Władysław.
Drzeworyt ludowy w Polsce. [The popular woodcut in Poland] Warszawa, J. Mortkowicz, 1933. 13, 100 p. (p. 1–99 mounted illus., part color). NE676.P6S55 Rare Book Coll.

Authored by the pioneer in the study of Polish popular prints. The prints originated in the second half of the eighteenth century. Facsimiles of ninety-nine woodcuts divided by subject, including foreign devotional images (Our Lady of Loreto).

737. Śląskie stroje ludowe.
[Silesian folk costumes] Katowice, Wydawnictwo "Śląsk," 1988. 150 p. 173 illus, 74 color plates. GT1060.B33 1988
By Barbara Bazielich.
Bibliographic references: p. 141–43.

The author provides an introduction to the history and development of the folk custume in Silesia, including not only its different forms and causes of variations, but also the manner in which the traditions have been handed down.

Clothing in Silesia was not substantially different from western European attire until about the end of the seventeenth century, when development of the Silesian folk costume began. From the thirteenth to the sixteenth century, the everyday attire consisted of a short tunic belted at the waist, a cloth cloak (or a hooded greatcoat in the winter), leg coverings, hard-soled slippers or shoes, and a hat (either of straw or cloth).

738. STRYJEŃSKA, Zofia.
Polish peasants' costumes; with introduction and notes by Thadée Seweryn. Nice (France), C. Szwedzicki, 1939. 16 p. 40 color plates. GT1060.S8 Rare Book Coll.
Issued in portfolio.

Forty serigraph plates of great artistry and charm by Zofia Stryjeńska. The plates are described by Tadeusz Seweryn, whose introduction poetically evokes the geographical features of Poland that brought forth the various ethnic forms. References to the ancient sources of the costumes.

739. UDZIELA, Seweryn.
Hafty kurpiowskie. Les broderies populaires des Kurpiens. Kraków, Nakładem Muzeum Etnograficznego w Krakowie, 1936. 8 p. illus. 40 color plates. (Wydawnictwa Muzeum Etnograficznego w Krakowie, no. 9) NK9271.P7U38
Summaries in French and German.

Drawings by Stanisława Czyżewska.

740. WIĘCKOWSKI, Tadeusz. Ginące piękno. Artystyczne rękodzieło ludowe w Polsce.

[Vanishing beauty. Artistic folk handicrafts in Poland] Warszawa, Wydawnictwo Spółdzielcze, 1987. 196 p. illus. (part color). NK1035.P6W54 1987
   Summary in English.
   Bibliography: p. 184–87.

The title notwithstanding, most crafts flourish due to the support of various organizations: not only "Cepelia" but regional artists' associations, museums, and cooperatives. Two vanishing crafts are carpentry and unglazed pottery.

Folk Art

Pijarska Street in Kraków passes
under the Floriańska Gate, which
was built in the fourteenth

the city. Looming behind the gate
is the St. Florian tower. From
Cracow by Edward Hartwig, 2d

VIII. Photography

❋

741. BEYER, Karol.
Karol Beyer 1818–1877; pionier fotografii polskiej. [Karol Beyer 1818–1877; pioneer of Polish photography] Muzeum Sztuki w Łodzi, październik-listopad 1984. Łódź, 1984. 93 p. illus. TR654.B487 1984

    Summary in English.
    Bibliography: p. 62.
    Exhibition catalog edited by Urszula Czartoryska.

Technically innovative and pictorially creative. Beyer opened a studio in Warsaw in 1844 and maintained a large and active practice. Exercising his recognized social and historical function, he recorded the 1861–1864 uprising against the Tsar. The catalog also lists his portraits, daguerrotypes, and ethnographic subjects, and discusses his personal outlook, views, and opinions.

742. BUŁHAK, Jan.
Fotografia ojczysta. [Photography of the motherland] Wrocław, Zakład Narodowy im. Ossolińskich, 1951. 152 p. illus., ports. TR185.B8

An author and photographer (1876–1950), Bułhak held a chair and lectured on photography at the Stefan Batory University in Wilno between 1919 and 1939. He combined a profound pictorial aesthetic with a deep love of country in all its aspects—land and cityscape, people, industrialization. He presents his philosophical and aesthetic values in six essays. One hundred fifty of his photographs are reproduced.

[455]. DŁUBAK, Zbigniew.
Zbigniew Dłubak, prace z lat 1945–1980. Works from 1945–1980. Muzeum Narodowe we Wrocławiu, luty–marzec 1981. February–March 1981. [Exhibition] Wrocław, Muzeum Narodowe we Wrocławiu, 1981. 107 p. illus. port. N7255.P63D482 1981

    Introduction by Adam Sobota in Polish and English.
    Bibliography: p. 100–102.

A painter and photographer, Dłubak (b. 1921) came under the direct influence, in 1947, of the Polish analytic constructivists Władysław Strzemiński and Henryk Stażewski. An outcome of their theory has been a two-tiered production: art serving its social function, and experimental art; or, social realism alongside—eventually—conceptual art. More recently, using photography, the artist has sought to desymbolize old myths. His theoretical speculations are quoted. Included is a biography, a list of significant events in his creative life, and a list of exhibitions. Approximately one hundred illustrations—only one in color—show the artist and his work.

743. Fotografia polska: featuring original masterworks from public and private collections in Poland, 1839–1945, and a selection of avant-garde photography, film, and video from 1945 to the present. International Center of Photography, July 26 through September 15, 1979. New York, 1979. 49 p. illus. (part color). TR646.U6N4816

    Exhibition catalog.

An exhibition catalog of Poland's photographic heritage Since 1839, including many works never before publicly exhibited, even in Poland. Principles on which the exhibition was organized by its director, William A. Ewing. A history of Polish photography of Juliusz Garztecki. Contemporary photographers reject the expressive and visual for the perceptual. Fifty-seven reproductions.

744. HARTWIG, Edward.
Tematy fotograficzne. [Photographic themes] Warszawa, Wydawnictwo Artystyczne i Filmowe, 1978. 143 p. illus. TR656.H39

Reproduced are 122 black and white photographs by an artist-photographer who was first active in Lublin, then received his education in Vienna at the Graphic Institute, and later worked in Warsaw. Specializing in landscape photography, Hartwig also developed a lively interest in theater personalities and scenes. Born in 1909, Hartwig was the author of numerous albums of photography—such as Moja ziemia, Lublin, Łazienki, Kulisy teatru, Kazimierz nad Wisłą, Cracow, and Żelazowa Wola (Chopin's birthplace)—and was the 1961 recipient of the highest art award of the city of Warsaw. Exhibited in the capitals of Western Europe as well as in Poland.

745. HARTWIG, Edward.

Wariacje fotograficzne. [Photographic variations] Warszawa, Krajowa Agencja Wydawnicza, 1978. port. 112 photograms. 11 p. of text. TR654.H374 1978

Text in Polish and English.

Black and white photograms from various periods, testifying to the artist's love of human beings, their emotions, and their artistic qualities. He appreciates nature with its changing scenery, and brings out its beauty and poetry to the viewer.

746. HERMANOWICZ, Henryk.

Kraków; cztery pory roku w fotografii. [Kraków; Four seasons of the year in the photographs of Henryk Hermanowicz] 4th rev. ed. Kraków, Wydawnictwo Literackie, 1978. xii, 174, 65 p. 16 color plates. DK4714.H47 1978

Edited by Jerzy Banach.

Summary in English, French, German, and Russian.

Captures architectural landmarks and monuments in excellent, large-scale photographs.

747. LATOŚ, Henryk.

Z historii fotografii wojennej. [From the history of war-time photography] Warszawa, Ministerstwo Obrony Narodowej, 1985. 316 p. illus. TR820.6.L38 1985

Of particular importance are the photographs of World War I, taken in France, Serbia, and Bulgaria, and of World War II taken in Poland and the USSR. Of interest also are those depicting Poland immediately

after World War II. More than two hundred photographs reproduced; only general sources are cited, except in a few cases.

748. LEJKO, Krystyna, *and* Jolanta Niklewska.

Warszawa, na starej fotografii 1850–1914. [Warsaw in old photographs 1850–1914] Warszawa, Państwowe Wydawnictwo Naukowe, 1978. 207 p. illus. DK4624.L44

The 736 photographs listed are divided by categories: panoramas, streets, parks, palaces, portraits (including family groups), and recreation (such as horse racing and boating). They were selected from the collection of the Warsaw Historical Museum, which has photographs from the seventy-seven Warsaw studios active between the second half of the nineteenth century and 1914. Another 126 studios were active in Warsaw at that time. Among the eighty-six photographs reproduced in this catalog are those by the Polish pioneer photographers Karol Beyer (1818–1877) and Konrad Brandel (1938–1920).

749. MIERZECKA, Janina.

Całe życie z fotografią. [Life-long photography] Kraków, Wydawnictwo Literackie, 1981. 272 p. 48 p. of plates. illus. TR95.P7M53 1981

Bibliographic references.

Memoirs of the photographer, born in Lwów, whose style was defined before World War II. She argues that Polish artistic photography was born in Lwów, and appends biographical notices on thirty-two Lwów photographers. Her photographs reproduced on thirty-five plates, those of her contemporaries on twenty-eight plates.

750. MOSSAKOWSKA, Wanda, *and* Anna Zeńczak.

Kraków na starej fotografii. [Kraków in old photographs] Kraków, Wydawnictwo Literackie, 1984. 224 p. illus. DK4714.H67 1984

The streets of Kraków, its public buildings, houses, monuments, parks, riverside, bridges, panoramas, and details, are captured in 205 photographs. Numerous interiors include a salon in the Palace of Art decorated by Stanisław Wyspiański, restaurants, and an elegant butcher shop. Each photograph is accompanied by a description.

751. MOSSAKOWSKA, Wanda.

Walery Rzewuski (1837–1888), fotograf. Studium warsztatu i twórczości. [Walery Rzewuski (1837–1888), photographer. A study of his workshop and creative work] Wrocław, Zakład Narodowy im. Ossolińskich, 1981. 252 p. of text, 131 plates, illus. TR140.R9M67

Summary in English.

Bibliography: p. 219–24.

Bibliographic references.

Walery Rzewuski began work as a professional photographer in Kraków around 1860. His subjects were conventional and commercial— portraits, mainly of society figures, actors, actresses, and artists. He also photographed the monuments of Kraków, the Tatra Mountains, ethnographic subjects, and paintings. He was the first photographer to lecture publicly (in 1869–1870) on the techniques of photography. Five chapters are devoted to the history of Rzewuski's three studios—their equipment, techniques, organization, and personnel.

752. La photographie polonaise
1900–1981. (Exposition) 21
Janvier–8 mars 1981. Centre
Georges Pompidou, Musée
national d'art moderne. Paris, Le
Centre, Herscher, 1981. 48 p.
illus. (part color). TR95.P7P47
1981

Introduction by Jean-Claude
Groshens and Pontus Hultén.

*Essays on the history of Polish
photography and the exhibition by
William A. Ewing, Alain Sayag,
Adam Sobota, Urszula Czartoryska,
and Stanislaw Kopf. Biographical
notices on sixty-eight photographers.
An exhibition of works chosen with
great aesthetic discernment, judging
from the thirty-five photographs
covering surrealism, constructivism,
documentation, photomontage, and
wartime photography.*

753. PŁAŻEWSKI, Ignacy.
Spojrzenie w przeszłość
polskiej fotografii. [A look at the
past of Polish photography]
Warszawa, Państwowy Instytut
Wydawniczy, 1982. 414 p. illus.,
ports. TR95.P7P53 1982

*A history of photography in Poland
to 1945, mainly pictorial and documentary. Photographers, their studies,
subjects, and the expressive possibil-
ities of their equipment.*

**754. Polska fotografia
krajobrazowa 1944–1984;**
wystawa problemowa. [Polish
landscape photography, 1944–
1984; a controversial exhibition]
Kielce, luty 1985, Galeria Biura
Wystaw Artystycznych. Kielce,
1985. 120 p. illus.
TR646.P72K543 1985

Exhibition catalog.

Includes a list of photographers and their major works.

*The controversy referred to in the
subtitle has to do with the nature of
the landscape photographer's creative
allegiance, whether it is to aesthetics,
documentation, photomontage, or
other. The history and theory of
landscape photography are discussed in
eight chapters. Over one hundred good
examples reproduced from the work
of the more than one hundred
photographers who participated in the
exhibition.*

**755. Polska współczesna
fotografia artystyczna:** styczeń
1985, Warszawa, Zachęta:
marzec–kwiecień 1985. [Polish
contemporary artistic photography: January 1985, Warsaw,
Zachęta: March–April, 1985]
Wrocław, Muzeum Narodowe.
Warszawa, Wydawnictwo
Centralnego Biura Wystaw
Artystycznych, 1985. 56 p. 122 p.
of plates, illus. TR646.P72W377
1985

Summary in English.

Exhibition catalog edited by
Romuald Niekrasz and Helena
Szustakowska.

*A brief text on the history of
photography in Poland since World
War II. Over five hundred works by
268 photographers are listed, with
fourteen reproductions in color and
more than one hundred in black and
white.*

756. SOBOTA, Adam.
Polska fotografia artystyczna
do roku 1939. [Polish artistic
photography before 1939]
Wrocław, Muzeum Narodowe,
1977. 15 p. 36 photographs.
TR653.S6

Summary in English.
Exhibition catalog.

*Reproduces photographs by Jan
Bułhak, Tadeusz Cyprian, Wojciech
Bujko, Antoni Wieczorek, Witold
Romer, Franciszek Groer, Henryk
Mikolasch, Jan Neuman, Edward
Hartwig, and others who represent
pictorialism, documentation (including ethnographic subjects), surrealism, and photomontage. Brief biographical notices on thirty photographers and a list of the photographs
exhibited.*

757. SZULC, Marian.
Materiały do historii fotografii
polskiej. [Materials related to the
history of Polish photography]
Wrocław, Zakład Narodowy im.
Ossolińskich, 1963+
TR95.P7S95

Vol. 1: Bibliografia 1836–1956.
[Bibliography 1836–1956] 590 p.
illus., facsims., ports.

Summary of the preface in
English, French, German, and
Russian.

*Over thirteen thousand entries divided
into theory, history, reportage and
sports, organizations, competitions,
prices and commerce, aesthetics, and
techniques and processes. Portraits of
seventy-five Polish photographers.*

**758. Witkiewicz, Stanisław
Ignacy.** Przeciw nicości.
Fotografie Stanisława Ignacego
Witkiewicza. [Against nothing-
ness. Stanisław Ignacy
Witkiewicz's photographs]
Kraków, Wydawnictwo
Literackie, 1986. 79 p. of text,
224 p. of plates, illus. (part
color). TR654.W58 1986

Edited by Jan Fejkiel, et al.
In English and Polish.

*An album of four hundred photo-
graphs taken by Witkiewicz, by*

❋

his father—a professional photographer—and by friends. Includes portraits of Witkiewicz from the years 1899 to 1903, taken by unidentified persons, and photographs of Witkiewicz's friends from 1910 to 1914 taken by Witkiewicz himself. The landscape photographs are mostly of the Zakopane area.

759. ŻDŻARSKI, Wacław.
Historia fotografii, warszawskiej. [History of Warsaw photography] Warszawa, Państwowe Wydawnictwo Naukowe, 1974. 373 p. illus. TR95.P7Z38

Bibliographic references.

The Daguerrotype was introduced into Poland in 1839 (the year of its official recognition in France) by means of Daguerre's book describing the process (Paris 1839); a Polish translation appeared in 1840. Karol Beyer was the pioneer Polish photographer. Four other chapters on the history up to 1972. Illustrated by a mere 109 plates.

IX. Art Collections

❁

[352]. AMEISENOWA, Zofia.
Les principaux manuscrits à peintures de la Bibliothèque Jagiellonienne de Cracovie. Paris, 1933. 119 p. xvi plates (including facsims.). (Bulletin de la Societé française de reproductions de manuscrits à peintures, année 17) ND3345.P16 no. 17

Holdings of the Jagiellonian University Library: fourteen illuminated manuscripts and eighty-six fragments (leaves, initial letters). The earliest manuscript is Paduan or Bolognese, circa 1200. Another is a Czech chronicle of 1531. The Behem codex is included. A concordance between the manuscripts and the twenty-six plates is on p. 119.

[645]. Arrasy flamandzkie w Zamku Królewskim na Wawelu. [The Flemish tapestries at the Wawel Royal Castle] Warszawa, Arkady; Antwerp, Fonds Mercator, 1975. 501 p. color illus. ports. NK3071.P63K72 folio

Edited by Jerzy Szablowski.

By Anna Missiąg-Bocheńska, Marie Hennel-Bernasikowa, Magdalena Piwocka, Sophie Schneebal-Perelman, and Adelbrecht L.J. Van De Walle.

Bibliography: p. *481–87.*

For English-language edition, 1972, see item 652.

[493]. BÓBR, Maciej, *and* Krzysztof Kruzel.
Katalog rycin Biblioteki Polskiej Akademii Nauk w Krakowie. Szkoła niemiecka XV i XVI w. [Catalog of prints in the Library of the Polish Academy of Sciences in Kraków. The German school of the fifteenth and sixteenth centuries] Wrocław, Zakład Narodowy im. Ossolińskich, 1987. 180 p. 115 p. of illus. NE651.B58 1987

Edited by Maria Macharska.
Summary in French.
Bibliography: p. 148–49.

Formed from the eighteenth-century Moszyński collection and a collection assembled in the nineteenth century at the Bibliothèque Polonaise in Paris that was transferred to Poland in 1931. Eight hundred eighteen prints that include not only the major artists, such as Schongauer, Dürer, Altdorfer, and Baldung, but also extremely obscure artists such as Wenzel von Olmutz, G. Zehender, Hans Leinberger, and the Monogramists MZ and ASG. Twenty-two pages on watermarks. Only minimal cataloging data.

[626]. BOCHNAK, Adam.
Mecenat Zygmunta Starego w zakresie rzemiosła artstycznego. [The patronage of crafts by King Sigismund I] Studia do dziejów Wawelu, vol. 2, 1961, p. 131–301. illus. NA7764.K7W27 v. 2

Summary in French.

An article of great importance for the breadth of material it covers and the quality of the archival documentation it provides to support the argument. These extensive accounts and inventories offer the means for a detailed insight into the patronage of Sigismund I (reigned 1506–1548) in the decorative arts. He introduced the Italian Renaissance to Poland, yet maintained contacts with Nuremberg. He ordered utensils, jewelry, and harnesses from Hungary. In Kraków he employed the goldsmith Martin Marciniec (1502, 1512) and commissioned an immense bell (1520) from Hans Beham, a Nuremberg founder who settled in Kraków. In 1535, for the occasion of his daughter's weddging to the Elector of Brandenburg, Sigismund I commissioned a silver casket enriched with enamels and precious stones, whose subsequent course to the collection in the Hermitage is then charted. A wealth of information on other large and important commissions is included in the article. The Nuremberg craftsmen supplied many art objects for the Sigismund Chapel in the Wawel Cathedral and for the church on Jasna Góra in Częstochowa.

760. BIAŁOSTOCKI, Jan, *and* Michał Walicki.
Malarstwo europejskie w zbiorach polskich 1300–1800. [European painting in Polish collections 1300–1800] Kraków, Państwowy Instytut Wydawniczy, 1955. 560 p. 12 mounted color illus. ND450.B5

Bibliography: p. 42–45.

A selection of paintings from early Tuscan painters to Ingres in museums, galleries, and some churches. Many paintings deserving of wider renown, as by Mazzolino, Luca

Giordano, and a large number of
Dutch seventeenth-century canvases.
Also available in a 1957 (Warsaw)
German-language edition.

761. BIAŁOSTOCKI, Jan, *and* Michał Walicki.
Europäische Malerei in
polnischen Sammlungen, 1300–
1800. Warszawa, Państwowy
Instytut Wydawniczy, 1957. 581
p. plates (12 mounted color),
illus. ND450.B515

German-language edition of item 760.

762. Chiaroscuro. Drzeworyty
światłocieniowe XVI, XVII,
i XVIII wieku w zbiorach
polskich. [Chiaroscuro.
Chiaroscuro woodcuts of the
sixteenth, seventeenth, and eighteenth century in Polish collec-
tions] Łódź, Muzeum Sztuki w
Łodzi, 1981. 56 p. 20 p. of plates,
illus. NE1300.2.C48 1981

Exhibition catalog by Elżbieta
Budzińska.

*One hundred sixty-eight works, as-
sembled from seven different collections, comprising a traditional range
of schools and dates, from Hans
Burgkmair to John Skippe.*

763. Collections of the Royal
Castle of Wawel. 2d enl. ed.
Warsaw, Arkady, 1975. 434
p. illus. (part color).
N9041.P62K7513 1975

Introduction by Jerzy
Szablowski.

Translation of *Zbiory zamku
królewskiego na Wawelu.*

Bibliography: p. 413–25.

*Uncommonly original choices of objects
reproduced on 281 excellent plates.
Among the many works shown are
eight tapestries designed by Michiel
Coxie; portraits of royal children,*

sixteenth century; the entry of Louise-
Marie Gonzaga, wife of King
Władysław IV, into Gdańsk, 1646;
Portrait of a Lady by Palma
Vecchio; Holy Family by J. van
Hemessen; a tomb by Jan Pfister,
School of Lwów, after 1636; splendid
objects of decorative arts of all
periods; numerous examples of the
renowned collection of arms and
armor, as well as seventeenth-century
Turkish tents.

764. Corpus vasorum
antiquorum. Pologne. Fasc.
1+ Warszawa, Państwowe
Wydawnictwo Naukowe, 1931+
NK4640.C6P6 folio

Publication suspended 1937–
59.

Issued by the Polish Academy
of Learning and the Union
Academique Internationale.

*Ancient vases—Greek, Egyptian,
etc.—in Polish museums in Kraków,
Warsaw, Wilanów, Poznań, Wilno,
and other places. The most recent,
fascicle 9, was published in 1976.*

[14]. Cracow, city of museums;
the most beautiful works of art
from seven museums. Warsaw,
Arkady, 1976. 54 p. 183 plates
(part color). AM70.P63K7413

A collective work edited by
Jerzy Banach.

Translation by Neil Jones and
C.S. Acheson-Waligórska of
Kraków, miasto muzeów.
*Incorporates the collections of the
Wawel (Royal Halls and Chambers,
Cathedral Treasury, Oriental art,
Armory), the National Museum
(including the Czartoryski collec-
tion), the Jagiellonian University
Museum and Library, the Museum of
Archeology and Ethnography, and the
Historical Museum of the City.*

*Museums were concentrated in
Kraków, the center of arts and
sciences in Poland, in the last decades
of the nineteenth century. Highly
literate text, and large-scale, generally
good reproductions.*

765. FIJAŁKOWSKI, Wojciech, *and* Irena Voisé.
Portrety polskie w Galerii
Wilanowskiej. [Polish portraits in
the Wilanów Palace Gallery]
Warszawa, Krajowa Agencja
Wydawnicza, 1978. 205 p. illus.
(part color). ND1301.P7W543
1978.

Summary in English.

List of illustrations also in
English.

Bibliography: p. 190–92.

*Fine reproductions of paintings in the
National Portrait Gallery. Portraits
by Marcello Bacciarelli (including a
self-portrait), Angelica Kauffmann,
Pompeo Batoni, Theodore Géricault,
Ary Scheffer, Franz Winterhalter,
and others.*

[370]. FLIK, Józef.
Toruńskie portrety
mieszczańskie drugiej połowy
XVI wieku z Muzeum w
Toruniu. [Toruń burghers' portraits of the second half of the
sixteenth century in the Toruń
Museum] Toruń, 1982. 130 p. 26
plates. ND1324.P62F55 1982

Summary in English, French,
and Russian.

Bibliography: p. 121–25.

*Media determine not only pictorial
appearance but, together with technological examination, make possible
hypotheses regarding the origins of a
portrait. That of Mikołaj Kopernik
(Copernicus), which has no counterpart among works of Polish origin,
may have been executed in England by*

a Netherlandish master, perhaps Marcus Gheeraert or Johann de Critz.

766. GĄSIOROWSKA, Maria (Jarosławiecka), *and* Marek Wierzbicki.
Oprawy artystyczne XIII–XVIII w. w zbiorach Czartoryskich w Krakowie. [Artistic bindings from the thirteenth to the eighteenth centuries in the Czartoryski collection in Kraków] Kraków, Muzeum Narodowe w Krakowie, 1952. 10 p. 38 plates of illus. Z274.G3
Brief account of a splendid collection of bindings. The earliest are Gothic, inlaid with Byzantine ivory reliefs. Other outstanding examples are French of the thirteenth and fourteenth century, Italian c.1400 and c.1500, Persian c.1490, and other important specimens of later Italian, French, German, English, and Spanish workmanship.

[646]. GĘBAROWICZ, Mieczysław, *and* Tadeusz Mańkowski.
Arrasy Zygmunta Augusta. [The tapestries of (King) Sigismund Augustus] Rocznik Krakowski, vol. 29, 1937. 220 p. illus. DB879.K8R58 v. 29
Summary in French.
Bibliographic references.
A fundamental scholarly study to which Szablowski et al. (no. 652) pay tribute. King Sigismund Augustus (reigned 1548–1572) owned about 350 tapestries at the time of his death. The research focuses mainly on the Genesis set: comparisons with analogous tapestries elsewhere; workshops where they were executed. Discussion of the eleven copies after various cartoons of the

three Kraków series (Stuttgart). Transcriptions of the extensive archival documents.*

767. GOETEL-KOPFF, Maria.
Polish mediaeval art in the National Museum in Cracow. The Connoisseur, vol. 182, no. 731, Jan 1973, p. 35–43. illus. (part color). N1.C75 v. 182
Among the National Museum treasures reproduced here are a panel painting (c. 1425), originally in the church at Ruszcza near Kraków and considered the oldest sepulcral preserved painting, and a beautiful sculpture (c. 1400), The Virgin and Child from Krużlowa, originally in the church in Krużlowa, that has been exhibited in Paris, London, and the U.S.

[497]. Grafika i rysunki polskie w zbiorach polskich. [Polish prints and drawings in Polish collections] Warszawa, Arkady, 1977. 130 p. 148 illus. (part color). NE735.P6G68
Edited by Maria Mrozińska and Stanisława Sawicka.
Introduced by Alina Chyczewska.
Summary and list of illustrations in French.
Bibliographies.
Prints and drawings by widely known artists along with works by artists virtually unknown to non-Polish historians of art. Among many works placed in the context of European art history are those by T.B. Lubieniecki (1654–1718?), J. Wall (1754–1798), Z. Vogel (1764–1826), P. Michałowski (1800–1855), A.T. Kwiatkowski (1809–1891), B. Zaleski (1819–1880), and J. Chełmoński (1849–1914).

768. Grafika japońska w zbiorach Muzeum Narodowego w Poznaniu; katalog wystawy. [Japanese prints in the collections of the National Museum in Poznań; exhibition catalog] Poznań, 1970. 120 p. illus. (part color). NE1318.P6P66
Bibliography: p. 75.
No closer date given for acquisition of the collection than "before World War I". No exact early inventory. Despite losses during two world wars, there are 198 sheets dating from the sixteenth to the twentieth century. Biographical notices on more than fifty artists.

769. Grafika szkół obcych w zbiorach polskich. [Prints of foreign schools in Polish collections] Warszawa, Arkady, 1978. 178 p. illus. (part color), ports. (Polskie zbiory graficzne) NE625.G73 1978
Catalog by Maria Mrozińska and Stanisława Sawicka.
Summary in French.

[355]. JAROSŁAWIECKA-GĄSIOROWSKA, Maria.
Les principaux manuscrits à peintures du Musée des Princes Czartoryski à Cracovie. Paris, 1935. 2 v. (Bulletin de la Societé française de reproductions de manuscrits à peintures, no. 18) ND3345.P16 no. 18
Vol. 1: Text. 203 p.; v. 2: 48 plates.
Bibliographic references in v. 1.
Describes thirty-six magnificent manuscripts with all scholarly probity. Thirty Western manuscripts (originating in France, the Low Countries, Germany, and Poland)

dating from the eleventh to the late sixteenth century. Six oriental manuscripts (Persian, Turkish, Indian). Concordances between manuscripts and illustrations on pp. 199–203.

[506]. Katalog rysunków z Gabinetu Rycin Biblioteki Uniwersyteckiej w Warszawie. [Catalog of drawings from the Print Room of the Warsaw University Library] Warszawa, Państwowe Wydawnictwo Naukowe, 1967–69. 2 v. illus. (Biblioteka Muzealnictwa i Ochrony Zabytków, Series A, vols. 4 and 5) AM70.P6B5 v. 4, 5

Vol. 1: Varsaviana. Rysunki architektoniczne, dekoracyjne, plany i widoki z XVIII i XIX wieku. [Varsaviana. Drawings of architecture and decoration, plans and views of the eighteenth and nineteenth centuries] 385 p.

V. 2: Miejscowości różne. Rysunki architektoniczne, dekoracyjne, plany i widoki z XVIII i XIX wieku. [Various locations. Drawings of architecture and decoration, plans and views of the eighteenth and nineteenth centuries] 379 p.

The core of the collection is the abundant and splendid material gathered by King Stanisław August Poniatowski (died 1798) that was acquired for the University Library in 1818. Part 1 of the scholarly catalog, prepared by Teresa Sulerzyska, Stanisława Sawicka, and Jadwiga Trenklerówna, consists of 1,394 items. Undertaken in large part for the monarch, they consist of building projects, including urban plans, churches, and chapels, palaces and other residences, academies, monuments, and architectural decorations (triumphal arches, festivals). Part 2,

prepared by Teresa Sulerzyska, catalogs nearly one thousand items— projects in Poland arranged topographically, and some designs for foreign locations (Tsarskoe Selo, Versailles). Indexes by person, place name, and by building type. Two hundred fourteen inadequate illustrations.

770. KIELCE, Poland.
Muzeum Świętokrzyskie w Kielcach. Zbiory malarstwa polskiego. [Collections of Polish paintings] Warszawa, Arkady, 1971. 90 p. illus. (part color). ND955.P6K54

Introduction in French.
Biographies of artists.
Catalog by Barbara Modrzejewska and Alojzy Oborny.

History of acquisitions and styles of paintings in the Museum of Kielce. Glossary of terms useful for placing Polish artists in the general European context, i.e., "Secesja" [Secession], "Postimpresjonizm," and in national art movements. Severely reduced format makes any aesthetic evaluation of paintings reproduced in black and white impossible.

771. Kolekcja imienia Jana
Pawła II fundacji Janiny i Zbigniewa Karola Porczyńskich. [Collection named after (Pope) John Paul II donated by Janina and Zbigniew Karol Porczyński] Warszawa, Krajowa Agencja Wydawnicza, 1988. 237 p. color illus. ND454.C37 1988

Edited by Maria Raczyńska, Barbara Deńca, and Małgorzata Pawlak.

An album of about four hundred paintings by European artists, including Rubens, Lucas Cranach,

J.B.C. Corot, Alfred Sisley, portraits by Rembrandt van Rijn, B.E. Murillo, P.G. Battoni, Joshua Reynolds, T. Gainsborough, etc.

The collection is arranged in five sections: the Bible and Saints, Portraits, Mother and Child, Mythology and Allegory, and Landscapes and Still Life. About five hundred color photographs are included in the album. There is a list of twenty paintings that are being held in conservation.

The collection is located on Plac Bankowy 1, 00139 Warsaw.

772. Kolekcja Porczyńskich.
[The Porczyński Collection] Projekt, no. 5, 1988. p. 1–72. illus. (part color). N6.P7 no. 5

Contents: Zielecki, Jan. Zbigniew-Karol Porczyński rozmowa z Redakcją. Interview with Zbigniew-Karol Porczyński.- Pasierb, Janusz St. Problematyka ikonograficzna Kolekcji Porczyńskich. Iconographic problems concerning the Porczyński Collection.- Rzepińska, Hanna. Rzut oka na Kolekcję Porczyńskich. A glance at the Porczyński Collection.- Porczyński, Zbigniew Karol. Obrazy z Królewskiej Kolekcji. Paintings from the Royal Collection.

The entire issue is devoted to a collection of paintings presented to the Muzeum Archidiecezjalne in Warsaw by Janina and Zbigniew-Karol Porczyński. Text in Polish and English.

The collection of nearly four hundred paintings was acquired mainly from 1982 to 1983 and was donated in 1987 to the Catholic Church in Poland. It consists of

European master paintings from the sixteenth century to Van Gogh, and is reported to contain paintings by artists of quality otherwise unavailable in Poland.

[357]. Kraków. Uniwersytet Jagielloński. Biblioteka. Rękopisy i pierwodruki iluminowane Biblioteki Jagiellońskiej. [Illuminated manuscripts and early printed books in the Jagiellonian Library] Wrocław, Zakład Narodowy im. Ossolińskich, 1958. 233 p. (154) p. of facsims., 12 mounted color illus. ND3177.K7K75 folio

By Zofia Ameisenowa. Bibliography: p. 228–31.

Catalog of 215 items of Italian, French, Czech, Polish, and other origin, from the mid-twelfth through the sixteenth century. Complete scholarly apparatus. Numerous appendices such as provenances, scribes, copyists, authors, artists, repositories of related materials, and detailed iconography. A publication of highest importance. Among the manuscripts is the famous Codex Picturatus Balthasaris Behem (c.1505) consisting of 372 leaves, illustrated with 26 multicolored miniatures.

773. Kraków. Wawel Castle. Państwowe Zbiory Sztuki na Wawelu. (The Orient in the Wawel collections; guide-book) Kraków, 1977. 88, 15 p. illus., map. N7262.K7 1977

By Jerzy T. Petrus, Maria Piątkiewicz-Dereniowa, Magdalena Piwocka. Translation by Krystyna Malczarek of *Wschód w zbiorach wawelskich.*

A brief introductory history to the role of Turkey and Persia, China and Japan, and Armenia in the life and art of Poland. Vigorous relations through trade, immigrant craftsmen, and war existed from the sixteenth century. Communications flourished, especially in the seventeenth century, survived to the end of the eighteenth century, and were revived in the historicism of the nineteenth century. The exhibition includes Turkish and Persian tents, carpets, arms and armor, and pottery and porcelain.

774. KRZEMIŃSKA, Marta. Muzeum sztuki w kulturze polskiej. [The art museum in Polish culture] Warszawa, Państwowe Wydawnictwo Naukowe, 1987. 347 p. 64 illus. N3150.K79 1987

Summary in English and German. Bibliographic references.

In the period of the Enlightenment, the purpose of Polish museums was to rally the people around their national heritage. Izabella Czartoryska's establishment at Puławy is an example. This pattern has continued essentially to the present. After World War II, the scholarly aims of museums were down-played in favor of the political system. The State bill of 1962 stresses the educational aims of museums. An exhibition such as "A Self-Portrait of the Poles" revivifies society's historical consciousness.

775. Łódź, Poland. Muzeum Sztuki. Malarstwo polskie w Galerii Muzeum Sztuki Łodzi; przewodnik, katalog. [Polish painting in the Gallery of the Art Museum in Łódź; a guide

and catalog] Warszawa, Sztuka, 1957. 135 p. 34 illus. ND691.L6

Bibliography: p. 132–34.

776. LORENTZ, Stanisław. Przewodnik po muzeach i zbiorach w Polsce. [Guide to museums and collections in Poland] 3d rev. ed. Warszawa, Interpress, 1982. 520 p. illus. (part color), plans. map. N3150.L6 1982

Bibliographic references.

Textually, a thoroughly admirable and valuable vade-mecum which, besides covering all the appropriate institutions, is studded with information on the history of the museum building, the collection, and the collecting mandate. Illustrations and graphics not equal to the text.

777. LORENTZ, Stanisław. Guide to museums and collections in Poland. Warsaw, Interpress, 1974. 360 p. 60 leaves of plates, illus. (part color), map. N3150.L613

Translation by Jan Aleksandrowicz of *Przewodnik po muzeach i zbiorach w Polsce.*

This unique English-language guide to art collections in Poland was authored by the former director of the National Museum of Art, Warsaw. Arranged alphabetically by city name, the collections in each city are surveyed in general. It is, however, the detailed particulars on both primary and secondary collections that the reader and/or traveler will find so valuable.

[50]. MAŃKOWSKI, Tadeusz. Mecenat artystyczny Stanisława Augusta. [The artistic patronage of (King) Stanislaus Augustus] Warszawa, Państwowe

Art Collections

Wydawnictwo Naukowe, 1976.
384 p. illus. N5280.P72S865

Edited by Zuzanna
Prószyńska.

Introduction by Władysław
Tatarkiewicz.

Summary in English.

Bibliographic references.

The present critical edition of a work written in the 1926–1938 era. Updates the status of research and makes the literature current. The text examines one of the most important of all royal patrons in Polish history and considers six aspects of his influence: (1) the spirit of the Enlightenment, where patronage functioned to improve the general welfare, while the King's refined personal taste promoted the creation of architectural masterpieces; (2) the King's agent, August Moszyński, who purchased prints, drawings, medals, and antiquities on an enormous scale; (3) the King's classicizing and Western taste as opposed to traditional Sarmatism, with the expansion of Greco-Roman taste being taken into account; (4) the production of porcelain in the Belvedere; (5) the program for the Knight's Hall to commemorate important events and persons in Polish history (inter alia with bronze busts, many of which are extant); (6) and—in the King's mercantile interest—the production of waist sashes.

778. MROZIŃSKA, Maria.

I Disegni del Codice Bonola del Museo di Varsavia. Catalogo della Mostra. Venezia, N. Pozza, 1959. 148 p. plates. NC255.M7

Sponsored by Fondazione Giorgio Cini, Venice. Centro di cultura e civiltà. Istituto di storia dell'arte. Cataloghi di mostre, 8.

Introduction by Giuseppe Fiocco.

Album of drawings assembled by the seventeenth-century Milanese artist and collector, Giorgio Bonola. Rich in the Lombard School (Camillo Boccaccino, B. Campi, Cambiaso, Cerano, Camillo, Giulio Cesare, and Ercole Procaccini, Morazzone, F. del Cairo, and others), and the Bologna School (Antonio Carracci, Domenichino, Franceschini, Cignani, Canuti), and Pordenone. Illustrations in 107 plates.

[563]. MROZOWSKA, Alina, and Tadeusz Majda.

Rysunki o tematyce tureckiej z kolekcji króla Stanisława Augusta w Gabinecie Rycin Biblioteki Uniwersyteckiej w Warszawie. [Drawings on Turkish themes from the collection of king Stanislaus Augustus in the archives of drawings of the Warsaw University Library] Warszawa, Wydawnictwo Uniwersytetu Warszawskiego, 1978. 79 p. illus. NC87.W37 1973 v. 2

Drawings by F.A. Lohrmann (c. 1735–after 1793), J.C. Kamsetzer (1750–1795), and others depicting life in Constantinople, its buildings, events at court, the coronation of the Sultan, the audiences of the English, Dutch, and Venetian ambassadors, etc. All fifty-one illustrations are described, but there is no numerical correlation between the catalog and the plates.

779. Museums of Cracow. New York, Newsweek, 1982. 171 p. illus. (part color). (Great Museums of the World) N7255.P62K77813 1982

Introduction by Tadeusz Chruścicki.

Texts by Franciszek Stolot.

Translation by Edward Rothert of *Muzea Krakowa*.

Bibliography: p. 168.

One of the most outstanding among many books on the Kraków museums. Superb color reproductions give a cross-section of the preeminent works of art, from the tenth to the twentieth century. Although many well-known works are illustrated, such as the Wit Stwosz altar and Renaissance tombs, the emphasis is on lesser-known objects. Some are fabulous, such as the silver tomb of St. Stanisław (1669–1671) by P. von der Rennen; others are illustrious, such as the altarpiece painted by J. Pencz and sculptured by P. Flötner, and the paintings by L. Lotto, A. Allori, J. van Noort, and Rembrandt. Extended commentaries on each plate. The quality of the commentary by F. Stolot matches the discerning choice of illustrations.

[723]. Muzeum im. Władysława Orkana w Rabce.

Katalog zbiorów sztuki w Muzeum im. Władysława Orkana w Rabce. [Catalog of the art collection in the Władysław Orkan Museum in Rabka] Rabka, 1977. 274 p. 212 plates, illus., maps. N7255.P6M893 1977

Introduction and catalog by Teresa Jabłońska.

Bibliographic references.

This ethnographic museum, founded in 1936, is devoted to the Gorce, Beskid Wyspowy, and northern Podhale regions. Established in the name of the first outstanding writer and poet of the Podhale area (Władysław Orkan, 1875–1930), its holdings represent all areas of folk art and culture, including one of the largest

Polish collections of folk sculpture and painting on glass, canvas, and paper.

The catalog of 459 works is arranged by technique: sculpture, painting (on glass and on all other materials), and prints. Under each technique, the arrangement is iconographic: Madonna, Christ, God the Father, Saints. A scholarly presentation that includes an index to places of origin of the works.

780. Muzeum im. Xawerego Dunikowskiego. Xawery Dunikowski; rzeźby, obrazy, rysunki; Katalog. [Xawery Dunikowski; sculptures, paintings, drawings; a catalog] Warszawa, Muzeum Narodowe, 1975. 201 p. 49 leaves of plates, illus. N7255.P63D854

Edited by Aleksandra Kodurowa.

Introduction, preface, and biography also in French.

Bibliographies.

Collected works of the artist (1875–1964) which span his career. Summary catalog of 947 sculptures, paintings, and drawings. Index of subjects. Located in Warsaw, in the eighteenth-century Królikarnia palace, as a branch of the National Museum.

[565]. Muzeum Narodowe we Wrocławiu. Gabinet Grafiki. Katalog zbiorów Gabinetu Grafiki. [Catalog of the collection of the Print Department (of the National Museum in Wrocław)] Wrocław, Muzeum Narodowe, 1983+ NE735.P6M87 1983

Vol. 1: Grafika polska w latach 1901–1939. [Polish prints, 1901–1939] Prepared by Irena Rylska. 240 p. illus.

Summary in English.
Bibliography: vol. 1, p. 38–42.
Bibliographic references.
Short biographies of artists.

A catalog of 819 works representing the best from the schools of Lwów and Kraków; few prints from the schools of Warsaw ad Poznań, none from Wilno. The poor quality of the reproductions fails to do justice to some interesting work.

781. Muzeum Narodowe we Wrocławiu. Polska sztuka współczesna; katalog zbiorów. [Polish contemporary art; catalog of the collection] Wrocław, Muzeum Narodowe, 1983. 409 p. illus. N7255.P6M896 1983

A collective work edited by Mariusz Hermansdorfer.

Introduction also in English.
Bibliography: p. 264–66.
Bibliographies of artists with description of their works.

This catalog includes over three hundred reproductions from collections of over 1,900 paintings, sculptures, drawings, and prints in the National Museum in Wrocław, which was established in 1948. Indexed by artists, the collection encompasses all media and documents conceptual as well as environmental art.

782. Muzeum Narodowe w Krakowie. The National Museum in Cracow. The Czartoryski Collection. A historical outline and selected objects. Warsaw, Arkady, 1980. 194 p. illus. (part color). N3152.32.C92M813 1980

A collective work edited by Marek Rostworowski.

Translation of *Muzeum*

Narodowe w Krakowie. Zbiory Czartoryskich.

Bibliographies.

A detailed history of the celebrated collection. The narration covers its founding by Izabela Czartoryska in the 1790s at Puławy, its enormous expansion until 1831, its dispersal at the failure of the November 1831 Uprising, its reconstruction at the Hôtel Lambert, Paris, and its restoration to Kraków in the 1870s. Many good color reproductions of the paintings (Leonardo, Lady with an Ermine; Rembrandt, Good Samaritan), drawings (Gerard David), miniatures, ivories, tapestries, goldsmithery, armor.

783. Muzeum Pomorskie w Gdańsku. Zbiory sztuki. [The Pomeranian Museum in Gdańsk. Collections of art] Gdańsk, Muzeum Pomorskie w Gdańsku, 1969. 119 plates, illus. (part color). N3150.5.M89

Introduction and catalog also in French, English, and Russian.

Respectable collection, strong in sixteenth and seventeenth century paintings from the Lowlands: Hans Memling, Frans Floris, Van Dyck. Outstanding objects, such as Angelo Bronzino's portrait of Catherine de Medici, a drawing by Holbein the Elder, sculpture by Giambologna, textiles, and goldsmithery. No scholarly apparatus.

784. Muzeum w Wilanowie. Artystyczne zbiory Wilanowa; katalog. [The art collection of Wilanów] 2. wyd. Warszawa, Auriga, 1979. [i.e. 1982] 228 p. chiefly illus. (part color). N3165.A55 1982

Edited by Irena Malinowska.

Introduction by Wojciech Fijałkowski.

Summary in English; list of illustrations also in English.

Bibliography: p. 30–32.

Excellent introduction to the collection founded by King Jan III Sobieski, and systematically enlarged by his heirs. The illustrations in 184 plates, with a brief but scholarly catalog of objects from the sixteenth to the nineteenth century. Over forty paintings reproduced, including those by Cima da Conegliano, Le Sueur, Batoni, and Winterhalter. Nearly thirty pieces of furniture are illustrated, along with clocks, porcelain, glass, bronze objects, and Far Eastern art. Altogether, the collection is one of quality and great interest.

[618]. Muzeum w Wilanowie.
Das polnische Plakat von 1892 bis Heute; aus den Sammlungen des Plakatmuseums Wilanów. Berlin u. d. Nationalmuseums Warschau, Hochschule der Kunste Berlin. Münsterschwarzach, Vier-Türme-Verlag, 1980. 92 p. illus. (part color).
NC1807.P6M86 1980

Edited by Anna Rutkiewicz and others.

Bibliography: p. 190–92.

Consists mainly of three hundred color reproductions of posters with a descriptive entry for each and biographical sketches of more than one hundred artists. Six short essays, such as "Structure, aesthetic, and semiotics of the Polish poster."

785. Muzeum w Wilanowie.
Galeria Malarstwa Stanisława Kostki Potockiego w Wilanowie. [Gallery of paintings of Stanisław Kostka Potocki in Wilanów]

Warszawa, Arkady, 1974. 241 p. illus. (part color). (Katalog zbiorów artystycznych, 1)
N3163.A54

Edited by Irena Voisé and Teresa Głowacka-Poheć.

Summary in French.

Bibliographic references.

Stanisław Kostka Potocki (1755–1821) was chiefly responsible for enlarging the collection. He is the subject of J.L. David's famous equestrian portrait (no. 21). The italian School is represented mainly by workshop or copies: original paintings by Cesare da Sesto, B. Dossi, B. Franco, B. Schedone, and G.F. Grimaldi. The French, Dutch, and Flemish Schools are also represented.

[631]. Muzeum w Wilanowie.
Rzemiosło artystyczne i plastyka w zbiorach wilanowskich. Katalog-Przewodnik po Galerii. [Decorative arts and sculpture in the Wilanów Museum. Catalog and guide to the Gallery] Warszawa, Muzeum Narodowe w Warszawie, 1980. 340 p. illus. (Katalog zbiorów artystycznych, 2) NK480.W54M89 1980

Edited by Włodzimierz Bałdowski, et al.

Bibliography: p. 15–16.

Arranged by materials: ceramics, including majolica and delftware, and an extensive collection of Meissen; glassware; silver; bronze; arms; furniture; Far Eastern objects; nineteenth-century medals. German, Dutch, English, Russian, Italian, and Polish schools are represented. Well-reproduced illustrations.

786. Najcenniejsze rysunki obce ze zbiorów polskich.
Katalog wystawy. [The most valuable foreign drawings from

Polish collections. Exhibition catalog] Warszawa, Muzeum Narodowe w Warszawie, 1980. 119 p. 102 p. of plates, illus. NC17.P6W36

Catalog prepared by Waldemar Baraniewski and others.

Edited by Justyna Guze and Anna Kozak.

Bibliography: p. 105–15.

By Maria Mrozińska, a short history on the collecting of drawings by foreign artists in Poland. A scholarly illustrated catalog, albeit in quarto format, that discusses and reproduces notable works by the following artists not included in Rysunki szkół obcych w zbiorach polskich *1976 (see no. 793): Carlo Cignani, pl. 18; Giovanni Domenico Tiepolo, pl. 96; Jean Louis Prieur the Elder, pl. 74; Victor Louis, pls. 75–76; Philip Otto Runge, pl. 98; Schnorr von Carolsfeld, pl. 99; and Karl Friedrich Schinkel, pls. 101–102.*

787. The National Museum in Cracow. A historical outline and selected objects. Warsaw, Arkady, 1987. 257 p. illus. (part color). N3160.A541813 1987

Introduction by Tadeusz Chruścicki.

Catalog and selection of objects by Franciszek Stolot.

Translated by Elżbieta Chrzanowska.

Valuable for the introduction on the founding of the museum and assemblage of the collections. These include paintings, prints and drawings, sculpture, and decorative arts of all periods and international origins. There are also a few rare and unusual objects: no. 79, engraved view of Kraków as a background to a plate of a volume on the horse, 1603; no. 93, Virgin and Child with Saints as by Lorenzo

Lotto. Most of the objects chosen for illustration are routine, even banal. Good photography.

788. 100 [i.e., one hundred] of the finest drawings from Polish collections; a loan exhibition under the patronage of Prof. Stanisław Lorentz, Director of the National Museum of Warsaw and the Rt. Hon. Kenneth Robinson, Chairman of the Arts Council of Great Britain. London, Heim Gallery, 1980. 108 p. 99 p. of plates, illus. (Heim exhibition catalogues, no. 32) N8640.H4, no. 32

Bibliography: p. 107–08.

Includes sheets by Dürer, Wolf Huber, Rembrandt, Jordaens, Pordenone, Ludovico Carracci, Cignani. Attributions updated: Lorenzo di Credi (Pouncey) from Boltraffio; Taddeo Zuccaro (Gere, no. 249); Rubens (Burchard and d'Hulst, no. 179). Architectural and ornament drawings by practitioners active in Poland (André LeBrun, Victor Louis, J.B. Pillement) and elsewhere (G.B. Piranesi, F. Rastrelli). Collections of foreign drawings in a Poland devastated by politics and war recounted in a preface by Maria Mrozińska.

Review by Nicholas Turner in Burlington Magazine, vol. 22, no. 924, March 1980, p. 213–14.

789. PIĄTKIEWICZ-DERENIOWA, Maria. Majolika włoska w zbiorach wawelskich. [Italian majolica in the Wawel castle collections] Kraków, Państwowe Zbiory Sztuki na Wawelu. 1975. 157 p. illus. (part color). (Państwowe Zbiory Sztuki na Wawelu.

Katalog zbiorów, 2). NK4315K73 1975

In Polish and French. Bibliography: p. 156–57.

790. PIĄTKIEWICZ-DERENIOWA, Maria. Porcelana miśnieńska w zbiorach wawelskich. [Meissen porcelain in the Wawel castle collections] Kraków, Państwowe Zbiory Sztuki na Wawelu, 1983. 2 v. illus. (part color). (Państwowe Zbiory Sztuki na Wawelu. Katalog zbiorów, 3) NK4380.P36 1983

In Polish and French. Bibliography: v. 2, p. 197–98.

[516]. Polskie kolekcjonerstwo grafiki i rysunku. [Collecting prints and drawings in Poland] (Polskie zbiory graficzne.) [Polish graphic arts collections] Warsawa, Arkady, 1980. 218 p. NE735.P6P64

Edited by Maria Mrozińska and Stanisława Sawicka.

Bibliography: p. 214–15. Bibliographic references. Summary in French.

Describes holdings of prints, some foreign, in forty-six collections in nineteen cities and towns, and traces the history of the collections. The oldest is the collection of King Stanisław August Poniatowski.

791. Primitifs flamands; Corpus de la peinture des anciens Pays-Bas méridionaux au quinzième siècle, no. 9. Les musées de Pologne. (Gdańsk, Kraków, Warszawa). Bruxelles, Centre national de Recherches "Primitifs flamands," 1966. 133 p. 240 plates. ND665.P66 no. 9

By Jan Białostocki. Bibliographies.

Emphasizes Memling's Last Judgement in Gdańsk. Also includes Bouts, Flémalle, and Coter groups. Extensive descriptions, documentation, and bibliography. Excellent illustrations with many details.

792. ROSTWOROWSKI, Marek. Netherlandish paintings in Polish collections. Burlington Magazine, vol. 102, July, 1960, p. 366–69. illus. N1.B95 v. 102

Reviews an exhibition of eighty-seven paintings (1450–1550) from some of Poland's major museum collections. Among the items discussed are the St. Reinhold retable by Joos van Cleve (National Museum, Warsaw) and Memling's Last Judgement, a three-panel scene in the retable in the Church of Our Lady (Gdańsk). Also included is the Crucifixion (Poznań Museum) by a Netherlandish artist, circa 1500.

793. Rysunki szkół obcych w zbiorach polskich. [Drawings of foreign schools in Polish collections] Warszawa, Arkady, 1976. 178 p. illus. (part color). (Polskie zbiory graficzne) NC23.P7R95

Edited by Maria Mrozińska and Stanisława Sawicka.

Summary and list of illustrations also in French.

By Maria Mrozińska, a short history on the collecting of drawings in Poland and abroad. Catalog, with scholarly apparatus, of 101 drawings, 25 reproduced in color, 126 in black and white. Some important drawings, many of great interest, by Italian, German, French, Dutch, and Flemish Schools, from Giovanni Boltraffio

to Paul Klee. *Among the artists
represented are Annibale Carracci,
no. 11; Ludovico Carracci, no. 12;
Bartholomaeus Spranger, no. 36;
Domenico Canuti, no. 49; Rubens,
no. 58; Abraham von Diepenbeeck,
no. 60; Rembrandt, nos. 67–76;
Giuseppe Galli Bibiena, no. 101; and
Piranesi, no. 107.*

[338]. RYSZKIEWICZ, Andrzej.
Zbieracze i obrazy. [Collectors
and paintings] Warszawa,
Państwowe Wydawnictwo
Naukowe, 1972. 326 p. illus.
ports. N7445.8.P7R97
Bibliographic references.
*Part one: Collectors of art:
Aleksander Chodkiewicz
(1776–1838); Józef K. Ossoliński
(1764–1838) who provided the first
public gallery in Warsaw; Ignacy
Korwin Milewski (1846–1922);
Henryk Hirszel, Warsaw
lithographer, print dealer and, from
1850, paintings dealer. Part two:
foreign artists in relation to Polish
subjects and collections: Antoine
Pesne (d. 1757); Stanisław August
Poniatowski as portrayed by such
French painters as Louis Tocque
(1696–1772) and Marie-Elisabeth-
Louise Vigée-Lebrun (1755–1842);
portraits of Poles by Anton Graff
(1736–1813); and pictures in Polish
collections by Wilhelm Schadow
(1788–1862). Numerous
documentary citations.*

[79]. Secesja. Wystawa ze
zbiorów Muzeum
Mazowieckiego w Płocku.
Katalog wystawy. [Secession: An
exhibition from the collections of
the Masovia Museum in Płock.
Catalog] Płock, Muzeum
Mazowieckie w Płocku, 1979. 24

p. illus., ports. N6465.A7M88
1979
Introduction by Tadeusz
Zaremba.
*Paintings, prints, drawings, sculp-
ture, medals, ceramics, glass, metal-
work, furniture, and costume. Orien-
tation of Polish style to that of
Austria and Germany evident from
preponderantly Austro-German ori-
gins of objects represented. Other
works shown are by Czechoslovak,
Russian, French, and Belgian artists.
Famous names include E. Gallé and
M. Thonet. Lesser-known Polish
artists include the painters K.
Krzyżanowski, K. Stabrowski, and
W. Wojtkiewicz; the sculptor W.
Szymanowski; and the ceramicist
J. Szczepkowski.*

794. SKUBISZEWSKA, Maria.
Malarstwo włoskie w zbiorach
wawelskich. [Italian paintings in
the Wawel Collections] Kraków,
1973. 188 p. illus. (part color).
(Państwowe Zbiory Sztuki na
Wawelu. Katalog zbiorów, 1)
ND614.S58
Sponsored by Ministerstwo
Kultury i Sztuki, Zarząd
Muzeów.
Edited by Jerzy Szablowski.
Bibliography: p. 182–85.
*Several interesting works, such as
A. Allori, Portrait of Francesco de
Medici holding a miniature portrait
of Joanne of Austria; Palma
Vecchio, Portrait of Woman in
White; Paris Bordone, Pietà with
donor; Guercino, Allegory of
Painting; a G.B. Tiepolo and a
Michele Marieschi. Minimal scholarly
discussion.*

795. STEINBORN, Bożenna.
Katalog zbiorów malarstwa
niderlandzkiego. [Catalog of

Netherlandish paintings (in the
National Museum of Wrocław)]
Wrocław, Muzeum Narodowe
we Wrocławiu, 1973. 110 p. 50
plates. ND644.S73
Text in Polish and French.
*Museum created in 1945. Collection
of Dutch and Flemish paintings
consists of a core of pictures existing
in pre-World War II Silesia, others
brought from Lwów (now in the
USSR), and contemporary purchases.
Although the historical representation
is fragmented, many of the fifty-two
pictures in the scholarly catalog
deserve close attention; several are
otherwise unpublished. Examples of
outstanding pictures are by Jan
Asselijn, Karel Dujardin, Frans
Floris, Salomon Koninck,
Bartholomaeus Spranger, J.B.
Weenix, and Emannuel de Witte.*

[652]. SZABLOWSKI, Jerzy.
The Flemish tapestries at
Wawel Castle in Cracow.
Treasures of King Sigismund
Augustus Jagiełło. Antwerp,
Fonds Mercator, 1972. 501 p.
color illus. NK3071.P63K78 folio
Various chapters by Anna
Missiąg-Bocheńska, Marie
Hennel-Bernasikowa, Magdalena
Piwocka, Sophie
Schneebal-Perelman, and
Adelbrecht L.J. Van De Walle.
Bibliography: p. 481–87.
Also published in French,
Flemish, and German. The Polish
edition published in 1975 (see
item 645).
*One of the finest books ever published
on art in Poland. Three sets of
tapestries commissioned by King
Sigismund II Augustus (1520–
1572) are illustrated in 136 un-
surpassed color plates. The text, of*

appropriate quality, furnishes the cultural and artistic circumstances that led to these commissions. One set consists of eighteen hangings with subjects from Genesis based on designs by Michiel Coxie; another is of forty-four verdures with real and fantastic animals, having antecedents in the work of Joachim Patinir, Pieter Brueghel the Elder, and Mathieu and Hieronymus Cock, among others, and anticipating mannerist landscapes; the third set is made up of sixty-two tapestries with grotesque subjects whose basis in ancient, Italian, and Netherlandish art is explored.

796. SZABLOWSKI, Jerzy.
The Royal Castle of Wawel and its collections. The Connoisseur, vol. 182, no. 731, Jan. 1973, p. 2–14. illus. (part color). N1.C75 v. 182

797. Sztuka francuska w zbiorach polskich, 1230–1830.
Katalog wystawy. [French art in Polish collections, 1230–1830. Exhibition catalog] Poznań, Muzeum Narodowe w Poznaniu, 1973. 187 p. illus. N6841.S96
  By Teresa Armółowicz-Kosecka, et al.
    Summary in French.
    Bibliography: p. 169–78.
Catalog entries totaling 471 by scholars specializing in painting, sculpture, prints, drawings, manuscripts, decorative arts (silver, clocks, enamels, furniture, porcelain, textiles), and medieval art. Represents the holdings of thirteen museums, libraries, and ecclesiastical collections. Besides well-known portraits by J.L. David and J.M. Nattier, there are memorable canvases by Simon Vouet,

Claude Vignon, Watteau, Chardin, Greuze, and Ingres. A Tournament Book by a follower of King René of Anjou dates around 1465. Silver is represented by M.G. Biennais and P.P. Thomire, among others.

798. Tkanina turecka XVI–XIX w. ze zbiorów polskich,
[Turkish textiles of the sixteenth to nineteenth centuries in Polish collections. Exhibition catalog] Muzeum Narodowe w Warszawie, wrzesień-listopad, 1983. Warszawa, Muzeum Narodowe 1983. 62 p. 125 plates, 16 color plates. NK8965.A1T58 1983
    Bibliography: p. 18.
A descriptive catalog of 136 items from twenty-six collections that include rugs, tapestries, tent fragments, sashes, chasubles, and attire. All are illustrated in sixteen color plates, plus the cover, and 125 black and white plates.

799. Ukiyo-e-dawny drzeworyt japoński ze zbiorów Muzeum Narodowego w Krakowie, Kolekcja Feliksa Jasieńskiego.
Ukiyo-e old Japanese woodblock print from the National Museum in Cracow, Feliks Jasieński Collection. [Katalog wystawy] 7 czerwca–31 lipca, 1988 r. Towarzystwo Przyjaciół Sztuk Pięknych, Pałac Sztuki. Kraków, Międzynarodowe Bieniale Grafiki, 1988. 235 p. illus. (part color). DLC
    By Zofia Alberowa, Maria Dzieduszycka, Małgorzata Martini.
Catalog of the exhibition of Japanese prints from the seventeenth, eighteenth, and nineteenth century.

800. Warsaw. Muzeum Narodowe w Warszawie.
Galeria Malarstwa Obcego. Galeria malarstwa obcego. [A gallery of foreign printing] Warszawa, Sztuka, 1954–55. 2 vols. illus. maps. N3690.P6W39
    Contents: Vol. 1. Malarstwo Niderlandzkie, Niemieckie, Flamandzkie i Holenderskie XV, XVI i XVII wieku. [Netherlandish, German, Flemish, and Dutch painting of the fifteenth, sixteenth and seventeenth century]
    Vol. 2. Malarstwo Włoskie, Hiszpańskie, Francuskie XV, XVI, XVII, XVIII wieku. [Italian, Spanish, French painting of the fifteenth, sixteenth, seventeenth, and eighteenth century]
    Bibliographies: Vol. 1, p. 99–101; v. 2, p. 68–78.
    The catalog is the collective work of Jan Białostocki, Benedykt Tyszkiewicz, Wanda Drecka, Andrzej Chudzikowski, and Janina Michałkowa.
Includes 124 paintings by Rembrandt, Joos van Cleve, Dürer, Jacob Jordaens, Bronzino, Strozzi, Watteau, and others.

801. Warsaw. Muzeum Narodowe w Warszawie.
Galeria Malarstwa Obcego. Malarstwo francuskie, niderlandzkie, włoskie do 1600. Katalog zbiorów. [French, Netherlandish, Italian paintings before 1600. Catalog of the collection] Warszawa, Muzeum Narodowe w Warszawie, 1979. 276 p. 221 illus. N3160.A54 1979
    By Jan Białostocki, Maria Skubiszewska, et al.
    Bibliography: p. 251–276.

[345]. Warsaw. Muzeum Narodowe w Warszawie.
Galeria Sztuki Polskiej. Miniatury polskie od XVII [i.e. siedemnastego] do XX [i.e. dwudziestego] wieku. [Polish miniatures from the seventeenth to the twentieth century] Warszawa, 1978. 113 p. 60 leaves of plates, 227 miniatures, illus. ND1337.P7W37 1978

Bibliography: p. 17–22.

Catalog of the collection prepared by Halina Kamińska-Krassowska.

A scholarly compendium, mainly of portraits (227 of them), published and reproduced for the first time, of historically important persons, sometimes in an informal guise (T. Kościuszko, nos. 134–35, for instance), or by unexpected artists (S. Chlebowski, painter to Sultan Abdul Aziz, Constantinople, from 1864, no. 22). Biographies of artists, including D. Chodowiecki and A. Orłowski, and sitters. Half of the original collection was lost during World War II.

[346]. Warsaw. Muzeum Narodowe w Warszawie.
Galeria Sztuki Polskiej. La peinture polonaise du XVIe au debut du XXe siècle. Catalogue. Varsovie, 1979. 539 p. illus., ports. ND955.P6W345 1979

Edited by Krystyna Sroczyńska.

Translated by Maria Cieszewska.

Bibliography: p. 39–52.

Approximately two hundred artists, arranged alphabetically. Informative biographies and discussions of paintings, 1,200 of which are illustrated. Summary, historical introduction.

[347]. Warsaw. Muzeum Narodowe w Warszawie.
Malarstwo. [The National Museum in Warsaw. Paintings] Warszawa, Arkady, 1984. 70 p. 168 plates of illus. (part color). N3160.A542 1984

History of the collection by Stanisław Lorentz.

Catalog by Tadeusz Dobrzeniecki and others.

Exceptionally fine reproductions of recently conserved paintings. Most are in color. Polish and Flemish Gothic masterpieces are introduced; an important triptych by Maerten van Heemskerck, paintings by Giovanni Battista Cima da Conegliano, Botticelli, Paris Bordone, Gaspare Diziani, and Jean Baptiste Greuze. Half of the pictures are by Polish nineteenth- and twentieth-century artists.

802. Warsaw. Muzeum Narodowe w Warszawie. The National Museum of Warsaw: Handbook of the collections. Warsaw, 1963. 84, 181 p. 230 illus. N3160.A543

Edited by Jan Białostocki.

Introduction by Stanisław Lorentz.

Translation by Maria Rogoyska of *Zbiory Muzeum Narodowego w Warszawie.*

Prepared by the curators and keepers of the galleries and departments.

Collection ranges from ancient Egyptian to Picasso. From among the most important objects of quality, 241 are selected for illustration. Represented are Greek, Roman, and Early Christian periods; paintings by Cima da Conegliano, B. Cavallino, M. Preti, S. van Ruysdael, Watteau,

Ingres, and Courbet; and decorative arts: Gothic, majolica, porcelain, coins, and medals. History of the collection.

803. Warsaw. Muzeum Narodowe w Warszawie. Szkła starożytne; katalog naczyń. [Ancient glass; catalog of vessels] Warszawa, Muzeum Narodowe w Warszawie, 1952. 254 p. illus. tables, plates. NK5107.W3

By Barbara Filarska.

Bibliography: p. 229–37.

Currently, the collection comprises 353 objects. The majority of these were purchased on the Balkan peninsula, Asia Minor, and Constantinople during the years 1900 to 1920 by Władysław Siemianowski, who donated the collection to the National Museum. Fifty-two plates illustrate the pitchers, bottles, bowls, plates, vases, vials, and glasses from antiquity that make up the collection. Most of the items were made in the East and in the east basin region of the Mediterranean. The book discusses the history of the production of glass in the area, the characteristics of the centers of production, and the technology of production and ornamentation.

804. Warsaw. Muzeum Narodowe w Warszawie.
Sztuka starożytna. [Ancient art] Warszawa, Wydawnictwo "Sztuka," 1955. 270 p. illus. (part color), maps. N5871.P6W3

By Kazimierz Michałowski.

Bibliography: p. 239–45.

A guide to the collections of ancient art in the National Museum in Warsaw. Opened to the public in 1938, the gallery of ancient art, made up of donated private collections, comprises the excavations from Polish

*expeditions led by Professor
Kazimierz Michałowski in Egypt,
the Crimea, the Sudan, and Cyprus.
The Coptic and Byzantine collection,
established in 1972, is the newest in
the museum. It has the famous mural
paintings from Faras, according to S.
Lorentz,* Guide to Museums and
Collections in Poland, *1974. The
results of the excavations at Tell
Edfu (Egypt) were published in*
Fouilles Franco-Polonaises Tell-
Edfou. *The excavations at Faras
(the Sudan) are discussed by K.
Michałowski in his two-volume*
Faras, fouilles polonaises
(Warsawa, 1961–62).

805. Warsaw. Muzeum Narodowe w Warszawie.
Widoki architektoniczne w
malarstwie polskim 1780–1880.
Katalog. [Architectonic views in
Polish painting 1780–1880.
Exhibition catalog] Warszawa,
Muzeum Narodowe, 1964. [132]
p. 80 plates. ND691.W346

Introduction by Krystyna
Sroczyńska and Maria
Suchodolska.

Bibliography: p. 23–25.

*The paintings exhibited are from the
National Museum in Warsaw and
from other Polish museums; included
are 476 architectonic views in oil,
watercolor, and drawings. Reproduced
in the catalog are eighty views, from
Warsaw, Kraków, Wilno, Lwów,
Gdańsk, Płock, and many other
locations. The painters include
Franciszek Kostrzewski (1826–
1911)—the Trinitarian Gate in
Lublin; Zygmunt Vogel (1764–
1826)—numerous views of Warsaw;
Franciszek Smuglewicz (1745–
1807)—views of Antokol, Wilno;
Jan Chrucki (1810–1885), who
painted the Wilno Calvary; and*

*Wojciech Gerson (1831–1901)—
a view of Płock.*

806. Warsaw. Muzeum Narodowe w Warszawie.
Wystawa Malarstwa Włoskiego
w Zbiorach Polskich
XVII–XVIII w. Mostra della
pittura Italiana nelle collezioni
Polacche XVII–XVIII sec.
Warszawa, 15 kwietnia–31maja
1956. Warszawa, 1956. 137 p. 114
plates. ND616.W35

Introduction by Juliusz
Starzyński.

Exhibition catalog by Jan
Białostocki.

*A brief, scholarly catalog arranged
alphabetically by artist. The following
list of artists indicates the scope of
the holdings: Jacopo and Francesco
Bassano, Domenico Tintoretto, Il
Cerano, Daniele Crespi, Carlo
Saraceni, Bernardo Cavallino,
Mattea Preti, Il Guercino, Carlo
Dolci, Bernardo Strozzi, Giovanni
Lanfranco, Cagnacci, E. Sirani,
Desiderio Monsu, Salvator Rosa,
Marco Ricci, Michale Marieschi,
Giovanni Battista Tiepolo, and many
others. Shortcomings of the collection
are mentioned in the introduction.*

807. Warsaw. Państwowe Muzeum Etnograficzne w Warszawie. Historia; Zbiory;
Ekspozycje. National Museum of
Ethnography in Warsaw.
History; Collections;
Expositions. Warszawa, 1973.
265 p. illus. (part color)
GN36.P72W377 1973.

A collective work edited by
Jan Krzysztof Makulski. In
Polish, English, and Russian.

*The museum has a large collection of
fabrics woven in Polish villages, folk*

*costumes, jewelry, wooden sculptures,
folk paintings, prints, crafts, toys,
and many objects connected with
annual celebrations of holidays and
traditions—crèches, Easter eggs, car-
nival masks, and costumes. It also
holds many objects from other parts of
the world (particularly notable is the
collection from Africa). The museum
suffered heavy losses during the war, so
the present collections have been
assembled during the past forty years.*

[532]. WITKE-JEŻEWSKI, Dominik.
Pamiętnik wystawy starych
rycin polskich ze zbioru
Dominika Witke-Jeżewskiego
urządzonej staraniem
Towarzystwa Opieki nad
Zabytkami Przeszłości w r. 1914.
[A souvenir catalog of the
exhibition of old Polish prints
from the collection of Dominik
Witke-Jeżewski, organized in
1914 by the Society for the
Preservation of Ancient
Documents] Warszawa, 1914. 143
p. illus. NE735.P6W5

Introduction by Józef
Weyssenhoff.

*A print collection of great artistic
and historical interest. Over one
thousand prints from all periods,
approximately fifty being reproduced.
Sheets of the greatest rarity are
illustrated, perhaps uniquely. A
Monument to Judaism, aquatint
by A.F. Dietrich; J. Ziarnko's great
Carrousel on the Place Royale,
1612; several views of the buildings at
Puławy, etched by C.A. Richter;
portraits of Polish subjects such as J.
Zamoyski by A. Oleszczyński, 1856,
as well as portraits of contemporaries
by J. Falck and W. Hondius.*

809. Zeichnungen alter Meister aus polnischen Sammlungen. Ausstellung im Herzog Anton Ulrich-Museum Braunschweig vom 29. November 1981 bis 17. Januar 1982; Ausstellung in den Kunstsammlungen der Veste Coburg vom 14. März bis 25. April 1982. [Exhibition catalog] Braunschweig, 1981. 236 p. illus. (part color). NC33.P6Z44 1981

Catalog by Jan Białostocki, Maria Mrozińska, et al.

[703]. ŻYGULSKI, Zdzisław, Jr. Stara broń w polskich zbiorach. [Old arms and armor in Polish collections] 2d rev. ed. Warszawa, Krajowa Agencja Wydawnicza, 1984. 274 p. color illus. NK6671.P6Z94 1984

Bibliography: p. 273–76.
Contents: I. Broń Polska. [Polish armor]; II. Broń obca w rękach polskich. [Foreign arms and armor in Poland]; III. Broń zachodnio-Europejska nabyta w XIX i XX wieku. [West European arms and armor acquired in the nineteenth and twentieth centuries]; IV. Broń wschodnia nabyta w XIX i XX wieku. [Eastern arms and armor acquired in the nineteenth and twentieth centuries]

The author includes swords, helmets, equestrian equipment, armor, sabers, and maces. Each item is fully described and the provenance is given; 274 fine color illustrations. The arms and armor come from the Museum of the Polish Army (Warsaw), the National Museum in Kraków, the State Collections of Art at Wawel, the National Museum in Poznań and the Kórnik Library, the Pauline Monastery at Jasna Góra in Częstochowa, and the Museum of Malbork Castle.

810. ŻYGULSKI, Zdzisław, Jr. Sztuka Islamu w zbiorach polskich. [Islamic art in Polish collections] Warszawa, Wydawnictwo Artystyczne i Filmowe, 1989. 42 p. 179 color plates. (Skarby Sztuki w Polsce) N6260.Z94 1989

Bibliography: p. 18–19.

The author provides a short sketch on the origin of the Islamic collections in Poland, and includes very good illustrations of all the objects discussed in the catalog: Persian and Mongolian miniature paintings, Turkish and Persian carpets and rugs, sashes, Turkish armor, saddles, knives, banners, etc. He emphasizes the special artistic qualities of the Turkish tents in the Wawel castle, the trophies of the victory at Vienna in 1683.

JOHANNIS HEVELII
MACHINA COELESTIS.

X. Periodicals

✺

811. Architektura. Polski przegląd architektury. [Architecture. The Polish review of architecture] Vol. 1+ Warszawa, Arkady, 1947+ illus. monthly. NA6.A7225

Summaries in English, French, German, and Russian.

Texts are often in English and Polish.

Publication of Stowarzyszenie Architektów Polskich [Association of Polish Architects] *Each issue of the review generally focuses on a single social, architectural, urbanistic problem such as the restoration of historic buildings (no. 6, 1980), "Architecture for social purposes" (no. 1, 1981), or designs by Polish architects implemented throughout the world (no. 2, 1981). Presents contemporary professional architectural issues in terms intelligible to the concerned layman.*

Includes articles on contemporary design in the applied and decorative arts.

812. Artium questiones. Vol. 1+ Poznań, Wydawnictwo Naukowe, 1979+ irregular. illus. N6.A79

Publication of the Art Institute of the Adam Mickiewicz University in Poznań.

Articles on art, architecture, iconography, and theory, both historical and contemporary. Some English summaries.

813. Biuletyn Historii Sztuki. [Bulletin of the history of art]

Vols. 1–7, 1932/33–1939; v. 8+ 1946+ Warszawa, Instytut Sztuki PAN oraz Stowarzyszenie Historyków Sztuki. illus. quarterly. N6.B5

Sponsored by the Art Institute of the Polish Academy of Sciences and the Association of Art Historians.

Summaries in French.

Subject matter addressed from theoretical and stylistic viewpoints. Covers Romanesque to modern, excluding contemporary art. Few non-Polish subjects. Emphasis on painting and architecture.

814. Chimera. Vol. 1, part 1, 1901–v. 10, parts 28–30, 1907. Warszawa. illus. irregular. AP54.C48

No more published.

A publication of the Polish art nouveau movement. Provides an abundance of illustrations, with head and tail pieces by artists such as Stanisław Dębski, Józef Mehoffer, Jan Stanisławski, Edward Okuń, and Stanisław Turbia-Krzyształowicz.

815. Folia historiae artium. Vol. 1+ Kraków, Państwowe Wydawnictwo Naukowe, 1964+ illus. irregular. N6.F6

Sponsored by the Polish Academy of Sciences.

Summaries in French.

Style and iconography—mainly of Polish art, although coverage extends to important studies of non-Polish material. Gothic to modern, painting,

prints, architecture, and decorative arts.

816. La France et la Pologne dans leurs relations artistiques. Vol. 1, no. 1–4, 1938. Paris, La Bibliothèque Polonaise de Paris. illus. N6991.F7

No more published.

Contains important articles on the monuments in France to Jan Sobieski—victor at the Battle of Vienna (1683)—whose queen was Marie-Casimire de la Grange d'Arquien; on painter and etcher Jan Ziarnko, and his work in Paris in the seventeenth century; and on King Stanisław August, who introduced Lyonnaise silk craftsmen into Poland around 1764 to produce the sashes traditional to Polish masculine attire. His aim was to supplant regressive, orient-inspired design influences.

817. Ikonotheka. Prace Instytutu Historii Sztuki Uniwersytetu Warszawskiego. [Ikonotheka. Works of the Institute of the History of Art of the Warsaw University] No. 1+ Warszawa, Uniwersytet Warszawski 1990+ illus.

Summaries in English.

818. Kwartalnik Architektury i Urbanistyki; Teoria i historia. [A quarterly of architecture and urbanism; theory and history] Vol. 1+ Warszawa, Państwowe Wydawnictwo Naukowe, 1956+ ills. NA6.K9

Issued by the Committee on Architecture and Urban Studies

of the Polish Academy of Sciences.

Tables of contents and summaries in English, Russian, and other languages.

A first-rate publication that covers Polish developments, medieval to contemporary, including gardens. Occasional foreign subject matter.

819. Poland; illustrated magazine. Vol. 1+ Warsaw, Interpress, 1954+ monthly. illus. DK401.P45

Also appears in French, German, Spanish, and Swedish. Includes articles on Polish history, literature, and art. Many color and black and white photographs of paintings and sculptures.

820. Polish art studies. Vol. 1+ Wrocław, Zakład Narodowy im. Ossolińskich. 1979+ annual. illus. NX571.P6P63

Publication of the Art Institute of the Polish Academy of Sciences.

A scholarly annual of articles and book reviews on art and architecture, theater, music, film, and folklore of all periods.

821. Polska Sztuka Ludowa. [Polish folk art] Vol. 1+ Warszawa, Państwowe Wydawnictwo Naukowe, 1947+ illus. quarterly. NK7P6

Sponsored by the Art Institute of the Polish Academy of Sciences.

Brief summaries of articles in English and Russian.

Bibliographic references.

Solid scholarly studies on all folk art media such as painting, sculpture

(including wayside crosses), woodcuts, festival decorations, costumes, and interior decorations.

822. Projekt. [Project] Vol. 1+ Warszawa, Wydawnictwo Artystyczno-Graficzne "Prasa." 1956+ bimonthly, illus. (part color). N6.P7

Articles in English, French, and other languages on the visual arts and design in Poland and elsewhere. Emphasis on contemporary art.

823. Przegląd Artystyczny; pismo Związku Polskich Artystów Plastyków.

[Art review; journal of the Association of Polish Visual Artists] Nos. 1–76; Warszawa, 1946–Nov./Dec. 1973. irregular, illus. N6.Z95

Superseded by *Sztuka.* (see entry no. 828)

824. Rocznik Historii Sztuki. [Yearbook of the history of art] Vol. 1+ Wrocław, Zakład Narodowy im. Ossolińskich, 1956+ illus., facsims., ports. N9.6.R58

Sponsored by the Art Institute of the Polish Academy of Sciences.

Theory and styles of art, mainly—but not exclusively—Polish. Has contained articles on subjects such as Renaissance and Baroque jewelry (1907) and a Warsaw skyscraper (1910). Vols. 4–10 (1964–1974) and vols. 12–13 (1981–1982) include a running bibliography on Polish art history.

825. Rocznik Krakowski. [Kraków yearbook] Vol. 1+ Kraków, Towarzystwo

Miłośników Historii i Zabytków Krakowa, 1898+ illus. DB879.K8R58

Published in parts.

Organ of the Society of Friends of Historical Monuments in Kraków. Vol. 1–31 (1898–1939); v. 31, 1952+

A scholarly journal. Articles on the history of the architecture, architectural decoration, and art of the city and its environs. Recent issues have achieved a high quality of production; for instance, reproductions in color of stained glass of the 1920s and 1930s, and a historical map.

826. Roczniki Sztuki Śląskiej. [Yearbooks of Silesian art] Vol. 1+ Wrocław, Muzeum Narodowe we Wrocławiu, 1959+ illus. annual. N9.6.R6

A well-edited and well-produced scholarly publication covering the visual arts and architecture of all periods. Examples: Vol. 10 (1976) has a fundamental article by Anna Ziomecka on the carved and painted altarpieces of the region, from the 1450s to the early 1500s; 156 altars are described and analyzed, with an index to artists and artisans. Vol. 11 (1977) has an article by Maria Starzewska on the Wrocław goldsmith Pawel Nitsch (1548–1609) in a period of flourishing goldsmithery.

827. Studia źródłoznawcze. Commentationes. [Studies on Polish history sources] Vol. 1+ Warszawa, Państwowe Wydawnictwo Naukowe, 1957+ D13.S853

Issued by the Institute of History of the Polish Academy of Sciences.

Summaries in French, English, or other languages.

Analyzes sources; includes reviews.

828. Sztuka. [Art] Vol. 1+ Warszawa, Krajowa Agencja Wydawnicza RSW Prasa-Książka-Ruch, 1974+ illus. bimonthly. N6.S87

Supersedes *Przegląd Artystyczny.*

Short summaries in English and Russian.

Deals almost exclusively with the modern and contemporary arts: painting, sculpture, architecture, photography, film, and video. Regularly features artists born before World War I such as Henryk Stażewski, Eugeniusz Eibisch, Piotr Potworowski, and Tadeusz Gronowski. Might be said to be overextended—for example, into education in the visual arts.

829. Sztuki Piękne; miesięcznik poświęcony architekturze, rzeźbie, malarstwu, grafice i zdobnictwu. [The Arts; a monthly devoted to architecture, sculpture, painting, graphics and dec-orations] Year 1–10; Kraków, Polski Instytut Sztuk Pięknych, 1924/25–1934. illus., plates (part color), ports. (part color). N6.S9

Organ of the Polish Institute of Arts.

A major publication that, while it heeded nineteenth-century roots, dealt principally with twentieth-century representational painting and sculpture, and occasionally with prints and decorative arts. Concentrated on Polish painters, yet it also covered the latest productions of Henri Matisse and Pierre Bonnard. Presented a chronicle of exhibitions in Poland and abroad. Typical articles include those on the prints of Leon Wyczółkowski (vol. 1, 1924–25); the paintings of Julian Fałat and the sculpture of Konstanty Laszczka (v. 2, 1925–26); the art of Józef Mehoffer (v. 2, 1926–27); and the paintings of Ludomir Sleńdziński (v. 4, 1927–28). An atypical piece is on the historical patrimony of the Castle in Podhorce, with photographs of interiors (v. 1, 1924–25).

830. Warsaw. Muzeum Narodowe. Bulletin du Musée National de Varsovie. Vol. 1+ Warszawa, 1960+ illus., quarterly. N3160.A2

In French.

A very informative Museum publication having substantial essays on a wide variety of works of art. Among many noteworthy articles are: M. Skubiszewska demonstrating S. Botticelli's authorship of a tondo in the Museum (v. 20, 1979); and A. Rottermund summarizing the themes and motifs that stimulated Polish art during the period of the partitions (v. 20, 1979). The publication issues a chronicle of exhibitions at the Museum and a periodic list of acquisitions.

831. Warsaw. Muzeum Narodowe. Rocznik. [Yearbook of the National Museum in Warsaw] Vol. 1+ Warszawa, 1938+ illus., ports. AM101.W3674

Summaries in French and Russian.

Bibliographic references.

Articles on all aspects of the Museum collection; covers Polish as well as foreign art. Also serves as a forum for discussing ancient art. Thirty-one volumes were published before 1987.

XI. Bibliography and Reference Works

XI. Bibliography and Reference Works

❁

832. GĘBCZAK, Józef.
Bibliografia historii sztuki na Śląsku za lata 1945–1963. [Bibliography of the history of art in Silesia in the years 1945–1963] Wrocław, Muzeum Śląskie we Wrocławiu, 1967. 120 p. (Rocznik Sztuki Śląskiej, vol. 5) N9.6.R6 1967

Continuation of the bibliography in *Rocznik Sztuki Śląskiej*, vol. 7+

A scholarly compendium covering theory, style, and iconography in all media, including architecture, applied arts, and conservation.

833. GRAJEWSKI, Ludwik.
Bibliografia ilustracji w czasopismach polskich XIX i pocz. XX w. (do 1918 r.). [A bibliography of illustrations in Polish periodicals of the nineteenth century and to the year 1918] Warszawa, Państwowe Wydawnictwo Naukowe, 1972. 553 p. Z5961.P57G73

The periodicals covered are listed on p. 9–11. The indexes are in six parts: (1) Painters, sculptors, graphic arts; (2) Portraits; (3) Tombs and free-standing sculpture; (4) Architecture; (5) Applied arts; and (6) Museums. Two additional indexes are arranged by surname and geographical location.

834. KROH, Magdalena.
Polska sztuka ludowa; bibliografia za lata 1947–1976. [Polish folk art; a bibliography for the years 1947–1976]

Wrocław, Zakład Narodowy im. Ossolińskich, 1979. 86 p. Z5956.F6K76

Sponsored by the Polish Academy of Sciences Art Institute.

The topic is discussed within various frameworks, such as theory and methodology, folk art within the general culture, geographically by province, and by medium, necrology, reviews, and other subdivisions. Films are included. There is a substantial index.

835. Polska bibliografia sztuki
1801–1944. [Polish art bibliography 1801–1944] Wrocław, Zakład Narodowy im. Ossolińskich, 1975+ Z5961.P57P64

Compiled by Janina Wiercińska and Maria Liczbińska.

Contents: Vol. 1: Malarstwo polskie [Polish painting], part 1. Prace ogólne. Historia. Malarze. A–K.—part 2. Malarze. L–Z.—v. 2 (1979): Rysunek, grafika, sztuka książki i druki [Drawing, graphics, the art of the book and printing]; v. 3 (1986): Rzeźba [Sculpture].

836. RYSZKIEWICZ, Andrzej, *and* **Janina Wiercińska.**
Bibliografia polskiej historii sztuki, 1945–1968. [Bibliography of Polish history of art] Rocznik Historii Sztuki, vol. 4, 1964, p. 215–337; v. 5, 1965, p. 213–307; v. 6, 1966, p. 304–400; v. 7, 1969, p. 317–78; v. 9, 1973, p.

337–468; v. 10, 1974, p. 256–351; v. 12, 1981, p. 265–374, compiled by Nawajka Cieślińska and Anna Rudzka; v. 13, 1981, p. 237–366 compiled by Hanna Fruba and Anna Rudzka. N9.6.R58

837. Allgemeines Lexikon der bildenden Künstler von der Antike bis zur Gegenwart. Begründet von Ulrich Thieme und Felix Becker. Unter Mitwirkung von etwa 400 Fachgelehrten bearbeitet und redigiert von H. Vollmer, B.C. Kreplin, J. Müller, L. Scheewe, H. Wolff, O. Kellner. Herausgegeben von Hans Vollmer. Leipzig, E.A. Seemann, 1978. 37 vols. N40.A64 1978

The most extensive biographical dictionary—commonly known as Thieme and Becker—of architects, painters, sculptors, engravers, and etchers, prepared by about four hundred specialists. The location of an artist's works is frequently given.

838. BÉNÉZIT, Emmanuel.
Dictionnaire critique et documentaire des peintres, sculpteurs, dessinateurs et graveurs de tous les temps et de tous pays. Revised ed. Paris, Gründ, 1976. 10 vols. ports. N40.B47 1976

A collective work edited by E. Bénézit in which the biographies of artists vary in length, some listing detailed information on prizes awarded to them and the locations of their works, while others provide only basic biographical data. The coverage ranges from the fifth century B.C. to the mid-twentieth century. Numerous Polish artists are included: painters, sculptors, draftsmen, etchers, and printmakers.

A previous edition, 1948–55, was in eight volumes.

839. ŁOZA, Stanisław.
Architekci i budowniczowie w Polsce. [Architects and builders in Poland] Warszawa, Budownictwo i Architektura, 1954. 424 p. 180 illus. NA60.P6L6 1954

Edited by Jolanta Maurin-Białostocka.

Bibliography: p. 4–5.

Bio-bibliographical dictionary of architects, builders, and masons— including some foreign—working in Poland from the Middle Ages to c. 1950. Includes an index to the locations of buildings. A revised edition of the author's Słownik architektów i budowniczych Polaków oraz cudzoziemców w Polsce pracujących *(1917). Good photographs.*

840. Polski słownik biograficzny. [A Polish biographical dictionary] Vol. 1–7, Kraków, Gebethner i Wolff, 1935–58; v. 8+ Warszawa, Zakład Narodowy im. Ossolińskich, 1959/60+ CT1230.P65 ERR

Vols. 1–7 sponsored by the Polska Akademia Umiejętności; vol. 8+ by the Historical Institute of the Polska Akademia Nauk.

Contains scholarly biographies of prominent deceased Poles. The most

recent volume, vol. 33 (1987), includes names beginning with the letter "R."

841. RASTAWIECKI, Edward.
Słownik malarzów polskich, tudzież obcych w Polsce osiadłych lub czasowo w niej przebywających. [Dictionary of Polish painters and foreign painters residing in Poland] Warszawa, Nakł. autora, 1850–1857. 3 v. ports. ND698.R3

Reprinted in 1979.

842. RASTAWIECKI, Edward.
Słownik rytowników polskich, tudzież obcych w Polsce osiadłych lub czasowo w niej pracujących. [Dictionary of Polish engravers and foreign engravers residing or temporarily working in Poland] Warszawa, Wydawnictwa Artystyczne i Filmowe, 1980. 316 p. plates, port. NE735.P6R3 1980

Reprint of the 1886 Poznań edition.

An important reference that gives biographical information, but is even more useful for its catalogs of prints and extensive quotations of legends. In the best tradition of nineteenth-century print catalogs.

843. Śląski słownik biograficzny. [A Silesian biographical dictionary] Katowice, Śląski Instytut Naukowy, 1977–79. 2 v. DK4600.S466S54

By Jan Kantyk and Władysław Zieliński.

Biographies of deceased nineteenth and twentieth century Silesian notables. Each volume alphabetically complete, each biography having bibliographic

references; there is an index to the whole in volume 2. Supplements the general biographical dictionary Polski słownik biograficzny.

844. Słownik artystów polskich i obcych w Polsce działających. Malarze, rzeźbiarze, graficy. [Dictionary of Polish artists and foreign artists working in Poland. Painters, sculptors, printmakers] Wrocław, Zakład Narodowy im. Ossolińskich, vol. 1+, 1971+ N7255.P6S59

Publication of the Art Institute of the Polish Academy of Sciences.

By Jolanta Maurin-Białostocka, et al.

Designed to be comprehensive with respect to the inclusion of artists working in the Polish Commonwealth at the height of its territorial extent, before 1772. Architects are omitted. Includes artists who died before 1966. The fourth volume appeared in 1986, covering names beginning with Kl–La.

A review of volume 4 by Andrew Ciechanowiecki appears in Burlington Magazine, *vol. 128, no. 1005, Dec. 1986, p. 910–11.*

845. Związek Polskich Artystów Plastyków. Okręg Warszawski. Słownik artystów plastyków; artyści plastycy okręgu Warszawskiego ZPAP, 1945–1970. [Dictionary of visual artists; artists of the Warsaw branch of the Union of Polish Visual Artists, 1945–1970] Warszawa, 1972. 714 p. illus. N7255.P62W39

By Maria Serafińska, et al.

Introduction in Polish, English, French, German, and Russian.

❋

Brief biographical sketches of about 2,600 artists. Over 2,000 photographs of their works.

846. DAVIES, Norman.
God's playground; a history of Poland. New York, Columbia University Press, 1982. 2 v. illus. maps. DK4140.D38 1982
   Vol. 1: The origins to 1795; v. 2: From 1795 to the present.
   Bibliographic references to each chapter.
   Chronology.

847. DAVIES, Norman.
Heart of Europe. A short history of Poland. Oxford, Clarendon Press, 1984. 511 p. illus., maps. DK4140.D385 1984
   Bibliographic notes.
   Chronological and genealogical tables.

The author begins his book with the most recent history of Poland, and concludes with a retrospective look to the medieval period. Emphasizing those elements of the Polish past that he believes have had great impact on present "attitudes," he stresses the Polish national elements: the Catholic Church, Polish literature, the intelligentsia, and Russian relations.

848. HALECKI, Oskar.
A history of Poland, with additional material by A. Polonsky. London, Kegan Paul, 1978, 407 p. maps. DK4140.H3413 1978
Originally published by the author in 1921–1933 as La Pologne de 963 à 1914. *First edition in English translation published in 1943. Subsequently updated through several editions.*

849. History of Poland, by
Aleksander Gieysztor and others. 2d ed. Warszawa, Państwowe Wydawnictwo Naukowe, 1979. 668 p. illus. color maps. DK4140.H58 1979
   Bibliography: p. 622–35.
   Chronological tables.
   Translated from the Polish manuscript by Krystyna Cękalska and others.
Contents: Introduction by S. Kieniewicz. Medieval Poland, by A. Gieysztor. The Commonwealth of the gentry, by J. Tazbir and E. Rostworowski. Poland under foreign rule 1795–1918, by S. Kieniewicz and H. Wereszycki. Poland 1918–1939, by H. Wereszycki. Conclusion by S. Kieniewicz.

850. HRUSHEVS'KYI, Mykhailo.
A history of Ukraine, by Michael Hrushevsky. Published for the Ukrainian National Association. [Hamden, Conn.] Archon Books, 1970. xviii, 629 p. maps. DK508.5.H683 1970
   Edited by O. J. Frederiksen.
   Preface by George Vernadsky.
   Reprint of the 1941 ed. published by Yale University Press.
   Bibliography: p. 585–600.

851. KAPLAN, Herbert H.
The first partition of Poland. New York, Columbia University Press, 1962. [New York, AMS Press, 1972] xvi, 215 p. DK434.K33 1972
   Original ed. issued in the series: East Central European Studies of Columbia University.
   Bibliography: p. 197–209.

852. LORD, Robert H.
The second partition of Poland; a study in diplomatic history. New York, AMS Press, 1969. xxx, 586 p. DK434.L7 1969
   Reprint of the 1915 ed.
   Bibliography: p. 557–72.
A classic work, unsurpassed.

853. WANDYCZ, Piotr S.
The lands of partitioned Poland, 1795–1918. Seattle, University of Washington Press, 1974, 431 p. maps. (A History of East Central Europe, vol. 7) DJK4.S93 v. 7
   Bibliography: p. 381–411.

854. KRZYŻANOWSKI, Julian.
A History of Polish literature. Warszawa, PWN Polish Scientific Publishers, 1978. 807 p. illus., ports., plates. PG7012.K7713 1978
   Translation by Doris Ronowicz of *Dzieje literatury polskiej od początków do czasów najnowszych.*
   Bibliography: p. 671–737.

855. MIŁOSZ, Czesław.
The history of Polish literature. 2d ed. Berkeley, University of California Press, 1983. 583 p. illus., ports. PG7012.M48 1983
   Bibliography: p. 545–61.

856. BYSTROŃ, Jan Stanisław.
Dzieje obyczajów w dawnej Polsce: wiek XVI–XVIII. [History of customs in Old Poland; the XVI–XVIII centuries] 2d rev. ed. Warszawa, Państwowy Instytut Wydawniczy, 1976. 2 v. illus. DK4188.2.B94 1976
Covers the history of Poland prior to 1795. Richly illustrated with drawings by Norblin and Chodowiecki.

857. The Columbia Lippincott gazetteer of the world. Morningside Heights, New York, Columbia University Press, 1962. 2148, 22 p. G103.L7 1962

Basic reference work for geographic place names.

858. KRAJEWSKI, Klemens. Mała encyklopedia architektury i wnętrz. [A short encyclopedia of architecture and interiors] Wrocław, Zakład Narodowy im. Ossolińskich, 1974. 493 p. illus. NA31.K72

In two parts. Part I is alphabetical by architects, builders, theoreticians, decorative artists. Part II consists of architectural terms. Chiefly of importance for its emphasis on Polish architects and Polish terms of architectural description.

859. Miasta polskie w tysiącleciu. [Polish cities and towns over a thousand-year period] Wrocław, Zakład Narodowy im. Ossolińskich, 1965–67. 2 vols. illus., facsims., col. coats of arms, maps, views. DK416.M5

Bibliography: vol. 2, p. 685–96.

Historical essays by Aleksander Gieysztor, Stanisław Herbst, Jerzy Michalski, Ryszard Kołodziejczyk, and Stanisław Arnold. Includes coats of arms, in color, of cities and towns.

860. Podział administracyjny Polskiej Rzeczypospolitej Ludowej. [Administrative Division of the Polish Peoples' Republic] 3d ed. Warszawa, Urząd Rady Ministrów, Biuro do Spraw Prezydiów Rad

Narodowych, 1965. 380 p. JS6131.A3A45

Official directory listing administrative divisions of Poland by provinces, cities, counties, and urban settlements.

861. POGONOWSKI, Iwo Cyprian. Poland; a historical atlas. Rev. ed. New York, Hippocrene Books, 1988. 321 p. maps. coats of arms. G1951.S1P34 1987

Bibliography: p. 261–62.

List of coats of arms of Polish towns.

The author includes 144 coats of arms, in color, of Polish towns, and a chronology of Poland's constitutional and political development from the tenth century to the year 1981. Numerous maps.

862. Polska Akademia Nauk. Instytut Geografii. Narodowy atlas Polski. [National atlas of Poland] Komitet redakcyjny: Stanisław Leszczycki [et al.] Wrocław, Zakład Narodowy im. Ossolińskich i Instytut Geografii i Przestrzennego Zagospodarowania, Polska Akademia Nauk, 1973–1978. 634 maps. G1950.P62 1973 G&M

Scale 1:2,000,000 for most of the maps.

Supplement: National Atlas of Poland. An English translation of Narodowy atlas Polski, without maps. 185 p. G1950.P62 1973 Suppl. G&M

863. Słownik geograficzny Królestwa Polskiego i innych krajów słowiańskich. [Geographic dictionary of the

Polish Kingdom and other Slavic countries] Warszawa, Wydawnictwa Artystyczne i Filmowe, 1975–77. 15 v. in 16. DJK7.S46 1975

By Filip Sulimierski, Bronisław Chlebowski, and Władysław Walewski.

Reprint of the 1880 edition.

Outdated, but still very useful for the history and geographic setting of localities.

864. Słownik terminologiczny sztuk pięknych. [Dictionary of terminology applied to visual arts] Warszawa, Państwowe Wydawnictwo Naukowe, 1976. 522 p. illus. N33.S55 1976

Edited by Stefan Kozakiewicz.

About four thousand terms, some accompanied by illustrations, explained and described by specialists in the fields.

865. SZOLGINIA, Witold. Ilustrowana encyklopedia dla wszystkich: Architektura i budownictwo. [An illustrated general encyclopedia: Architecture and building] Warszawa, Wydawnictwa Naukowo-Techniczne, 1975. 458 p. illus. NA31.S94

A useful reference for biographies, especially of Polish and foreign architects working in Poland, for architectural terminology that is illustrated with numerous photographs or diagrams, and for ancient and modern sites of architectural importance in Poland.

866. TRZASKA, Evert i Michalski. Encyklopedia staropolska.

[Encyclopedia of Old Poland]
Warszawa, Nakładem Księgarnia
Trzaski, Everta i Michalskiego,
1939. 2 vols. illus. (part color),
plates, facsims., ports.
DK412.3.T7

By Aleksander Brückner.

Vol. 1. A–M. 955 p., 2,003
illus., 18 plates; v. 2. N–Z.
1,070 p., 1,941 illus., 17 plates.

Reprint of the 1900–1903
edition.

Can be supplemented by Zygmunt
Gloger. Encyklopedia staropolska
ilustrowana. [Illustrated encyclopedia
of old Poland] Warszawa, Wiedza
Powszechna, 1958. 4 vols. in 2.
illus., music, ports. AE53.G62

867. Wielka encyklopedia
powszechna PWN. [The great
universal encyclopedia of
Pánstwowe Wydawnictwo
Naukowe] Warszawa,
Pánstwowe Wydawnictwo
Naukowe, 1962–70. 13 v. illus.,
maps, plates, ports. AE53.W44

Supplement in v. 13.

Editorial Committee: Bohdan
Suchodolski et al.

868. ZWOLIŃSKA, Krystyna,
and Zasław Malicki.
Mały słownik terminów
Plastycznych. [A concise
dictionary of visual arts
terminology] Warszawa, Wiedza
Powszechna, 1974. 438 p. illus.
N33.Z96

The dictionary contains over fifteen
hundred terms used in Poland in
architecture, painting, sculpture,
printmaking, and the decorative and
applied arts. Concise explanatory
entries in alphabetical order. Index of
names.

The Barbican in Kraków, built at
the end of the fifteenth century to
strengthen the defense of the city
at the walls. From *Cracow* by
Edward Hartwig, 2d ed. (Kraków,
1956)

Name Index

✿

❀

❋

✳

❀

❀